T0380444

A JOURNEY THROUGH TIMES

A sequential political history of Nigeria's Fourth Republic
from Olusegun Obasanjo to Muhammadu Buhari
– with introductory commentaries represented in articles.

FRISKY LARR

authorHOUSE®

AuthorHouse™ UK
1663 Liberty Drive
Bloomington, IN 47403 USA
www.authorhouse.co.uk
Phone: 0800.197.4150

Published by AuthorHouse 09/26/2018

ISBN: 978-1-5462-9848-9 (sc)
ISBN: 978-1-5462-9849-6 (e)

Print information available on the last page.

This book is printed on acid-free paper.

Contents

I
The Run-up to the Fourth Republic

The various phases of Republican governance in Nigeria mark the periods of homegrown constitutional dispositions under civilian leadership. It is the post-independence era. The country gained independence from British colonial rule on October 01st, 1960 and set itself the onerous task of self-governance in the wholesome belief in its abilities and capabilities. The actors were sure, they would live up to the impending challenges. Ethnic divisions and squabbles across the geographical spectrum, however, soon saw the overthrow of the constitutional order in a military coup d'etat six years into independence. The subsequent imposition of successive military governments that competed in a chain of illicit coups became a part of its political history.

While the promise of a quick transition to civilian rule became a routine in the inauguration of military rules immediately after overthrowing a government, the military government of the then General Olusegun Obasanjo was the first to have followed through on the promise to transit and truly installed the second Republic of civilian constitutional democracy in 1979.

The civilian experiment very soon exposed the political immaturity of local actors in this inherited system of the colonial masters of old. Bitterness and acrimonies were allowed a free flow without arresting mechanisms. Systematic developmental structures installed by military regimes were brazenly allowed to wither away in the face of greed and uncontrolled self-enrichment. It was a matter of time before the military rebelled again in its 'self-imposed' but poorly executed role of custodian of good governance.

One name stood out at this initial stage. It was a major personality, who served a bridging role in the experimental democracy through the resultant military intervention or interregnum as it were, and the repeated transition to the short-lived dream of a third but failed republic and the subsequent advent of the fourth Republic in 1999.

Moshood Kashimawo Olawale Abiola was a major player in the consolidation and demise of the Second Republic. He was a major player in the hastily-managed and disentangled Third Republic and in the transition to the presently tapered and pressurized Fourth Republic in its contrived state of bumpiness.

Moshood Abiola, his political ambitions, the aftermath of these tragic and unmitigated ambitions, his dubious rise to wealth and fame on the heels of marketing the multinational telecommunications giant – ITT in Africa and his use of this wealth and fame to foster his personal political dreams, all symbolize a part of the problems that Africa contends with in building a workable democracy till the present day.

Enjoy reading the first article "No Tears for Abiola" that I wrote in one of my first adventurous leaps into public space. It was written and published in several online portals as from December 12, 2006.

No Tears for Abiola

By Frisky Larr

The sun neither rises in the north nor does it ever set in the south. The solar system has its own set of rules. No one plants an apple tree and reaps cherry fruits in harvest time. Nature's own dynamics runs in ordered consistence. Therefore, what the night holds is usually what the day sets to achieve.

Thoughts indeed, that would have reshaped the entire biography of the man Moshood Abiola had they been made to serve as the paramount credo of his political dealings.

Before embarking on this dangerous analogy though, I will like to point out that repeated references these days, to the annulment of the June 12th, 1993 elections that would have seen the installation of Moshood Abiola as President of Nigeria, in the condemnation of General Ibrahim Badamosi Babangida underscore the relevance of this issue at this point in time.

The project of analyzing the man Abiola is one that is fraught with challenges and the risk of encroaching on, albeit usurping the emotional territories of many political observers alike. Given a place in political analysis, it is an open secret that emotions always have their own dynamics of setting facts and logical reasoning aside. It is therefore, regrettable if extraneous emotions are perceived as violated in the process of this discourse.

Without pretending to be a sage in the observation of the Nigerian political scene however, it may be pertinent to highlight the extremely personal and therefore, limited nature of my observations.

The M. K. O. Abiola that I know shot to the limelight of political activities round about 1979 in the wake of political activities to determine a successor for the Murtala/Obasanjo junta. Indeed, I was only a teenager at the time and my mind was yet unpolluted in terms of ideological leanings. The intellect was set on the path of growth and future direction was to be shaped by whatever the prevailing system that fed my brain in ethical, moral and intellectual conduct, portends. In other words, such names as Akintola, Awolowo, Azikiwe, Sarduana of Sokoto, Herbert Marcaulay etc. who played active roles in pre-independence and perhaps also in the early post-independence years, were nothing more than just names to me. I heard a lot about their importance but never knew what they represented in their individual capacities.

So, when suddenly, names like Chief Obafemi Awolowo and Dr. Nnamdi Azikiwe emerged in the flurry of political activities that greeted the lifting of the ban on political parties by General Olusegun Obasanjo, I had a first-hand opportunity to get to know a few prominent characters all on my own.

I soon found out that the man Obafemi Awolowo did a sound homework preparing for the ultimate lifting of the said ban on political activities. The organization of his party the Unity Party of Nigeria (UPN), the ideological framework which was largely left-leaning, the lieutenants with which he surrounded himself etc. were a resounding evidence of cohesion and a streamlined coordination of a group's identity. His four-cardinal program "Free Education at all levels", "Free medical Services", "Integrated Rural Development" and "Gainful Employment" bore the hallmarks of the equitable distribution of wealth and the re-organization of infrastructures. Nigeria was not known to be wanting at the time in terms of finances. The discovery of oil and the crisis it meant to European and American states translated into high proceeds for Nigeria's finances. Nigeria had money.

Quite interestingly, lessons in Economics were beginning to take hold of my perception in understanding political developments. I was reading that conservative (right-leaning) ideologies were regarded as more suitable to the healing of ailing economies because the right-wing does not care much for public welfare and is as such, less involved in public spending. On the contrary, left-wingers were deemed more suited for the handling of a robust economy because they traditionally hold the program for social welfare and the distribution of wealth. In short, conservatives generate capital and the socialists disburse capital. That was the simplified version that permeated my mind at the time.

So, not caring much for the ethnic divide that seemed to have characterized the existing political parties, I sought to understand what the parties had to offer in terms of program.

In addition to the Unity Party of Nigeria, the National Party of Nigeria (NPN) was most prominent. Its tendency was elitist and right wing. Its most popular slogan was "Qualitative Education" not "Free Education". It backed it up with one more program: "Green Revolution". In fact, the Green Revolution had a long-term objective of making Nigeria self-sufficient in agriculture. In sharp contrast to the UPN though, the NPN – in my views – is comparable to the PDP of today in its formation. It had no single person that could be seen as its long-term architect. It showed no traces of a party that had long been planned in expectation of the lifting of the ban. It was systematically organized with lots of eminent personalities.

The Nigerian People's Party (NPP), which was most tribal-oriented like the UPN, served the Ibo base. In fact, if anything, the NPP far surpassed the NPN in its resemblance of today's PDP in terms of formation. The flag-bearer of the NPP Dr. Nnamdi Azikiwe was desperately begged to take back his words on withdrawing from politics to lead the party. This is even more similar to the positioning of Obasanjo (who though, was not begged) at the peak of the PDP.

What all the other parties had in common in contrast to the UPN was that they lacked programmatic ideological cohesion. They were sustained by tribal affiliations. The UPN had both. The UPN then, was predominantly Yoruba-based. Its ideology centered on its founder's (Obafemi Awolowo's) preliminary homework. Everyone in positions of importance identified with the ideology.

Then came the lust for power. The right-wing tendency of the NPN was even underscored by the number of (vocal and silent) millionaires it had in its ranks. Most prominent and vocal was Moshood Abiola. As a Yoruba, one would have naturally expected him to tow the Awolowo line in his choice of party. Not only did their ideological leaning obviously differ there, however, seemed to have been no place for Abiola in the UPN to advance his political ambitions.

Given the array of candidates presented to the nation (Shehu Shagari for the NPN, Obafemi Awolowo for the UPN, Nnamdi Azikiwe for the NPP, Aminu Kano for the PRP – *People's Redemption Party, largely Kano-based* and one other flag-bearer (Waziri Ibrahim) for the GNPP – *Great Nigeria People's Party, also north-based)* many observers agreed and rated Shehu Shagari as an intellectual lightweight in the political arena. Aminu Kano of the PRP and the flag-bearer for the GNPP (Waziri Ibrahim) indeed, stood no realistic chance of winning the game. The real battle was between the UPN and the NPN.

Given heightened tension between the Ibos and the Yorubas, it came as no surprise that neither Azikiwe nor Awolowo would pave way for each other as historical gladiators. They both ended up as spoilers to their own interests and left the country at the mercy of the strong northern base and military sympathy of the NPN.

The only formula that didn't fit much into this equation however, was Moshood Abiola. A Yoruba who personally knew the gravity of tribal influences in Nigerian politics, Abiola decided to team up with the north-dominated NPN shrugging aside the obvious traits of cohesive intellectual deficiency, viable party program and the long-term development of the fatherland. Apparently, the quality of being a Muslim and the dream of getting nominated as NPN's presidential candidate for the four-year term following the first, made Abiola believe he was better off finding a home in the NPN.

The truth in my perception is that Awolowo had a party and a program. Shagari was elected to represent a party. He had no program of his own except the party program. Azikiwe even had no party. He was virtually begged to join a party and lead it. On the other hand, program and party was a matter of personal conviction and heart-felt commitment for Obafemi Awolowo. Observers agreed that he was poised to unleash an agenda, whose implementation would have been easy for him to oversee as every follower (e.g. Tai Solarin) was also an ardent believer in his objectives. I held the view in my teenage years that Awolowo stood out for a vivid project named uplifting Nigeria.

Many disagree with this assessment partly for their sentimental dislike of Obafemi Awolowo, tribal call of duty and far less on the basis of factual and intellectual observations.

In fact, months after Shagari's lieutenants looted Nigeria's treasury and drained the foreign reserves, Awolowo was first to cry foul calling on Shagari to tell the nation the true story of the plague that was hitting the Nigerian economy. Shagari initially denied anything wrong with the economy until we all stood on the verge of seeing the report to be released by a world financial institution (IMF or the World Bank) on the true state of Nigeria's economy. Shagari finally came out and grudgingly too, to admit what Awolowo had been echoing over several months.

In the case of Moshood Abiola, personal ambition and probably personal animosities meant a diversion from facts and objective analysis. The NPN's internal regulation provided for the zoning system. Each political zone was to be entitled to only a four-year term as presidential candidate. In the analysis, Shagari was to serve only one four-year term. Thereafter, Abiola – in his own reckoning – would have stood a brilliant chance of succeeding him for the next four-year term.

Full of high hopes, multi-millionaire Abiola founded the Concord Group of Newspapers to counter Awolowo's well prepared leap into the political playground with his Tribune newspaper. Indeed, Abiola seemed to have been so badly carried away in his dining with the devil that he chose to unleash a ferocious attack on Awolowo that went far below the belt line. The credo being the destruction of the myth built around the name "Awolowo". The dirty face of politics was indeed represented by the battle of the Concord and Tribune newspapers. Abiola spent a huge amount of money on NPN in the hope that he may end up as a presidential candidate of the following term. Money, which would have done him much service, spent on philanthropy.

However, the day of reckoning came and Shagari amended the rules to allow him a second term as the NPN candidate for President. Abiola was left in the dark and in emptiness.

Rumors also did their rounds on how Abiola earned his millions. Though unproven till date, he was said to have played a fast one on ITT to defraud them of a huge sum of capital. These rumors did spread like wildfire. Abiola was not held in high esteem during the second Republic. His fallout with Fela Kuti culminating in "Give me shit I give you shit" should be fresh in everybody's memory that experienced those days of political bickering.

In the rapid deterioration into decadence that followed the Babangida days, Nigeria had lost almost all political heavyweights of intellectual substance. Azikiwe had died and was no longer there and Awolowo too. Idiagbon had been driven into oblivion and the light at the end of the tunnel could only fall on Abiola. Here, time seemed to have healed the wound he inflicted on the stature of Nigeria by helping install the NPN and Shagari.

The truth is that anyone that represented anything different from the accustomed northern oligarchy and the absolute decadent filth that is reminiscent of Babangida and all that followed his reign was sufficient for Nigerians to embrace as a break from the past. Last minute attempts to remedy his own image by embarking on philanthropic activities seemed to have lured people away from deeply scrutinizing Abiola's credentials. Or probably the absence of a more credible alternative did the trick for him. Else, in an equitable field of balanced competition there is hardly any place in my reckoning, for an Abiola's victory in any Nigerian election without the decadence perpetrated by Babangida and his cohorts.

While the Yorubas were ready to forgive Obasanjo for turning his back on Awolowo in the legal battle that ensued in the aftermath of the 1980 elections, Abiola's case was one of an independent dynamic. Obasanjo was known in his days as the stooge of the northern oligarchy. Sharper tongues even contend that the real rulers of the Obasanjo days were the Yar A'duas and the Danjumas!

Even though no one would have been able to stop the north-driven military government of Obasanjo from handing over power to the north in the person of Shagari, the view was largely held that Abiola should not have been involved in enhancing this process.

Intellectually, Abiola was an average Nigerian who happened to have been rich and in a position of influence. His calling was based on the philosophy of "anything goes"! What matters most was his personal aspiration. He sought to have a sun that would rise in the north and set in the south. Little did he know that the northern mafia is a collection of skillful dribblers for whom his stature did not stand a chance in spite of his millions. Indeed, the annulment of the June 12th elections by "Maradona" (as Babangida was famously called) was Abiola reaping in the evening what he had sown in the morning. Babangida, on his own, will also pay for his evils, which include that annulment in disregard for the people's choice. But in hindsight, it is difficult to avoid observing how the dynamics of nature can play out on individuals in reminiscence of the karmic justice. I do not shed my tears for Abiola's misfortune on the electoral field!

May his soul rest in peace!

***

Indeed, when tragedy struck, Moshood Abiola died under mysterious circumstances and June 12, 1993 became a landmark date in the history of Nigeria. It was the day that the presidential election was held, which was presumed to be the freest and fairest ever and post-humously declared won by Moshood Abiola. Ever since, June 12 has become a political date that is commemorated year-in, year-out.

Alongside Moshood Abiola died General Tunde Idiagbon – a renown disciplinarian of the Muahmmadu Buhari junta days – and every attempt to launch the Third Republic was nipped in the bud in spite of the temporary installation of one Ernest Shonekan of minimum political clout and the Fourth Republic was hastily ushered in. The need to pacify the Yoruba as one major ethnic group, from which Abiola stemmed informed the machinations that saw the quick installation of former General Olusegun Obasanjo, from his prison abode, by the northern establishment that controlled the politics of the country.

***

II
The Obasanjo Days

The retired General was not a stranger to the leadership of the country and was also not a stranger to the control of the political establishment. As a military General, he had succeeded a northern General on the heels of assassination. He was widely believed to have been under the strict control of members of the northern establishment, flanked by two nominally junior but very powerful Generals, who held key positions in the cabinet – the defense portfolio and Chief of Army Staff.

Lieutenant-General Theophilus Danjuma as the Federal Commissioner of Defense and General Shehu Musa Yar'Adua, who was the General Chief of Army Staff both from the northern region of the country, were widely believed to be calling the shots behind the scene.

The installation of this Yoruba President Olusegun Obasanjo in 1999 to launch the Fourth Republic was widely seen as a move to sooth tensions and calm frail nerves in the aftermath of the perceived marginalization of other ethnic groups by the powerful northern block. No doubt, the new President would draw from his past experience as military Head of State, with the widespread perception of having been remote-controlled by more powerful junior Generals of northern descent who flanked him on all sides in the junta cabinet. This was even more important in view of the fact that his ascension in 1999 was again, widely seen as the political maneuver of another former junior General Ibrahim Badamosi Babaginda, who is believed to have orchestrated the release of General Obasanjo straight from prison and a date with the executioner's strings on trumped up treason charges by the late General Sani Abacha, to the throne of the Presidency.

Again, he was flanked by a northern Vice President, who had ambitions of his own. His facilitator (General Ibrahim Badamosi Babangida) also had dreams of his own having helped a tried and tested hand of the military days that would be easy to remote-control and perhaps, who may pass the baton on to him (Babangida) when his term is up. That was the general perception by many neutral observers.

Alas Olusegun Obasanjo refused to play ball and bit the fingers that fed him. He became color-blind in terms of ethnicity. He broke with taboos in appointing cabinet ministers and people into key positions that were hitherto exclusively reserved for the North. The Governor of the Central Bank became an Easterner for the first time in ages as was the Minister of Finance etc. He reorganized the military to render military coups d'etat much more difficult. In a nutshell, he tipped the scale in favor of a more geographically equitable distribution of political offices.

Above all else, he declared war on corruption by establishing the special Economic and Financial Crimes Commission. But the war on corruption was perceived to be one-sided, caging the President's enemies and letting the President's friends off the hook. But for stepping on powerful toes though, vested interests descended on him and the general public was hardly sobering enough to separate the wheat from the chaff and in the aftermath, several manipulated ordinary persons joined the bandwagon of verbally lynching the new President with the most despicable weapons and in the most horrifying terms.

I wrote the following article that attracted a lot of attention in the new online world of citizen's journalism (published on www.nigeriaworld.com, the long defunct www.nigeria.com and several other websites):

OBASANJO SHOULD NOT STAND ACCUSED OF CORRUPTION!

Frisky Larr   December 01, 2006

"Kan davasi" is a phrase in Turkish language. It roughly equates with the English word "Vendetta". It is indeed, one ugly side of traditional and rural Turkey that no modern Turk is proud to talk about. It is the face of deep-felt fanaticism, abhorrence, misplaced family pride and a climax in bloodshed vis-à-vis the erasure of a complete family lineage. "Kan davasi" is indeed the face of primitive vengeance and the quest for vindication and undeserved honor.

The emotional state of extreme anger, frustration and humiliation is indeed as human as human nature can ever be. The easiest remedy for anger, frustration and humiliation has always been vengeance - at best in a tit for tat manner. Many of us were witnesses, in the early days of the spate of Sharia declaration that swept over the north, to scores - indeed hundreds - of souls that were aimlessly sacrificed in the aftermath of emotional outbursts in the north and the east of Nigeria. It was all about efforts to restore honor in the spirit of "kan davasi".

The English man says "Time heals all sorrows". But does it really? Psychologists in psychotherapy have always sought to advance the theory that sorrows should not be left to time alone for a healthy healing process. There has to be a vent to let out anger and cumulated destructive energy. Time does the rest thereafter. So the psychologists say.

However, bloodshed is seen as one way of venting anger in the spirit of "kan davasi". In the political arena though, "kan davasi" has not done much to help societies.

Before dealing with the specifics of the Nigerian society and the present tendency of exacerbated hatred for the man Obasanjo and his actions, I will like to quickly illustrate two national examples of how "kan davasi" is capable of reducing a society to complete ruins.

Afghanistan of the 1980's was under Soviet occupation that was fiercely resisted with the stinger missiles of the Reagan era. The typical symptoms of communism translating into the few elitist "haves" and the very many "have nots" meant a deeply felt resentment and abhorrence of the government of President Najib Ullah who was largely seen as a Kremlin puppet. However, when the Soviets finally quit and the Afghans were left to themselves, the day of reckoning began. The Mujaheddins had to vent their anger and leave the rest of their sorrows for time to heal. They sought to have the head of President Najib Ullah to vent their anger. The revolution was unstoppable. The President sought refuge at the Soviet embassy! In a flagrant violation of diplomatic tradition, the Mujaheddins broke into the Soviet embassy, seized Dr. Najib Ullah, slew him and dismembered the President's body. The President's head was finally held high and paraded through the streets of Kabul in a motorcade amid celebrations and jubilant fanfare! It was all about honor in the spirit of "kan davasi".

Liberia in the early eighties was under the siege of a young Master Sergeant-turn-General Samuel Doe. His brutality, illiteracy, arrogance and God-like sense of complacency brewed boundless anger against this young, ruthless dictator. Many would settle for nothing but his head. So widespread was anger against Doe that he was elected post mortem as Dictator of the month "November 2003". Pushed to a corner in the midst of mounting civil war in 1990, General Doe begged Nigeria's General Babangida for military assistance. Babangida responded with a 4000-man peace-keeping force under the banner of ECOWAS. The peace-keepers were not active warriors, they were peace-keepers only. Doe's forces were overrun by the forces of Charles Taylor. Doe sought refuge in the sanctuary of the ECOWAS peace-keeping force. General Prince Yormie Johnson broke into the headquarters of the peace-keeping force in circumstances unclarified till date and seized President Samuel Doe on September 09th, 1990. The President was beaten and that was only the beginning of a sadistic orgy. They started from his ear, which was cut off in slow, agonizing pain. The fingers followed etc., etc. before his remains were left to bleed to death in unequalled agony and barbarism. It was all documented on video all in the spirit of venting anger, satisfying bruised ego and waiting for time to heal all sorrows. It was the spirit of "kan davasi".

Funnily though, none of these circumstances helped either Afghanistan or Liberia. What followed in both countries in continents far apart, was more carnage, social destruction and a steady backward progression towards the stone age. The radical Talebans were removed from Afghanistan only four years ago by external intervention and Liberia is currently experimenting on democracy after narrowly skipping anarchy.

Events in Nigeria have been fraught with anger, frustration and humiliation in very many directions! People are stuck in blind alleys. Virtual points of no return? Egos have been bruised and people have sought and still seek to restore honor. Atrocities too have been committed. Dele Giwa, Moshood Abiola, Bola Ige count among such atrocities. Thank God though, that the scale does not compare in any way with the Mujahidins, Talibans or the Samuel Does.

One begins to wonder, however, what vicious crime Obasanjo has so committed to justify the intensity of prevailing bitterness and fanaticism against his person away from facts and substance from many popular sources! Where are the wise and the prudent to summon moderation and balance in the prevailing sense of judgment? Returning from Nigeria only on the November 25th, 2006, I was impressed with what I saw of improvements in the banking sector. It takes an intellectual with a sense of economic and financial operations to understand the progress made in the banking sector under President Obasanjo.

Telecommunication has witnessed a buoyant and explosive growth in the Nigerian market. NITEL's grip on the telephone market with its uncontrolled range of flagrant corruption has been broken. Today, owning a conventional telephone line is a matter of choice and affordability and not a matter for some NITEL clerk on the strength of whims and caprices with illicit cash-flow. Mobile phones did the trick.

Ribadu's courageous and gallant fight against corrupt people of political substance is not a non-starter. (Indeed, I have long been nursing a futile expectation for voices to call on Ribadu to run for President.) All these are happening under the Presidency of Obasanjo.

There are many more accomplishments that are not readily known to me and can be counted by the perpetrators of such projects. All these are achievements that should be juxtaposed against the failures and inefficiencies of the Obasanjo regime in any attempt to reach a balanced academic judgment.

Power and water supply as two crucial sectors of public welfare have characterized the glaring failures of the Obasanjo administration not because the administration did not know what to do about them but because it seems to have chosen the wrong approach at some crucial points in time in the aftermath of wrong assessment. The killing of Bola Ige and other spate of unsolved political killings still remain one issue I am unable to comprehend. It is still a mystery why the killing of Bola Ige has not been solved till today. The agitation for tenure elongation against all strains of logical imagination is a marked flaw of the Obasanjo's calculation and political judgment. The chain of flaws may extend endlessly if we choose to count in pessimism. However, I will dare say that corruption is not one of such weaknesses and failures of which Obasanjo should stand accused.

The practice of corruption is not an Obasanjo invention in the history of Nigeria. When Obasanjo handed over military power to an elected civilian government in 1980, there was no report of empty coffers and a drained foreign reserve. In fact, the treasury was so buoyant that the left-wing Obafemi Awolowo was able to promise free education at all levels and free medical care for all. The ruling conservatives of the NPN sought to diversify the economy through the Green Revolution in the agricultural sector. These are all projects that pre-supposed the existence of the necessary resources in government coffers.

However, it took the likes of Umaru Dikko, Joseph Wayas et. al. to run down the economy under the watchful eyes of President Shehu Shagari. Still Nigeria was not completely grounded economically. The subsequent 'sweep-clean' mentality that was ushered in during successive military regimes is culminating today, in the activities of new-breed politicians all over the country.

Obasanjo cannot solve the deeply-rooted problem of corruption in the Nigerian psyche overnight. In fact, he cannot even be realistically expected not to be a part of the corrupt process even though we will choose to pretend that we expect him not to be. The paramount realistic question should therefore, always be how to control the scale of corruption at this opening stage.

This, in fact, is Obasanjo's drive in the installation of the EFCC and Ribadu. Nigerians are not so stupid not to understand that there is never any such society with a zero-level of corruption. Not in this world. But the "winner-takes-it-all" attitude of having not even a single road maintenance to show for eight years of governance like in Edo State is not an uncommon phenomenon today. With reports surfacing, of wealth owned by the Igbinedions, the Ibori's in England, South Africa and perhaps in the USA to say the least of Nigeria, I wonder why Obasanjo should not be allowed to start-off a quiet process of tracking down fellow thieves gone mad, without being chastised and excessively brandished as corrupt. The scale of corruption has now reached an excruciating and obnoxious climax that one should honestly and realistically differentiate only between the moderately corrupt and the chronically corrupt if we are to make any headway at all. This indeed, is a reason, why Obasanjo's level of corruption does not seem to bother his admirers when they unleash venom on Abubakar Atiku. The scale has indeed, taken a turn for lunacy. The selectivity in Obasanjo's probes notwithstanding, the achievement of triggering off a process that no one (not even IBB if he eventually becomes President) would dare halt, deserves positive acknowledgement. In fact, if so corrupt in the scale propagated, Obasanjo may himself, one day appear in the dock and be haunted by the same machinery that he set up for Ribadu to run only if it is allowed to function without unnecessary obstacles. The ultimate goal being a social cleansing of public ethics.

Given the multiplicity of politicians that choose to cheat and steal with impunity and relegate public works to the barest minimum of practicality, no doubt, the end of Nigeria may be a popular uprising. A revolution that seems to be reluctant to unfold in the face of ethnic diversity and multifarious political composition. I dare say in pessimism that the day that a common goal is identified cutting across ethnic divide, may be the defining moment for an unstoppable mob justice, which velocity will surely redefine the history of all Nigeria - Muslim or Christian. We will need all the bishops and priests, evangelists and imams as well as ritualistic chief priests of the world to pray for Nigeria not to toe the path of Afghanistan and Liberia. We will have so many Najib Ullahs and Samuel Does to hang and parade along the streets that the carnage will ultimately, not be worth the revolution.

Let us all hope and pray that time will heal all wounds and help us all forgive and forget in the spirit of constructive advancement and help Nigeria forge its path. After all, who remembers the role attributed to General Yakubu Gowon these days in the Dimka group that killed Murtala Mohammed? At a point in time, Gowon was stripped of his rank of General precisely for this perceived role. Today, it is only an issue for the archives. Perhaps, time will do the trick.

***

Reactions to this article marked my very first encounter with the brutal face of Nigeria's world of amateur political punditry. It was the brazen face of unmitigated perception in black-and-white. You're either for it or against it – whatever the issue is. No middle grounds, no shades of gray.

I had tried in this article, to remind my readers, where we, as a nation, were coming from and where we may be heading to if we choose the wrong priorities. I had tried to underscore the need to tread cautiously and achieve our goals step-by-step.

Unfortunately, the problem was just beginning. A Nigeria of blind hatred drawn across ethnic lines has been born. Eastern Nigerians seem to hate the man Obasanjo, with passion for having been a part of the Nigerian military formation that brought down the Biafra insurgency partly with methods that were not purely military. Time did not seem to have healed wounds as oral history seems to have related a single version of events down to subsequent generations.

Western Nigerians hated Obasanjo – their own man – with passion for his failure to make his impact felt on the region while he was a military head of state. Above all, he led the military government that denied their own son – Obafemi Awolowo – the Presidency of the Second Republic in 1979 and favored the Northern Shehu Shagari.

The Northerners developed their own grievances, because Olusegun Obasanjo committed himself to dismantling the structures that virtually made Nigeria the political property of the northern establishment.

In other words, the President was basically an enemy of all the regions for different reasons. The maxim "the enemy of my enemy is automatically my friend" informed the coalition of odd bed-fellows that stood up against the President. You were either for them or against them. Reasoning in neutrality was seen as pretended rationality and sponsored image-laundering. You were tagged a propagandist and a cheap apologist.

It marked the start of attacks against my person, by persons, who categorically refused to weigh the good sides against the bad ones when it comes to the name Obasanjo.

I wrote the next article that was also published on www.nigeriaworld.com, the long defunct www.nigeria.com and several other websites.

POOR OBASANJO: A HELPLESS PUNCHING BAG FOR WANNABE PHILOSOPHERS

By Frisky Larr   January 04, 2007

In my days as a student, I remember going through a course in "Political thoughts and Philosophy". My lecturer, was a popular Turkish Professor who later became a government functionary and was subsequently assassinated with a car bomb by Islamic fundamentalists. Prof. Ahmet Taner Kışlalı started off that semester by calling on students to visualize themselves sitting in a circle with a huge lamp at the center of the floor. Sitting in one segment of the circle, the Prof. continued, students were to imagine him (the Prof.) calling out to the student sitting opposite him to identify the color of the lamp. From his vantage point, the student opposite would clearly identify the color as "red". At the side of the Prof. though, everyone including the Prof. himself, is identifying the color as "black".

Murmurs begin to make the round. Students begin to accuse themselves and the Prof. of having faulty eyesight. Some recommend that the Prof. and the student opposite him should consult an eye doctor as a matter of priority because other students were seeing the "yellow" and "green" colors respectively from two other vantage positions. Ringing the bell and signaling "order" the Prof. brings an end to the murmurs and grumbles. He orders the students to swap their sitting positions and take the respective places of their counterparts. Only thereafter, did a sigh of relief make the round.

The student who identified a red color can now see that the lamp was truly painted black at the Prof.'s vantage position. Others that saw yellow and green are now able to see that the lamp was indeed, painted red at the vantage position of the other student.

The lesson from this illustrative exercise according to Prof. Kışlalı was to be on our guard as aspiring intellectuals. Never reach any conclusion on any issue without swapping positions with your opponent and viewing issues from his vantage point.

In the past, holders of academic degrees were highly valued and adored in Nigeria of the seventies and early eighties. The reason was simple. Intellectuals were made out of academic drills. There was hardly any degree holder of those years that did not command respect, at least, through the quality of their utterances. There was a sense of awe and myth about them if one did not have the academic qualification to cope with them in discussions.

At that time, academic training seemed to be boosting the intellectual potentials of individuals. It forged analytical reasoning and the empirically undisputable presentation of facts.

Methodology in research teaches every student only two ways of achieving these objectives: Qualitative and/or Quantitative reasoning and analysis. Personal comments serve to interpret facts and figures not obscure them.

At undergraduate level, one is just being introduced into the world of empiricism like the Neophyte of Rosicrucian fame. At the graduate level of pursuing a master degree, on should have passed through series of exercises in scientific and analytical reasoning through semester papers, individual research topics etc. This is then concluded by the ultimate post-graduate aspiration of acquiring a doctorate degree. It is at this stage, that a candidate is expected to be routinely perfected in objective reasoning, scientific analysis and the empirical dissection of facts. The path may then be towed at the individual's discretion, to become an actively researching scientist and end up as a professor or stop at the doctorate level and impart knowledge on others around him.

Qualifications in each of these categories were indeed, defining moments for the Nigerian intellectual of the seventies and early eighties.

Today though, many Nigerian holders of high academic qualification excel by being at best, mere embarrassment to the qualification they hold. Many Internet forums for the dissemination of information are being flooded these days, by highly paper-qualified individuals who cherish just one subject: Obasanjo and the Presidency. They focus exceedingly on Obasanjo-bashing.

The alarming rate at which Obasanjo has these days, become a helpless punching bag for every aspiring verbal pugilist, is indeed, throwing the direction of the Nigerian democratic development into serious question. Particularly at the sight of Doctorate titles as displayed by some of the Obasanjo-bashing authors, I am always excited and in high expectation of a taste of qualitative or quantitative analysis. Much too often, I end up in disappointment at the overwhelming dose of personal caprices and hate-filled subjective manifestations.

Before identifying the ethnic divide along which most of many meaningless attacks seem to play out, I will first like to observe that a large part of these hate preachers with high academic qualifications lives in the USA.

Outside the USA, where I am personally, not exposed to many of the domestic American news media, I am content with the CNN, Newsweek and TIME to give a glimpse of what American journalism may look like. In none of these media have I ever seen such blatant echo of insults and abuses on political office holders like Nigerians choose to pour on Obasanjo through the news media. Indeed, the present administration of George Bush would find his ways of settling scores with anyone who chooses to rain aimless abuses on him by straying too far away from facts. Even a fellow President (Hugo Chavez of Venezuela) who insulted George Bush (no matter how justified he was) at the podium of the UNO general assembly knows what he went through in the aftermath thereof. Never have I seen Larry King insult his guests in the name of boldness and courage.

Tai Solarin rose to fame for constructive criticisms based on facts and figures. Air Iyare of the old Mid-West State was well known for intellectual attacks that left his targets looking for explanations. None of these men excelled with insults and abuses. The only prominent Nigerian critic that was known for abusive and insulting criticisms was the veteran Fela Anikulapo Kuti. But he was not a journalist and never pretended to be one. He even symbolically sang in Pidgin English to shed off any semblance of intellectualism (even though intelligent he was).

When some over-ambitious and no doubt, intelligent but hate-filled young and elderly men of Nigerian origin then pick their pen or PC keyboard to write and address the President of their own country as a "Serpent head", a "Village tyrant", "demon", "madness ruling the land" etc. no intellectual postulant of substance would react to such superficial Tarzans of the intellectual jungle. But when exalted and clearly identified degree holders come up with extremely imbalanced and overtly flawed products of empiricism, one wonders why the degrees they hold deserve such a huge embarrassment.

Most often, a large and vocal section of the Yorubas, who seem to be well acquainted with the man Obasanjo from his hometown (or wherever) are mostly in the forefront of raining insults on him and demonizing him in the most despicable fashion. I have often heard the saying that a Prophet is never accepted in his own home. But that too, should not give consolation because the rejection of a single prophet should not be tantamount to the rejection of objectivity and fairness.

On the opposite spectrum of the unholy divide stands a huge number of the Ibos (definitely not all Ibos) who traditionally abhor anything Yoruba.

What these two parties have in common is the absolute rejection of anything factual, objective or fair about the man Obasanjo. In private conversations, articles, public forums of all kinds, they will pick on any given opportunity to rain hell and damnation on the poor fellow. Sometimes, I ask myself if the keyboard of the computer on which the articles are written do not feel the pains of the written insults?

There has been such an extreme turn of events that anyone who dares to experiment on objectivity in connection with Obasanjo ends up being branded a paid Obasanjo-supporter.

People feel bold and courageous, get the feeling of 'making noise' to be heard by picking on Obasanjo with the weirdest of expressions. I have, however, asked myself on countless occasions, where these people were at the time Abacha raged uncontrolled.

I ask myself if anyone would be true to himself to assert that Obasanjo has brought nothing but destruction to Nigeria. In counting the failures if not blunders of Obasanjo (seeking a third term through the ill-advised project of constitutional amendment, presiding over incessant price hikes on fuel and commodity products, not doing much to fix countless numbers of bad roads, helplessly watching the surge in crime rate that is killing dozens of innocent Nigerians, failing to account for the death of Bola Ige [in which fingers are also pointed at him], failing to resolve the long-standing issue of power supply, social chaos and indiscipline now leaving Nigeria even rated far behind Ghana, wanton corruption as alleged and apparently being proved by Atiku, etc.), has Obasanjo - in spite of all that - done nothing at all to account for his eight years in office? Just nothing?

People are always cautioned to look back at where the Obasanjo government started from. What Abacha inherited from IBB, further destroyed and left behind for onward transmission to Obasanjo. Has Obasanjo really achieved nothing and absolutely nothing?

Check the issue of Atiku Abubakar. Is anyone out there that can give me an example of an insubordinate Vice President in the history of any democracy worldwide? We have a constitution that asks a President to handpick his running mate but failed to address the issue of dealing with him when he becomes insubordinate, a liability and even a threat and an opponent to the President. I bet no one involved in the drafting of this constitution ever dreamt of such an issue occurring. I know of no single precedent. Nowhere in the world. Now, rather than seeking to address this loophole in the constitution in a fair and equitable manner to forestall a future repeat of such ugly situations, voices are busy blaming the President as if it was so impossible to swap positions to figure out how it feels to have an insubordinate and threatening deputy hanging on one's heels. Rather than friends of Atiku cautioning the Vice President in the loudest term possible and drawing his attention to the truth that a Vice President is on no account, meant to be an opposition force against his own President, they are busy applauding him through his own political suicide. Rather than making him realize that a Vice President is supposed to rise and fall with his President, they are accusing the President of breaching the constitution.

The truth though, is that the constitution has not been breached. A process of seeking an interpretation of the constitution has only been set in motion. For this purpose, the semblance of breach had to be created as one of several options. The removal of the Vice President, who adamantly refuses to resign in disagreement with the President, is meant to trigger a constitutional debate at the doorstep of the Supreme Court. If the Vice President fails to challenge the President's decision in court, the decision automatically becomes an unwritten part of the constitution and will be emulated by future Presidents of the country. This too, is a process that is not strange to normal democratic practices. The constitution in Great Britain today, is a product of trial and error, not mandatory drafting. That is how democracies can also function. By challenging Obasanjo's decision in court, the loophole in the constitution will be mended by a decision of the Supreme Court.

Rather than focusing on the intellectual aspect of bridging this glaring constitutional gap, many Ph.D holders are doing what they cherish most: Obasanjo-bashing. They fail to ask themselves, if it pays more for the democracy of the country to encourage an attitude like Atiku Abubakar's or to focus on bridging the constitutional gap to prevent such a universally unprecedented act of intra-governmental indiscipline in the name of democracy.

No one for once (not even the Ph.D holders), seeks to swap position to view the issue from the other side of the fence. All that matters most seems to be Obasanjo-bashing. Poor old Obasanjo.

***

Reactions to this article were mixed. While many neutral-minded observers, who were vocally in the minority, showed a great deal of understanding for my angry disposition, the die-hard haters of the President saw confirmation of their suspicions that I was a paid agent of the President, working against the vocal opposition. At that time though, I had never met the President or anyone in his inner or outer circle and was fully reliant on media information for my independent opinion.

One of the leading online forums for written opinions at the time was the website "Nigeria World", in which I considered myself lucky to be published. The brains behind this website (largely based in North America) were a combination of ambitious self-styled 'gifted' writers of Yoruba and Ibo descent. They were largely, hardcore Obasanjo-haters. Some of them truly paraded the doctorate degree and fell into the category of people that I had brutally chastised in my article, unknowingly and unintentionally. But I realized this only in hindsight without regrets. They went mad at me and were led by one Ibo fellow that I simply identified as "Wabuz".

They put an immediate stop to further publication of my articles on "Nigeria World" and it didn't matter that I pointed out to them that they were refusing to accommodate my divergent opinion – a point for which they had repeatedly attacked the President so viciously. They proceeded to have someone write the following rejoinder to my article, have it dissected to contradict every single point I raised therein and denied me the right of subsequent reply.

OUR OWN OBASANJO: NOT A HELPLESS PUNCHING BAG!

By John Ayodele
bishopbode@hotmail.com
Atlanta, GA, USA

Tuesday, January 9, 2007

One very interesting piece was in the Nigeriaworld recently titled: *"Poor Obasanjo: A helpless punching Bag For Wannabe Philosophers"* and evokes some discussions amongst some of us here who always review events in Nigeria. Those of us who also enjoy all the information and contributions by Nigerians on the internet which go a long way in involving more people in the affairs of that part of the world and importantly sensitizing hitherto lukewarm Nigerians.

There were well made points by all those who have had to criticize the utterances, comportment and actions of the Nigerian President, Chief Olusegun Obasanjo. It is believed that the article in question is not saying that OBJ has been turned to a helpless punching bag as a result of well-intentioned criticisms.

Mr. President of Nigeria, our own Mathew Okikiola Olusegun Obasanjo is never a helpless man. He has never been, except during the days of Abacha when things completely fell apart! It was an unusual period and any one could be helpless when faced with dark goggled man and we all chose to ignore the fact that the strongest of men would cry if handled by Mustapha and company.

Apart from being an Owu man who ''will never give in'' (''Unn o ni gba''). A typical Owu man will tell you this. OBJ, the President of Nigeria is never helpless with so many people at his beck and call to run errands for him, take care of his public relations, handle his stocks or buying Transcorp shares (ask Onyiuke Okereke of NSE), special assistants to give fire for fire (Femi Fani-Kayode told the Senators that he was specifically hired to do this) and other guys all over Aso Rock or Presidency whose job is to give a 24/7 all protection to our own OBJ and many more. How can he be helpless?

Again, he is not poor. He is the number one man and the most powerful in Nigeria. He told the whole world that his ministers or advisers could give their opinions but he had the options of taking or ignoring them as he knew which way(s) to go. He is indeed the Commander in chief of the Armed Forces of Nigeria (sorry excluding those of the Niger Delta, OPC,

MASSOB, Arewa and of course several armed robbery Forces in Nigeria) but his Forces have full legitimacy. He is also the real brain and power of the ruling party - People's Democratic Party where his candidates are always unopposed for Chairmanship or other elective positions. If OBJ does not like a face anymore, such person or persons should vacate office. It therefore follows that to be in favor, obey OBJ commandments! If there is any doubt, ask Gemade or Awoniyi or Ogbeh or some elected officials who could not keep pace with 'Babacratic' policies.

How can he be helpless or poor?

The President from the literal point has become richer than he has ever been in his life. His farms now make 30million naira monthly (that was the figure given but nothing on taxes), a big leap from a near dead farm in 1999! Obasanjo has been able to purchase more than 200-million-naira worth of shares in a Microsoft type of mega Company named Transcorp in Nigeria while the President's family is going to be rich enough to live riches for their future generations. How can he be poor?

There have been donations running to billions into the coffers of Olusegun Obasanjo by all the richest men and women in Nigeria and this translates into huge wealth for the person of Obasanjo. Several governors have been doing stiffest competition to give gifts to him and this is different from the man who was out from Abacha gulag in 1999 and had to rely on the widow's mite of some men to rehabilitate.

These should not take any credit away from OBJ's undoubtable strides toward bringing some discipline to Nigeria's Finances as he had secured a creditworthiness for Nigeria as per the liquidation of debts with the Paris Club and the laudable move to cancel that of London. He also deserves commendation with the establishment of the Economic and Financial Crimes Commission which is a trail blazer. It is not impossible that the Commission may be used in future to throw more lights on some alleged serious financial misdemeanors of Obasanjo and his men.

Far away from being helpless or poor, OBJ remains very intransigent in his ways since he moved from the Anambra crisis in which a sitting governor was detained with covert support from Aso Rock to the drama with his party Chairman who forcefully resigned and to a defeat over the Third Term debacle. The actual beginning of his 'war' with Atiku started when Ngige was supported by the Vice President while OBJ was cleverly away from home at the turn of Chris Uba riots in Anambra.

There is no doubt that the President has involved himself in many unnecessary squabbles which will not be the case elsewhere as the article of note would want us to look at the situation in Europe and United States. His allegations and counter allegations which Reuben Abati likened to 'bolekaja' has done incalculable harm to the image of the office of the President and has ridiculed Nigeria as a country in the comity of nations around the world.

Nothing will take credits away from OBJ in his handling of the debt repayment of Nigeria and his firm control of the retired but not tired big Khaki boys who still want to come back. Great kudos for his removing the tight ropes of the World creditors from the neck of Nigeria and other achievements under his watch.

Still there are many misnomers under the watch of OBJ which continue to befuddle Nigerians at home and abroad. Nigerians have become hungrier than ever without benefiting from the great savings in the International purse, the Nigeria Police has become more unreliable as it is today in the face of alarming political assassination, armed robbery and even Police slaughtering. The Niger Delta problem is a gathering threat to the continued oneness of the country which seems to have gone beyond the President's comprehension. Many times in the early life of OBJ's first term, Nigerians witnessed his globetrotting in search of investors for the home economy, now with the rate of assassination which has not elucidated any serious action from him, most of his targeted investors will not budge while those who chose to consider must have changed their minds.

If Mr. President became a punching bag as the piece said, the issues at hand caused it. The stringent criticism of Economic and Financial Crimes Commission is because the Commission, with due respect to Mallam Nuhu Ribadu's lion heart, has glaringly been perceived as being under the whims and caprices of Obasanjo. The war against graft seems to have some sacred and untouchable 'cows'. Mr. President himself by his actions such as purchasing 200 million shares in a mega Company which purchased some of the biggest parastatals in the Nigerian economy, being in the middle of a Library Fund raising in which some of the big men seeking patronage from his government donated huge sums of money to 'him' and the banana peel from Atiku's counter allegations - some of those documents very convincing, has done more harm to his personal image, and also that of the President's office. Our simple romance with modern States tells that there should be some equality before the law. The law which catches an Alamiyisegha or Dariye over money laundry should not be made different for a Daniels or an Odili or OBJ or any of the Presidential Assistants or Advisers caught with unexplainable money. This is where the United States of America has always been a good example. An Assistant of the Vice President of America resigned over some classified information and his matter still hanging in the Court while the reverse will be the case in Nigeria as there will always be some protections from the top for some crimes committed by cronies of powerful men in Nigeria.

Posterity will be there to reappraise the years of Obasanjo and then Nigerians will be able to see if the war on corruption was all inclusive or selective or if the hunter of corrupt people is also dirty. It will also allow us all to know why the President has kept quiet despite the haplessness of the Nigeria Police in the mounting wave of assassinations and why some political shenanigans or touts are allowed to hold the country or their States to ransom with the President continuing to give them carrots instead of the sticks. Why is it difficult to arrest the incessant armed robbery acts and endangered security of lives in Nigeria under the watch of a retired General Obasanjo?

In our days too at the Great UI, we practiced what was then known as amateur journalism in which we tried to emulate some of the doyens of the industry either by going with aliases or fake names or some unreal names. Some of us picked names like 'aiyekoto' – pen-name for the late civilian governor of Ogun State, 'periscope' – Ebenezer Babatope, 'searchlight' - Lam Adesina, 'Pendulum' – Ofeimum and others. We did give hints as to our real names like the popular people above.

It is therefore rite for some people to use aliases or surreal names to pen articles in the papers or on the Internet. On the other hand, some people hide under fake names to defend some payers while there have been examples of people who work under some governments as civil servants but who do public image laundry jobs under some fictitious names.

The writers who have had one or other bone to pick with the way OBJ has mishandled some issues in Nigeria are not less patriotic and the choice of some wrong or out of line words by some authors (not this writer) does not make them less patriotic or respectful to the person of the President. However, learning is a continuum and hoping these few out of line phrases or adjectives will cease to be applied by all the concerned.

There is nothing wrong in every opinion being represented or portrayed as the internet has allowed. It is not every opinion published in the Nigeriaworld for example or any media that is read. There is no doubt that name calling by contributors in any type of media is wrong. Names such as 'serpent head', 'ugly man' and others are unnecessary in any objective analysis or article contribution. Open insults and abuses should indeed, as the piece in the Nigeriaworld advised, be ostracized from all debates. The issue of nation building which is at stake should be done without hate filled opinions or debates.

Empirical analysis teaches that one should be totally convinced and to involve all evidences, while the study of existentialism makes everyone responsible for his actions. Obasanjo takes full responsibilities for his actions as the President of Nigeria because these affect millions of people within and outside the country. Nigerians whether outside or inside have the right to aspire to a better country under a better leadership. The joy of Nigerians outside or inside will be complete when whoever occupies the Office of the President is sensitive about all his actions or inactions.

Writing is a passion especially to those who have had one or other relationship with any of the mass media particularly the pen media. It is kudos to those who write on burning topics touching the sleeping country Nigeria suffering under some mumbo-jumbo kind of leadership since Independence.

There is nothing wrong in people appraising their leaders, but such should be done without any abusive words. This is done even in United States and at least in England. It is also the case in Germany where we citizens employ several means to disagree with their leaders.

Nigeria cannot and will not be an exception.

Nigerians should always be on the march for strict obeisance of the laws while no man should be allowed to turn the laws of the land into his. Democracy involves dialogue or debates and 'is for the people, by the people and of the people' and not just for the powerful.

***

This article marked the last mention of my name on the platform of NigeriaWorld. A fellow, who I identified as "Wabuz", who later engaged in further communications with another reader, was vocal in claiming credit for having "taken care of" Frisky Larr. A few days later, the above article was released on the website.

While this article stands out today, for a complete balance and neutrality in its appraisal of the article it refers to, I must admit, I had a completely different impression of its content at the time it was released. Indeed, I nurse the profound suspicion that the article has been modified and doctored over time to reflect a milder and more neutral demeanor. It's initial intention was to reflect bias on my part in favor of the incumbent President, advance reasons for the suspected bias and accuse me of recklessness in the things I wrote. Today, no such trace is left in the article. In fact, the boastful architect and mastermind of its release, Mr "Wabuz", who also masterminded my expulsion from the "Nigeria World" forum did not have such a mild and friendly article on the top of his wish-list, when he sought to have me discredited.

As is my usual habit in consuming media information, I focused basically, more on the content than on the author. I was, therefore, full of surprises, when almost eight years later, I ran into someone on Facebook, who had long been a friend and shared much cerebral common grounds with me, and introduced himself in a casual chat down the line, as the author of the above rejoinder.

Today, John Ayodele is one writer, with whom I enjoy a very cordial and mutually respectful relationship.

Having been kicked out of "Nigeria World", I went out in search of a new home-base to continue writing my articles and expressing my views. I finally found the free-for-all portal "Nigerian Village Square". I had virtually jumped from the frypan directly into fire.

The Nigerian Village Square, as I subsequently found out, was partly populated by people, who like me, were shown the way out of "Nigeria World" for different reasons. I had no clue then that this portal had a special reputation for a huge nuisance value, which it took time to correct several years later after inflicting a massive damage on its own reputation.

Every individual was allowed to register on the portal and post his/her own article whenever desired. Readers were allowed to comment directly below articles with only theoretical restriction on language, abuses and obscenity.

As in every free-for-all venture however, the Nigerian element will never be complete without abuses. There were seemingly, professional readers, who hardly played any other role but to write comments with the primary motive of discrediting and ridiculing writers and articles. Even though the portal was guided by clear rules, the administrators of the website were extremely reluctant to enforce such rules. In fact, in one casual comment, I spotted one of the administrators reveling delightfully in the abuses and characterizing them as the "baptismal" ushering-in, of new writers.

Worse still, a huge part of such readers, who devoted themselves to abusive comments and vitriols, were Yorubas and Igbos, who formed a staunch and uncompromising anti-Obasanjo block. They would engage in no constructive reasoning to view the then leader of the country from a position of neutrality. Any such call at the time, was considered sacrilegious and one that could be advanced only by paid agents and spies of the President.

Unaware of all these and with the zeal to go on writing, I posted my very first article on Nigerian Village Square lambasting Nigeria's new-found appetite for cross-border military operations in Sierra Leone and the like.

Nigeria's Hunger for Peacekeeping: Ain't seen nothing yet!

By Frisky Larr

When Bruce Willis starred in the motion picture "Black Hawk down", the watching audience was well aware of the epoch-making quality of the storyboard that was translated into electronic motion on the movie screen. It was one of America's earliest outlandish combat adventures since Vietnam. Until I read critical reviews about the movie though, I didn't think I knew precisely what Black Hawk was. Commentaries and analyses told the tale that the Black Hawk is the name of a particularly, valued specie of America's combat helicopters used for tactical troop transportation, electronic warfare and aero-medical evacuation. Until it was shot down in Somalia, no common man knew that American Helicopters had names for identification.

How did it start? American troops led the United Nation's military intervention in Somalia in the year 1993 to enforce the pacification of the war-torn country that has never known peace since the overthrow of Siad Barre on January 26th, 1991. America's giant stride in warfare electronics and space exploration for military intelligence had developed an auto-dynamic scare in the psyche of beholders with a sense of awe and invincibility. Some exaggerated perceptions even contended at the time that the Americans were capable of spotting the movement of any rat in far-away Saharan desert. When news broke out that the Americans were leading the UN intervention troop, warlords were scared to their panties and I guess many would have boozed and ingested every possible courage-inducing substance to stand on their feet. The Americans however came and unleashed the power of their military might, identified the principal troublemaker in the person of warlord General Aidid, who was declared wanted and never caught. He finally prided himself for having stood up to the most powerful country in the world. The worst however happened when someone somehow managed to shoot down the Black Hawk while the Americans were caught in the midst of a civil war. The Americans withdrew their troops in the aftermath and this was largely seen as a failed mission as subsequent development proved.

Today though, having seen the downing of the Stealth bomber in the Yugoslavian war and the repeated shooting down of the Black Hawk over Iraq, no film on this issue will have any epoch-making character any more.

In sanitizing and pacifying Sierra Leone, Nigeria played a major role with its contingent of forces. The resultant order that is currently seeing Sierra Leone through to the gradual process of recovery away from civil war and trade in child-soldiers is evidence of a job well done. The dark side of this mission, which also gave Nigeria one of its worst images on the black continent, is hardly talked about. Nigerian soldiers were accused of indiscriminate raping with a huge number of young innocent girls impregnated and condemned to bringing up fatherless children as single mothers in a financially and socially hostile society. Worse still, Nigerian soldiers were accused of involvement in all sorts of crimes including the smuggling of the now notorious "blood diamonds".

The same scenario played out in Liberia with the resultant political stability that is currently pushing Liberia through under the captainship of a technocrat, who was more or less, installed with the prominent contribution of Nigeria.

In both cases, the dark side of the peacekeeping forces particularly, alleged atrocities of Nigerian soldiers, was overshadowed by success on the political front.

When this project succeeded in Sierra Leone, the Americans were pleased and highly gratified for now having an Assistant to pull the chestnuts out of the fire. Somalia taught the Americans to dread the jungles of Africa and the tricky landscape that should better be left to the indigenes of the continent.

In fact, one of the achievements that the Olusegun Obasanjo administration is credited with today, is that of making Nigeria acceptable in polite societies. The one-time pariah state under Sani Abacha is now a major regional power with some global muscle-flexing capability. Is that really true?

The impotence of Nigeria's muscle is much evident in Darfur in Sudan where the Arabic and government-sponsored Janjaweed militia keeps on slaughtering our black brothers and sisters under the helpless and watchful eyes of Nigerian soldiers amongst others, under the banner of African Union Peacekeeping.

So, if Nigeria is claimed to be having some muscle-flexing capability on the international stage, that stage is indeed, highly limited to the black African continent and the capability badly 'limited' in the real sense of the word. Faced with scattered groups of militias that are well armed with conventional weapons without the least or semblance of current structure in modern weaponry, it took for instance, a country like Ethiopia to dislodge fighters of the Islamic Court from Mogadishu with basic (and nothing near sophisticated) air power. The rebels that were strong in conventional warfare on the land did not even have the least anti-aircraft missile to match. Compared with the Mujaheedin warfare of the eighties against the Soviet Union in Afghanistan where the rebels carried American-made shoulder-borne stinger missiles to upset the superior air power of the Soviet Union, the Somalia game is a mere child's play.

In other words, with a moderately equipped air and naval force, it doesn't take much to be a major military player in Africa faced with scantily equipped rebel forces as long as the powers behind them are not Russia, EU or the USA. At home, Nigeria is struggling to confront marauding rebels in the Niger Delta because the cost of wiping them off with superior air and naval power will be too high to lives in the entire region. Let's make no mistake. The battle for the emancipation of the Niger Delta has now turned from emancipation to the common criminality of kidnapping for ransoms and mere terrorism. Since this is not our issue in this essay, it will be sufficient to see the difficulties of the Nigerian combat forces in fighting conventional battles with no clearly visible enemy. This is even more exacerbated in Somalia if the terror-trained individual fighters of Al-Qaeda with their cell-type structures, are involved.

After major combat dominated by Ethiopian feeble air attacks by modern standards, the Americans led the cry at the corridors of the United Nations seeking to have regional powers take over the peacekeeping mission to stabilize the newly won position of the government in Mogadishu.

Now watch it! Who was first to volunteer troops for the mission? Nigeria of course! Before examining the underlying motive in this case, it may be interesting to note the immediate aftermath of Ethiopia's military success in Somalia.

Following Ethiopia's successful battle, the Americans could not do more than covertly support Ethiopia and itself launch some sporadic hit-and-run air strikes to eliminate any residual radical Islamic potential in a form of mopping-up operation, having learnt lessons from the downing of the black hawk. But fighting is still raging today, no matter how low-keyed.

The Americans, however, immediately backed up the military angle with a diplomatic move by dispatching a State Department's envoy to the region to rally neighboring countries to contribute substantial troop numbers. All of a sudden, the focus was shifted from requiring an African peacekeeping force, to demanding a peacekeeping force that is contributed by immediate neighboring countries of Somalia. Given the instability of the military situation, a lot of the work was cladded in secrecy. The American envoy shuttled between Mogadishu, Nairobi and Kampala and sometimes presumably, reached out to Dar Es Salaam to rein-in neighbors in the search for troops. This was all playing out long after Nigeria had declared its readiness to contribute a substantial troop number. Suddenly, no one was talking about Nigeria's offer anymore. Unfortunately, however, Uganda, Kenya and the rest of them have either had their military capacity either decimated in civil wars of their own or simply do not have the acceptable basics of military intervention.

Agreed that a lot happens behind the scene in diplomatic negotiations that do not meet the eyes, it is still a mystery why this semblance of snobbery against Nigeria was deemed necessary or allowed to appear the way it did. Our records in Sierra Leone and in Liberia did not hold the most glorious moral banner. Aside that though, the question arises if there was possibly any attempt to carefully trim Nigeria's wings?

Furthermore, a neutral observer may want to know if Nigeria has anything to gain from sending troops all over Africa to keep political houses in order when its own house has hardly been properly cleaned. One speculation that glaringly meets the eyes is the desire to keep the soldiers busy. Their attention will thus be diverted from any thought of coup plotting. Unfortunately, however, all these ventures are characterized by the inevitable aftertaste of colonial adventurism. Political psychology teaches us that no country is gladly and thankfully inferior and militarily muscled around.

At the moment, our immediate neighbor Ghana, has a more robust economy and a resilient social order as opposed to our cash-in-hand and economic potential. Experts and observers agree that Ghana is on a sound path to sustainable economic growth. Yet, the focus in the management of the country is not on militarism and colonial adventure. South Africa is by far Africa's most technologically advanced and richest country in all senses of economic and military analyses. President Thabo Mbeki has, however, categorically ruled out contributing forces to Somalia.

What then is Nigeria's motive in reiterating its desire to contribute forces after the dust on the emphasis on "neighboring countries" had settled down? What are the prospects in dragging Nigeria into a country where religious sectarianism and particularly Islamic fundamentalism with a touch of Al-Qaeda's involvement looms? What is the long-term benefit in presenting Nigeria as a stooge of the Americans in a country where America itself shies away from fighting the battle for its own interest directly but will only arm the nations it is sending only in line with its own whims and caprices? What does Nigeria stand to gain in exposing itself to Somalia's Muslim militants as siding with one of the parties to the conflicts?

I bet the President of the country is aware that South Africa's explicit rejection of any direct involvement is informed by sound and professional advisory calculations! Where are the wise and the prudent political and diplomatic advisers in Nigeria?

Nigeria's goodwill towards Somalia has been well demonstrated and documented on several occasions not the least, in the acceptance of Asylum for President Siad Barre after his overthrow before he finally died of heart attack in Lagos on January 02nd 1995. Wouldn't it be better off stopping at that?

***

While reactions to this article were largely positive and full of praises, the professional team of baptismal fire, was itching for a point of attack. I remember one reader's comment, which took me on to drive home a point that the American military helicopter that was downed in Somalia was not called Black Hawk. I remember the aggressive tone of the comment that failed to tell me the correct name but kept pounding the phrase the Blackhawk is not called Black Hawk. When I finally realized what he meant that "Black" and "Hawk" were not spelt in separation the American style, I politely acknowledged this, and he repeated that the Blackhawk is not called Black Hawk. That was my baptism of fire at the Nigerian Village Square portal.

As time progressed, it became obvious to the professional audience of this portal that I was not naturally disposed to antagonizing President Olusegun Obasanjo on a blanket basis. Of course, the heroes of this portal were Reuben Abati, who was a Guardian columnist and Chairman of the Guardian Editorial Board at the time, and Okey Ndibe, who was a Sun columnist at the time. The Sun belongs to Orji Uzor Kalu, then Governor of Abia State, who was a sworn enemy of President Olusegun Obasanjo. Reuben Abati and Okey Ndibe had one thing in common. They were die-hard Obasanjo haters (not critics, since critics display senses of academic rationality and objectivity). The duo was revered by the audience of the Nigerian Village Square and they never failed to deliver in their competition to outdo each other in the venom of their poisonous arrows.

One of my most popular articles that was published in several online platforms at the time, was:

Atiku Abubakar: A Harakiri fighter?

By Frisky Larr

The phrase "Harakiri" is a slang word widely used in the United States and Europe, more than in Japan. It is originally, a Japanese word depicting ritual suicide by self-disembowelment on a sword. It derives from "Hara" – for bowel and "Kiru" – for tearing. In fact, it is merely a facet of an old Samurai tradition called "Seppuku", which was dominant amongst the Samurai in the middle of the twelfth century. A manly action depicting manhood at its gallant height, it was a way of restoring honor to a man and his family that has lost face and dignity through a breach of service and official duty. Rather than walk around in shame and feel the humiliation of letting down his personal sense of pride, a Samurai would rather drive the sword deep into his own stomach, tear it apart, feel the wildest pain and stand up to it in the spirit of manhood and finally drop dead. Seppuku was officially outlawed in Japan in the year 1868.

However, Harakiri as a segment of Seppuku cannot be outlawed from the human mind in the depth of shallow reasoning and egoistic calculations.

I remember the American presidential elections that saw George W. Bush through to his first term in office. Many blacks were reportedly denied voting. Many votes were said to have been wrongly counted in the face of faulted machines and ballot papers. Intimidation was said to have been used as a weapon against voters to the detriment of the democrats, etc. etc. The first Supreme Court judgment in the aftermath of the legal challenge filed by Al Gore, ruled in favor of the Republicans, by a controversial margin. Al Gore vowed to take the fight through the length of all judicial challenges, because he figured there were reasons and facts enough to push his case. One required no experienced political analyst to figure out the political ramifications this would have had on the already dented image of the mighty America. The inauguration of the new President was scheduled for a few weeks after polling. A protracted legal battle would have translated into recounts and probably rescheduling of elections in some constituencies if the rule of law was followed to the last. Emerging democracies laughed. People jeered. *"If elections could not be hitch-free in one of the oldest and most stable democracies in the world, who are we in the third world?"* many asked.

Fellow democrats saw these loose stones flying wild from all directions. Priorities had to be defined. No one wanted to see America continuing to be a laughing stock in the face of perceived "vassals" that were regularly lectured on democracy. Friends and fellow democrats reined-in Al Gore. Pressure was brought to bear. Gore finally rescinded his vow. The interest of the nation mattered most.

Rumors have it that Atiku Abubakar was installed as Vice President in the aftermath of traditional horse-trading to pacify the north in a Presidency that was graciously ceded to the South out of the "kindness of the heart" of omnipotent Northerners. We choose to ignore the fact though, that no law foresees the inevitability of northern involvement (or do we call it domination?) in every government to rule Nigeria. Rumors also have it that Obasanjo as the accustomed marionette in a northern power game, was chosen as a trusted gatekeeper in a window-dressing exercise to camouflage occasional southern ascendancy to the presidency. Atiku was to be the real power broker from behind the scene while Obasanjo did the bidding to the outside world, so the rumors say. However, Obasanjo was said to have "grown wings" after the first term in office and would no longer "play ball". The aggrieved Atiku who, as the rumors say, actually saw Obasanjo as his subordinate by illegal contractual deal, then set out to teach Obasanjo a lesson to make him realize who installed him (Obasanjo) in power.

Since we will never have any way of verifying the amount of truth in wild political rumors, we can only pick on indicative validations. The bitterness with which Atiku is presently selling even his own grandmother to fight a senseless battle against the President seems to give credence to the theory that Atiku is badly offended about an Obasanjo who seems to have stepped on his toes, even though the fellow Obasanjo is supposed to have been nothing but a worthless rat. Everything Atiku has been doing bears the hallmark of wanting to prove to Obasanjo that the world will see Obasanjo for the worthless rat that he is. This seems to validate the idea that Atiku has never at any time, regarded Obasanjo as his superior officer.

Unfortunately, however, none of us spectators on the wider field was party or even witness to any clandestine behind-the-scene arrangement. As electorates though, we are a major party to an election that voted Obasanjo into the office of President (not puppet President). Quite recently, a Nigerian writer highlighted a well-known fact of which we all needed to be reminded. Musa Yar'Adua was recently elected as presidential candidate in his own party. He subsequently handpicked a running mate that had nothing to do with his election. Buhari did the same in his own party. In selecting a running mate as candidate for the Vice Presidency, a presidential candidate justifiably expects unflinching loyalty and personal commitment no matter the horse-trading behind the scene.

George Bush Snr. as Vice President of Ronald Reagan is down in history as having disagreed with Ronald Reagan on several policy issues. None of these issues came out in the open. Fragments of such information trickled out in the press at the end of Reagan's second term while George Bush ran to succeed Reagan. Bush wanted to be rewarded for his blind loyalty to Reagan with unflinching support from the Reagan family in his own campaign.

President Corazon Aquino of the Philippines ascended to the highest office after a people's power revolt that ousted Ferdinand Marcus. As a vote-winning candidate of the time, the opposition picked on her with some window-dressing motives to remind voters of her charismatic husband Nino Aquino, who was brutally murdered by Ferdinand Marcus' death squad. In the pre-election horse-trading that brought Corazon Aquino to power, General Fidel Ramos and General Juan Ponce Enrile were allegedly assured by her that they would be the real power brokers behind the scene. She was said to have characterized herself as a mere housewife who understood nothing of politics. Upon becoming President though, Corazon Aquino gave both Generals important appointments and went ahead to exercise her full authority as President. General Enrile was aggrieved, embittered and sought to organize a palace coup. General Ramos kept his cool and accepted the status quo irrespective of pre-election horse-trading. The Generals were pitched against each other and General Ramos prevailed. He frustrated all efforts by Enrile to oust President Aquino. In the democratic dispensation, General Enrile ended up only as a Senator rather than as President, which he badly wanted to be. In rewarding General Ramos, Mrs. Aquino made General Ramos her crown prince and Ramos succeeded Aquino as President at the time her term was over.

The question becomes pertinent most often, if Atiku Abubakar has well-meaning friends who wish him well. Friends that should be having the political wisdom of the American democrats who cautioned Al Gore to put his personal ambitions aside and put the interest of the nation first. Friends, with the wisdom of General Fidel Ramos to inject the benefits of loyalty in the man.

Elementary logic should tell anyone that dissatisfaction in government should translate into departure from the government. When the conscience is clear, people fear no accusation. They will indeed, launch a cleansing crusade from outside the government either at home or from a foreign country if they fear undue persecution. Unfortunately, however, Atiku Abubakar wants to be taken seriously as a clean crusader hiding behind the cloak of immunity. While Vice President, he cannot be prosecuted. If he wins the election to become President, his immunity will continue, and he will have time to reorganize the political structure to kill the notion of ever prosecuting him. What is Atiku afraid of? To achieve his aim the man is stopping at nothing.

Knowing fully well that his opponents will always device counter-strategies, he continues to behave as if he had a monopoly of intelligence and political machinations to outsmart his enemies. Standing elected alongside a President that selected him to run as Vice President, he swaps political party amid regular trading of insults and counter-accusations. Thereafter, he expects to sit beside the same President on daily basis as if nothing has happened. He starts a battle, which he, under normal circumstances, can never win.

Atiku seems to count on the polarizing strength and sympathy of the northern oligarchy that probably placed him there. However, indicative validations seem to suggest that the northern oligarchy is not necessarily comfortable with him. Who knows if they ever wanted him to nurture presidential ambitions as he was made to represent the northern interest in the Obasanjo's presidency.

No doubt Atiku would have been far more credible if he resigned his office early enough, went on exile to England, USA or elsewhere and launched a crusade against the purported corruption of the Obasanjo's Presidency with the embarrassing facts and figures he has so far been presenting. Unfortunately, however, no matter the evidences presented by him to indict President Obasanjo right now, people cannot help but see him as a drowning desperado merely wanting to take as many people as possible with him to his irreversible death. The more prominent the victim he takes along the better it is for his ego.

With the interest of the nation at heart, Atiku would have known the consequences of his action and save the nation such a dirty development. He is unfortunately, being applauded and urged forward by friends mainly powered by their common hatred for the man Obasanjo or the obvious material benefit of their actions. Much as I wish to remain balanced in my assessment of this troubling issue, it is very difficult to put the blame on Obasanjo in any obvious way. He is the President and the boss. If one falls out of favor with him as his subordinate, one should quit and tell his story in a different terrain. The President and the President alone bears responsibility for the failure or success of his administration not the Vice President. No one talks of Dr. Alex Ekueme today, who was the Vice President of Shehu Shagari.

Atiku's posturing creates the impression of a man hallucinating and seeing himself as a Co-President or a parallel President that is subordinate to no one, ignoring the fact that he was selected to assist and not to fight. He basks in the attitude of spoiling the party if he has to go. He simply doesn't want to go alone.

The brave and valiant Samurai, however, never seeks to drag others to their own death. It is a matter of honor. If he were to be lectured by the ancient Samurais, many would have told him that his actions are symbolic of his own sword, which he is deliberately driving into his own stomach. With every passing day, he is tearing and ripping his stomach apart. The game of harakiri also requires some proficiency and a sense of dignity and honor. One can only hope that Atiku realizes this fast. Only a miracle can ever see him become President of Nigeria. So, what is all the fuss about? Vengeance? Ignorance or willful malice? He will probably count his success by the amount of collateral damages he is able to inflict on Obasanjo. But history may not take kindly to him in the final analysis.

***

While articles like this, heralded to the audience of Nigerian Village Square that I was not an enemy of the President, it was enough for them to brand me a friend and praise-singer of the President, which I was not.

Parallel to the Nigerian Village Square, was www.Nigeria.com (now defunct in that form because the owners obviously did not continue to pay for the portal). No one knew who owned the portal. It was also free-for-all but without an administrator known to bloggers, who were allowed free usage of the platform. Views were freely expressed and posted, and alliances built. Here too, an anti-Obasanjo block was dominant as in many other portals of the Internet. Indeed, the Nigerian media landscape controlled by political forces, was awash with anti-Obasanjo tendencies since the man had stepped brutally on toes without fear of repercussions.

While attacks on me on www.Nigeria.com were yet in their budding stage, I remember one contributor from Canada, who blogged under the name "Afari Korodo", coming out to make a very passionate plea on the forum, on my behalf, explaining to co-bloggers that I was not an Obasanjo-apologist. He advanced his arguments and elaborated the reasons that made him believe that I was a "philosopher" – a term that humbled me tremendously. This plea took me by surprise. Funnily, this fellow enjoyed reading my writings but was not in any mood to grow any private friendship with me whatsoever, in spite of my private overtures. His plea worked as many co-bloggers moderated their attitude towards me thereafter, until www.Nigeria.com was shut down and I lost contact with all co-bloggers on that platform. One subsequently appeared again on the Nigerian Village Square however, to continue the unfinished business of tormenting me with his ill-conceived notion of me being a paid Obasanjo propagandist.

On Nigerian Village Square, very few people sympathized with my views or my approach. Very few seemed to have given it a thought, whether or not, I was truly a paid image-launderer. To the vast majority of those, who held the portal hostage, it was a done deal.

Parallel to these two portals, I sent my articles to different websites that were managed by administrators, amongst which was www.NigerianNews.com. The owner of this website, Dr. Michael Oladimeji, who I fondly referred to as Uncle Mike, was favorably disposed to the government of the day and did not have any problem publishing my articles and the website was widely read, mostly by people in North America. In fact, he had a special appreciation of my works and encouraged me to write more. He had a caveat. Articles published on NigerianNews could be published elsewhere only after 72 hours. He soon gathered a few more writers that shared a passion for writing too and made us special columnists with no regular timeframe.

Since every writer naturally seeks to attract wide readership and followership, the instinctive need to release articles in as many platforms as possible, began to militate against the NigerianNews caveat of a 72-hour bar. This term soon began to put a strain on the relationship between the site owner and his writers, who he, by the way, was not paying but preferred to handle like employees. As already said, that was by the way.

The government of President Olusegun Obasanjo was characterized by four major issues that will forever define the regime through the history of the country: 1.) The complete repayment of Nigeria's debt to the Paris Club, 2) – The declaration of a parallel regime of Muslim laws (The Sharia Law) in some regions of the country in addition to the western legal structure of the country, 3) – The Niger Delta militancy that was sponsored by aggrieved politicians to teach a President a lesson, who they largely considered too arrogant and egomaniacal, 4) – The running battle between the President and his Vice President that trailed him till the end of his tenure.

While the very first issue remains valid till the present day and features more frequently in references that are relevant to the days in question, issue number 2 (The Sharia Law) seems to have largely caused a political earthquake only in the days it happened. It seems to have paled into political insignificance and fizzled away from the scene of relevance as time progressed. Yet, these first two items featured repeatedly and sporadically, in many of my articles depending on the issue I was addressing.

More importantly though, was the issue of the Niger Delta militancy, which started seemingly harmlessly and slowly spiraled almost out of control. It prompted me to write the following article primarily for NigerianNews and had it published in other platforms afterwards:

The vicious circle of the Niger Delta: Shame of a Nation!

By Frisky Larr

It started like a child's play. It was a struggle in the interest of the suffering masses. The highlight of the struggle was characterized by environmental pollution. A serious development that ended up denying the local folks their erstwhile fertile farming land and healthy fishing waters. The environment was badly polluted by oil drilling business magnates of multinational identity. The symbol of the struggle in the days of its holy peak was Ken Saro-Wiwa. The folks rose to their feet and stood up against the profit hyena of multinational acclaim. Resources were exploited much to the detriment of the local folks.

But indiscretion and misguided political judgment led to the execution of the symbol of the struggle. He dared the military government of Sani Abacha to stand up for truth and justice. In the end, the bright and promising writer with the scholarly gift of literary excellence Ken Saro-Wiwa was killed against all pleas. He was murdered by Sani Abacha, who now stands at the center of a regionally choreographed debate as Nigeria's best political leader ever. Unfortunately, however, these days were thought to be long gone. Painful memories were thought to have been soothed in the spirit of national reconciliation.

But alas, little had anyone known in the days of Saro-Wiwa's murder that his struggle was to open another avenue for a different form of homegrown terrorism in the guise of justified separatism. For close to seven years now, Nigeria has been held to ransom by some armed mob and helpless lunatics of Niger Delta origin. But first, some fact-checking.

The so-called struggle for the emancipation of the Niger-Delta is sold internationally today, as the frantic and last resort to the power of force by the oppressed and downtrodden masses of the Niger Delta. Many of Ken Saro-Wiwa's arguments are being invoked and spread today in the search for the justice that is so fraudulently and desperately propagated. The need for the region, on which milk the entire nation feeds, to be granted a better share of accruing revenue has been persistently highlighted, not the least, for the improvement of the lot of the common Niger-Delta masses suffering pathetically from the impacts of pollution and inequitable revenue allocation.

A lot has also been done to address the anomaly. Revenue allocation has been consistently revisited, adjusted and fine-tuned to favor the region in dramatic hikes. Commissions have been established to focus on the concerted elevation of the standard of living of a folk that is not alone in sharing the collective plight of a nation's shame. The shame of underdevelopment in the face of glaring abundance! Numerous public works-projects are on course in the Niger Delta far more than anywhere else in the country. The systematic self-service mentality geared towards personal enrichment away from the universal understanding of the essence of governance has long been a household tradition of political leadership in Nigeria. It has excelled in a consistent pace of steady metamorphosis for the worse throwing Nigeria into darkness and hunger in the midst of dusty roads and dry taps.

Reasons abound to take the ruling elite to task. But what is the emancipation of the Niger Delta all about? Is it a battle to wrest Nigeria from the hands of a filthy political elite that has long been a national liability and an obstacle to affluence? If it were, many more regions would have joined the struggle. Is it a fight to save the Niger Delta from the rest of the country that has been very well developed and advanced at the expense of the Niger-Delta that is still wallowing in poverty? If that were true, many international voices would have spoken out.

Unfortunately, none of these is the case. If anything, this movement is the banditry of cowardice born out of greed and utter disregard for damning consequences. Observers have long been asking where on earth these so-called holy emancipators were when Sani Abacha murdered their son in cold blood? They chickened out in fear from confronting a military government. Indeed, it will be no surprise to understand that many of the retired senior military personnel training these bandits today were collaborators of the murderous system.

It all started as a joke. Politicians sought to make a point and provided finances as long as the fight was aimed at their opponents. Disgruntled operatives who felt left out of what they saw as the "kill and divide" insider practice of the Olusegun Obasanjo administration financed the acquisition of weapons. Everything was deemed legitimate that taught Obasanjo a lesson that he was not god. Many who could have intervened to stop the dangerous insurgency at its budding stage either kept mute, supported it actively or jubilated at the sight of Obasanjo been in serious trouble. All these were being fostered under a civilian experiment that was condemned to cautious reaction in handling civil strife. It was cowardice indeed.

No observer has been in doubt today that a battle of this sort launched against Sani Abacha's killing machine would have been blessed with nationwide support. Today, what started in the collateral impact of destabilizing a hated government and dressed in the cloak of seeking justice is threatening to take apocalyptic dimensions away from the sphere of control of its founding fathers.

In fact, while claiming to be fighting for and representing the interest of the Niger Delta, millions of dollars were extorted through the arbitrary kidnapping of foreigners at the height of anti-Obasanjo agitations. None of these millions of extorted monies ever found their ways to public work projects in the interest of the Niger Delta. They were spent on more weapons and shared amongst the big guns, who grew richer by the day. Indeed, Orji Uzor Kalu was more than cynical and could not disguise a sly grin of malicious pleasure in a BBC interview while stressing that Olusegun Obasanjo only didn't know how to solve the problem of Niger Delta militancy. Indeed, the pleasure with which he expressed confidence that he as a President, would have the key to unravel the impasse, prompted suspicion of his clandestine involvement in fanning the flame of violence. Today, Orji Uzor Kalu has a friend in Umaru Musa Yar'Adua doing his best to shield him from corruption-based prosecution.

A governor in Rivers State that was not democratically elected and imposed on his folks by the supreme judges of a supreme court has long taken up the daring task of getting to the root of the problem in the state under his governance. Thanks to Governor Rotimi Amaechi's Truth and Reconciliation Commission, the nation today, has not only gained a brief insight into the machinations and mechanisms of this murderous militancy, it now knows a few names of those who perpetrated militancy in that part of the nation. A retired military operative has even been named, who was said to have been spotted training some militants. Yet no judicial investigation of any sort has been insinuated by a government wielding the mantra of the rule of law.

What has changed today since the exit of Obasanjo and the inauguration of a more Kalu-friendly regime has been the discontinuation of hostage taking. Like Obasanjo, talks have been held by the present regime. Stakeholders have been consulted. Efforts intensified at pacifying and appeasing emotions in the region.

Unfortunately, however, something always goes wrong. There is always a reason to disagree with one point or the other. The consequence is a sudden flare-up of violence, thank God, no longer with hostage taking.

Indeed, there are simply two possible solutions. An all-out war or the prevalence of the voice of reason! Since Nigerians are characteristically known for overdoing every venture embarked upon without the subtle feeling of identifying the crucial threshold of apocalypses, every move at appeasement and pacifying the Niger Delta always seems to be identified as weakness or is it truly weakness? If anything, the Niger Delta militants are revealing general military weaknesses in the armed establishment of Nigeria – in the navy and ground forces.

In the aftermath of Odi and Zaki-Biam, Obasanjo was careful to avoid a blanket onslaught. In the exaggerated self-estimation of the militants and their backers, they seem to forget that an all-out war with the navy, air force and ground forces set out against them to resolve this issue once and for all will only end up in a carnage of sort and the destruction of innocent civilians in whose names the militants claim to operate. It is certain that Nigeria has passed the stage of separatism and disintegration. If these daydreaming agitators of separatism knew what they were up against, no doubt they would better be advised to revisit Biafra of the 1970s to comprehend the enormity of public hardship and wastage in lives and resources that will accompany a senseless civil war. They should have known by now that the notion of a sovereign Niger Delta nation will never be an issue for any roundtable or squared-table discussion by any political instance as long as Nigeria lives.

Unfortunately, however, the longer an all-out war is ruled out, the stronger the militants may get with time and thus become even more audacious. It may be apocalyptic if one day, an airport or a place of public gathering becomes the target of this mob-gone-wild. In other words, while every further audacious strike by the militants on oil installations may heighten the pressure on government to narrow down the day of reckoning for an all-out war, this reality alone should be pressure enough on the militants and their sponsors to understand that they will not forever enjoy this obnoxious jester's license *ad infinitum*.

The secret fear of becoming politically irrelevant shall not forever hold the nation completely hostage. European countries will readily come to the aid of any country at their backyard in Europe faced with the threat of civil war and destruction to arrest a deteriorating situation. History has however taught the lesson that they will readily provide food aid and medical assistants to victims of war in any African country. But contrary to what they would in their own backyard, they would seek to improve their own economic growth by also selling arms to warring parties in Africa and ensure that wars drag on for as long as possible. Sometimes they add diplomatic recognitions to their arsenal of war-promoting weapons.

If the Niger Delta militants are dreaming of any rosy future in separatism, they will definitely have a sorry story coming their way and only the poor folks will pay the bills with their precious lives. Enough is enough!

***

It was just the beginning. The senseless cycle of kidnappings, bombing and armed gangsterism went on in Nigeria to intimidate the President, who was perceived as arrogant. His enemies saw the need to send him a strong message and no one was backing down. Soon, a media theatrics followed. It was a media highlight that was stage-managed by none other than the American CNN with its then African correspondent, the Kenyan Jeff Koinange. It Prompted me to write this primarily for NigerianNews and had it published in other platforms afterwards including the Nigerian Village Square:

TV Journalism, CNN and the MEND Dispute

By Frisky Larr

I must admit that I am not well acquainted with eminent personalities in Nigeria today. Else I would have by now, learned to appreciate the worth and integrity of Dr. Reuben Abati. My interest in closely monitoring events in Nigeria from far away Germany dates back only to very recent years. The reputation of individual news organs in Nigeria cannot be lost on anyone. The Guardian stands out in this light, as one respected news establishment that I have always known even before my 27 years of migration out of Nigeria. Having been attracted to this News portal by a friend with a passion for writing, one of the first faces I noticed on board was that of Reuben Abati. It took some time to sort out the proper status of every feature on this News portal's opener. Among these was sorting out who Dr. Abati is.

Having read a few of his expressed opinions and comments made by readers of the News portal, I soon found out that Dr. Reuben Abati is held in high esteem and regards with a huge reputation as a very senior and leading decision-maker in the Guardian establishment. One notable quality in his essays is the ease, with which he puts his ideas across. In today's Nigeria though, where we all seem to live in a world of cruel reflections and crude classifications, Reuben Abati comes across as one that would easily be categorized as anti-establishmentarian. I perceive him as a critic of the present administration, most often with precise facts and figure, until I read his take on Nigeria's current dispute with the CNN.

After reading an article by one writer disagreeing with Reuben Abati on the CNN's dispute with Nigeria, I scrolled far down again to find the initial article in dispute. In both articles, I found a great deal of misinformed deviation from the substance of the matter. While this writer focused basically on the incompetence of Nigerian journalists in their adoration and general exaltation of anything American to the detriment of national pride and Nigeria's own security considerations, Reuben Abati concentrated more on defending a fellow news organ while highlighting the flaws of Nigeria's approach in tackling the CNN's menace.

One writer rightly drew attention, in my views, to a pathetic quality of journalism in today's Nigeria highlighting the glaring absence of background reporting and in-depth investigative journalism. True to it, there would have been nothing out of place if Nigerian journalists had done quality features on the armed insurgency of the Niger Delta, uncovering the true multifarious facets to the obscured conflict. Unfortunately, though, no rebel in the Niger Delta would trust any Nigerian journalist to cover its hideout for fear of betrayal against cash.

One writer's tenor of Reuben Abati subscribing to the tendency of exalting Americanism to the detriment of Nigeria's own national security is an issue that should be foremost in the mind of every critic of the Niger Delta. This is an issue on which the Americans themselves would accept no compromise. Not even in the name of freedom of expression or free press for that matter. The Arabic news station Al-Jazeera will have a solid tale of persecution in the hands of the Americans to tell on an issue like this. Unfortunately for this writer however, there was clearly no such evidence of exalting or glorifying Americanism or the CNN in Reuben Abati's article. I do not hold the view that he was "in awe of CNN and America".

One salient note was however struck by this writer in his criticism of one Mr. Laolu Akande, who I know absolutely nothing about. He addressed the notion of fair and balanced journalism. Here indeed, is where Reuben Abati does have a case to answer. But before touching on this issue, I will like to give a brief hint on Television journalism. One basic issue in obtaining a quality material for professional television reporting is the effect of the motion picture. Getting a scene from the proper perspective with the proper effect of light and sound are major considerations in setting a scene as a newsworthy material. While a journalist of the print media may simply observe a scene and take notes with probably one or two pictures that also have to be expressive and demonstrative, the television journalist is far more reliant on the proper pictures to match the commentary of the journalist. In other words, a lot is pre-conceived in the mind of a television journalist. The ideal picture of the scenery that may best convey the journalist's message in a newsworthy report is usually worked out in advance of any move. It is like the storyboard of a moviemaker. On the ground however, a lot does not work out as planned and adjustments are made through improvisation.

In the case of Jeff Koinange and the CNN, many of the scenes shown in the footage from the encounter in the middle of the river to the display of the hostages were most likely agreed scenes. To catch the picture of the boat of the rebels intercepting Jeff Koinange's speedboat (apparently from nowhere), the cameraman should have switched on his camera and be ready for recording, all along the journey probably from Lagos or wherever the journey started. That is most unlikely. Not the least, the scare of the rebels shooting above their heads would have ultimately made filming the least priority and issue of interest to the Jeff Koinange's crew amid the fear of life and the ultimate risk of even being taken hostage by the rebels. This is where Reuben Abati is most obviously unbalanced in his judgment. He feared for instance, that a tour of CNN's reporters of the Niger Delta guided by the Nigerian government may be fraught with the danger of the Americans being taken hostage. If Jeff Koinange and his crew without armed escort were not taken hostage, why should that be the case with the guided tour?

Indeed, a lot must have been agreed between Jeff Koinange and the rebels before setting out on the dangerous mission to the Niger Delta. The most plausible and likely agreement should bother on the scenes that would best convey the message of the rebels and the intended newsworthy report. Whether or not money changed hands is another issue that is likely but must not be categorically true. It is, therefore, astounding that Reuben Abati finds scenarios like this unusual or even unlikely to imagine. Every practicing journalist should indeed, have a clue on how television journalism functions. Reuben Abati's claim that the Nigerian government found a MEND' spokesman in Jomo Gbomo to confirm that Jeff Koinange bribed militants to stage a show is another unusual comment. Unless Abati has other information, I am not aware of any instance in which a MEND's spokesperson asserted that anyone was bribed. I remember an assertion that Jeff Koinange asked MEND to stage a show. But bribe? The MEND's Press Release even challenged Jeff Koinange to deny the claims. It specified the origin of the rebel group that Jeff Koinange met. In the end, stage a show, the rebels did. The war dance, the parade of the hostages, the speech on the speedboat in the middle of the water and all that. That was stage-show *par excellence*.

I do agree with Abati, that the statement of Nigeria's Information Minister on CNN that Jeff Koinange went around seeking armed volunteers to stage his show on Nigerian soil was tantamount to an expression of virtual juristic impotence. Abati wrote: *"How on earth would a foreign correspondent enter Nigeria, go about offering money for an anti-Nigeria media show, to be recorded on Nigerian soil, and the government would come later to tell the world that it was aware that this was happening, and did nothing?"*

For God's sake would Abati not be first to cry foul, if Jeff Koinange was indeed arrested and imprisoned for such activities that several governments in the world would term 'subversive', if it actually happened the way the Minister presented it? Now, if Nigeria decides on sanction to express its indignation why should that be wrong? Nigeria will not be the first country in the world to play the toothless bulldog. Right or wrong, it is in my own views, a non-issue. It doesn't alter a thing on the practical situation and therefore, not worthy of a media debate. After all, what other means does Nigeria have at its disposal to raise a warning finger? This is not unusual in international dealings except that it provides ever-ready critics a subject for attack and decapitation. Ask Al-Jazeera and they'll tell you what they have suffered in the hands of the American government. No one laughed at the Americans.

One glaring contradiction that baffled me in Reuben Abati playing the spokesman of CNN is the statement that CNN was not interested in propaganda by going on a government-sponsored tour of the Niger Delta. At the same time however, he acknowledged "They (the rebels) got free advertisement for their cause. They didn't need to be bribed for them to realize the importance of CNN coverage." Does this mean that CNN was involuntarily used for propaganda purposes? Forgetting here, that Abati chose the wrong word in using 'advertisement' in connection with the rebels, he has said nothing other than pure propaganda for the rebels. In Public Relations, advertisement is defined as measures of profit-maximization in the marketing of commercial products, while propaganda is simply focused on the maximization of positive image in public view. It is obviously, the latter that applies to the rebels. If CNN did the propaganda work for the rebels, would an establishment with the reputable professional magnitude of CNN not have seen this coming? Come on now, Mr. Abati!

In insinuating that Jeff Koinange's footage was balanced, accurate and true, Dr. Abati referred to the truism of a crisis in the Niger Delta. So regrettable if that is all Dr. Abati could see in the Niger Delta. As long as representatives of the news media continue to turn a blind eye to one part of the problem and focus only on the other, Nigeria will continue to boil into disintegration. Dr. Abati has no word to spare on the rightness or wrongness of criminal hostage taking nor has he any word on the description of the rebel group as Robin Hood in Koinange's footage. Oh, there is also the case of politicians involved in arming and fueling the insurgency. Where is objective reporting à la Nigeria? Even though it*s is widely agreed in the world of journalism that the concept of objectivity is an impossible task, Dr. Abati declared the interview granted to the Nigerian Information Minister to get the government's own side of the story as gracious. Laughable. Attempt at objectivity is one valuable credo in journalism. It is indeed, an obligation. It is incumbent upon any media organization that seeks to wear the mantle of seriousness and responsible journalism to present the other side of the story for a complete take. This may be a gracious act in the Guardian newspaper and Nigeria at large, but not in the world of civilized journalism. I was glad when I heard Jeff Koinange say, he was unable to reach the Nigerian authorities for their own side of the story before airing his footage. It shows that this is a basic rule in CNN. Two sides to a story. That indeed, is what is glaringly missing in Reuben Abati's exercise in compromising the reputation of honorable journalism including his personal reputation as a veteran think-tank. I once raised this concern about his 7th take on the "Gbolekaja Presidency" (whatever Gbolekaja means). There is none of his articles, in which I have ever seen any attempt at viewing the other side of the story with some credible appraisal before finally dissecting the facts with his own conclusion. It is always bashing galore! Unfortunately, however, objectivity and a minimum of two sides to a story is what one is taught in elementary journalism.

***

When this article was released on Nigerian Village Square, I became the refuse bin of all regime haters trying their best in the creative dumping of moral trash. Many unprintable and unspeakable words were used in the casual practice of deep-sinking, toxic exercise of individual freedom. Many regime haters made haste to call CNN, write CNN and overwhelm CNN with praises and thanks for its "absolute objectivity" as some put it, upon the airing of the controversial 'fake' footage on the Niger Delta militants, by Jeff Koinange. Their priority was to celebrate every embarrassment of the President, who they hated to their bone. My attempt to keep it all real and pull down the mole in the eyes, was simply a sacrilege. It did not matter that I was a Radio-TV journalist by training and was likely naturally disposed to spot anomalies in the report presented by the CNN correspondent. As usual, the reaction was abuses and scorn with many continuing to accuse me of being the President's paid agent.

When the so-called Movement for the Emancipation of the Niger Delta (MEND) finally came out to refute the authenticity of the CNN footage, however, the defensive bricks of elated and excited haters of the President began to crumble. I wrote this article for the NigerianNews and subsequently released it in other Portals:

MEND's Disclaimer, its Consequences and the Role of CNN in the Niger-Delta Dispute

By Frisky Larr

The day September 11th 2001 is one date that television viewers all over the world will never forget so easily. Many sat in front of their motion picture sets to see the vivid picture of two airplanes thrusting one after the other and with chirurgical precision, into the heart of skyscraper buildings like a sharp arrow penetrating the middle of a standing butter pack! It was the assault on the twin towers in New York. In fact, skeptics of the authenticity of this terrorist attack ask today, where, indeed those cameras were positioned that shot such vivid and clear pictures. Were the cameras positioned in anticipation of something to happen? The quality of the pictures seems to dispel every possibility of a routine surveillance camera positioned so high (at the right place) to capture such brilliant pictures by coincidence. Inasmuch as I do not subscribe to this skepticism, I bet there will definitely, be cogent explanations by those who hold the key to the answers as there are surely, plenty possible explanations to explain the whys and how's!

The importance of this episode however, does not only lie in the illustration of the power of moving images on mass communication media, it also highlights the growing suspicion with which consumers of information view the media, newsmen and all other factors with the power of media manipulation.

A few days ago, the American news channel CNN aired its highly sensational take on the scary insight into the looks of our Niger Delta militants. Indeed, the information in that piece should be a highly valued one as this party to the conflict has long remained a faceless entity in its ominous tidings. While news of its criminal kidnappings is commonplace, who they are, what they look like and what they stand for, are issues that have long been too critically concealed. No doubt, this understanding played a prominent role in the consideration of the CNN correspondent Jeff Koinange in deciding to establish contacts with rebel leaders and furnish their own side of the story.

As a correspondent for a news station in a foreign country, one is by and large, an independent Program Director and Producer. Choices on the subject of reports are made freely as long as the employer does not disagree with the content. Better still, the choice of style belongs wholly to the producer who is mostly the person of the correspondent. A documentary may be chosen, filled with archive pictures and lots of narratives. It could be serial, choosing to present one party after the other in succession, etc. In short, like the author of an article in the print media who has an idea to write about, the Television journalist requires his cameraman to put his idea on the screen. Therefore, before Jeff Koinange set out on his obviously, well-prepared trip to the Niger Delta on his speedboat, do doubt, he had established his contacts and had a clear idea what he wanted to have on the television screen.

The beautiful piece of journalistic work that Koinange finally came up with had one general impact on its viewers. It was generally scary as Monita Rajpal correctly remarked. Amongst Nigerians though, this report either unleashed outrage at that blatant and naked and primitive show of provocative riverside militarism or it triggered admiration in the eyes of such beholders as welcome the sacrifices of daring young men finally standing up to what is perceived as naturally theirs. Indeed, it bore all the hallmarks of an articulate and heroic journalism.

When MEND however, came up with its disclaimer of Koinange's report though, one would have thought there was a tactical dimension to this obviously transparent ploy. A military show of strength and some diplomatic nicety to match. All in the spirit of hitting and petting. But taking a close look at the MEND's Press Release, it soon became clear that our black brother Jeff Koinange may have possibly, been guilty of inciting this show of barbaric misrepresentation.

MEND emphatically contends, so it was reported, that Jeff *"requested we **stage some scenes** for a very important CNN program which was supposed to air in the first week of February."*

In fact, in the USA much like in Germany, a law enforcement agent who leads and encourages a cocaine dealer to a cocaine producer to buy cocaine only to end up arresting the dealer and the producer, may himself either end up being arrested or will be sure to lose his case on prosecution. Such a law enforcement agent will be accused of inciting crime as well as aiding and abetting same.

When Jeff Koinange's speedboat was itself, suddenly intercepted by militant speedboats that seemed to have emerged from nowhere in the middle of the vast river, MEND's rebuttal seems to be suggesting that the armed young men were indeed playing out Jeff Koinange's movie script. It's not so much MEND's denial that is so sensational and intriguing but the emphatic and categorical nature of that denial. They challenge Jeff Koinange to deny their rebuttal and they'll release all the email correspondences that were exchanged between them.

That's a pity indeed. If that is the method of securing sensational reporting to outsmart competitors in the news market, then its goodbye to substance and responsible reporting. It is indeed such a challenge to human logic, why any kidnapper with the amount of weaponry displayed and the number of young men, who no doubt, were floating in phantom midair under the inspiration of Jah most high in the imaginary cloud of marijuana smoke, would let such a prized American hostage like Jeff Koinange slip through their net. In the end, all that intimidating war dance, all that hostage parade with the fear-stricken grief written on faces of young Filipino men close to tears were merely playing out Jeff Koinange's movie script? Pity and shame indeed, if that was true.

If anything, though, the whole incident as it unfolded seems to be leaving more questions than providing answers. The most significant question being 'who were these young militants if not MEND?' The MEND Press Release claims that they are nothing but "...*a collection of thugs, pirates and bunkerers...*". How would Koinange have managed to put them together as MEND claims he did? That indeed, is one unbelievable part of MEND's statement that seems to be unfair on Jeff Koinange and may lack credibility.

On the other hand, however, MEND provided a clear and unmistakable answer to a long-held speculation and suspicion in the mind of neutral observers. Apart from denying the abduction of the current Filipino hostages, MEND even went further to identify the hostage takers as "*...a community in Gbaramatu with the connivance of FNDIC in Warri who were paid by local politicians to blackmail the government into annulling the PDP primaries in Delta State.*"

If anyone has ever been seeking the handwriting of politicians in this reckless game of emancipating the Niger Delta through atrocious sabotage and hostage taking, this was the ultimate proof.

Indeed, with one more statement in that Press Release, MEND gained my admiration as a group that does not seem to be made up purely of thugs and the marijuana-smoking mob of hopeless youngsters. They criticized the hostage takers and accused them of desperation in hostage taking, saying: "*[In a bid to] lend credence to their fraud and cover up this disgraceful act carried out in the name of the struggle for the liberation of the Niger Delta, they added our original list of demands to their intended goals.*"

If this is MEND talking, then it sure has some intellectuals among its ranks who seem to be recognizing the amount of danger these criminal acts in the name of emancipation is doing to their comprehensible cause. If sanity is to be restored to the Niger Delta, MEND owes the nation the duty of joining hands with the forces of the State in fighting these criminal elements. The long-term impact of such careless acts if allowed to go uncontrolled will be the ultimate disintegration of Nigeria. If the example of Yugoslavia is anything to go by, secession will be easy but survival and sustenance will be another daunting task. Even the breakaway tiny states of former Yugoslavia at the backyard (if not the heart) of the European Union have problems today securing acceptable living standards for their citizens despite massive aid from the European Union who detests instability in that region. Nigeria stands at the backyard of no major power. If we fall as a nation, we will fall for real. The best to expect will be numerous oil-hungry powers that will gladly supply weapons of secession in exchange for oil and leave seceding Banana Republics to face their own corrupt leaders and destiny.

On this note, it may be worthwhile to remind MEND that it owes the world a duty to fight local politicians in the Delta region to make them understand the need for putting their people first. If MEND succeeds in a project of this type, no doubt, their movement will be setting a benchmark for a new sort of sociopolitical awareness throughout Nigeria. Improved derivation for the Niger Delta will then be easier to negotiate and push through thereafter!

***

Then the news broke in early June 2007. Many American news outlets including the **New York Post** reported the sudden dismissal of the CNN correspondent Jeff Koinange from the CNN's payroll, on account of precisely the same footage that many Nigerian callers described as objective and sound. Writing for the New York Post of June 08, 2007, one Leonhard Greene referred to several sources, which claimed that the correspondent had indeed, paid militants "to help him stage a story". The writer reported on the exchange of a series of private emails between the correspondent and an estranged Swiss girlfriend, who finally blew the lid on him and his methods.

Sequel to strong objections from the Nigerian authorities at one point, CNN was forced to offer a rebuttal *"during a February broadcast"* anchored by John Roberts, contending that *"CNN did not pay for or stage any part of the report. CNN does not pay for interviews"*. The latter part of this contention became a sloganeering phrase that was also repeatedly echoed by the correspondent himself in several defensive interviews that he granted several outlets to wash himself clean. In the privacy of email exchange however, he had bragged to his Swiss lover:

"Of course, I had to pay certain people to get the story, … But everything was done in agreement with CNN and in accordance with their usual standards. But you do not get such a story without bribing … You have to have financial resources. But at the end, it was worth it. CNN has its story and I have my 'fame.'"[1]

The Swiss lover, Marianne Briner, who had personal and romantic reasons to be aggrieved, had bared all email communications between her and the correspondent, to the then CNN Worldwide President, Jim Walton, with the looming risk of a disgraceful scandal since CNN had repeatedly claimed that it had no hand in "faking" the story or buying the interviews.

This whole development did not teach Nigerian readers and viewers and most especially, the abusers of the President, any lesson in life. It failed to pave the way for added intellectual maturity. The fun of bashing the President and government of the day under the bandwagon spell of group dynamics, no matter the odds, got the better of several senses.

While all these happened, and the President fought a running battle with his deputy and the nation was polarized from top to bottom, between the friends and enemies of the President, 2007 was to mark the end of the regime's constitutional lifetime. The battle to amend the constitution to allow the President a third term had raged with the President making no public pronouncement on the subject until the idea was voted down in the legislature. This further exacerbated the anger of the President's enemies. It was an issue that I wrote virtually nothing about for lack of sufficient facts.

The end of the regime finally drew closer in the shadow of an unprecedented discord between the President of the country and his Vice President, who changed party and challenged his boss for supremacy. He was impatient to succeed his boss and the impression could not be avoided that he laid claim to a natural entitlement to being the crown prince. The deeply polarized nation was torn between the two parties with the Vice President seizing the moment to declare himself the last hope of the common man fighting to stabilize democracy in the face of a dictatorial one-man show.

The President sought to calm the temperature by taking the unprecedented action of dismissing his Vice President not only hoping to get the blessing of the judiciary to seal the deal and sail the ship of governance in calmer waters but also creating a constitutional crisis. There were many on the other side of the divide, who hoped too that the courts would deal the President a major blow and they really did. The judiciary backed the Vice President's insubordination and recipe for a constitutional crisis by leaving the President's party, making himself an open enemy of the President but still remaining Vice President.

I wrote this article in the unfortunate aftermath of the judgment of the Court of Appeal:

Atiku Judgment: Reckless and Dangerous

By Frisky Larr

The judgment by the Abuja Court of Appeal declaring Vice President Atiku's loyalty to the constitution as opposed to his party and President is by all senses of objective reasoning, the most dangerous, reckless and latest in a chain of impediments to the advancement of democracy in our country. A judgment that is largely applauded by a segment of society that is unfortunately, strongly polarized along lines of sympathy but obviously veiling the dramatic nature of strife and tribulations that are yet to face the nation.

A higher instance of judicature, in which highly learned judges agree in unanimity on a judgment that is not just sensibly and legally flawed but also obviously falls out of point in all aspects of logical comprehension seems to smell badly of subjectivity. The glaring absence of a single dissenting voice among the judges can only fuel already exacerbated speculations and debate on conspiracy. Not even the split in the society at large is reflected in the conduct of the judges.

After all, it is none of the business of the judges what happens to the future of an already fragile national union of multi-ethnicity.

By implication, the ruling of the appeal court has left more questions unanswered. Worse still, it has raised further questions begging for answers as well. While it is incumbent on constitutional courts to perform the near impossible balancing act of reconstructing scenes and issues of a constituent assembly that was responsible for the drafting of the constitution, the court is never expected to perform wonders or re-enact the impossible. What is expected is basic logic and fundamental rules. Rules based on objectivity rather the persons of office holders.

Unfortunately, the learned Justice Abdullahi Umaru and his colleagues rather chose to focus on the persons of the Vice President and the President. In reference to the Vice President, the presiding judge said: *"He did not swear to hold allegiance to the President."* Focusing on the office and not the holder of the office would, indeed, have warranted some degree of relativism in the judge's choice of gender to describe the Office of Vice President since the office of Vice President can be held by either a "He" or a "She". It was obviously lost on the judges that the nation expected ruling on the Presidency and not on Atiku or Obasanjo. While a landmark judgment was expected, the nation was served a piecemeal that looked only narrowly at the present administration by referring to what Vice President Atiku swore to uphold. In fact, many more Vice Presidents are yet to come if the system is allowed to grow. The direct implication of this narrow-minded focus on precise and prevailing incidents almost automatically entails entrapment in the bond of partisan sympathies. In the end, the presiding judge came across as providing a defense for Atiku like the defense counsels themselves, would never have done.

What is left is a pile of broken glasses on which the nation is expected to continue its dreadful walk on its already difficult path to democratic advancement. The blisters and sores and if not total collapse that may usher in its end in the process, seems to be lost on the unfortunate judges.

The judges emphasized that the Vice President swore allegiance to the constitution and not the President. True to it. What do Ministers swear to? I doubt if any Minister would swear to destroy the constitution. This will however, not give them the constitutional authority to be disloyal to the President even though are not elected.

Funnily, the judges refused to rule on the restoration of the privileges of the Vice President that were withdrawn by the President. Obviously, because the constitution authorizes the President to define the responsibilities and schedule of duties of his deputy. Now, the nation is told that the deputy is independent of his boss. It is a deep mystery where the political jurisdiction of the Vice President lies. Each governor has a political jurisdiction over his state. Since they rule autonomously, they owe the President no allegiance.

Nigeria is by implication, now granted a parallel Presidency, even though the Vice President is handpicked by the President as a running mate – a deputy. The appeal court in Abuja now seems to have taken advantage of the lapse in concentration on the part of the fathers of the constitution to authorize future Vice Presidents to henceforth package a parallel agenda of their own and simply bollocks to whatever plans any damn imbecile, wannabe President may cook up in a party program. After all, once in power, the President will have no single power to keep his Vice President under control! Future Presidents will then be at the mercy of their Vice Presidents in terms of loyalty and rivalry. Moreover, since money rules the world and Nigeria in particular, it will only take a few grand to keep the roaring school-boy-type rascals at the corridors of the National Assembly quiet to forestall anything in the semblance of impeachment. What a brilliant precedence indeed! "First time in the whole world" as Fela would say.

The court has now authorized Atiku and all future Vice Presidents to be disloyal to the President and be answerable only to the voters. Astounding that the learned judges only stopped at that. What about authorizing the Vice President to appoint a Vice Presidential cabinet – a parallel Executive Council to be in direct competition with the President?

Besides throwing all these questions open, the learned judges also failed to answer why the fathers of the constitution required the Vice President to be nominated from the same party as the President. A key sentence with which the authors of the constitution did not intend to decorate any page of the legal document. The American constitution that we, by and large, sought to copy, does not mandate membership of the same party for the President and the Vice President. If the judges in Abuja want to make believe that this clause ends only at the doorstep of the electoral commission and has no significance of any sort after the swearing-in of the Vice President, then we should, as Nigerians, begin to restudy fundamental logic from pilots of the UFO.

The often-cited example that several governors have defected to other parties and were not relieved of their positions doesn't seem to take cognizance of the fact that the constitution did not mandate any common party for the President and any governor.

A position of unease is now created for any President that is ever chosen to occupy the high office in Nigeria. Even the choice of one's own wife or child as Vice President for the sake of loyalty cannot guaranty peace and the calm sailing of the ship of government. All because the judges chose to focus on a person for whom they sympathize and a person that they despise.

While many agree that Atiku is not a saint or innocent for that matter, there seems to be widespread consensus that the President's move to remove the Vice President for carpet crossing was wrong. In the end, people jubilate too loudly in the obsession of seeing the court reduce the President to a size that they widely cherish to see him in. They however, seem to lose sight of the fact that even if the judgment was right, the arguments in its justification were outright flawed and at best amateur. The delicate balancing act of rescinding the President's authority and highlighting the Vice President's subordination was lost on the learned judges.

The most unfortunate aspect of this drama is that old Obasanjo, who is partly responsible for some of his own predicament, does not represent perpetual Presidency, which was at stake in the issue before the court. I will even bet that the Supreme Court, on which all the President's hopes now rest will not deviate an inch from the judgment of the appeal court but I sincerely hope they will come up with better arguments.

Whichever way this judgment goes, as I opined in a previous essay, the President is in trouble.

All things being equal, President Obasanjo would here and now, have been advised to resign in honor and leave a country to its fate that refuses to accept anything good in every step he has made. A country, in which forces seem to be united in seeking his and their own destruction. Leaving the country unto Atiku for the few months left of the legislative Period would probably unleash a new lease of life and the birth of a newfound Messiah on our dear incorrigible nation. But the equation may not be that easy. The end of one battle marks the preparation for the start of the next.

For now, the court of appeal has succeeded in saving Atiku from the waiting fangs of law enforcement, which in itself was actually not a certainty. But conspiracy along whatever line, with the ultimate motive of uplifting one party at the expense of the other can only warrant extreme reactions in an already charged and tense political atmosphere. It remains a mystery how long the drama will continue to unfold.

***

The final word was reserved for the Supreme Court and it went the way of the Vice President and the constitutional crisis was no more a matter of speculation. All efforts by the President to frustrate the candidature of the Vice President were frustrated by the judiciary.

This article summed up my views on the state of affairs at the time:

My Problem with the President and his Enemies!

By Frisky Larr

I may be old fashioned and out of touch with mainstream political reality. I am however, proud to be a journalist of the old school. Old school journalism that was taught in institutions of learning as late as the early to mid-eighties laid emphasis on objectivity and balance in reporting and commentaries. Modern journalism however, assumes to have outgrown this old trend, which is currently coined "obsolete". Modern journalism contends that there is no such thing as objectivity because it is relative and individually construed. Modern journalism contends that objectivity may be attempted but never attained. The conclusive impact of this confusionist psychological maneuver is the dwindling trend of journalists even attempting objectivity these days. The genesis of the Iraq war and the high dose of nationalist and pro-western coverage, which urged George Bush on to the ultimate marginalization of the USA in international politics, is arguably, one strong evidence of the manifestation of modern journalism.

When it comes to Nigeria however, old school or modern journalism doesn't seem to play any single role. Envelopes of different colors in conjunction with the consuming power of any diabolic cheerleader to sway the media men and women in all convenient directions are enough to do the trick. In the midst of all that though, I submit in all humbleness that even though both parties in the current political divide in Nigeria have axes to grind, the anti-establishmentarian forces have taken their game far too far!

General Obasanjo has my highest respect and honor as a man of visionary political calculations. Contrary to all that have been said and are being said, Obasanjo did not start off in 1999 without a clue on how to rule Nigeria or where Nigeria needs changes. In his eight years of leadership, he has taken bold steps in restructuring the political equation from the grass root to the highest echelon. He has audaciously taken on forces that have always had the might and wherewithal to make or mar. Forces that have made and marred Nigeria's future throughout years and decades since independence. Forces that sought to teach him a lesson by almost plunging the nation into a civil war in the wake of the Sharia waterloo. In fact, Obasanjo bit the fingers that fed him in violation of generally accepted ethos across the board in the Nigerian cultural divide. All in the interest of salvaging a fair and balanced distribution of power for Nigeria. Obasanjo has headed a government that has offered proof that Nigeria does have qualified and competent technocrats after all the years of helpless brain drain and intellectual bankruptcy. Technocrats have made their fingerprints a landmark in the shaping of economic and financial reforms that will definitely elevate Nigeria's future to affluence if consistently followed upon. Various institutions that saw the light of day in the fight against economic and financial crimes are parts of the legacies for which Obasanjo will be remembered much to the anger of his hate-filled adversaries.

In this appraisal, I will cautiously deviate from addressing the failures of Obasanjo's eight-year administration in healing the infrastructural malaise that has inherently plagued the country's social identity for ages. These have been and are being exhaustively addressed almost on daily basis. The focus of my problem with Obasanjo will however, center on partly more serious and sometimes, more pertinent issues of his eight-year governance.

I strongly implore the President to educate me in all fairness, detail and candor on what really happened to Bola Ige. The life of this flamboyant politician with the stubborn attitude of wanting to walk through an impermeable wall to achieve what he believes is right, may have been lost. But his soul remains imprisoned as long as the truth is not known about the circumstances surrounding the criminal termination of his life. His soul remains with every well-meaning Nigerian who knows that Bola Ige was a "Zero Tolerance" advocate of Ribadu's caliber with a slightly more confrontational treat than Nuhu Ribadu. To set his soul free from the hands of fellow Nigerians seeking to know why Bola Ige had to die, I strongly implore the President to open up Bola Ige's Dossier for public dissection. It is extremely incomprehensible to figure out the failure of law enforcement in solving the riddle of Bola's killing several years thereafter.

I desperately implore the President to educate me wholeheartedly on the rationale behind his affiliation with and tolerance of a thug like Adedibu in Oyo State. I beg the President in desperation to help me out with explanations on the real story and truth surrounding the person of Andy Uba. The story of money laundering linked with facilities for the President's farm is hanging in the balance.

While no one expects the President to be perfect like his enemies seem to be doing, answers to these three simple questions will go a long way in smoothening out several wrinkles in the President's biography that simply do not fit.

Given the reality that post-Obasanjo Nigeria will never be the same again, the zero tolerance attitudes that have now taken hold of Nigeria have long overdriven a wave of social frenzy across the nation that has been hijacked, misused and ultimately overblown by enemies of the President. All of a sudden, the President now personalizes evil, madness, corruption, civil disobedience and social and political destruction all in one, in the eyes of his detractors.

It is on this note that I say good morning to former Governor Balarabe Musa of Aminu Kano's PRP. Balarabe Musa as a personification of effective and efficient hate propagandists of the Atiku Abubakar's camp now seems to be waking up from a long, dreary sleep of political fantasies. Suddenly he is waking up to the reality that Atiku may not end up becoming President of Nigeria.

How on earth did anyone imagine anywhere in Nigeria that Atiku could afford such a high-profile humiliation and ridiculing of the Presidency and end up triumphant? The focus on Atiku and his camp in this case is informed by the symbolic posture he has come to assume these days, for enemies of the President.

As a harakiri political fighter, the signs were on the wall for Atiku to read that taking on the President in an extremely albeit childish open battle from within and outside the government is the start of a long-drawn political suicide. I have long wondered in several essays and analysis, where the Vice President's psyche derived. I cited the example of Vice President Al Gore and the sacrifice he had to make in the face of a Presidency that was hijacked by George Bush, which arguably, failed to meet the explicit provisions of the constitution in various ramifications. To avoid ridiculing the nation, party friends and well-wishers advised Al Gore to back down. He made this sacrifice, withdrew his legal cases even though he could have gone on and on, and is standing high today in the triumphant pose of a successful and high-profile environmentalist. Former German Chancellor Schröder of Germany could have remained Chancellor today if he had stubbornly insisted on political doggedness in personal interest.

Unfortunately, the likes of Balarabe Musa urged Atiku on. They could be literally heard chanting "Go Atiku, Go!!" while the man steadily headed for his own political destruction. In hindsight, I will refuse to lay the blame squarely on Atiku. Events that have unfolded over the past weeks and months have unleashed a lot of realities. Atiku may have been quietly smiling and laughing at people like me, who cautioned him to consider personal sacrifices in the interest of Nigeria and the growth of constitutional democracy. He had Judges to rely on. He had the President of the Association of Nigerian lawyers to rely on and above all, he had a sufficient number of senators and representatives that will not send him to his premature death. He had all he needed to carry on with the fight even though the invaluable support of a united North eluded him.

As the most prominent figure to stand up against the President, Atiku Abubakar ended up building a coalition of extremely incompatible bedfellows. All united in the quest to destroy Obasanjo. Court judgments after court judgment went on fueling Atiku's strength and the power of his opposition machine. No one took cognizance of the ultimate weapons available to the President in the event that such official and partly unjustified humiliations are allowed to succeed. The most prominent and controversial product of the Kingdom of "Absurdistan" in this respect once contended that the Vice President owed the President no allegiance because he swore only by the constitution. This absurd judgment vomited hatred of the President and forgot to understand that the hated Olusegun Obasanjo will not forever occupy the Nigerian Presidency.

Balarabe Musa who gained public sympathy in the wake of his illegal impeachment as Governor in the second Republic was highly revered as a pillar of the "Progressives" – a movement that stood for social justice and political advancement in the second Republic. Now, he has ended up squandering all those useful assets by leaning too far out of the window in support of one section of the political equation at the expense of personal credibility.

There will definitely come a time when the Nigerian Bar Association will openly beg for questions to be answered. Questions on what deal existed or still exists (if at all) between the current leadership of this highly honored body of learned intellectuals and a party to the ensuing political dispute culminating in the reality that the Nigerian Bar Association is now overtly and ostentatiously in betrayal of the high ideals of judicial objectivity. The neurosis for political relevance informing the drive for profiling a political identity on the part of individuals leading the Nigerian Bar Association has long been speculated as an explanation for the NBA's presently undeniable partisanship. The Agbakobas, the Balarabes and the "incorruptible" judges of the Nigerian establishment all await the day of reckoning.

A day of reckoning that should teach every party to the democratic agreement that law and order is not defined by hatred, not the least, in a country like Nigeria, where government should occasionally be allowed the benefit of treading the critical boundary for the purpose of instilling sanity. A day of reckoning that will teach politicians that arming jobless youngsters and dedicated followers of "Ghana must go" in political insurgency will spell their own destruction. A day of reckoning that should teach everyone to judge Obasanjo by his success and his failures and not by any undue amplification of his failures alone.

Obasanjo's enemies have long relied on a pathetic press that remains overtly silent in the face of hate-filled destruction. They watched high-level Nigerian political tourists traveling to America and Great Britain to ridicule the government of their country. They applaud a sitting Vice President recklessly remaining Vice President and decamping to another party. All is well as long as it seeks to destroy Obasanjo.

In a press landscape featuring learned colleagues that are unable to differentiate normal Public Opinion Polling from Exit Polls, there are only a handful of luminaries to show. When even an exemplary and learned colleague like Reuben Abati (who stands out for Obasanjo-bashing rather than balanced appraisal) makes the unforgivable error of characterizing a journalistic attempt at objectivity (as done by CNN in interviewing the Nigerian Minister of Information to balance up a reporter's footage on the Niger Delta) as benevolent, then the state of journalism in Nigeria is questionable indeed. Neither old school journalism nor modern journalism seems to have caught up with the present breed of Nigerian journalists. Pity indeed!

***

This ultimately became the psychological basis for writing my first book "Nigeria's Journalistic Militantism" with an elaborate treatise on the failing of the Nigerian media in the birthing of the democratic system of government in the country with the requisite duties of the fourth estate.

I summed up the election year 2007 that marked the end of the regime thus:

Election Year 2007: The Realistic Options Now and After

By Frisky Larr

When Flight lieutenant John Jerry Rawlings overthrew the Supreme Military Council of Ghana and installed the Armed Forces Revolutionary Council in June 1979, he was cheered and received with open arms by the Ghanaian populace. His bloody revolutionary reckoning that cost the lives of several leading political figures prompted speculations along all lines in Nigeria. The general tenor was that something like that could never happen in Nigeria. Rawlings barely ruled for three months and handed over power to an elected President Hilla Liman on September 24th, 1979. When he however observed from the sideline that things were not progressing the way he expected, he overthrew President Liman in a second coup on December 31st, 1981. From then on, he held the scepter of power till the year 2000 before he was succeeded by President John Kuffour. Within this period, Rawlings steered the boat of leadership with the help of technocrats and military men and adopted a largely centrist, market economy policy. The groundwork of economic growth and infrastructural advancement that Rawlings left behind was a showpiece for future developments. Today, the fear of this dangerous man becoming mischievous again is a thorn in the flesh of his successor, who cannot afford to under-perform.

It is worth noting that John Jerry Rawlings did not command popular support at the turn of the millennium when his tenure ended. Many of his reforms did not alter the prevailing poverty level. He was largely jeered and insulted by domestic observers and commentators while international economic and financial experts applauded the parameters they saw with lots of hope for the future.

Knowing fully well that many commentators and observers will rather stone me to death than hear me out in peace, I will take the risk of opining here that there are many ideological parallels between Olusegun Obasanjo and John Jerry Rawlings.

Even though I have never met this retired General Obasanjo or any of his policy advisers at any point in my life, it is rather a less daunting task to catch a glimpse of his mindset with a bit of goodwill and neutrality.

The reality that President Obasanjo reaped only partial success in all that he initially set out to achieve for Nigeria is probably one pain that may torment him to the end of his political career. The initial failed intention of sanitizing the energy sector with an action man Bola Ige and all the aftermath thereof is history today. The incompetent attempt to rejuvenate old power structures as the Vice President has now reported is one clear evidence that the President indeed knew where he sought to set the pace of development. The alleged lamentation before the Vice President thereafter (which, by the way, has never been denied), regretting not having accepted the Vice President's initial suggestion on how best to solve the problem of power shortage underscores the incompetent execution of a project that was commenced with good intention.

Seeing how quickly eight years go by in two administrative terms that seem to fly with the wind, Obasanjo could read the writing on the wall. A lot has been achieved in terms of reform. Debts have been paid away and resources can now be concentrated on inward development. Banks have been restructured and foreign investors can now be confidently wooed etc. Unfortunately, however, roads are in dire states, power and water supply remains a persistent problem. The idea of picking up the power grid project from zero commenced too late. Now that the relevant projects are on course, the Associated Press reported only last week that the final completion of projects in the energy sector alone is expected to take about twenty-five years. This may go through a gradual process of the phased launching of partial completions. Obviously succeeding governments will then claim credit for every partial launching that is realized in their term, in a project that was started by the Obasanjo administration.

On top of that is the fear that no one can predict the direction that a succeeding government may take. It may turn out to be more corrupt. It may turn out to be even more focused. If there is anything I may bet on however, it is the fact that if Olusegun Obasanjo could turn back time, he would never again hand over power to any Shehu Shagari in 1979. Having helplessly watched the dismantling of his pre-1979 achievements by successive governments, the worst he could do today would be to refuse to act and impact the situation in any meaningful manner.

The power to overthrow a regime afterwards if things do not progress the way they are expected is no longer there since the status is now that of a retired and not active General. What Rawlings could do with ease, Obasanjo will now only be able to watch in helplessness.

That (in my mind) is one of several factors that seem to have prompted Obasanjo to seek a third term in office. A constitutional coup attempt that was to see his project through. In the process though, he seems to have insinuated that he alone and no one else can steer Nigeria to the harbor of affluence. For this insinuation alone, he was jeered and scorned particularly in the dream talk of an Internet columnist. For the purpose of comparison, a similar incident occurred in Hungary during the past summer. The tape of a private conversation between the Prime Minister of that country and some party henchmen surfaced in the media, in which the Prime Minister admitted having lied to the electorates to win the last election. This sparked off a violent demonstration lasting several weeks with protesters placing the parliament in Budapest under siege. The Prime Minister vehemently and stubbornly refused to resign claiming openly in a World Service broadcast that he is the only one that can steer his country through all the necessary economic reforms.

The truth though is that only Obasanjo can implement Obasanjo's reforms in Nigeria much like only Gyurcsány can implement Gyurcsány's reforms in Hungary.

Today, while Obasanjo is being loudly abused and desecrated at home in the news media and Internet, international financial and economic experts express general satisfaction at the economic parameters available to them showing a ray of hope in the long dark tunnel of untold human misery.

Politically though, the options at our disposal are anything but promising. To retain some leverage of sort on the continuation of his agenda, Obasanjo seems to have subjected his party to his tight grips. A risky venture that may place him at loggerheads with the President if his party's candidate wins the presidential election.

Obasanjo has learnt the lesson today that ruling with the military uniform is far easier than maneuvering his ways through the labyrinth of constitutional democracy. While the judiciary and the legislature each have a say in the running of the country, none of them however, is given responsibility for failures in achievement. Then comes a fully unnecessary domestic battle with a rebellious Vice President, which keeps subjecting the President to series of judicial humiliations that are obviously largely politically motivated. Whichever way the President goes there are always hurdles to overcome. Yet he bears all the blames for the failure of the experiment.

In the aftermath of all these though, there are now voices openly hoping that the military will take control sooner than later. This may even be exacerbated if the Supreme Court ruling on the excesses of the Vice President adds one more humiliation to the President's woes.

Not long ago, a Nigerian newspaper reported that disgruntled lawmakers have picked up the rejected legislation on the Third Term Agenda once again. Since they were not nominated for another term in their own parties, constitutional amendment may be the only way for them to extend their grip on political relevance. Alongside this, protagonists of impeachment are bracing themselves for a showdown in the intended malicious dumping of the combined team – President/Vice President.

Politicians are promoting their social and political relevance by arming banditry and hobby separatism in the Niger Delta. Others are vowing that there will be no elections if they are disqualified.

One pertinent question seeks to uncover what the future holds for Nigeria in the weeks and months ahead. How can all these disputes be contained and how can development be advanced in environments of this nature?

The most horrendous scenario may be history repeating itself in the like of the Sani Abacha led coup that overthrew Shehu Shagari shortly after commencing his second term in power. Should Nigeria be greeted by post-election chaos in the form of bloodshed and endless expectation of election results or even a vicious rejection thereof with protracted litigations, I foresee a President that may invoke his constitutional powers of declaring a national state of emergency and suspending all democratic institutions to restore law and order. Since the President has however vowed that he will not stay in Aso Rock beyond May 2007, handing over power to a military administration is a very viable and realistic option. Then and then alone can we truly hope that a Nigerian Rawlings will be borne with all the dire and positive consequences it may entail.

***

Elections were held in the very tense atmosphere that gave every observer the impression of an impending warfare. For President Obasanjo, it was overtly a do-or-die affair since two serious contenders on the ballot list were avowed personal enemies: Retired General Muhammadu Buhari and the serving Vice President, Abubakar Atiku.

I wrote this article to sum up, what transpired before and during the elections. The article was basically published on my online column and several other outlets.

Nigeria's Rapid Drift Towards Anarchy: A Big Thanks to the President and Atiku

By Frisky Larr

A lot has been philosophized in the run-up to the elections, on what shape Nigeria may take in the post-election era. The crystal ball was rolled over and over again and many commentators agreed on just one point: The future is not rosy. But the speed, at which this obvious drift and free fall down the bottomless pit and the sheer imagination of how intensive this may be unleashed, is beginning to scare the hell out of even the direst of pessimists. It is one thing to foresee. It is wholly another to be faced with the reality. Where is Nigeria heading and where are all the redeemers gone?

Irrespective of attacks and abuses that were mutually exchanged by observers and commentators in the badly charged atmosphere ahead of April 14th, 2007, in which polarization was not only accepted as the norm, but also in which many paid political activists and party loyalists intermingled with authentic observers, thus rendering it difficult to differentiate the real from the fake, tensions now seem to by dying down slowly. A new sense of calm seems to be dawning. But true to it, it doesn't take long to see beyond the façade. It strongly feels like the calm before the storm.

At center stage are just two personalities, who fought their battle in the public arena of private interest, in which the interest of the nation has been fully relegated to the background.

As I have consistently opined and will continue to say, the Presidency of General Olusegun Obasanjo has done Nigeria enormous credit in revamping the financial and economic stature of the country. General Olusegun Obasanjo has led a government with a very clear idea on how to solve the problems of the country but lacked the forceful competence to see through with the implementation of the simplest formula. A team of competent technocrats confronted the most difficult problems nations could ever have in these modern days of cold capitalist interest lost in globalization and mastered them with confidence and enviable skills.

What will now destroy President Obasanjo's legacy of these positive technocratic achievements is not his failure to fix social infrastructure or improve the daily life of the common man as many may think. Definitely no! Even though these failures should not be trivialized because they should have been the easiest problems to solve, it should also be highlighted that they form the cornerstone of the irrelevance of party political programs in Nigeria today. Even the most unimaginative of party founders these days requires just one political program: "Electricity, Water and Roads".

The President's nemesis has a name: Abubakar Atiku. Either by virtue of being surrounded by incompetent advisers or sheer miscalculation, the entire dispute with the rebellious Vice President has now unleashed a chain of deadly reactions on the nation that neither of the two men will stand to gain from.

The inadequacy of the constitution was first unearthed through the rebellion of the Vice President. A novelty in universal suffrage that no country has ever witnessed.

Courts took to obvious partisan politics and guidance by public sentiments in passing judgments and the helpless President seeing the integrity of his power being audaciously eroded, obviously rested his final hopes on bringing his party back to power in a do-or-die fashion.

So far so good! When do-or-die however, begins to translate into wanton killings in the name of votes, the question will become inevitable, whose interest is being served in a game of collective lies. Soldiers were deployed in hotspots ahead of gubernatorial elections. Yet ballot boxes were robbed and apparently replaced. People were killed and maimed to secure the victory of private individuals. Faced with the reality that election rigging and attempts at same are all attendant characters of Nigerianism in electoral charades, no one will be fooled into believing that they are confined to the ruling party alone.

Unfortunately, however, the government of the day bears ultimate responsibility for security and safety in elections. The pertinent question must be addressed, where soldiers were deployed, how ballot boxes could be stolen with impunity and nothing is being done till the present moment, to launch investigations to address the situation. On the contrary, results are being declared in constituencies, where crimes characterized electioneering. What is all this game about and where are we heading?

As if Nigerians have not been sufficiently subjected to the burden and pains of routine crime wave in everyday life, special election crime seems to be turning into another casual way of life as well.

Without wishing to question the integrity of the ruling party and its followership, I am nonetheless prone to airing my unease at the strength of the party's victory in so many states fully against the trend of outright public hatred of the ruling party. How on earth, can I be assured that victory in Adedibu's Oyo state was free and fair?

Victory that has become an inevitable do-or-die outcome for the ruling party in the desperate bid to checkmate a self-centered Vice President that is hell bent on fostering his personal interests in the unmistakable spirit of a novice to the prerequisites of a successful democratic practice.

Will someone summon courage and ask Atiku Abubakar where he will finally stand if he ends up winning all the court battles of this world and the nation ends up in perils.

Agreed that there was no way the ball could have been stopped by Atiku once it was set rolling, the Vice President should bear in mind that the successes he has achieved so far have been the exposure of the inadequacies of our constitution. Democracy can never grow in Nigeria until the removal of a rebellious Vice President is finally addressed in the Nigerian Constitution without decimating the President's powers no matter who that President is. Democracy will definitely have a problem growing if an Independent National Electoral Commission – fully independent of the publicly hated General Obasanjo and Prof. Iwu – is not allowed the power to disqualify candidates without resort to the judiciary. Democracy can never grow in Nigeria as long as disgruntled party members are not granted the constitutional rights to contest as independents.

Many of these facts are the collateral aftermath of Atiku's battle with the President. The largely advanced argument that Atiku was oppressed and merely fought for his right cannot but be dismissed with contempt. A member of any government that served for seven years, who comes to the ultimate realization that he does not belong in the team amid malicious marginalization, has no choice in every democracy that I know, but to quit the administration.

Let us forget for once that unverified claims contend that Atiku was to represent specific interests in a remote-controlled Obasanjo's Presidency. Let us forget the unverified claims of horse-trading that was said to have brought Obasanjo to power through the help of General Babaginda and Atiku with all the clandestine agreements reached and Atiku's hopes for a different role than the one he finally got. In the course of grieves and disappointments, Atiku as the clean crusader did not quit the regime to fight the corruption and disrespect for the rule of law which he had helped nurture over seven years. No. His desire to have it both ways by remaining Vice President and belonging to another party underscores the urgency of a constitutional amendment.

Now the Supreme Court has not so surprisingly ruled to strip the Independent National Electoral Commission of its right to disqualify unqualified candidates just a few days to the Presidential elections. Candidates cheated out of election victory are understandably, fueling unrest. Presidential candidates are seeking a viable strategy to wrest power from the ruling party, which they will apparently be unable to outdo in election rigging. The President's camp will be watching quietly with strategy plans behind closed doors. Strategy that will definitely not seek to advance lovemaking with opposition candidates.

The writing on the wall is clear. If General Buhari is hell bent on becoming President like Abubakar Atiku at all cost, the opposition will never find a consensus candidate and that will spell their ultimate destruction. This cannot be disguised by even an overt call for the postponement of the Presidential elections in the aftermath of their own deadlocked negotiations. The expected rejection of this call by the ruling party will not but further exacerbate an already tense situation. Should the opposition however, choose to unleash its own reactionary potential in frustration, the answer will be bloodshed within the next few days after April 21st, 2007.

Many Nigerians are however basking in the illusion that Nigeria has passed the stage of a military coup d'etat.

Agreed that what we badly need today is not a coup d'etat but a fundamental revolution to cleanse the system per se, the question persists however "who will lead the way?" Revolutions are borne of spontaneity in the midst of miniature organizations and petty ringleaders. While petty ringleaders these days tend to focus more on what they can reap off the political establishments on the short-run to support their livelihood, the overriding interest of the nation is pushed down the priority scale.

If the President does not eventually get fed up with the situation at one point in time and give the military the green light to intervene, the sleeky and unpredictable Babanginda effect may take the day. Alternatively, a junior revolution may become the impending risk in the spirit of Jerry Rawlings.

The only credible alternative that however sounds far more realistic in the face of current developments may be a dramatic resolution of the Atiku problem either through his ultimate arrest with massive unrest in its aftermath or the voluntary and timely exit of Atiku from the scene thus laying the groundwork for a new start. If tensions finally calm down with a great deal of foreign intervention, working out a credible and face-saving formula for Atiku and Obasanjo, a good government over four years with good roads, power and water supply, may wipe off all these upheavals from public memory. But the scars will remain and mopping-up operation on the constitution may begin in earnest. I fear a scenario where many judges will be sacrificed on the long run to match the ideology of the prevailing party. Quietly and away from the limelight. The name may be honorable retirement.

Democracy will ultimately grow if this realistic scenario prevails. This does not mean however, that democracy will not grow in the event of a disciplined military intervention.

Such an intervention that may spell a welcome intermezzo from the current confusion and threat of Armageddon may help the reorganization of the democratic process if kept short with a great deal of political discipline.

***

The government ultimately came to an end and was marked by a near-anarchical upheaval occasioned by the influence of the vast array of the President's enemies. President Obasanjo played rough and tough precisely the way many Nigerians (except his die-hard haters) miss a decisive Presidency today in 2017. He stepped on toes, defied counseling and made his views, his perceptions and his choices the paramount feature of his style of governance. His enemies were everywhere, who sought to teach him a lesson for playing God. They were in the judiciary. They were foremost in the legislature. They were in the fourth estate and they were vast among the ordinary population who formed opinions through the fourth estate.

One issue is not represented in the articles published above to reflect the days of former President Olusegun Obasanjo. I wrote no article on the wave of Sharia Law declarations that started from Zamfara State and pervaded the entire northern states as the first of its kind in the open challenge that was posed by a section of the political establishment, to the perceived "Arrogance" of the former President. I was sure it was a stage in Nigeria's political evolution that was designed to pale into insignificance as time went on.

Summing up the Presidency of Olusegun Obasanjo's 8-year term, the popular Vanguard daily newspaper perfectly wrote the following in a résumé of a lively Presidency that the nation is still waiting to experience ever since, even in a mimicked format:

"Obasanjo has done very well or performed woefully, depending on which level of the economy you're operating. To ordinary Nigerians, most of whom are at the fringes of the economy, he has done nothing, especially when they weigh the impact of fuel deregulation and the comatose electric power situation on their lives. If you're at the core of the economy, Obasanjo is a messiah who has stabilized exchange rate, wiped out the debt burden, got Nigeria off the FATF list, consolidated the banks, and inveigled foreign investors to come in. To many therefore, his tenure is a mixed gruel of conflicting tastes — peppery, sour, sweet, sugary, bitter." [2]

***

III
The Yar'Adua Days

The transition from one democratically-elected civilian government to another was successfully completed for the very first time in the history of Nigeria, on May 27, 2007. In every preceding democratic experiment that was labeled with numbers as the first, second or third Republics, the processes were always disrupted by military coups d'etat.

The new President was hand-picked but not groomed for the new office, by his predecessor and was formally pushed through the intra-party caucus stages and obviously rubber-stamped by the rank and file under the influence of the constitutionally overbearing incumbent. It was the former President's only fragile insurance against persecution and vindictive prosecution in a field that was dominated by his enemies and sworn avengers. The little-known new President Umaru Musa Yar'Adua, came from a family that is very well-known to and highly respected by the northern political establishment and was a serving Governor in one of the northern states.

His elder brother General Shehu Musa Yar'Adua was one of President Obasanjo's powerful deputies in the military days of the then General Obasanjo. In fact, he, alongside General Theophilus Danjuma, was highly rumored to have been the true power that remote-controlled General Olusegun Obasanjo from behind the scene and on behalf of the northern political mafia during the military regime of General Obasanjo. As a civilian President caged by constitutional limitations this time though, there is no doubt that President Obasanjo stretched the limits of the constitution to earn himself so many enemies. His groomed and designated President, who, unconfirmed rumors claim to have been Nasir El-Rufai, had to make way for

Umaru Musa Yar'Adua at short notice given the hostility and threats posed by other candidates and the northern establishment, to the incumbent President at the time. The choice of Umaru Musa Yar'Adua was compelling and could not be rejected by the northerners.

The little-known candidate thus won the election and had to master a delicate balancing act. One of my very first articles on the new President that was, first and foremost, published in my online column at NigerianNews.com and subsequently in other sources, reads as follows:

The New Government's Term: A Whole Lot is Going Wrong!

By Frisky Larr

One of William Shakespeare's plays is revered for the saying: "Some are born great, some achieve greatness, some have greatness thrust upon them!" If William Shakespeare were asked to comment on the Nigerian political scene, no doubt, he would probably have identified a pattern of Nigerian leaders, who seem to be having greatness thrust upon them and those who achieve greatness by the butt of the gun. Thank goodness though that the apex of political leadership of the country at large is now getting used to leaders, who have greatness thrust upon them. From a prison inmate-turn-President to a low-keyed provincial governor who had no Presidential ambitions, the center is slowly building up a discernible pattern.

Whether or not the identical characters of this pattern will end at the point of personnel selection will surely be a matter of subtle appraisal in a period of four years. At the moment however, the current President of Nigeria vividly stands out for trying to make the best of a delicate balancing act. An act that is slowly but steadily beginning to betray the emergence of a peculiar and personal tendency.

But first, to the background. In the run-up to May 29th, 2007 and perhaps today still, President Umaru Musa Yar'Adua was (or is) largely regarded as an undisputed proxy of his predecessor Olusegun Obasanjo. Sharp-tongued derogators even took to the length of seeing in him, an appointee to do the bidding of his foster father.

Therefore, the very minute that followed the proclamation of the inaugural words "…so help me God" in the swearing-in ceremony definitely marked the birth of a huge challenge for Umaru Musa Yar'Adua. The compelling burden of having to establish beyond reasonable doubt, that he is out to run a government of his own and not one that is remote-controlled by his predecessor, and the high moral pinch on human conscience of maintaining the hallmarks of gratitude to the man who made him great, clearly defines the depth of the abyss that he overlooks from the thin long rope, on which he balances his acts.

The necessity of defining priorities however, has now seen the President within his first few days in office, giving priority to consolidating his position, identity and authority over allegiance and gratitude to his immediate predecessor. This is precisely the point that is

73

marking the course on which President Umaru Musa Yar'Adua will steer the ship of the nation in the next few years.

That this course is one that is bound to stir up trouble sooner or later has been highlighted in a recent statement attributed to Yoruba leaders flaying the President's choice of appointees that seem to smell of tribal leanings as opposed to the more pronounced federal character reflected in the appointments made by his strongly hated predecessor. The President is obviously bowing to the agitations of disgruntled northern stalwarts like former military President Ibrahim Babangida, who are making a big deal of the return of the Presidency to a northerner. A dangerous direction indeed.

A deliberate act of adding more insults to the injuries of a collectively disgruntled southern region by ignoring the federal character in political appointments will definitely spell plenty of trouble for the President as his tenure progresses. On the other hand, it may be pertinent to ask what usefulness a precedence of this sort will constitute, when any eventual Southern successor to Yar'Adua (as theoretically agreed in the zoning policy) would start another process of reversing northern domination all over again. Could this be the vision of forward movement and national progress desired for the political future of Nigeria? Umaru Musa Yar'Adua may sooner or later, come to understand that a dose of Obasanjo's stubbornness (which he at the moment, cannot yet afford) will be required by him in confronting his northern power base on the long run.

This is simply one in a chain of potential seeds of trouble that are presently (knowingly or mistakenly) being sown by the President in these early days of a four-year term.

Another crucial problem is the fight against corruption. One newspaper reported very recently that the President has halted the aggressive momentum in this groundbreaking fight against graft and other forms of corruption. It was reported that by doing so, he was merely fulfilling the terms of a secret deal between himself and several foreign governments, which provided him the legitimacy of early recognition, while detractors at home were still singing from the hymns of fraud. If this is proven to be true, the consequence will be grim indeed.

Massively corrupt leaders like Lucky Igbinedion and many other previous governors are still roaming free to enjoy the fruits of corruption while many common Nigerians remain locked in the perpetual incarceration of structural oppression. To mark a clear departure from the unmistakable signs of selective prosecution (as was allegedly agreed with the said foreign governments), the President is said to have now decreed that he will be henceforth directly involved in any future decision on EFCC's arrests. Even though there was no innocent Nigerian that has so far, been selectively prosecuted or arrested by the EFCC, the President has now succeeded in giving a new lease of life to fear-ridden notorious agents of corruption, while at the same time robbing the EFCC further of its (badly needed) institutional independence frantically agitated by many. This is indeed, a highly flawed approach. In the event of dissatisfaction with the EFCC's *modus operandi,* the President has a choice of either reconstituting the commission completely or letting it operate with the usual aggressive momentum. Everything else will be tantamount to making a mockery of the fight against corruption.

Former Vice President Atiku Abubakar has thus, found sufficient reasons to be thankful to the President for temporarily saving him from the claws of Nuhu Ribadu. While sources are contending that the American government stands at the forefront of impacting the President to trim Ribadu's wings, the President is obviously not seeing the double standards in America's concern for corruption in Nigeria. Agreed though that there is very little the President can do even if he saw the double standards in the American conduct, he is (as of today) yet to devise an effective substitute to the deterrent element in Ribadu's aggressive drive.

In the wake of the Jefferson scandal in the USA, the double-edged sword the indictment of Congressman Jefferson meant to the Americans, was all too transparent to see. For whatever reason though, there is obviously a vested interest high up in the American leadership to avoid the incarceration of Abubakar Atiku. Else, it is difficult to comprehend the reference to the initials "A" in describing someone who is obviously Atiku as well as his crimes of corruption in the indictment of Jefferson. Whenever, the issue in the bill of indictment, came to the Nigerian named "A", who is said to be high up in the Executive of the Nigerian government, the offence was presented in a wishy-washy manner. The indictment of Congressman Jefferson was so carefully framed to avoid any explicit reference to Abubakar Atiku in any offensive form. Obviously, the Americans would have had no further excuse for not arresting Atiku if all the cards were laid bare and open. At the same time though, the Americans are obviously happy that Atiku Abubakar is not President of Nigeria given the hasty recognition they accorded the election of Yar'Adua despite all the credible reports of massive fraud. I am therefore, beginning to wonder aloud, if indeed, there is any truth to a long-standing rumor that many leading Nigerian politicians are agents of one American interest or the other, given the strange level of protection they seem to receive. But come to think of it though, what would that have meant to us as Nigerians today, if Atiku Abubakar had won the Presidential election and we were ruled by a President today, who would now, have been standing in the shadow of involvement in the corruption indictment of an American Congressman?

Be that as it may, in his traditionally obstinate fashion, Abubakar Atiku is steadfastly slapping down the hand of fellowship extended to him by President Umaru Musa Yar'Adua. He is hell bent on pursuing his petition before the electoral tribunal right up to the Supreme Court. All these coming at a time, in which Buhari's ANPP and very many elements of the AC are willing to join the President in bringing Nigeria forward. One is indeed, tempted to ask what the basis of Atiku's obstinacy is. Many observers are indeed wondering on what assurance or chances of juristic success, Atiku is basing this obstinate optimism.

Against the backdrop of the present quality of the Nigerian judiciary though, Atiku may be banking on the absence of objective and material cohesion as exemplified by the Supreme Court of Nigeria in recent judgments.

In many other matured and exemplary democracies all over the world, constitutional courts utilize the weapon of precedence to fill loopholes in constitutions and save the process the option of a weary and long-drawn political debate. Alternatively, constitutional courts order the legislature to draw complex and detailed legislation on specific issues to cover an existing juristic loophole. In today's Nigeria however, we have a judiciary that simply plays to the gallery as if it lacked the substance of jurisprudence. Nigeria's judiciary does nothing substantial these days other than aggravate if not add to the existing constitutional crises of the country.

One clear example is the removal of an elected governor Uba for the fortunate and at the same time, unfortunate Peter Obi in Anambra State. This delicate issue is one that is fraught with a multifaceted manifestation of historical dimension.

While I personally congratulate Governor Peter Obi as a true child of destiny, who God obviously doesn't wish to abandon, I cannot disguise my pleasure at seeing the back of Andy Uba who won the office of Governor with a thick cloud of money laundering on a Presidential jet hanging over his head. While I do not wish to see the influence of suspected criminals prevailing in crucial political positions, I will agree that the much-acclaimed law of karmic justice was probably co-authored by Peter Obi for him to be seeing so much of the sunny side of destiny.

Now jokes aside. While the moral instance in the sufferings meted out on Peter Obi through his political career, underscores how much he deserves to serve as a politician in this important position of governor, law and jurisprudence is however, neither about wishes, morals nor are they about karma. The law is simply put, an ass!

Now, every serious student of political science should have learnt at one point in time or the other that democracy is a system that functions on a collection of constants and variables. While democratic institutions, temporal frameworks and the quantity of participants amongst others, are usually identified as constants, participants themselves are the most notable examples of variables. Therefore, while legislators may change from period to period, the number of legislators in a parliament is a constant factor. Even in a country like the United Kingdom with an unwritten constitution, the time frame of political activities is an accepted constant. In other words, the fact of a democratic tenure lasting for four years is a traditionally accepted reality. While the number of years constituting a tenure may differ from one society to another, the tradition of a temporal framework is widely accepted in every democracy.

Even though a written constitution may be short on explicitness or the proper punctuation at the right place on the validity of a fixed time frame, the divinity and untouchable character thereof is a traditionally accepted fact of political scientific relevance. The inevitability thereof is clearly informed by the need for constancy and stability for the proper function of a democratic process.

By willfully declaring the removal of Andy Uba as governor and the tenure continuity of Peter Obi, the judges of our supreme court have virtually and unceremoniously turned a constant in the democratic process into a variable. With utter disregard for the consequences such a systemic upset may cause to the entire democratic experiment in the country, the judges of the Nigerian Supreme Court seem to be leaving every objective observer astounded as to the level of their knowledge of the underlying principles of democracy. The ensuing chaos of now being unable to define the start and end of a political term with absolute certainty has only ended up playing in to the applause of many Nigerians, who rightfully rejoice at undoing the perceived evil of Andy Uba by way of karmic but not jurisprudent justice. Telling a tale of this or that in the constitution that was drafted by authors that would never in their dream, have expected difficulties of this nature does not compensate for the obvious political illiteracy of our learned judges. The political responsibility of closing constitutional loopholes with court judgments is simply one fact that is sadly unknown to our highly placed judges. This is precisely where constitutional law differs explicitly from criminal law and every other aspect of jurisprudence. Indeed, Nigeria obviously, does not have jurists with explicit training in handling constitutional matters. This is obviously a very new terrain for our judges, which they will never admit openly. This is further underscored by the fact of Nigeria not having a separate constitutional court that is explicitly manned by experts in constitutional law (as in several matured democracies). In its place, the Supreme Court – the highest instance of judicature on all legal issues from criminal law to matrimonial law (my exaggeration) – is being improvised as a constitutional judicial instance and the judges are simply pretending to be experts in constitutional law.

Indeed, seeing the amount of applause generated amongst intellectual Nigerians and the speed of the emergence of such applause at an extremely outlandish judgment of this sort, I begin to wonder aloud, if the level of education that has steadily deteriorated over the past years is now beginning to take its toll on the general quality of intellectual reasoning in Nigeria. No doubt, this will earn me some serious verbal lynching amongst our folks, I'd be sounding untruthful though if I claimed not to be used to such personal attacks.

People may then want to ask what solution jurisprudence should have had in resolving the dispute in Anambra State if not the one propounded by the Supreme Court. To avoid upsetting the political process, the law indeed holds several options handy. First, it is so incomprehensible that INEC is held responsible for the malaise because it conducted elections when the time was due. If it was as simple as that to frustrate INEC from performing its duties when election times are near, any citizen could merely proceed to the court of law to file a case against the electoral instance and every election should be kept on hold. This can definitely not have been intended by the learned judges of the Supreme Court.

The truth of the matter however, is that former governor Ngige and his henchmen are the culprits responsible for the entire trouble. Having publicly confessed to stealing an electoral mandate and not facing prosecution of any kind, it may be safe to assume that Ngige and co. probably, did not break any law of the country by stealing a mandate that did not belong to them. Upon ascertaining however, that governor Peter Obi is vindicated in his legal action, the law court of a functioning democracy – rather than upsetting a system and awarding the continuation of tenure (which is juristically extremely laughable) – would have granted the unfortunate governor Peter Obi the right to sue for damages against the parties that were responsible for the political deprivation, since the existing tenure cannot be overturned as a political constant. Even if INEC were (in my views) wrongly determined as the culpable party to the confusion by conducting elections when it should not have done so, INEC as a proxy of the federal government should have been subjected to paying damages to Peter Obi.

In this way, Mr. Ngige and his associates or INEC would have been made to realize the costly implication of stealing mandates or conducting elections at the wrong time. At the present moment however, those who openly confessed to the circumvention of the political and democratic process are sitting in prominence and comfort while the system is now being sacrificed to the utter detriment of the overall experiment. Should it however occur that the culpable parties that should have been made to pay through their nose to feel the pain and sensitivity of their crime, fail to comply with the payment of compensation, the prison would have been the tenable alternative. In no country in the world would the divinity of democratic timeframe have been sacrificed for a cause like this in a manner reminiscent of systemic illiteracy.

In all of these equations, Andy Uba would have gone scot-free and that would have marked the dark side of the judicial equation, with which the law is always qualified as being an ass and that would have been our one and only sacrifice.

A whole lot is simply going wrong. These developments on the judicial front clearly underscore the urgency of amending the constitution in crucial areas to leave our judges no more room for outlandish pronouncements.

As for President Umaru Musa Yar'Adua, the tenure is still young, and a lot will change in his attitude and actions. My disappointment in the President at the moment though, borders more prominently on my impatience to see the large-scale launching of massive infrastructural projects to reach out to the poor masses as quickly as possible. Only by achievements in this area will he be ultimately judged and only thus will the shortage of the federal character in presidential appointments be ultimately ignored!

***

Knowing what I know today, I will take a huge distance from a part of the opinion that I aired in this article. Today, I will understand the need to not reward electoral fraudsters, who steal elections by allowing them to remain in office while the victim of such blatant crime is merely compensated with financial rewards. I do understand today, that the need to uphold a uniformed electoral timetable nationwide, must be given a backseat.

Be that as it may, this highly controversial issue that split the country in two, like many other issues before it in the nascent democratic experiment of the time, was soon to be followed by another in a series of explosive political landmarks. The Governorship of a State was abruptly terminated in the wake of protracted legal battles that ended at the highest court of the land – the Supreme Court. The elected Governor of Rivers State, Celestine Omehia, was dismissed from office by judicial proclamation and replaced by a person, whose name was not even on the ballot list. This article was primarily published in my online column on NigerianNews as well as on the toxic Nigerian Village Square but also lifted onto other sites.

Supreme Court Oh Supreme Court!! Cry the Beloved Justice!

By Frisky Larr

If Nigeria is currently experimenting on the creation of a democratic tradition *en route* to political stability, then the Supreme Court – the country's highest judicial instance – is fast becoming a tragic figure and a major impediment to the achievement of these objectives. The latest in its most recent chain of destructive judgments is no doubt, one that spells heinous disaster for the growth of justice in our beloved country. Unfortunately painful, is the current reality that a large section of the country's self-styled elite is still choosing to remain blinded by residues of emotional agitation against the immediate past President Olusegun Obasanjo rather than seeing the easily foreseeable long-term impact of these despicable pronouncements of the apex court.

It is becoming increasingly outrageous and damn right frustrating that an extremely low level of kindergarten judiciary is strongly taking hold of the process in Nigeria in broad daylight and before the very eyes of self-professed intellectuals and worse still, to the delight of same. The issue at stake is simple. A party (the Peoples Democratic Party) conducts its primaries. A candidate (Chibuike Amaechi) wins, perhaps convincingly too. Subsequently, the party withdraws the name of the winning candidate on grounds of criminal investigations (cooked up or not) against the candidate, who under such circumstances is correctly perceived as untenable. The candidate is substituted (perhaps, by the runner-up Celestine Omehia), who proceeds to win the election and is elected as Executive Governor of a Federal State.

Disagreeing with his own substitution, Mr. Amaechi rightly challenges the legality of his substitution in court. Not contending that he was robbed of victory as Gubernatorial candidate, it should be noted that his challenge is and can only focus logically on being denied the right to be a Gubernatorial candidate of his party in the very first place. Whether or not Mr. Amaechi would have ended up being elected Governor of Rivers State is, by virtue of logical comprehension, another issue altogether.

By all standards of democratic and judicial practice known all over the world, an election that is contested with the wrong and unqualified candidate is logically and characteristically null and void. In the best of scenarios imaginable to juristic novices like myself, such elections are either repeated or the race is awarded to the runner-up of the election.

Today however, the Nigerian Supreme Court is leaving no stone unturned, making outstanding negative history and a mockery of itself worldwide with a chain of illogical, irrational and outright outlandish judgments of far-reaching consequences on the democratic experiment. While a lower court of appeal (rightly or wrongly) dismissed the actions filed by Mr. Amaechi, the Supreme Court is not even saying that Mr. Amaechi should have been the rightful candidate and in effect fault the replacement of the candidate by the Electoral Commission at the request of his party, the Supreme Court through Justice Aloysius Katsina-Alu is now saying categorically that Mr. Amaechi was indeed, the candidate himself and has therefore, declared Mr. Amaechi the new elected Governor of the state.

For God's sake, how far more shall we proceed in this country with this raving avalanche of chicanery? A daylight abracadabra of turning green to white!

While debates may rage as to the legality of the candidate's substitution, records have it that the Independent National Electoral Commission (biased or not, collaborating or not) was informed in writing by the home-party of Mr. Amaechi that Mr. Amaechi was mistakenly put forward as a candidate and presented a replacement. Records also have it that the Economic and Financial Crimes Commission (EFCC) indicted Mr. Amaechi as former Speaker of the State Legislative chamber on charges of corruption. Now, the Supreme Court is reported as disowning the EFCC's indictment on the grounds that only a court of law had the right to *__indict__* and *__bar__* candidates from election (Nigerian Tribune online, October 26th, 2007). While the court alone may have the undisputed power to bar candidates, there are questions as to the implication of the word "indictment". In fact, the word "indictment" means nothing else than charging to court by the prosecuting instance. If the report of the Nigerian Tribune is accurate, the Supreme Court now seems to be adding a new dimension to the functions of the Nigerian courts of law namely, the power of prosecution.

It may be pertinent to recall a similar judgment in the recent past that allows for a split Presidency by granting a Vice President the right to swap parties while in office and comfortably be in diametrical opposition to the elected President. The laughers and jeers that greeted this judgment at the time from behind the scene in other solidified democratic environments could and can hardly be overheard, even today. The only thunderous applause came from within Nigeria itself. Another laughable judgment soon followed in the arbitrary and chaotic extension of the tenure of another unfortunate Governor that was cheated out of victory. The bottom line in all these cases, is the suspicion that someone somewhere is strongly bent on teaching the overpowering and perceived evil machinery of Olusegun Obasanjo (whose fingerprint is seen in all of these losing cases) an unforgettable lesson. Another controversial issue indeed, which (even though without proof) should in itself, have had nothing in common with the rule of law.

Given the reality that the practice of democracy is by no means a Nigerian invention, the question is fast gaining relevance if some Nigerian Judges should not be deployed for special training in constitutional law in conducive environments to seal a glaring loophole. Amateur and destructive judgments of this nature from the highest court of the land will definitely do democracy no good on the long run.

While acknowledging the truth that Mr. Amaechi (who on personal basis, should be congratulated for this manna from heaven) may well have been cheated out of contesting the governorship race, the duty of judicial institutions can and should not be that of a ruthless avenger á la Robin Hood. Like every arm of government in the separation of powers, the judiciary clearly has its limits. Occurrences in today's Nigeria seem to be refusing to take any notice of the limits of judicial powers. Enlightened legal luminaries will surely appear anytime soon to provide their views on this outlandish judgment. Many learned voices will jubilate; many will lament the tragic course the judicial boat is sailing. The constitutional provision that grants the Supreme Court of Nigeria the authority to willfully award the office of State Governor to a person that did not contest the election in the first place, is yet to be discovered.

Granted the hypothetical legal tenability of the Supreme Court's judgment, the underlying premise would be seen in the assumption that it was the party PDP that won the gubernatorial election in Rivers State not the candidate Celestine Omehia. In other words, it does not matter which candidate the party fields, the PDP was destined to win the election in Rivers state anyway. Refusing to field Amaechi as a candidate was thus denying him his predestinated victory under the canopy of the PDP. Basic laws of nature teach us however, that this can be nothing other than a glaring poppycock product of the kingdom of *Absurd'istan*. There is no indication whatsoever that Mr. Amaechi would have been as acceptable a gubernatorial choice for the electorates as Mr. Omehia was. Awarding him the office of governorship through the back door by virtue of mere supreme pronouncement of some god-feeling justices is not only a rape of justice in excess of the powers of the Supreme Court, it is simply a fraud that is audaciously visited on the politically matured electorate in broad daylight.

In the absence of ruling in favor of fresh elections with Mr. Amaechi as the enforced PDP's candidate, another logical ruling would have been to declare the defeated candidate of the opposition party in Rivers state as winner of the election since the PDP had a flawed selection process that should have rendered the PDP's candidature invalid. These are alternatives that do sound quite plausible to me as a novice of jurisprudence.

Constitutional courts like the Supreme Court of Nigeria are usually made to seal constitutional loopholes as a short cut to the tedious legislative process of constitutional amendment. In today's Nigeria however, the Supreme Court as a *de facto* Constitutional Court has ended up creating far more substantial constitutional problems for the country than it has ever done on the contrary.

The most embarrassing development however, is the emotional deafening applause given the pronouncements of the Supreme Court each step of the way by our pseudo-intellectuals, who simply do not seem to understand what jurisprudence and democracy is truly about.

And then we will all want to rise up in gallantry to prove Prof. Watson wrong?

***

The central message of this article cannot be lost on the prudent observer and analyst. The Amaechi decision as it was taken by the Supreme Court at the time drew attention to three major issues. The first was the length some characters were prepared to go to deal former President Olusegun Obasanjo an indelible punch. Second was perhaps, the need to also have experts of constitutional law as judges of the Supreme Court or the need to create a separate Constitutional Court that is exclusively responsible for adjudicating matters of constitutional relevance. A model of this sort is practiced in Turkey. Third is the completely childish implication of the decision itself, which imposed a solution that the plaintiff did not even request for. It was a brutal overreach.

So dominant was the anti-Obasanjo factor in the early days of the Yar'Adua's Presidency that leading pundits cared little about the political program that the government had to offer. Anti-Obasanjoism was the central political program of President Umaru Musa Yar'Adua. Obasanjo was the talking point. He was at the center of executive, judicial and legislative actions. While the government was busy reversing the federal character gains made under Obasanjo, the judiciary was busy making pronouncements that were basically aimed at undermining the former President. The legislature set up committees of inquiry (suspected to have been incited by the President) to dislodge any semblance of sanity attributable to the Obasanjo era.

It was in the heat of the early days of the Yar'Adua Presidency that I wrote the following article that was basically published on my column in NigerianNews, the Nigerian Village Square and a host of other websites.

Indeed, no Evidence of Financial Wrongdoing against Olusegun Obasanjo?

By Frisky Larr

Reading through very recent media reports on comments made by leading political figures, anyone would stumble onto statements made by Orji Uzor Kalu. The former governor of Abia state made one single comment that sent me thinking deep and trying to get a vision of his mindset. I ended up in a mental state of partially sharing Kalu's frustration at the glaring spirit of defeatism staring him in his naked face. I was able to figure out the exasperation in Kalu's composure. A sense of helplessness that greets a daylight robber when he is made to face the music while other big-time crooks hang out on the side-line wielding the smiles of joy and gloating smirk. A terrible irritation indeed!

Orji Uzor Kalu made just this statement: *"I am surprised that by now the so-called EFCC and ICPC are coming to a state like Abia when the total budget of the state in eight years is just one parastatal in the Federal Government. One year budget of a parastatal in a Federal Ministry is the total budget of Abia in eight years. I think the right thing to do is for the Federal Government to institute a different body to try this case, to try ex-president Obasanjo."*

While Governor Kalu does not admit stealing any state fund under his care, he went a long way to emphasize that he was a millionaire in the days preceding his governorship that he needed no state funds to get rich any longer. Mr. Kalu even quoted how many jobs he was able to offer Nigerians. No doubt charges of financial impropriety filed against him are neither cooked up nor are there no Nigerians that can provide a long list of suspected misappropriation on his part.

In a honest paraphrase, Orji Uzor Kalu expressed nothing else than his failure to understand the rationale behind running after far smaller thieves in the form of state governors managing funds that are way lesser than the annual budget of just one Federal parastatal while the big-time thieves running the Federal capital and its institutions are left untouched. The truth that many comments have so far, been made and the fact being self-explanatory that a thief will always remain a thief – big or small – are reasons enough for the avoidance of details on this aspect of our discourse.

Felt beyond the skin and down through the flesh till deep in the bone, anyone would sympathize with the ex-Governor and understand his frustration.

This is indeed, an issue that hits the raw nerve of the lame duck government presently running the nation from the federal capital. A lame duck government with due and comprehensible reasons for maintaining the status of standing still! True to it, it is a daunting task to take on Olusegun Obasanjo without standing up against political dilemmas of sort.

In dealing with President Olusegun Obasanjo, everyone is faced with a largely unguarded leader, who achieved a great deal for his country. This is a man who negotiated debt forgiveness and paid off the rest of the country's major debt with improved oil revenues that he could also well have stolen. This is a leader who laid the groundwork for independence in telecommunications by engineering the construction of Nigeria's own satellite launch. Let us forget for once the rejuvenation of the banking sector, the airways etc. There are a lot more achievements that are simply groundbreaking and attributable to the labor of this ex-President's government. It is distressing to observe critics and sworn enemies simply denying these achievements and focusing solely on his perceived evils that are also all too numerous.

Olusegun Obasanjo is largely unguarded because he gives no damn about decorum and mutual respect. Open and unguarded insults and abuses on his fellow man were all too common in a larger than God fashion

Many of Obasanjo's enemies are people who were either denied political appointments or denied the opportunity of stealing public funds. No doubt, such persons will be doubly aggrieved when they not only perceive but (perhaps) also openly see how this same President is alleged to have stolen the public funds that he denied them the opportunity of stealing, while he even goes after them and disgrace them publicly as enemies of Nigeria's progress. These enemies in fact, are always all too happy and pleased when they find any little fact to lay their hands on to disgrace the ex-President in public view.

It is therefore highly understandable that the present government is extremely reluctant to bring General Olusegun Obasanjo to any public dock for the sole purpose of disgracing him before many of his sworn and unforgiving enemies.

Alas there comes a time though, when decisions have to be made. Times when priorities have to be defined!

For all the achievements in the world, no ruler has the right to steal from the coffers that were trustfully kept under his humble watch. It is on this note, that the cries of corruption against the former President should be honestly investigated.

In a furious reaction to one of my recent essays on the ex-President, one compatriot wrote to give me a list of concrete questions on perceived financial wrongdoings on the part of the ex-President. The reader asks: 1. Why were 200 million Transcorp shares given away at ridiculously low rates? 2. How was Otta farm miraculously transformed from a scrap yard in 1999 to a state of the art farmyard today? 3. How were $10 billion spent on electricity while there is nothing to show for it? 4. How were N300 billion spent on roads that are worse off today? 5. What were the underlying guidelines for the allocation and revocation of oil blocks? 6. How were N754 billion worth of oil contracts awarded only in the twilight of the regime? 7. Why were secret accounts operated without the knowledge of the National Assembly? 8. How did Andy Uba transform from a Massage Parlor operator in Los Angeles into one of Nigeria's wealthiest men within a spate of 8 years? 9. How were steel rolling companies sold to parties that did not participate in the bidding process?

While answers to some of the questions above can hardly go any step close to the proof of corruption, they may at best, uncover administrative improprieties. Given the shrewd and crafty manner of Olusegun Obasanjo as we have come to understand in the past few years, I would indeed, not be surprised at all, to figure out that there is absolutely nothing available to nail him on. While bank credits may have solved very many issues from farm refurbishment to the acquisition of several private companies, questions may however, be asked if a head of state may not end up compromising his exalted position by being too hugely indebted to private economic interests. There is no doubt that many banks will be all too happy to grant a President as much loan as he requires. It should be recalled that several co-politicians at lesser level were often ending up making gifts of stolen money to the President for one favor or the other.

However, answers to some other questions will indeed, go a long way to quell anxieties and speculations about the activities of the ex-President.

Orji Uzor Kalu, who is himself closer to the corridors of power than myself and many of my readers put together remarked that about 79% of corruption occurs at Federal level while the remaining 21% can be sought at state level. No doubt the Governor had more tangible and near-irrefutable questions to ask the regime of President Obasanjo since he *"wrote several petitions to Ribadu on corruption against Obasanjo. Ribadu never investigated any of the petitions."*

Precisely this point it is that brings us to the illusionary issue of high expectations on Nuhu Ribadu and his exceptional anti-graft commission. Many Nigerians like Orji Uzor Kalu seemed to have basked in the unforgivable illusion that Nigeria was operating a traditional democracy of several centuries as in the United States, in which the President may appoint a Special Investigator, who would be free to investigate any issue within his scheme of reference including the President himself.

Nigerians simply lacked the wisdom to detect the courage and boldness in the man Ribadu and nurture this element in utmost tranquility until a period that would have been fit enough to carry our democracy forward at least, in the field of investigations across the board. What Nigerians were and are still very good at is the so-called "Gra-gra" mentality of knowing it all and wanting to have it all in one fell swoop.

In the end, we succeeded in trimming down and decimating one viable human weapon that we had at our disposal that would have led the nation through a major distance in curtailing the perpetrators of evils that we seek to eradicate.

Thank goodness even Orji Uzor Kalu has now come around to admit in all openness that Nuhu Ribadu started well and did a good job. It is so strange how people now come around to state that Nuhu Ribadu played politics because he refused to commit suicide by moving into Aso Rock in handcuffs to arrest the serving President, who was his boss and employer. A clear goal incongruence that sets expectation in diametrical opposition to reality!

And when Nigerians start to bash, they usually know no "stop!" Not even at a point when the web was slowly beginning to strengthen and tighten up did some critics recognize Ribadu's slow and cautious movement in all directions. Hardliners would settle for nothing but Ribadu's head. The likes of Orji Uzor Kalu believe it is injustice when corrupt officers are arraigned for public disgrace while the higher ones at Federal level remain untouched. And of course, a friend of Governor Kalu it was who taught the world in public lecturing of sort, of the difference between equity and justice. That equity is not evenly served on all criminals at the same time should not mean that a lesser criminal is not getting justice for his lesser crime because the higher criminal has not been arraigned. The powerful forces at the corridor of power finally made it through and Ribadu was criminalized for being cautiously courageous.

One question will ever loom though: is it really true that no single financial wrongdoing can be established against the ex-President? It may be one thing to be unable to establish a case of outright corruption and looting of public treasury. It will definitely be another issue when nepotism and favoritism take center stage as the circus-hall charges from Gbenga & co. currently indicate!

To the enemies of the ex-President too, the question will always ever loom: What do they all stand to gain from this mob-type call for probe? If a probe is finally installed and President Olusegun Obasanjo publicly disgraced even in a manner worse that the current diabolical charge of incestuous conduct, would the mob be satisfied and get a holy audience with God in heaven?

***

Three issues stand out at the end of this article, that highlight major actions during the short-lived Yar'adua government in its early days: The victimization of Nuhu Ribadu. The witch-hunt for the ex-President's daughter Senator Iyabo Obasanjo-Bello the unnecessary outburst of the ex-President's son, Gbenga Obasanjo, using the newspaper outlet of a sworn enemy of the ex-President.

Let us begin with the sensational removal of the legendary Nuhu Ribadu, the founding Chairman of the Economic and Financial Crimes Commission (EFCC) that western powers aided the former President in founding. Under the former President and given a relatively free hand in the exercise of his duties, Nuhu Ribadu gained a reputation for fearlessness, not the least, in his bold move to indict his own boss and friend of the President – the Inspector-General of Police – on charges of corruption and have him arrested in handcuffs. Like the President that he served, he stepped on toes and had countless enemies.

In the era of President Yar'Adua, in which the single political program was the dismantling of the Obasanjo legacy, Nuhu Ribadu, was target No. 1. I wrote the following two articles in the heat of the moment and principally released them on my web column and on countless other outlets.

Killing Ribadu Softly: Who Will Pay the Price?

By Frisky Larr

It took two acts. Just two acts. The megaphones were silenced. The trumpets are taking over. Just with utter caution!

It took the act of closure. The closure of a media house! The arrest of journalists! All in the aftermath of hoaxes and arguably, malicious reports on the President's health! It took a second act. The arrest of a blogger in a newfound hobby that is not so new. Internet blogging is a few years old, transforming the face of media expression in the landscape of political commentary in Nigeria. Self-imposed writers or public commentators with no clue of journalistic mechanisms have been no strangers to the Nigerian scene for the past few years. Many are remnants of megaphone writers and hobby critics of the past regime. They were mostly abusers of the instruments of writing speaking in bile, gruesome and despicable languages all in the guise of courage and stoic resilience.

For the first time though, one of them was picked up at the Nigerian airport on a visit to his motherland from overseas. Not by Idi Amin. Not by agents of Sani Abacha or agents of the hated Olusegun Obasanjo. No. He picked by agents of the allegedly democratically elected government of President Umaru Musa Yar'Adua. His crime: too critical of the present regime.

This new twist has kept voices restrained in the face of arrests and media closure. Those abusive languages and hate-filled venom that trailed the last year of the past regime are a rarity today in the columns of professionals in the home scene.

Caution, diplomacy and objective criticism have all become a hallmark of critical contents these days. And that is how it should have been since anger against a brother is paradoxically felt in the flesh and not in the bone. But reasons enough the media do have to unleash venom on the present government of Umaru Musa Yar'Adua.

Observers are no stranger to the traditional illustration of our past leaders in figurative characterization. In fact, one such case portrayed General Ibrahim Babanginda as one strange leader in Nigeria who would slap his detractor and offer him his shoulder to cry upon in a mockery of solace and tactful comforting. On the contrary, General Muhammadu Buhari is generally portrayed as one bizarre personality that would slap his detractor and dare him to cry.

The latter is unfortunately, the image that meets the eye today in the actions of the Nigerian Police Force (obviously tele-guided by the maximo-leader President Umaru Musa Yar'Adua) against a prominent and outstanding son of forceful devotion – Nuhu Ribadu.

While history reflects that many leading names in the hierarchy of the Nigerian Police Force have at one point or the other, benefited from rapid promotion for reasons that were not subjected to public scrutiny, a weird argument bearing on due process is being advanced today as reasons enough to reverse the promotion of Nuhu Ribadu from AIG to DCP. Unlike previous benefactors – amongst whose names Mike Okiro often features – reasons for the accelerated promotion of Nuhu Ribadu is highly appreciated by many reasonable Nigerians and foreign observers alike because they were there for all to see.

Having beaten this rare symbol of anti-corruption decorum in a desperate bid to invoke some elusive public disgrace by demoting him in Public Square, they are now daring him to cry by seeking to know who authorized him to challenge his demotion in the court of law.

Indeed, when Olusegun Obasanjo fought tooth and nail to install Umaru Musa Yar'Adua as President to succeed him, he – do doubt – had at the top of his mind, the fear of the persecution he would suffer if he was succeeded by Muhammadu Buhari or Atiku Abubakar. Alongside this fear though, were some vital assurances that political operatives in traditional democracies characterize as "Gentleman's Agreement". It has been reported that the retention of Nuhu Ribadu in his position for the continuation of the good work he was doing, was part of such vital assurances made by Umaru Musa Yar'Adua to his predecessor. It may be pertinent to observe that some will rightly contend that nemesis served Obasanjo right for having himself, reneged on previous phantom deals with the mentors that installed him in power. Unfortunately, though, Obasanjo neither succeeded IBB nor did he succeed Abubakar Atiku as President. The gravity of reneging on words or the disposal of prudent continuity in the handover and takeover of policy-making positions has been all but clearly exemplified in the disaster called President George W. Bush of the United States. The same scenario is now playing out in the Nigerian domestic scene.

Reneging on agreement with IBB and his cohorts was dangerous enough for national unity as Sharia and Atiku subsequently tried to vindicate. But breaking words in policy-making positions however, is always done at the expense of the destiny of policy direction and the mechanism of governance. Today, a chain reaction has been set in motion with Nuhu Ribadu declared as a free game for Michael Aondoakaa and Inspector-General Okiro and perhaps sooner than later, Mrs. Waziri as well.

But what reasons on earth does Umaru Musa Yar'Adua have for launching this massive war of attrition against Ribadu?

It is easy to understand – thank goodness – a dwindling minority of Nigerians who claim in all soberness that Ribadu is getting back what he did to others. After all, such people (much like the leadership of the Action Congress headed by Abubakar Atiku) have either had axes of corruption to grind with Ribadu in the course of his courageous fight or are sympathizers of those who fell victim to the no-nonsense stance. Many voices have highlighted in all clarity thus far, that Nuhu Ribadu unfortunately did the bidding of his erstwhile boss by being blind on one eye and seeing all too clearly on the other. This reality has never been lost on wise and prudent observers from within and outside the nation. Foreign financial sponsors of the EFCC under Ribadu's leadership saw this as well. It was in fact, no novelty to the world's political scene to see the victimization of political opponents with authentic crimes committed by them. Hear echoes of multi-millionaire Khordokowski behind bars in the Russian Federation! The bottom line in the views of observers is simply to determine if the crime for which charges are made were truly committed or not. Till today, no single person that was prosecuted by Nuhu Ribadu has been discharged and acquitted or declared innocently prosecuted by any court of law.

Indeed, it is easy to understand the frustration-induced bitterness expressed by these culprits and their sympathizers when they claim that Nuhu Ribadu went after them and left out others, whose innocence was their personal proximity to the power of the day.

But what problem does Umaru Musa Yar'Adua have? Has he become so much of a captive of circumstances and influences that he would simply stop at nothing to destroy Nuhu Ribadu?

Today, analysts are puzzled and raise endless questions on why one action or the other is being served on Ribadu for no discernible crime. In fact, many analysts are addressing the symptoms of the ailment while the real issue has nothing in the main, to do with uniform or lack thereof at the NIPPS graduation ceremony, or qualification for the rank of AIG. It is simply vendetta for real.

But again, why? For what reason on earth is Umaru Musa Yar'Adua bent on undoing Nuhu Ribadu? The picture simply does not fit.

Ribadu did his utmost to investigate corrupt politicians across a broad spectrum. Many voluntarily opted out of competition for the Presidency upon persuasion with the volume of corruption dossier piled up against them. The benefactor was Umaru Musa Yar'Adua and the nation at large that was spared known corrupt leaders. Umaru Musa Yar'Adua was widely believed to be clean at heart and in bank account. No Ribadu dossier, no shrinking eyebrow showed him as corrupt. He was a promising figure. To consolidate power and position in a volatile political arrangement, the President no doubt, needed power brokers to avert social and political upheaval. But where is the President's guts to let people be tried in public, who are widely believed to have made no secret of their obnoxious mission to drain the public coffers? Why do Lucky Igbinedion, Orji Uzor Kalu or former governor Ibori count among the President's best friends today? More painfully and disturbing too is the shortage of any attempt whatsoever, to disguise this trait. Ibori who bears the wrath of his people for arbitrary personal wealth and extremely disproportionate minimal achievement as Governor! Lucky Igbinedion who patiently and stoically watched and laughed at a whole state reversing deeper into the Stone Age and abject poverty while his own family burgeoned in wealth and progress!

Obasanjo the devil-incarnate surrounded himself with people like Ngozi Okonjo-Iweala, Soludo, El-Rufai and Nuhu Ribadu – all appraised for positive achievements but are collectively being derided today. The most prominent actor in Saint Umaru Musa Yar'Adua's government today is Michael Aondoakaa and his principal agenda is "Bringing down Ribadu"!

What on earth is Yar'Adua's problem? Power and position have been consolidated almost two years into a four-year tenure. Where are the guts? There has been a public yearning for the Supreme Court to play it easy on Yar'Adua on the legitimacy of his election. After all, the signs will be dismal if instability is ushered in, in the wake of a negative judgment. Unfortunately, however, the government seems bent on chewing more than it can swallow. Never has headline been made with milestone achievements in the power sector, transport sector or water supply. When headline is made, it is a diversionary reversal of a predecessor's policy or the humiliation of a predecessor. Thus far, Umaru Musa Yar'Adua has been applauded by a public that is increasingly turning around to recognize that no action taken by the President has thus far translated into public benefit.

Labor Unions are watching and Students Unions too. The bellwether goals have become "money in my pocket" and the deal is done. Students are locked in cultism and are hardly students anymore.

But today, major columnists in Nigeria have done Nigeria proud by rallying round Nuhu Ribadu. Caution in their choice of words notwithstanding, the message has all been clear. Nuhu is not Ribadu. Ribadu is not the man. And the man is not the issue. Ribadu is a name. It stands for anti-corruption. Kill Ribadu and the project will be killed. At least for now! But when it rises again, it will wear a different cloak and the victims will be different.

Close the media house. Arrest the journalists. Arrest the bloggers too. But there are Fawehinmis whose soul will never die no matter the chains of arrests. NigerianNews will speak out – Unbridled and Unafraid. Set the secret service loose – the truth will never die! Some will take to the streets with a little bit of courage. They will ask you loud and clear: "Kill Ribadu slowly but who will pay the price?"

***

What if Ribadu's Reputation has been Compromised like Obasanjo's?

By Frisky Larr

The saying "What the eye doesn't see, the heart doesn't grieve over" is an old saying of the wise in English language. In routine usage it is in common circulation amongst lovers in the nest of emotional interaction. As long as a lover is not aware that he or she is being cheated upon by the counterpart, the heart would not grieve. Therefore, most lovers would just not want to know as long as the feeling of love remains true to its nature of barren purity.

It is precisely on this basis that lovers, admirers and objective observers of the activities of Chairman Nuhu Ribadu in the past few years and months will have much, not only to grieve but also to bleed over if the reputation of this young courageous man has indeed been compromised.

The **NigerianNews** has been placed on alert in ample time and by several reliable sources many months ago, that a huge dossier has long been prepared on Nuhu Ribadu that houses a can of worms. Since this information can by and large, only qualify as a rumor, which authenticity can hardly be verified at a snap, the **NigerianNews** opted to steer clear of reporting any such story. Amongst professionals in journalistic circles though, the rumor has long persisted with all tenacity. Sources are usually such quarters as can hardly be characterized as friendly disposed to the cause and person of Nuhu Ribadu. The question however, has never been whether or not there is truly any such dossier in existence or if there is any truth to the content of any such dossier, but when the dossier itself will be finally blown open to see the light of day.

Even though no one who is not an insider to the sinister or patriotic ploy (as the case may be) would know the precise content of this dossier, it may be safe to assume that recent events unfolding in the corridors of jurisprudence provide a hint of things to come by way of any imaginary or real Ribadu-dossier. A team of legal practitioners has been reported to have prayed an Abuja High Court Judge to mandate the investigation of the private financial capacity of the man Nuhu Ribadu in the face of incompatible ownership of a villa in Dubai and a house in Abuja (all valuing millions of dollars).

The issue remains particularly disturbing in view of the potentially damaging impact such information is bound to have not only on the image of the man Nuhu Ribadu but also on the long-drawn fight against corruption led by him and his EFCC on several Nigerian battlefronts.

Funnily, no point of substance can be made on Ribadu today, without reference to his previous boss and 'discoverer' Olusegun Obasanjo. It should be recalled that one minor segment of vocal and badly embittered critics of the ex-President are those people who seem to know him at close range with a better insight at the running of Aso Rock during the tenure of the former General.

Their one-sided focus mainly on hypocrisy and deceit in the activities of Olusegun Obasanjo has most often, always left observers like me furious at the shortage of some sense of objectivity. But this camp has always been resilient in hammering home some credible points of the ex-President's hilarious and ludicrous acquisition of unspeakable wealth within a short pace of time. While the neutral observer sought to have emphasis equally placed on failures and achievements as they related to the ex-President, such critics as were close to the crux of Presidential activities at the time understandably remained bitter at what they claim to have seen of systematic looting by the ex-President and were therefore, not prepared to acknowledge anything positive in the semblance of achievement. But chains of milestone achievements the ex-President does have in his favor.

The ultimate result however, is currently, a badly dented image of a beleaguered ex-President. While foreign debt repayment, satellite launch, bank reform, telecommunication breakthrough etc. count in favor of the former President, ownership of a big university with unexplained source of finance, expanded commercial empire of enterprises with unknown financial sources in addition to alleged questionable financial interests in several commercial entities credibly count against the ex-President until judicially resolved for good.

Precisely this route is the envisaged path that the author(s) of some Ribadu dossier intend to tow. In a recent discourse, I remember warning of days to come that will bear witness to accusations flying wildly Ribadu's way. It did not require a sage to smell the plot. Ribadu will very soon stand on the dock of public conscience standing accused of corruption in dimensions ever unheard of. No doubt such perpetrators will stand out like those alleged insiders of Presidential conduct in the days of Olusegun Obasanjo claiming to be aware of Ribadu's hypocrisy as a tangible reason for stubbornly refusing to credit him with any worthy success.

Even though it cannot be discounted that the EFCC as a body may have operated with a great deal of imperfection if not outright thievery perpetrated among the ranks, it may sound too simplistic to lodge all misdeeds of an entire commission squarely at the feet of a Chairman. Information now abounds that the EFCC suddenly surged into a position of extreme preference for the ranks of the police force with very many officers suddenly wanting to serve at the EFCC. This alone no doubt, smells of some skeleton in the closet.

Even though history is fortunately, unemotional and will credit Nuhu Ribadu with his courageous and daring stride in marking a huge thaw on the stiff ice of some endemic corruption, something will surely stick in this equally daring campaign against the wave of public sympathy for an imperfect, young and inspiring Ribadu.

He it was, who remarked that corruption has its own way of fighting back if you fight it too hard. But that was mere rhetoric. What the eye doesn't see, the heart will surely, not grieve over. True or untrue, an allegation remains an allegation until completely dispelled. Once heard by the public, something must be done.

There is no doubt, that Nuhu Ribadu can never in his life, have earned millions of dollars as a senior Nigerian Police Officer to buy a house in Abuja to say the least of a villa in Dubai. If this were not brought to the public's attention, no heart would grieve. As soon as this accusation sees the light of day though, nothing short of absolute clearance will address the impending damage.

The Speaker of the House of Representatives Mr. Bankole gave a shining example lately on how to confront mongers of mischievous rumors. It sounded clear and irrefutable when the rumor became public information that the Speaker did not serve in the NYSC (as if that mattered to the discharge of his duties though). I was one of those who expressed personal fascination at the depth of sound investigations some Nigerian media houses were now capable of expediting. When the Speaker finally emerged however, to release his photo as a corper in his days as well as furnish a pictured copy of his certificate of discharge, I finally learnt to take any investigation associated with Nigerian public figures with a pinch of salt.

Even though no accusation should be dismissed with a wave of the hand, extreme caution should however, be exercised in good faith, in digesting the volume and intensity of accusations that may fly Ribadu's ways in the days ahead. If such serious charges turn out to be true, nothing will be able to subvert veracity. If not – as one good friend of mine puts it – such perpetrators should bear in mind that they will surely answer up to the living God when their time is due!

Many are Ribadu's enemies – born of envy and anger. Envy at rapid promotion above some ranks and anger at being exposed in the cage of corruption. At the center of all these scenarios is the bared inefficiency of the serving President who was obviously unable to make a crafty move with the sophistication of at least appearing to contain Ribadu – no matter the differences – at least for the sake of governmental expediency! Today, we reap scorn and suspicion from beyond the borders of our land for the mismanaged project of backdoor appeasement. The conclusion is anyone's guess.

But if Nuhu Ribadu finally turns out to have been corrupt however, then let it be on record that many hearts will be broken. History may still remain fair and balanced on him. Posterity will not.

***

Nuhu Ribadu was finally ejected from the commission that he served from inception in a most cowardly manner. He was sent off on the pretext of a compulsory advanced training program, where he became the subject of harassments and humiliation attempts. He had dared dock and lock up the powerful ex-Governor of Delta State on corruption charges. James Ibori foretold Ribadu's fate in the wake of his own arrest and Nuhu Ribadu had to flee the land to skip the fulfillment of the conclusive prediction, namely jail. An attempt was also reportedly made on his life.

There was a chain of events in the anti-Obasanjo frenzy, whose sequential order I can no longer reproduce. The ex-President's eldest son, Gbenga Obasanjo, had made a spectacular public allegation against his father claiming his father was going to bed with his (the son's) wife. This was a massive talk-of-the-town in a massive operation to humiliate the former President. There was also the case of the President's daughter, who was a Senator and ridiculously accused of corruption without substantiation.

I wrote the following two articles on the subject and tried as much as I could to get a neutral appraisal. The articles were basically released on my column on NigerianNews, on the Nigerian Village Square and on several other websites.

The Iyabo Scandal: EFCC's Case is Weak!!

By Frisky Larr

Day-by-day, details are trickling out of the 'EFCC versus Iyabo' scandal currently rocking political Nollywood in Abuja. In the latest round, it was the EFCC's turn to tear its can open and bare up the contents of its own view. What has thus far, become obvious and comprehensible is that the EFCC operatives have reasons enough – plenty of it too – to be dead angry with Iyabo Obasanjo-Bello.

One age-long traditional adage seeking to address the problem of the human factor in handling matters of public interest says that scratching the skin in reaction to itching should willfully not follow the intensity of the itching felt. Else, the skin may be torn open before the realization of pains while the irritating itching stimulus allows for a pleasant scratching feel for a considerable stretch of time.

In practice, this adage says nothing else than cautioning against conscious or unconscious overreaction in the aftermath of malicious provocation, for which humans are characteristic in the quest to assert power and gain edges over their fellow beings. It therefore goes that public service is a calling that presupposes some super-human qualities with expectations of the near impossible.

The issue at stake as reported in the latest media takes, presents a picture of an EFCC that is vowing to arrest and prosecute Senator Iyabo Obasanjo-Bello for posing as if she was above the law and almost ridiculing the Economic and Financial Crimes Commission, come what may. Her attention was said to have been drawn to the illegality of the N10 million given to her committee by the Ministry of Health in ample time ahead of the so-called retreat in far-away Ghana. She is quoted as having agreed to return the money quietly. For whatever reason there is, she should have reneged on her words and went ahead to spend the money on the retreat.

No doubt anyone would be aggrieved, as this conduct reflected in the EFCC's version of the story is tantamount to questioning the authority of the anti-graft commission. A position that usually doesn't go down well with any African, to say the least of Nigerians!

An EFCC operative is further quoted to have vented his anger in the words: *"Is it part of the oversight function of the Senate to go for workshop in Ghana? What manner of workshop is it that cannot be done in Nigeria?"*

The same operative was reported in the Vanguard daily, to have summed up the issue by reiterating that Senator Iyabo's defiance and breach of prior agreement constituted *"a brazen act of disrespect to the anti-graft agency and the Federal Government."* He continues: *"Senator Iyabo Obasanjo still went ahead, organized some of her colleagues, shared the money and embarked on the trip to Ghana for the so-called workshop even after she had been interrogated and told to return the stolen money."*

It is precisely at this juncture that common sense is strictly required to prevail as a matter of priority. While the anti-graft commission is established to enforce the law, the law is definitely not the EFCC itself nor is it the persons making up the institution. Many stones that were thrown Ribadu's way in advance of his infamous study leave at Kuru often echoed charges of personalizing the EFCC. He was said to have overshadowed the cause of the struggle with the charisma of his personality. It was the fear of the creation of a demi-god that pervaded the air. Enemies of Ribadu got their way and Ribadu is not there today.

It therefore, becomes pertinent to ask if disrespect for the EFCC and the Federal Government is the financial crime for which Iyabo Obasanjo now deserves to be arrested and detained. No doubt, this EFCC operative, who wisely chose to remain anonymous while speaking to the press, would have been up against an avalanche of internal enemies here and now for this disastrous public relations blunder.

While it is very much legitimate upon any citizen of the country, whose money is being sunk down the drain, to question the rationale behind holding a legislative retreat, workshop, seminar (whatever they call it) in Ghana, it is a troubling puzzle for a spokesman and professional operative of the EFCC to advance this argument in seeking to convince the public of the need to arrest the embattled senator. When has it become a financial and economic crime to participate in a workshop in a foreign country?

While the EFCC now reports that Senator Iyabo Obasanjo-Bello is required for interrogation and clarification of ambiguous facts, records also reflect the intervention of the Presidency in preempting the intended detention of the senator during her first report for interrogation, probably in advance of the so-called retreat. The question should therefore loom on why there is so much desperation in efforts and commitment to arrest and detain Iyabo Obasanjo-Bello.

To set the records straight: judging by the facts allowed in public domain so far, Iyabo Obasanjo-Bello has a clear case to answer in her capacity as Chairman of the Senate's Health Committee. She and her committee did not only fail to prevail on the Ministry of Health over which they exercise legislative control function, to return unspent budget money to the Presidency, they even aided and abetted the illegal disbursement of such money definitely in breach of laws that jurisprudents will be precisely able to specify. In her favor however, no evidence has yet revealed that she embezzled the said amount. Illegal actions in this respect can therefore be seen to be in official capacities.

Even though reports are heard, of grumbles by some members of the Senate Health committee alleging that they did not benefit from the N10 million spent, it may be pertinent to probe into their understanding of the word "benefit". They may probably be in a position to furnish proof of embezzlement of the money on the part of senator Iyabo.

So far, no evidence in public domain supports the EFCC's anonymous claim that she went ahead "to share the money" where the vocabularies "spend the money" would have been more adequate. So far, the upper chamber of the legislative house has not bared open, its evidences that prompted the issuance of a clean bill of health.

The pressing question therefore is why the EFCC is stubbornly focused on Iyabo Obasanjo-Bello as a person rather than indicting the Health Committee made up of 13 members, of which 11 were said to have attended the Ghana workshop, and by implication, the senate directly.

If the EFCC is interested in prosecuting cases with a touch of professionalism and not with glimpses of wounded pride and conceitedness, it should come up with a better focus. It will come to no one as a surprise if the EFCC loses the case against Iyabo Obasanjo in court. The actual surprise would be an EFCC-victory on this issue. With a judiciary that is growing more independent and unpredictable by the day however, surprises are indeed, no surprises any longer.

One fact is certain though: the EFCC operative who spoke with the press on Tuesday April the 22nd of 2008, seems to belong to a camp of hardliners within the EFCC, whose focus is not necessarily the challenge of legality and due process, but the sheer will to have anger vented and embarrassment served. Ultimately, these gentlemen of honor will have to realize pretty fast that they ought to tread softly in seeking to scratch their skins with the brutality of the itching felt. They may end up simply having to stop upon seeing their own blood when the skin is scratched open. They may simply outsmart themselves running faster than their own feet can take them in the frantic attempt to utilize the current momentum generated by the wind of hate intensely blowing the Obasanjo's in the face.

**

Iyabo doesn't Sound Wrong but...!

By Frisky Larr

No doubt, Senator Iyabo Obasanjo has these days, been receiving solicited and unsolicited, private and public counseling from the right, from the left, from the center and from above and below. A few days ago, in an unsolicited act, we released a commentary on the ex-President's favorite daughter questioning where she thinks she can hide in the face of agitated sentiments. As if Iyabo Obasanjo read NigerianNews on Monday the 21st of 2008, the answer came just one day later, publicized in other news media.

Indeed, a lot of questions have been raised on why the Senator chose to flee rather than submit herself voluntarily for questioning and clearing the air once and for all. This at least, is the general impression pervading the air in the battle for public sympathy.

Having had negative psychological strings attached to her name as the blockbuster movie star perfecting disguises and scaling fences spontaneously in the style of an Olympian athlete, Iyabo Obasanjo's response truly gives every objective and fair-minded observer sufficient food for thought.

What is Iyabo Obasanjo being truly prosecuted for? It has been reported that a huge amount of unspent budget money was misappropriated at the Ministry of Health. Is the Senate's Health Committee now being docked for failing in its oversight functions and for failing to prevail on the Minister of Health to return unspent budget money rather than joining the Ministry officials in the willful and arbitrary disbursement of the said budget money?

This would sound perfectly logical, as the EFCC in its counter-oversight function owes a duty to follow every lead.

In all of this, the Chairperson of the Senate's Health Committee owes a public duty to blow the whistle on the Ministry of Health to have unspent budget money returned without delay and even threaten to initiate criminalizing legislation on the issue if the system functions without hitches. Instead, the existing situation is such that the crime investigation instance is blowing the whistle on the Chairperson of the Health Committee for even aiding and abetting the illegal disbursement of unspent budget money. This is shameful indeed.

One way or the other, there is definitely unmistakable illegality involving the Senate's Health Committee's conduct on the Health Ministry's scandal.

But why for God's sake is this being so badly personalized? Why is Iyabo Obasanjo and not the committee itself being required to pay back N10 million that was spent by the committee headed by her and not embezzled by her?

In seeking to seal the loopholes – which democracy is all about – uncovered by this conduct of the Senate committee, legislative or judicial remedies are adopted. Since the EFCC is not a legislative organ, it goes without saying that the only option at its disposal is the judicial remedy.

But why should the Chairperson of the Committee be arrested and detained in her personal capacity? Aside from the reality that there was no immediate risk of the Senator fleeing the country, it is extremely questionable, what purpose an arrest and detention of the Senator is expected to serve, i.e. assuming it makes sense to arrest and detain her in the first place for allowing her committee to accept money that was spent on official duties.

This complex knot is not only becoming puzzling by the day, it smells very much of vendetta and cheap populism at its best.

If indeed, Iyabo Obasanjo has filed a court case challenging the legality of holding her personally responsible for the N10 million saga, it will then be truly bemusing what gallery the EFCC is playing to. If the Health Committee is officially charged for breaking the law, it will be the duty of the Senate as an institution to stand up to the charges and challenges since the committee did not constitute itself all on its own. Indeed, the committee acts on behalf of the Senate and it is the senate that should be held accountable by all logical comprehension. It would therefore be left to the Senate to sort out erring characters from within its own ranks and subject them to internal disciplinary mechanisms before penal prosecution.

As is typical of Nigeria's Hollywood-type politics however, it will come as no surprise that every possible avenue and opportunity is exploited to settle political scores. Who is best suited for the role of a prominent and high-profile victim than the daughter of an erstwhile badly hated President?

Yet, we hear no call from hypocritical self-styled apostles of due process called Aondoakaa or Olisa Agbakogba, who would have wasted no time to descend heavily on the erring side if his name bore the semblance of Obasanjo. Thank goodness, voices of reason are beginning to come up lately, to point out that the morally acceptable threshold of decency is gradually being overstepped in lambasting ex-President Obasanjo. Thank goodness many also agree that all his evils (brought upon himself and by himself alone) notwithstanding, the legacy of Obasanjo the ex-President far exceeds this maliciously designed focus on negative coverage.

One thing is certain so far, while evidences of impropriety and financially untenable practices abound, there has so far, been no single indication of the willful stealing of public funds on the part of Olusegun Obasanjo or Iyabo Obasanjo-Bello.

Disgrace Iyabo Obasanjo-Bello all you can by locking her up and proving to the world that her father can do just nothing about it, but will it be moving Nigeria forward any bit? If an Obasanjo-leaning power takes over the helm of affairs in days to come, will the seed of vendetta not have been perfectly sown? Above all, is the reason for seeking Iyabo-Obasanjo's head justified in the first place? If Olusegun Obasanjo is truly proven to have masterminded several unjustified political killings and victimization, should his sins be visited on Iyabo?

One cannot help but remember past instances, in which the son of a former powerful head of state by the name of Ibrahim Babangida was arrested under the watchful eyes of Olusegun Obasanjo in a move that was widely interpreted as testing the waters to ascertain how much influence the General was still able to wield. Many agreed that Olusegun Obasanjo was on a self-acclaimed mission to decimate the powers of Ibrahim Babaginda.

Whoever kills by the sword dies by the sword. So is the saying of the wise in centuries past. Primitive philosophies, however, hardly have a place in our modern world of progressive advancement. The result of this ancient philosophy in the past had always been one of vendetta. A vicious circle of wiping off successive families in endless orgies!

First, there is an endless spate of media revelations highlighting charges of duping and financial scams with contracts awarded, paid for and never executed. There is a huge crowd that pre-concludes that these are money stolen by Obasanjo and his proxies by tricky dispensations. After all, Obasanjo was transformed into a multi-millionaire in eight years.

The ex-President may chant how much loan he obtained from banks as much he will, it will and continue to fall on deaf ears until proof is furnished of what happened to that huge sum expended on the power sector without results. Unfortunately, however, none of these charges have been competently investigated. But judgments have been passed. Volitionally. Pitiably, these cries are coming out from those sectors of governance that are themselves, stinking a stench of impurity.

Then, there is a sudden frenzy in reaching out for the jailing of a serving senator for an official misconduct being sold to the world as corruption. Who has a mole in the eyes not to see vendetta?

What credibility can Aondoakaa claim to possess today, if all he knows about due process is to volubly demand the head of Nuhu Ribadu and turn a blind eye to undue process in seeking to jail a serving senator? It wouldn't or shouldn't matter as long as the senator in question answers any name in the semblance of Obasanjo.

While anyone – Obasanjo or not – deserves to be duly punished for any proven crime, should the system be made to devour the innocent? If Obasanjo and Ribadu misused the EFCC as an instrument against political opponents, at least they did not cook up accusations against innocent souls. No one victimized by the EFCC under Obasanjo – political enemy or not – can claim innocence of the crimes for which they stood accused. Besides, who says two wrongs make a right, when one claims to be on a mission to correct the evils of the past?

The Nigeria that we seek to build should by all academic standards of practicality stand the test of time and the rugged test of credibility. It should be a Nigeria for every one of us – the deviants and the conformists. Creating a Nigeria for vagabonds in power no matter the shape and color or period in question, definitely means the construction of high-fly towers on a sandy foundation.

***

The obsession with the humiliation of the former President as the unspoken political program of his successor, continued unabated. Policies were reversed without viable replacements. The sale of dilapidated refineries was reversed. Deported foreign fraudsters, who posed as friends of the nation and sapped the nation's resources with impunity, were called back as long as it serves the humiliation of the central figure. The replacement of Governor's that were suspected loyal to the former President was encouraged even in cases that smacked of anti-party activities by the incumbent President. Appointments made by the former President to address geographical imbalance in the distribution of key public offices were reversed to reflect the tilted old order.

The Governor of the Central Bank of Nigeria, who has traditionally come from the northern part of the country much like some other crucial public offices, had been tampered with by the ex-President. For the first time, he had appointed an eastern Nigerian to head the apex bank. Now, that a part of the incumbent President's agenda was to return power back to the north and tilt the balance back to the diabolic status quo pre-Obasanjo, the next crucial office to be filled by a northerner was the office of the Governor of the Central Bank. The mission to dismantle the eastern Chukwuma Soludo from the office was launched.

The following article details the controversy that served as a prelude to the final removal of this Governor. It was published on my column, on the Nigerian Village Square and several other online platforms.

Even if Soludo was Wrong, the President Should Listen and Perhaps More Carefully!

By Frisky Larr

One good thing for which the Nigerian intelligentsia (as reflected in the Nigerian mass media) gains my admiration these days, is its inexhaustible expertise on issues of public controversy. No sooner does an issue become publicly controversial in this experimental democratic set-up than the center stage begins to produce countless number of homegrown experts. Theories begin to fly in all directions as if the dormant proponents of such opinions knew everything far better from the very start. Soludo has unfortunately become the latest culprit of such gracious geniuses in the open field of self-aggrandizement.

Without mincing words and subscribing to further forms of acrobatic verbal pageantry, I would love to call into question, the various forms of public contradictions that are slowly but clearly becoming a clear characteristic of governance imminent in President Umaru Musa Yar'Adua's presidential repertoire. Without invoking the debacle of the Attorney General's politically suicidal attempt (driven by anti-Obasanjo sentiments) at derailing and marginalizing the EFCC and Nuhu Ribadu and the President's rather amateur performance in mastering and calling the Attorney-General to a limited order, I would rather focus on the current issue centering on the Governor of the Central Bank. That the President on occasions, has cause to rigmarole, backtrack and even play a diplomatic somersault has so far, been appraised as a human trait and sold as admirable and contrary to everything his predecessor (General Obasanjo) stood for. There is undeniably, a whole lot of political goodwill at play. In the modern world of consolidated democratic practice however, rigmarole, backtracking, diplomatic somersaults and administrative U-turns may turn out to be slippery political banana skins, incompetence, poor preparation for the complex challenge of the office held and above all, potent boomerang on the perpetrator without much ado, from the opposition. Western democracies have a good number of high-profile victims to show.

When a few days back, the Governor of the Central Bank of Nigeria unveiled the bombshell of re-denominating the Naira, the academic finesse behind the exercise that was greeted by a huge wave of controversy, was absolutely new territory for me in spite of my university years on mass communication and various semesters on Micro and Macro-Economics. I am sure,

I am not alone in this terrain. Many who hastened to unleash their comments in favor of or against Soludo's move definitely share the position I am in. In an initial reaction however, the President's office reiterated that it would study the situation and in no way, intervene in the actions of the Governor of the Central Bank emphasizing that the law setting up the institution clearly empowers the Governor to take such actions. Riding on the wave of sentiments in the course of time however, it soon became clear that the balance of public debate, had slowly drifted to the direction of characterizing the Governor's action as unnecessary, wasteful and unproductive.

Then the coincidence. The President's office suddenly opined in a public statement that the Governor's action was after all, subject to Presidential approval. An elaborate study of the law by, and counseling received from various experts surrounding the President was said to have done the trick for the double somersault and roundabout turn.

For analysts and political observers, no doubt, the process of political metamorphosis currently underway in Nigeria is spelling a historically defining moment in the future course of consolidating the resultant shape of the final constitutional product. Our highly revered and idealized points of reference have always been the United States of America and Europe – a region that has recently embarked on a cumbersome journey to the destination of a European United States.

With this in mind, I have no doubt that observers will clearly see the ambitious psychological contribution behind the bold and indeed daring watershed unveiled by the Governor of the Central Bank.

A financial gatekeeper and security guard of Nigeria's monetary policies that the Central Bank Governor undoubtedly is, reminds me personally of the powerful position of the American Chairman of the Federal Reserves and the President of the European Central Bank. Before throwing more light on the immateriality of any perceived personal ambition on the part of Governor Soludo, let me hasten to highlight the importance of a financial gatekeeper for monetary policies in functioning democracies.

It is generally believed in every stable democracy that monetary policy is one sensitive aspect of general economic management that may impact inflationary tendencies independent of the overall performance of the economy as a whole. There is, therefore, a general preference – for even more scientifically viable reasons that are well known to experts who are more at home with the subject than I am – of keeping monetary policies away from political impacts. In other words, professional politicians and political decision makers are kept far away from anything monetary and a more neutral and capable technocratic instance is vested with the power of independence on policies of this sort outside the control of the Executive and Legislature. The power of the Executive and Legislature is never allowed to exceed the appointment and screening of office-holders as monetary gatekeeper. This is the ideal situation that is true of the

United States and is also true of Europe. In the days of Alan Greenspan much like the present days of Bernd Bernanke in the United States, a simple sigh or cough by the Chairman of the Federal Reserves Board is said to send chills and jitters down the spine of stock market waves.

In the course of German reunification, I remember the then President of the West German Bundesbank (Central Bank) refusing to approve a common Deutschemark currency based on the strength of the West German Deutschemark for the newly absorbed East Germany. At the time, Chancellor Helmut Kohl, who had literally promised the East Germans a land flowing with milk and honey *(blühende Landschaften – literally, "blossoming landscapes")* after reunification, with a common currency, did not know what to do after meeting the resistance of the President of the Bundesbank. In the heat of the confusion, the President of the Bundesbank emerged from several hours of consultation with the Chancellor withdrawing his objection and emphasizing loud and clear for the history books that this was a political decision that he was forced to accept for reasons of political patriotism since he could not shoulder the economic responsibility of a such a misguided monetary policy. In the aftermath thereof, the overall economic indicators slumped drastically, and Germany is today, more than 10 years after reunification, struggling to come to terms with the impacts of a one-to-one exchange rate of the East German Mark against the West German Mark.

In the wake of presidential campaign in France that saw the sweeping victory of the present hardline President Sarkozy, the overriding campaign promise in his camp was to curtail the powers of the President of the European Central Bank that currently holds overall gatekeeping function for the European Euro. The stiff resistance of Mrs. Angela Merkel (Chancellor of Germany) and other powerful heads of government is presently keeping the overzealous drives of the French President in check.

January 01st 2005 was the date on which Turkey implemented a policy of discarding six zeroes from its currency that hitherto read millions. Turkey was a land of virtually worthless millionaires. Today, the Yeni Türk Lirasi (New Turkish Lira) reads 1.70 to 1.00 against the Euro as opposed to the previous old TL 1,700,000.00 to € 1.00. Today, inflation is under control. There was no single know-it-all voice that echoed a tale of needlessness and wastefulness. With the Italian Lire reading millions and sometimes, also billions, the same policy was preempted in Italy thanks to the introduction of a common European currency in today's Euro zone. Let me however underscore that this view does not qualify for a tacit acceptance of Soludo's position on my part since I am not well versed on the specifics of Nigeria's situation.

The entire picture before the observer in this case, however, is one of unmistakable dilemma and confusion on the part of Nigeria's President and his team of advisers.

Seeing the implicit model of Governor Soludo's dream is not at all a difficult task for any capable observer or adviser. The dilemma of the President lies in either understanding the usefulness of a powerful financial gatekeeper for monetary policies operating alongside a constitutionally designated Alpha-and-Omega President, or politicizing the issue at stake and trimming the Governor's wings once and for all like was attempted on Nuhu Ribadu. Funnily though, The President is always obviously swayed in the direction of trimming wings, when it comes to matters of overall public interest. Indeed, consultations with colleagues in the United States of America and several countries of Europe on the economic or financial necessity of maintaining a power Governor of the Central Bank for monetary policies would have done President Umaru Musa Yar'Adua far more good than consultations with his personal and local advisers. Political power struggle as an option would thus, have been waived in favor of the institutionalization of technocracy in the Central Bank. Even if the law in question was found insufficient, the President would even be moving to empower the Governor of the Central Bank. Unfortunately, however, the President initially appreciated the actions of the Governor as being within the bounds of the law setting up the institution and finally came out to assert the opposite. This is an open betrayal of the direction in which the President's advisers have steered the President. Until the President acknowledges the fact that governance will not augur well for him as long he allows himself to be dictated to by the misguided stance of reflecting the opposite of anything Obasanjo stood for and riding on the wave of positive public opinion, he will not require long to spot the political quagmire of a political Bermuda triangle in the horizon that is steadily manned by power-hungry and suicidal Janjaweeds. I hope the Nigerian Presidency will not consolidate a tradition of harboring poor advisers in every aspect of governance as Abubakar Atiku mercilessly exposed in the dying days of President Olusegun Obasanjo.

Professional colleagues of the like of Reuben Abati who pay less attention to substance and unleash venom on one party or the other (like was recently unearthed on Soludo) with an eye on public applause in the fashion of the ancient President of a Palmwine Drinkers Club of the late seventies, will sooner or later also detect the disservice they are doing to the Nigerian intelligentsia and the shaping of public opinion. Soludo was virtually called upon to either deny the validity of the clause mandating presidential approval in the law establishing the institution or face the wrath of public anger for not knowing better from the very onset. However, given the sound currency-stability-based philosophy underlying the actions of the Governor of the Central Bank, it remains to be seen where a confrontation and chaos-fueling pattern of Reuben Abati's sense of journalistic commitment will lead the nation. Substance and meaningful contribution to the advancement and solidification of the political promised land of general aspirations do not seem to matter.

I will dare opine that the prominence of the likes of Reuben Abati in the present-day's media scene, is not a good sign of things to come in the future of the country's intellectual growth, no matter how much friendly missiles will be fired my way by like-minded admirers of the zeitgeist.

**

In the final analysis, the Governor of the Central Bank was removed and replaced by a northerner intellectual, who, luckily turned out to be a very brilliant and country-loving mind. Even though the Sanusi Lamido Sanusi, who succeeded Chukwuma Soludo as Governor of the Central Bank soon began advocating Islamic Banking, Nigerians were, by and large, happy to have had his services for the country. This, nonetheless, did not serve to diminish the perception and suspicion that Sanusi Lamido Sanusi was just one more building block in the overall architecture of a northernizing agenda.

But the narrative soon changed in a sudden reversal of fortunes. The President's health suffered such a rapid deterioration that he was only partly able to steer the vehicle of state with limited efficiency. As is common in such cases, the public is the last to know, often when the mechanism of damage-control also gets out of control. People began to ask questions and I had mine too.

As usual, this article was meant principally for my column and appeared in several other platforms and perhaps, in one of the prominent dailies, This Day, too.

Where, For Crying Out Loud, is Our President?

By Frisky Larr

The now infamous election rally call is no doubt, still resounding throughout the land: *"Umaru, are you dead?" "No sir!"* Little did anyone know however, that Olusegun Obasanjo's public reassurance gag in the heat of the presidential campaign a few months ago will bear some significant political hallmarks more than half a year into the Presidency of the former governor of Katsina.

Understandably, it will be recalled that Umaru Musa Yar'Adua was at the time, taken to a German hospital for urgent treatment in a cloak-and-dagger operation. The suddenness of his disappearance from public view at the time, did not only fuel speculations about the death or otherwise, of the designated presidential candidate of the ruling party, it also called into question the secrecy that cladded the departure obviously, under cover of darkness. Many were delighted, who would have wished him nothing but death simply for being the anointed heir apparent of his predecessor. Malicious rumors made the round. He was declared so badly ill that his anointment was portrayed as a clandestine ploy by his predecessor to facilitate his continued grip on power even beyond his tenure.

To reassure well-wishers and put adversaries to perpetual shame, ex-President Obasanjo stage-managed a grand but simple high-tech show linking a telephone conversation with the candidate on his hospital bed in far-away Germany, to a public-address system. It was loud and clear for all to hear. Umaru was not dead. Indeed, he was talking to the President.

Today however, the call and cry for the whereabouts of the President has a different quality altogether. Thank goodness, Umaru is alive and kicking or so it seems at face value. All rumors to the contrary notwithstanding, it is clear that the President does have international functions to attend to in the coming weeks that a very frail health would have ruled out the scheduling of any long-haul flights for state visits. Even though rumors contend that the President had been to Germany lately for medical examination with the consequence of dire medical warning against tight schedules and a grim prognosis, thank goodness, there has so far, been no need to take him to any foreign country for dialysis operations in the dead of night. The President seems healthy and the nation is happy. But where the hell is the President? Indeed, I almost laughed to death only today, upon reading a newly coined phrase used by a reader in commenting on my last essay. The phrase described our President as Mr. "Yar'Ado nothing"!

I have no doubt, that President Yar'Adua can and will not claim to be unaware of the dire problems facing the nation in all areas of infrastructure under present-day terms. Indeed, ex-President Obasanjo could simply have abdicated on May 29th, 2007 without a successor and the state of affairs would probably have been very much the same as it is today.

What the damn hell is President Umaru Musa Yar'Adua doing for crying out loud?

For the first time ever, I have seen myself very much in agreement with Atiku Abubakar's AC's assessment that the current administration is still groping in the dark more than six months into its tenure.

Agreed that a solution to the most pressing problem of power and water cannot come overnight as it requires sound structural and technical planning as well as execution. But where are evidences of progress on the ground? What single project is the President's government undertaking at the moment to provide some sign of life and hope to the long-suffering masses?

Is the President unable to launch a drive with proactive commitment to galvanizing action in a conference of governors? Is the President unable to devise a policy focus encouraging regular meeting with governors to coordinate infrastructural upgrade and subject the entire project to a national priority? Is the President unable to strike a crucial note of color blindness in the perception of party colors and urging all stakeholders to join regularly in a proactive drive to advance the country? What is all this talk of 2020?

What lofty height does President Yar'Adua intend to attain by simply staying colorless and invisible? The President's best friends and admirers today, are Orji Uzor Kalu, Aondokaa, James Ibori, Lucky Igbinedion and a host of others. A bandwagon of corruption suspects whose friendship the President openly courts regardless of the consequences. What does Umaru Musa Yar'Adua intend to achieve in the face of an action that may be perceived as arrogantly insensitive? What are the stakes in the President's compelling friendship with perceived enemies of national progress?

Today, news abound that a nationwide blackout is a formidable reality in the impending holiday period of religious festivities. Vandals are reported to be flourishing in acts of sabotage disrupting gas supply to already weak power stations. Unfortunately, there is hardly any talk of practical safeguards in spite of wealth amassed in recently accrued revenues. Indeed, the absence of these anti-vandal safeguards is already a fundamental failure at the lowest ebb of governance.

The most voluble and exposed government functionary today is the Attorney General of the Federation aggressively pursuing and implementing a policy yielding a result that is so far, representative of stagnation and inertia if not a slow but unnoticed backward drift. Unfortunately, all actions and pronouncements for which the present administration has gained prominence so far, are all turning out to be for all the wrong reasons there can be. The rule of law as a slogan and alleged policy correction has simply played into the hands of the wrong quarters altogether. Deliberately or coincidentally! And the President is mute!

Now I hear that contracts awarded to the leading telecommunications giant Siemens have been revoked in the aftermath of involvement in a corruption scandal. What an immaculate sanctity. Fighting glaring symptoms and leaving the disease intact to bite deeper into the wholesome structure. No single political heavyweight accused of receiving bribes from Siemens has been charged for any offense in Nigeria to say the least of conviction. In fact, prominent Nigerians with evidential involvement in money laundering facing the law in other countries are systematically left off the hook with the clever oratory invocation of technical deficiencies. Unfortunately, no such technical deficiency is brought to bear on Siemens. The idea being *"bribe your way through but thou shall not be caught!"* Punitive sanctions shall be imposed on softer targets. That may fetch some desired cheap points in public admiration. It is of course easier to make the scapegoat of foreign targets no matter how much we may stand on the losing end in the forfeiture of desired technology. Chicanery at its best!

Is the President aware how many more foreign companies may have bribed their way through Nigeria's contract jungle? What may be left if all contracts were called off? Are we simply opting to call a spade a spoon rather than facing the crust of our own domestic problem?

But there are roads begging to be fixed long before the coming of the President. Can the President see them? Since all roads are not Federal projects, is the government leading by example to state governments by commencing massive works at least on federal roads? Is it impossible to strike a deal with governors on mutual progress reports as relates to projects jointly agreed with the central government? Can someone call on our President to indulge in more action and push the rule of law camouflage to the background?

There is a debate to hike the price of fuel and this has not been ruled out for good. Ask Venezuela and find out the joy of being a citizen of an oil-producing country. Year-for-year Nigeria complains about the burden of fuel subsidy. Yet there is no remedial infrastructure in place to justify subsidy revisionism. Just what is the President doing?

What is the President doing to translate wealth into practical affluence? Umaru Musa Yar'Adua was praised for sanitizing the finances of Katsina from deficit to surpluses. But critics cried out early enough that surpluses were useless if they do not translate into practical and useful suffering-alleviating infrastructure. Is that the President's current strategy at the Federal level as well?

What is the President doing to have action expedited on the prosecution of treasury looters? When is Umaru Musa Yar'Adua going to creep out of the comfort of Aso Rock and hit his chest before the nation chanting loud *"now is the time to act and fast as well?"*

Seeking cheap political points in reversing previous policies including those that had long been reversed, as political window-dressing will not mean a thing to the large masses. The aftermath of the revolution-thirst that rocked the political establishment led by the largely anti-establishmentarian intelligentsia and was shunned by the common man in the post-election days, should be lessons enough to educate Mr. President that the intellectual focus on policy reversals and the rule of law, is least noticed by the common man. The nation expects leadership and not a perfect blending into oblivion and colorless inertia. Shagari'ism and the resultant aftermath of Dikko'ism are still very fresh in political perception. Where is the President?

Where is the sense of direction that the President is elected to spearhead? Will the President forever stay quiet as the gentle likeable darling of heaven and earth? If this is the President's dream, which can definitely not be true, then he may come up against a startling surprise as time progresses.

Now they say Ibrahim Babangida is standing on the verge of a second coming. Rumors, rumors everywhere and nothing to hold. The invisible President is lost upon the nation!

***

Time passed by and it became increasingly difficult to conceal the depth of the President's health condition from the public. The President traveled to foreign countries repeatedly for medical treatment. Every visit was apparently visited by increasingly bad tidings on the President's health-related prognosis. His family knew what that portended for the Presidency. The kitchen cabinet knew it too. A period of desperate concealment and ruling by proxies was ushered in.

The airwaves got taken over by speculations and conspiracy theories. One argument began to take center stage to sensitize and boost public awareness. It was the argument of the zoning of the Presidency to the North as an internal arrangement of the ruling party. The heightening of this debate was deliberate upon the goal of preparing minds for the battle ahead.

I wrote this article, as usual, primarily for my online column at NigerianNews.com. It was also released in several other platforms particularly the Nigerian Village Square.

112

The Zoning Poison and the Risk of Balkanizing Nigeria

By Frisky Larr

Never in the history of Nigeria has a clause in the constitution of a single political party become such a lethal and volatile minefield that is strongly seeking to explode on the corporate existence of the already fragile union. Never in history has Nigeria been so exposed to the project of a desperate stranglehold on the nerves of its roots by a determined geographical mafia fighting for a sustained power status. Never too, has the identity of this desperate mafia and its desperate godfathers has been so hopelessly laid bare than it is today in the wake of the national debate on the zoning poising.

When, at the collapse of the third term bid by General Olusegun Obasanjo as President in the democratic experiment, the issue of succession came up, many blamed the General for not grooming a successor through his good eight years at the peak of this populous nation. The President made a hasty firework of domestic diplomatic consultations and Jeannie was conjured out of the bottle sitting on the throne at the State House in Katsina. Many cried "foul" because General Obasanjo seemed to have crucified most of his opponents at the time, on a virile double-cross. Umaru Musa Yar'Adua was credible enough to dissuade another erstwhile General Ibrahim Babaginda to beat a face-saving retreat. On this day it was, that the then dissident Vice President Atiku Abubakar knew that his position in the active determination of the course of events in the body politics of Nigeria was being counted out. "Powerful" northern backgrounders also launched a silent retreat to re-strategize. Time revealed what their strategy was.

Umaru Musa Yar'Adua simply had to strike a deal. It was a deal that reassured the backgrounders that the dominance of the North in the running of Nigerian political affairs will be reinstated after eight years of daring and perfidious rearrangement in the spirit of the Federal character. All that followed in the form of amateurish policy reversals, appointments into strategic positions without caring for geographical distribution, etc. is now history. The man died! It was death in the valley of fate and the fate was the destiny of our dearest nation.

Sometime in the nineteen eighties, the phrase "Kaduna Mafia" was talk of the town and on everybody's lips. The phrase never had a face for public identification. But news made the round somehow in the spirit of perfidy, that the Kaduna Mafia was the heart of Nigerian politics, without which any act in the art of leadership may survive the test of crucial times.

The events that however unfolded in the run-up to the demise of Umaru Musa Yar'Adua brought us many steps closer to the age-long mystery of the so-called Kaduna Mafia. Then, they were called "The Cabal"! We thought we knew them all. Indeed, we thought we had seen everything.

Today, we can understand and speculate on what indeed transpired behind the iron curtains in the debate on $12^2/_3$ in the year 1979. It is no longer far-fetched to understand that on no account, was the Southerner Obafemi Awolowo to be allowed to succeed another Southerner General Olusegun Obasanjo who fate catapulted to the realms of glory with the hands of the Kaduna Mafia virtually tied. It didn't seem to have mattered then that Obafemi Awolowo was the more qualified candidate to steer the course of Nigeria's destiny. What seemed to have mattered was to keep the power equilibrium slanted northwards.

There was obviously no way Olusegun Obasanjo could have been denied succession to the assassinated Murtala Muhammed of blessed memory without causing uproar in the hierarchy and upsetting the smooth-sailing course of the mafia manipulations. The trick seemed perfect and obviously worked without blemishes. Olusegun Obasanjo – even though superficially the Head of State – was then made to serve virtually under the leadership of the duo named Theophillus Danjuma and Shehu Musa Yar'Adua. Obasanjo was therefore, a tried and tested figure in the art of Puppet Management.

There were no challenges. No dissent either. The popular level of enlightenment was yet marginal. Moreover, the bid to keep northern influence above all else was not as blatant and arrogantly flagrant as it has become today. The change? If you ask me, the position is now seriously threatened.

It started with the cabal that the backgrounders installed beside Umaru Musa Yar'Adua. They were certain, that the process of reversing Obasanjo's demolition of the northern influence and the impacts of the mafia that was now, no longer based in Kaduna alone, would be a gradual process that was to be completed in a minimum period of eight years. Occasional outcries against regional and geographical marginalization were expected and they simply to weather the storm and proceed with the marching orders. Unfortunately, though, they reckoned that the President's health would survive the eight strenuous years of dubious complicity.

When it became obvious however that the President was steadily on his way to the realms beyond, desperation became crass, flagrant and shamelessly disrespectful. the Vice President had hitherto been regarded by the cabal – playing the script of the backgrounders – as a simple decorative non-starter and the constitution was obviously a trash of academic hullabaloos compiled and authored by a bunch of ego-soothing Wisenheimers in the search for relevance.

We thought we knew the traitors. We pounced on the Aondoakaas and the Turais and a bunch of copycat vuvuzela blowers! The constitutionally inevitable had to happen unless they killed Jonathan.

For the second time in a short period, the military did not dare to execute a perfected coup plan. The world had warned military leaders at the end of 2008 as information made the round that a coup was imminent. The risk of ruling in pageantry and ending up in The Hague as Charles Taylor is now experiencing became a dreadful lever to deter the courageous risk of "Fellow Nigerians…"! Suddenly Barack Obama realized his mistake in sidelining Nigeria to visit Ghana in his maiden call on Africa as a serving Head of State. Even though it was made to teach Nigerian leaders a lesson that they deserved, it was nonetheless strengthening the encapsulation of the northern mafia. Nigeria became the scene of intense diplomatic activities.

In the end, the constitution prevailed when the man ultimately died. Jonathan became the President. Immediately after, the battlefront shifted, and the actors simply became different.

There was no more Aondoakaa! There was no more Turai Yar'Adua! Suddenly the battlefront shifted. No more Legalese! No more housewife rule on visits to an ailing husband. The battle immediately shifted to succession. Succession to the throne that Jonathan had barely ascended! The new kids on the block suddenly became Ibrahim Bademosi Babangida, the Sarakis and a host of other copycat vuvuzela fellas.

The issue became zoning. It doesn't seem to matter that this zoning issue is an intra-party issue predicated on a clause in the PDP constitution that openly violates the constitution of the country. Definitely no! It is important enough to have other northern governors who are not even members of the PDP voice their support for the zoning arrangement.

The face of the present debate is now Ibrahim Babangida who surprisingly, was also a quiet and background player at the time Nigeria became the scene of a flurry of international diplomatic activities to avert a military coup while Yar'Adua was in Saudi Arabia. Visiting envoys mediating between the Jonathan camp and the northern backgrounders frequently called on Ibrahim Badamosi Babangida.

Now that Aondoakaa is no more, the backgrounders seem to be doing the dirty job more on their own than through proxies and surrogates.

The common trait that today shares with yesterday when the cabal reigned supreme, is the desperate bid to keep the north empowered. The arguments employed are different from time to time. While the constitutional limitations on the exercise of Vice Presidential powers dominated yesterday and kept the northern cabal calling the shots in the name of the dying Yar'Adua, today it is zoning as entrenched in the internal constitution of the PDP.

This is the reason I am surprised that my idol and admired free-thinker Dele Momodu did a brilliant article on ThisDay today advancing cogent reasons to dissuade Jonathan from running for President. He argued principally on the filth in the system and the PDP that will inadvertently compromise Jonathan's credibility as an achiever.

Unfortunately, however, all the parties are run in the same old filth. The actors are products of the same old filthy system – PDP or not. Should this be a reason to willfully surrender to the aggressive northern drive of perpetually enslaving the rest of the nation after so many years of rulership and nothing to show? Should this be a reason to resign and tell IBB to proceed with the same old tricks in the system to which filth he contributed immensely either as a direct and indirect leader/coup plotter and mafia backgrounder?

Definitely no! Today, the nation is on the brink and waiting for a lethal catalyst. Invisible military groups are nurtured in regional hideouts and kept alive with armed robbery and kidnappings. The opponents are intransigent. Thank goodness, the Jonathan camp seems determined to pick up the gauntlet and stand up to the challenge.

If the ultimate risk of tearing Nigeria apart does not dawn on the northerners who are clearly the aggressors in this case, then so be Nigeria's destiny.

If for the sole purpose of proving the point that Nigeria belongs to us all – north and south – and that rulership is not the birthright of the northern mafia alone, who seeks to fight tooth and nail to dominate the country, I will urge Jonathan to run and damn the consequences.

Kill Jonathan and face the consequences! The Republic of Warri or The Republic of Bayelsa will no longer be unimaginable phenomena. After all, Europe has such city-states like Lichtenstein and San Marino!

***

The North had strategized and re-strategized. The banner of leadership that the British colonial power handed the region upon the granting of independence to Nigeria in 1960, was based on the fear of leaving the more academically potent South to embrace Socialism that was *en vogue* in budding nations of the days. Details of this claims and many others can be found with proof, in my book "Nigeria's Journalistic Militantism". Today, though, the Northern region of Nigeria has been badly spoiled in the power game to seemingly assume a birthright to political power in the country.

My next article, which, as usual, was written basically, for my online column details the strategy of the northern establishment.

The Northern Agenda: Spinmeisters at Work and Breeding a Revolution

By Frisky Larr

When Ex-President Olusegun Obasanjo picked on Umaru Musa Yar'Adua as his successor in Aso Rock, he had a lot of ideas in mind and a clear vision as well, of what he wanted the little known and ailing Governor of provincial Katsina to achieve as President. Allowing a more qualified and competent personality from other geographical zone to succeed him in the Presidency in breach of tacit gentleman's agreement would be risking the unity of the country. The Sharia drive had once shown how far northerners would go to make their impact felt when they feel slighted and marginalized for once in the history of Nigeria.

Olusegun Obasanjo knew quite well that he was not only fulfilling a pledge of shifting geographical positions, he was keen on protecting Nigeria's hard-earned treasury resources from willful plunderers counting on the purity of a man with the reputation of religious devotion and honesty. Above all else, President Obasanjo sought protection against a mob-gone-wild that haunted him from the press, the judiciary and the legislature. This latter motivation it was that superseded all other considerations in such a way that the election of the Ex-President's man was a do-or-die affair. Events unfolding today have truly justified this sentiment as the chameleonic attitude of strategic glorification has now seen erstwhile friends of the Ex-President teaming up with his foes and launching futile wars against the President's image.

The extremely charged, poisonously hostile and volatile political atmosphere that characterized the dying days of the last administration was single-handedly responsible for the reality that no President in his right senses would have allowed for the free and fair election of his own successor. Political suicide I guess, was not on Olusegun Obasanjo's agenda.

If anything was lost on or underrated by President Obasanjo, it is definitely the extent of the bond of brotherhood shared by northern political stalwarts. While northerners by design continue to teach the Southerners day-by-day how not to go about the game of sectional bickering, southerners are loudest when it comes to summoning the guillotine to the national stadium to hack off the head of their few elites that were permitted by the Grace of *"Allah"* to mount the saddle of leadership. When northerners of substance disagree, it is done behind closed doors. The megaphone voices of discontent amongst northerners are most often, politically irrelevant in mapping out geographical strategies by consensus. Who speaks today of the renegade Muhammadu Buhari or Abubakar Rimi (notable megaphone dissenters) as northern powerbrokers?

The last administration left a vibrant economy with growth rates of continental envy thanks to export revenue. Foreign reserves were figured at unparalleled amounts. Projects were commenced and launched requiring follow-up efforts in continuative moves of managerial and constructive complementation.

Unfortunately, however, the succeeding President Umaru Musa Yar'Adua's most remarkable achievement till today, has been shielding his predecessor from the mob's guillotine often using precisely this same predecessor to play his strategic game of populist appeal in a two-steps-forward, one-step-backward ploy.

Today, Nigerians know that the war against corruption has drawn to a standstill because a northern *rascal* named Nuhu Ribadu dared to join forces with a declared enemy of the north who betrayed the trust of northern powerbrokers. It didn't matter if his cause was noble. He was sacrificed to the applause of narrow-minded and truly intellectually blinded mob of the present century. Occasionally, a power-drunk Minister of Justice would face the press and cough out a stench of ignorant vituperations often as a prelude to Presidential actions. When the dust settles down however, President Yar'Ado nothing will emerge from nowhere and declare: *"Obasanjo is my leader"* and withdraw for a while leaving the stage for rats to dance and wine!

Obasanjo's administration tried its best to display a Federal character in the constitution of its leadership team. A Yoruba President was not surrounded by Yorubas. The closest personal confidant – even though, a controversial suspect of fraud – was an Easterner. Major players in key positions were geographically evenly distributed such that even indigenes of Edo state (Anenih, Obaseki) were allowed to feature prominently. Today, a President in the grip of northern interest is obsessed with the filling of strategic positions with northerners and northerners alone.

The last prominent politician that was judiciously brought to book to give account of criminal stewardship was Lucky Igbinedion of Edo State. Ever since, a lot has quickly died down on the corruption front. Wielding the enigmatic mantra of the rule of law and due process, some hobby writers who may be forgiven for ignorance in the art of writing, come forward to advance the unfortunate thought-crime of the rule of law being more important than fighting unconventional causes with unconventional means.

Thank goodness, the Special Anti-Robbery Squad (SARS) adopted the unconventional method of shooting known criminals and cultists at sight in Benin City to calm down the infamous crime wave that had been rocking that city in recent years. So much for the rule of law in a lawless society!

A President that is weird in all ramifications chooses to send an active public servant out of public view because he was pursuing a noble cause without close consultation with the President. Now the cause has been killed to pursue window-dressing projects like prosecuting Iyabo Obasanjo. A cause that goes down far better with the brainless mob of Causcescu's fame. With Ribadu not formally relieved of his position as Gani Fawehinmi has rightly pointed out, the President has appointed a replacement almost in circumvention of his megaphone '*due process*' policy until the senate blew the whistle on him.

But "*for every bad move that this Johanna makes, they've got a good explanation*" Eddy Grant once said in an Apartheid-related parody. They say it is a sinister plot against the appointment of Waziri that the due process of removal (and not study leave for one year) of Nuhu Ribadu is demanded by Gani Fawehinmi before the appointment of Waziri can be pursued. The Spinmeisters are everywhere selling the blockbuster President as the best thing to ever happen to Nigeria. They not only foolishly, maliciously and dishonestly point out that Umaru Musa Yar'Adua inherited a rotten Nigeria from his predecessor, they conveniently ignore the state of Nigeria inherited by Olusegun Obasanjo, who left the same nation in a different state, 20 years before.

Also, willfully ignoring the state of the buoyant economy handed over to the present administration, they put a neophyte spin on facts to ignore the burgeoning volume of our balance of trade and balance of overall budget left behind by the past administration. The least uncontested contention is the state of power stations begging for follow-up investments and installation-hardware wasting away in our ports. Yet the Spinmeisters say one year is not enough to get a grasp of situation and define an independent course.

The next man on the line will definitely be Governor Soludo of the Central Bank. A brilliant technocrat, who together with Okonjo-Iweala authored Nigeria's economic success of the past eight years, Governor Soludo is obviously too independent-minded for a President, who will do nothing tangible but have his two hands on deck in every nook and corner.

One foolish hobby author with his brains at the peripheral end of his physique wonderfully opined that launching infrastructural projects by awarding the relevant contracts after twelve months of leadership was not the crust of the matter. Today, the nation is virtually in darkness with sections that have not seen electricity for the past one month. While the self-styled intellects are able to afford generators and diesel to match, contract award will not matter much as long as political power is kept with the north and the north alone.

Historical facts were revisited recently, and colonial agenda uncovered, bordering on the fear of a more intellectual and enlightened south embracing communism as opposed to a more conservative, religious and less educated northern population. This notion and this notion alone it was that saw the British colonialists opting to manipulate processes in favor of empowering northerners into the political leadership of Nigeria, which the north now erroneously seem to perceive as a natural right of fortune.

Unfortunately, however, the world has come a long way. Awareness and the means of spreading them are growing by the day. The volatility of public order engineered by discontent and elitist indifference has laid a fertile groundwork for an ultimate revolution of the downtrodden.

The hope for a public uprising died woefully in the aftermath of the flawed elections of April 2007 because the public did not wish to fight any war of attrition as surrogates of some selfish politicians. With an intellectually comprehensive social stratum making up a negligibly small fraction of overall popular strength, media hostility was not enough to steer public sentiment in one direction and unjustly against a single target.

With jobless surrogates of political criminals up in arms at the Niger Delta openly threatening the unity of Nigeria, and a misguided and disgruntled Movement for the Actualization of the Sovereign State of Biafra brandishing weapons and the Biafran flag in broad daylight, President Umaru Musa Yar'Adua is still not able to see the writing on the wall and work towards national unity.

He is busy filling strategic positions with loyalists to the northern agenda. Infrastructure is declared a subordinate project in this agenda of priority and regional segregation is uplifted to the realms of urgency. With two regions however, accustomed to the routine use of weapons, in political dealings and the level of intellectual awareness growing by the day, Nigeria is sitting on a powder keg waiting to be blown.

When it finally blows however, there will be millions who have nothing to lose. Soldiers will be out shooting. Hundreds will die. Hundreds more will move ahead until soldiers are out of weapon, overwhelmed or wisely choose to turn on Aso Rock.

When this dreadful scenario becomes reality though, the north and the north alone shall bear the blame for focusing too much on solitary hegemony without the will to share for real. Umaru Musa Yar'Adua will have questions to answer for deliberate weakness and the propagation of an elusive mirage and erection of phantom castles.

***

At this point, the nation was virtually being ruled by the President's cabal without the knowledge of the now incapacitated President in a Saudi hospital bed following the alleged proclamation of a hopeless recovery prognosis by German doctors. Calls began to grow, for a handover of power to the Vice President as mandated by the constitution. The first most prominent voice of reason sounded from the most beautiful gift of nature with a reputation for action that followed her from the government of former President Obasanjo into the cabinet of the now ailing President Yar'Adua. It was the indomitable lion of competence and of blessed memory, Dora Akunyili.

Her action partly prompted me to pen the following article:

Is Aondoakaa a Decorated Illiterate?

By Frisky Larr

It requires the knowledge of a language to decipher the message encoded in a collection of individual words. Some languages are simple in structure and some are more complex. The Chinese, Greek and Russian languages are in their order, regarded as the most complex in the world. The English language on the other hand, is not the simplest language on earth. It also doesn't count among the most complex. Linguists with the gift of the multiple knowledge of diverse tongues across geographical divide will surely attest to this simple reality.

With the knowledge of several languages, one no doubt, sometimes gets confused when the expression of one language is packaged in the words of another to transmit a message that a speaker has in mind. If the listener understands the multiple languages commanded by the speaker, it is often easier to follow the pattern of thought of the speaker by identifying the language in which the pattern of thought is more at home. Listen to a non-native speaker of the English language from any Western European country (Germany, Holland, Denmark, etc.) speaking English with expressions that are typical of his cultural background but packaged in English words that are comprehensible but pretty much unusual of English language and you'd understand what I'm talking about. When you tell a German "Thank you!" and you get the reply "Please!" it may sound like a gesture of "Oh please, nothing to be thankful about". May be! What is however irrefutable is the fact that the word "Please" in German ("Bitte") in response to "Thank you", is the equivalent of the traditional "Don't mention" in English language.

It was against this backdrop that I hesitated a bit when the recent outburst of Chief Michael Aondoakaa against Dora Akunyili hit the headlines in Nigerian mass media. It will be recalled that Mrs. Akunyili in a desperate bid to break the impasse occasioned by the long health-induced absence of President Yar'Adua from Nigeria, took a radical departure from the conspiratorial consensus of self-serving compliance within the Federal Executive Council. She called for the constitutional handover of power to the Vice President by the ailing President barely one week after the same Federal Executive Council had unanimously concluded that the President was healthy enough to continue as a bedridden ruler from "Thine Kingdom Come".

For the few years that Umaru Musa Yar'Adua has been President of Nigeria, it has been no secret that the centerpiece of his so-called Kitchen Cabinet (the inner circle of Yar'Adua's power base) has been Michael Aondoakaa. He had gained notoriety for unprecedented audacity in the face of vehement adversity. He would voice out a position that is so strongly against the waves of reason that one would think he didn't give a damn driving at a speed of 120 kilometers per hour against the direction of traffic flow on an expressway irrespective of the hundreds of other vehicles heading his way from the opposite direction at the same speed. It is a boldness for which he has always gained my admiration.

But much like his defiance of logic in many legal pronouncements that he has made till the present day, I have never leaned towards the belief that he may be capable of defying the English grammar or the conventional understanding of the English language against all odds of human wisdom.

I had to hesitate a bit because I know that every Nigerian is at least, naturally and traditionally bilingual in the national set-up. The uneducated Nigerian has a sound and unflinching command of at least, the Pidgin English in addition to his/her native language. The educated ones also add at least, something close to the grammatically refined version of English language as known to the rest of the world, to their native language and the Pidgin English. Chief Michael Aondoakaa has no doubt, a sound command of his native language from the north, a sound command of the Pidgin English and **at least**, a weak version of Standard English. No doubt, the conflict of thinking in one language and speaking in another, thus packaging thoughts made in his native northern language in English words may quickly become a problem as everyone of us may have experienced at one point or the other.

In condemning Dora Akunyili's position that clearly betrayed a consensus cabinet position barely a week before, Aondoakaa lashed out at her in the following words: *"I think she was trying to make herself a cheap hero out of that. If you see what the Senate said, the Senate made an appeal. She does not need the FEC to make an appeal; she can also appeal. … The Senate said it was appealing. You saw the spokesman of the Senate eventually came out and said they have no power to compel the man. Now, there is even a court decision that says that transmission of letter shall be voluntary. It is within the President. … Bringing the memo to the FEC is just to make herself an angel. She wants to be seen as a populist. Whatever she wants to gain from it is still personal. None of the FEC members has disrespect for the Vice-President. As far as we are concerned, the VP is our leader and he is leading us. What she is trying to do is self-seeking; **let her go and <u>confront</u> herself with what happened in NAFDAC."***

In fact, the quality of his spoken English would make one believe that he is very well educated by Nigerian standard and seems to be thinking in English while formulating his sentences.

His refutal barely two days later, however, leaves room for disbelief and wonderment. Wonderment, seeking to know the language in which Mr. Aondoakaa may have been processing his thoughts in his own mind while formulating those hard words on his cabinet colleague in English. Forgetting the linguistic analysis of semantics and the correlation of facts and sentences as ordered in a message, Mr. Aondoakaa states clearly that the sentence *"let her go and confront herself with what happened in NAFDAC"* was indeed supposed to transmit a positive connotation urging Mrs. Akunyili to go and rest on her past glories in NAFDAC. But does the word "confront" as grammatically and conventionally used in English language agree with this reasoning? Having just referred to Mrs. Akunyili with words like "cheap hero", "make herself an angel" "be seen as a populist" "self-serving" etc., asking her to confront herself with what happened in NAFDAC could mean nothing other than asking her to first go and clear up the mess she laid in NAFDAC before anything else.

How asking someone to confront herself with what happened in the past can magically translate into the eulogy of urging comfort in the glories of the past can only be imaginable if such thoughts were made in Tiv or Hausa language and ambiguously packaged in English words in a manner that is liable to misunderstanding.

The renowned Word Reference Online dictionary describes the word "confront" in the following words: *"deal with (something unpleasant) head on"*. In its description of "confront", the reputable Merrian-Webster online dictionary says *"to face especially in challenge: OPPOSE <confront an enemy>"*

These indeed, are the negative connotations that the word "confront" usually entails in conventional English language usage. It is puzzling indeed, where Mr. Aondoakaa found the positive content of the word in English if not in his native language.

Indeed, if I had not been privileged to hear him speak and be convinced that he has a good command of the English language, I would have refused outright to dismiss the insinuation that he was an illiterate traditional cattle-rearer who was accidentally decorated with the office of Attorney-General and Minister of Justice.

Given his physical disposition with constantly flashy and colored eyes whilst not a victim of yellow fever or jaundice, I have always refused to subscribe to general insinuation in public debates amongst Nigerians here in Germany that the traditional Gworo or other stimulants may have played a role in many of Aondoakaa's public utterances.

Far-fetched arguments may be adopted to stand logic on its head in proving legal points because the law is generally believed to be an ass. But is language also an ass? Can language be so subjected to such a brutal rape in the daylight sorcery of transforming "confrontation" to "consultation"?

Flippant languages, shrewd, naughty and stinky gutter and abusive qualifications hardly drew any attention to something wrong with Aondoakaa's psyche as long as they were directed at popularly hated figures at the start of Yar'Adua's term. When this fellow however, began to bite more than he can chew by setting obnoxious rules for Nuhu Ribadu's EFCC, the society began to get split down the middle. His true color finally emerged upon his vehement defiance of the British judiciary in defense of James Ibori. The final fallout with Farida Waziri totally aroused sleeping heads to wake up and take a closer look. The days of Yar'Adua's unceremonious and speedy departure from Nigeria spelt Aondoakaa's final hours of desperation. Standing linguistic logic on its head is only the latest in his chain of woes that should unfold pretty soon.

If some disgruntled Nigerians had rejoiced at the demise of Nuhu Ribadu in self-serving jubilation with legendary phrases like "what goes round comes around" "the bird has finally come home to roost", what Nigeria is about to witness in Aondoakaa in the very near future will surely tell Nigerians "You ain't seen nothing yet".

By the way, are we slowly seeing the role of women in Nigeria? I hope the role of competence in technocracy played by Ngozi Okonjo-Iweala, the courage of Dora Akunyili in NAFDAC and in belling the cat at the Federal Executive Council as well as the marginal courage displayed by Farida Waziri in telling Aondoakaa "Enough is enough" is not lost on credible observers. As of today, I see two competent and qualified individuals for the Nigerian Presidency if Nigeria would let them be: **Nuhu Ribadu** and **Ngozi Okonjo-Iweala**. Dora Akunyili in her present state will qualify for the Vice Presidency any day, anytime until other names appear. But of course, that is just my dream only for the day that Nigeria will be ruled on Meritocracy.

***

One major death-knell that was dealt the Presidency of Umaru Musa Yar'Adua, came again, from his predecessor, President Olusegun Obasanjo.

The state of the nation had become tense. A few notches more dangerous than the run-up to 2007! People in the know were certain that the incumbent President was spending his last days alive in a Saudi hospital bed. Indeed, he had transformed into a vegetative state with little or no cognitive perception of the world around him. His immediate political allies took advantage of the situation, blocking access to him and peddling wrong information that the President's recovery was progressing. Led by his wife, Turai, they took the reins of political leadership backed by the norther establishment.

The notion of maintaining the northern slot to political leadership at all costs following a two-term Presidency of a southern President, was considered a must-do. The fear of a civil war was as palpable as ever.

It took the external political influence of former President Olusegun Obasanjo to break the visit barrier imposed by the cabal of the incumbent and ailing President, to visit the vegetative incumbent at his hospital bed. Rumors had it that the former American President Bill Clinton was instrumental in having the Saudi authorities facilitate the visit by Nigeria's former President Olusegun Obasanjo. It was a game-changing visit. Having obtained the certainty that the incumbent President was terminally ill and irreversibly in a vegetative state, the former President spoke out and called for his resignation. It was much to the displeasure of the northern political elite, who believed the same Olusegun Obasanjo had handpicked the incumbent Umaru Musa Yar'Adua because he knew the man was terminally ill and wanted him to die in office, so he could be succeeded by yet another southerner since the southern Vice President would automatically become President if the incumbent died.

The dangerous resistance was pervasive. I wrote the following articles as usual, for my online column and the Nigerian Village Square. Like several of my writings at the time, it may also have appeared on the prominent daily This Day.

Yar'Adua's Condition Worsens, Succession battle Heats Up!

By Frisky Larr

Information coming out of sources close to Aso Rock is painting a dismal and grim picture of President Yar'Adua's condition on his Saudi hospital bed. This could not have come at a worse time for loyalists and members of the President's kitchen cabinet jostling for a quick return of the President to the seat of power at all cost. The need for a quick return is basically informed by the urge to calm a highly agitated polity amid a state of political uncertainty that is fast spiraling out of control. Early optimism fed by Yar'Adua's positive response to administered treatment suffered a huge setback yesterday as cautious medical voices echoed a backslide in the President's condition.

Latest information from reliable sources failing to provide further details is now however suggesting that the President has currently been placed on life support on his hospital bed. A condition which normally indicates that a vital organ is failing to function perfectly without external machine support!

As can be expected, the consequence is dire and is intensely fueling the rumor mill and political actions behind the iron curtain. Prominently pitched against each other at the moment, seems to be the camp of former President Olusegun Obasanjo and loyalists of the ailing President. The voluble echoes trickling out of the invisible and clandestine northern group clamoring for the completion of the northern term on the zonal arrangement had initially favored a scenario seeking Vice President Jonathan's resignation in the event of an irreversible Yar'Adua's incapacitation. Stern and unmistakable signals emerging from southern reaction have however indicated dire consequences in the event that the Vice President is unconstitutionally coerced into premature resignation.

There has obviously been a clear backtracking from this position which seems to have made way for Jonathan's completion of the few months left of Yar'Adua's term. The key to succession is now focused on who would eventually emerge as Goodluck Jonathan's deputy. While the Obasanjo camp is reported to be strongly canvassing for Governor Sule Lamido of Jigawa State, the camp of Yar'Adua's loyalist is obviously throwing its political weight behind Governor Isa Juguda of Bauchi State. The calculation being the eventual discontinuation of Jonathan in 2011, thus paving way for the eventual deputy to assume the rudder of governance!

It will be recalled that Sule Lamido is viewed as a close confidant of Olusegun Obasanjo who served in the latter's cabinet as Minister of Foreign Affairs. The former President is also widely believed to have facilitated Lamido's ascension to the office of Governor. Isa Yuguda on the other hand, is the Governor at the center of a recent marriage event, in which one of President Yar'Adua's daughters was betrothed to him as the latest in a polygamous household. Whichever way it goes, each of these Governors is regarded as a staunch loyalist of the camp they represent.

Grumbles reaching out of the Delta region are however sounding another unmistakable warning that the northern cabals should desist from playing God. Their argument is founded on the reasoning that an internal PDP zonal arrangement should not be allowed to supersede the constitutional sovereignty of the land which clearly regulates the issue of succession in the event of a President's death. It is therefore resounding the warning that withdrawal on the part of Jonathan from the presidential throne in 2011 in the aftermath of invisible northern pressure to make way for succession by any eventual deputy will not be tolerated. Stakeholders are now eyeing an Obasanjo-Atiku model, in which Atiku Abubakar largely called the shots in Obsanjo's first term.

Meantime, the ailing President is said to be lying under the watchful eyes of strong affiliates who may stand to lose a huge stake upon the demise of the resilient President. Prominent among such affiliates is said to be ex-Governor James Ibori who features among the very few entourage of the President's men hanging out with him from the very first day.

***

The Yar'Adua Mafia: One Last Desperate Move!

By Frisky Larr

In one last albeit giant stride to salvage what is left of hope for presidential powers, the Yar'Adua mafia unleashed Wednesday, an unconstitutional *coup de main* to underscore the hint of the possible *man-in-charge*. For the avoidance of doubt, a *coup de main* is nothing but an attack without warning. A warning shot of sort that seeks to destabilize the camp of the opponent that will initially seek to identify the direction from which the shot was fired.

The peculiar character of this warning shot this time though, is the unconstitutional packaging of its peripheral elements. From all we know in the public arena, neither Goodluck Jonathan nor at least, the upper chamber of the National Assembly was pre-informed of the hastily arranged return of President Umaru Musa Yar'Adua.

Reports claim that information reached Jonathan of the imminent return of the ailing President only through diplomatic channels. To add insult upon an already painful injury, the inner circle of the Yar'Adua mafia obviously made microscopically pointed contacts with platoon leaders or commanders within the military for the release of soldiers to man the airport and the route to the President's home. All without the knowledge of Goodluck Jonathan!

I deliberately use the name Goodluck Jonathan in this context without the formal designation "Acting President" for obvious reasons. As long as Umaru Musa Yar'Adua returns to town and keeps hope alive that he may write a letter to the National Assembly that he is ready to resume office, Goodluck Jonathan remains his Vice President. As long as Umaru Musa Yar'Adua bears the title "President" (both formally and informally), Goodluck Jonathan will always remain his Vice President not "Acting President"! It is as simple as that. Finally, as long as legal challenges persist, and judgment is yet to be passed on the legality or otherwise, of Goodluck Jonathan's ascension to the seat of Acting President, Goodluck Jonathan will always remain Yar'Adua's Vice President. It is against this background that anger should be muted as a matter of necessity, over Yar'Adua's spokesperson Segun Adeniyi's reference to Goodluck Jonathan as Vice President.

Indeed, we are all, as Nigerians only now, beginning to reap the seed of misplaced convenience and expediency that we have tried to sow in our democratic environment over the past few years. We have deceitfully attempted to create a democratic tradition of permitting emotionally convenient realities to go for legalities. Now, the price is being demanded.

Not long ago, Nigerian Supreme Court Judges passed an amateurish judgment pronouncing the constitutionality of a Vice President swapping parties and still remaining Vice President. Legal experts who should have known better applauded the judgment because the victim of the judgment was their public enemy. They knew too well that if the President of the time had passed away, a new President with a different party that the electorates never voted for, would have taken over the Presidency. It was however, emotionally expedient and the judgment passed as law.

Shortly thereafter, a candidate for election, whose name did not appear on the ballot paper was declared the winner of a Governorship election even though he never filed any motion that prayed the Judges to declare him Governor. Experts applauded the judgment rather than knowing better. The victim, once again, was public enemy No. 1 and that was sufficient to make illegality the reality of law.

A Governor's term was illegally extended for the frivolous reason of late ascension to power at the expense of constitutionally defined tenure and framework. The denial of his rights was prudently attributed to criminal acts. The criminals were never identified, and no one faced prosecution. Constitutionally defined tenure was sacrificed. It was all accepted because public enemy No. 1 was at the receiving end.

The elected Governor whose term was kept on hold was denied the status of Governor-in-waiting because he was popularly hated. This too has become law.

The ensuing election of Peter Obi to a second term was visibly shown to have been badly flawed with even registered and prominent candidates failing to see their names on the list of voters. A minimal fraction of qualified voters was said to have been registered and allowed to vote and they determined who won the ensuing election. We accepted this whimsically as long as the wrong party did not win the elections.

The past days and weeks have been bearing witness to an ailing President on vegetative conditions, whose inner circle is taking the nation for a ride. They have trampled on the constitution perhaps without the knowledge of the ailing President. To fill the power vacuum, the legislative chambers passed non-binding resolutions and took a Radio interview as fulfilling a constitutional requirement demanding a written letter from the ailing President. The result was satisfactory. It calmed down tension and the body politics of an agitated land was up on its feet and the Acting President was to hit the ground running. Still it was illegal. There is never a legal framework on earth in which a Radio Interview can be taken in lieu of a written notification.

We now live in a country, in which expediencies take the place of strict legality. Whatever soothes our ego and satisfies our emotions is given the twist and turns of manipulated legality and funnily becomes the ultimate law.

Do we now understand the reasoning of the Yar'Adua mafia? We laid the groundwork and showed them the path to toe. This time however, we did not give them a viable public enemy No. 1 behind which they can rally and galvanize public sympathy.

Today's developments sadly and perhaps, fortunately too, bear the hallmarks of a positive twist. A historical watershed! It may be all that we have needed to take us back to the path of strict legality.

On the other hand, it may also mark the start of a radical overhaul weighing in, in the direction of partisanship. It may translate into a violent intervention to help the cause of the cabal that is holding us hostage.

Barring the absence of a military coup d'etat to restore the loudly propagated northern interest in a two-term Presidency, the present dynamics may hasten the demise of President Umaru Musa Yar'Adua.

On his recent visit to Nigeria in the run-up to the National Assembly's resolution to empower Jonathan, the American Assistant Secretary of State for African Affairs Ambassador Johnnie Carson was reported to have held a closed-door parley with retired General Ibrahim Babaginda – a man with no official designation. A non-office-holder, who has so far refused to make a public pronouncement on the boiling state of the nation at a time all former Heads of State have made their positions known! Ambassador Carson was reported to have helped defused a planned coup that had reached implementation stage.

In its recent public hearing at the American Senate's Foreign Relations Committee, Committee Chairman Senator Feingold stunned observers like me with the remark that a rumored military coup that was planned in Nigeria for December 31st, 2009 had to be called off due to the realization of impending fierce resistance by the international community.

Today, it remains to be seen what message the Nigerian military is sending its entire population, by having unit commanders release troops to receive a bed-ridden presidential patient from Saudi Arabia without the knowledge of the Acting President who was the tentative Commander-in-Chief at the time of arrival.

Recent reports have cried foul in the appointment of combat commanders of northern origin in the strategic positioning of high-level military personnel. The writing was clear on the wall. Military leaders have come out openly to deny this fact pointing assiduously to invisible rules and regulations that they have adhered to. Actions are however, speaking a very different language.

In this last desperate bid to hold on to power, the Yar'Adua mafia with the support of some non-office holding elements from the North may try out the last trump card – a military intimidation. A coup would definitely bear far-reaching and unforeseeable consequences and the cabal may end up ruling over Northern Nigeria alone on the long run. If a coup is successful, the resultant government may be destabilized by incessant rebel sabotage until the nation falls apart. On top of this, will be sustained international resistance led by a vehement and determined American diplomatic machine. No military government will thrive on this.

In the light of all these, the Yar'Adua mafia may end up falling straight down on their own erected sword. The game is being stretched too far. The military option is resting on a base of thawing ice. It is extremely unlikely to help them out. If anything, it will hasten the resolve of the Jonathan camp with the invisible hands of Olusegun Obasanjo, some eminent Northerners and many elements in the National Assembly to advance and seal the legal removal of Yar'Adua from the Presidency on health grounds. The American diplomatic machine will rally and should by now, have started rallying several loyalists in all segments of the leadership and the Senate amendment of section 144 of the constitution as proclaimed only some hours ago will be just the beginning.

Turai should then be careful not to witness the forcible removal of the patient from the presidential wing of Aso Rock when the time is due for the enthronement of national stability at the expense of the power-hungry cabal.

***

In fact, the end-game came out as predicted in the conclusion of this article. A large part of the nation stood up to resist the actions of the cabal. While several groups fought for constitutionality and the empowerment of the serving Vice President in the face of the deceitful validation of an unconscious President in a vegetative state, former President Olusegun Obasanjo intensified his battle to protect the legal status and value of the Vice and Acting President Goodluck Jonathan.

Time passed by and the incumbent President eventually died. The serious battle to ensure the continuation of the northern slot to the Presidency took several forms with suggested models. One of the most prominent models suggested was for the Acting President to resign to pave way for the constitutional ascension to the Presidency, of the President of the Senate, who was a Northerner.

Before this though, the battle had reached a peak and escalation had to be nipped in the bud. The international community weighed in. The United Nations Special Envoy for the Middle East and former British Prime Minister, Tony Blair, the serving Secretary of State of the United States, Hillary Clinton and her Assistant Secretary of State Ambassador Carson launched direct shuttle diplomacy missions. They consulted with all the names in the North and the only name in the South. They worked magic and managed to defuse the tension. The ultimate result was the Doctrine of Necessity that paved the way for the crowning of Goodluck Jonathan as the Acting President.

The death of the incumbent President thereafter, meant the completion of his tenure by the Acting President. The need for fresh elections became a compulsion thereafter. When the hues and cries finally subsided, the Acting President was permitted to feature as his party's nominee for President. He had the strong backing of his predecessor and mentor, Olusegun Obasanjo, the intelligentsia and several other organized associations and groupings.

Read this:

Now That the Die is Cast!

By Frisky Larr

Now that the rumble is ending, and we are counting the costs in material and human losses, sober reflection is begging to crave in when the die is cast in a matter of days. It has been a hectic few weeks of campaigning and soliciting voters' attention and patronage.

President Goodluck Jonathan started well in advance. His opponents were still busy fighting over the adequate running mate and the suitable format of an impressive campaign train. Architect Sambo had long become a household name in the realms of the incumbency's routine.

One after the other, the opponents of the President pulled one disappointment in systematic succession. The voting populace often greeted every action with consternation and endless frustration. Buhari pulled the first surprise in his choice of a running mate. Observers expected anyone, but not an extremely inexperienced celestial megaphone of mock-politicking. The preacher man who was well known and perhaps most desired in the theatre stage of playing the political conscience of a visionless playground, was suddenly declared a Vice Presidential candidate. A candidate to whom the destiny and future of Nigeria should be entrusted in the event that something happens to incapacitate Muhammadu Buhari – assuming he wins the Presidency! Tunde Bakare is a Preacher man and the head of a celestial church known for prophesies, visions and militant prayers. He heads a church that is a symbol of the credibility crisis rocking the Christian religion of today's Nigeria. A section of society filled with fake prophets, prophesies, visions and mass deception.

Buhari had a different mindset and followed a different line of reasoning. He had carved out a profile for his VP to be. A Southerner, non-Muslim (to shed the persistent media ballast of portraying Buhari as a Muslim fanatic) and a well exposed radical! But Buhari considered little of the credibility angle. The first voices that unleashed venom on the BB – for Buhari/Bakare – team (now ridiculed as Bed and Breakfast team) accused Bakare of having used the status of the man of God with visions and prophesies (that were not always true) and vocal frontliner of the Save Nigeria Group as a launching pad for political ambitions. Some saw it as blasphemy. Many admirers however, see his inexperience as an asset that keeps him off the line of fire since he has no track record of stealing government funds. All-in-all, Buhari pulled a surprise that was not pleasant to an overwhelming majority of political analysts and learned observers.

The ACN quickly followed suit. It denied zoning the Presidency to northern Nigeria. Yet it had no single candidate from any other geographical region to color its intra-party voting routine.

Candidates were imposed at different levels by party leaders in a mafia commando style. And they did not deny it. They came out openly and tried to make sense of all the awkward actions. Dramatically, all candidates pulled back and only one Presidential candidate was left. His name was Nuhu Ribadu. I jubilated personally and praised the day that this man was given to the common voter. But my joy soon gave way to shocking sobriety. News made the round that the beneficiary was someone else. His name was Asiwaju Tinubu. He led his party to working assiduously with a view to fusing up with Buhari's CPC. The reckoning was to have Tinubu as Buhari's running mate, while Ribadu would have stepped down graciously.

In the end, personal association with Nuhu Ribadu would have boosted his credibility rating while Ribadu himself would have gotten the exposure he needed, and three good birds would have been killed with just one stone. Tinubu was a man of the game. But Buhari's obstinacy and commitment to principle stood in Tinubu's way. Tinubu then ate the humble pie and let Ribadu be. But not before opening another controversial chapter. I was sure that Nuhu Ribadu would be a formidable opponent for President Jonathan. I thought he and the people around him were serious about the business of becoming President. They messed it all up in their choice of a running mate. As if they had taken leave of all their senses, they settled for a name, which I still do not know as I am writing and today is Sunday the 27th of March 2011. A few days away from polling and there are many more like me! For the handlers of Ribadu, Ngozi Okonjo-Iweala was too strong a personality to work with and therefore, does not qualify for a running mate. In plain language, it means she is too strong to manipulate. That was the day they began to kill Ribadu in installments. Nuhu Ribadu finally killed his candidacy when he began to attack Jonathan for not honoring the zoning arrangement and thus contesting the Presidency.

For one, it was a Party affair that concerned the President's party and not Ribadu's ACN. Secondly, as a gallant figure widely perceived as detribalized, Ribadu should have known better, if he had to express an opinion on the issue at all. I, as a campaign adviser, would have cautioned him to be deliberately ambiguous in any public statement on zoning. He should perhaps have criticized Jonathan alright but never fail to add too that the North should as well take a back seat having ruled Nigeria for so long. This singular message would have endeared Ribadu to the heart of very many admirers from different camps given his previous antecedents. Ribadu should have fought a campaign deliberately reminiscing on John Jerry Rawlings for public perception. But his advisers misled him into focusing on efforts to position himself as an alternative Northern Consensus candidate following the clearly foreseeable demise of Atiku Abubakar who killed and buried his presidential dreams in his Harakiri fight of 2006. Ribadu was misled into suddenly attacking Jonathan rather than concentrating on an issue-based campaign and promoting himself with all seriousness.

While all these were happening, Jonathan's campaign train was already reaching out into several corners of the country attracting followers and patronizing traditional rulers in chameleonic costuming. It does not help much that faint-hearted attempts were made to capitalize on Jonathan's blunders of addressing people as "Rascals". The campaign gift of the release of Bode George and the frenetic reception accorded him by a party seeking to be taken seriously as a redeeming leader came too little and too late for the opposition parties because the opposition parties were too clueless on how to capitalize on the manna from heaven. The fracas in Ogun state was obviously not recognized by the opposition as an issue that could have been reflected, exemplified and exacerbated to mold an adequate picture of a party that is tied with the multi-directional figments of conflicting interest groups. Buhari did not use it. Neither did Ribadu.

A few days ago, Acting President Jonathan rounded up his campaign and the Presidential debate boycotted by Ribadu and Buhari (by prior announcement) will be the finishing line.

But the campaign trail leaves a path of blood that has been spilled in broad daylight by careless campaigners. Powers are usurped in government and in opposition. The state's monopoly of force and power is openly challenged by thuggery and private armies and militancy. A trail of arson, looting and maiming is the track that we can see. Vehicles burnt, and houses set ablaze. It is a bad omen for the target date of April 9, 2011.

In spite of all that though, there seems to have been an involuntary collaboration to handover the Presidency to Goodluck Jonathan. Buhari's seeming arrogance, taking for granted that the voters know his antecedents in the hope that a pastor's followership will be of help and Ribadu's absolute amateurish organization and campaign movement all represent a virtual handover on a platter of Gold, of the Presidency to Goodluck Jonathan.

It does not matter at all that the self-imposed Northern elders' forum led by Adamu Ciroma is withholding its support for Goodluck Jonathan. The time is simply too short for any meaningful harmful manipulation to stop a Jonathan's victory. The Acting President was now confident enough, having consolidated his hold on power over the past few months, to now defy the northern mafia and call off negotiations with them in their bid to secure assurances from the President. Who would have imagined that in November 2010 when the cabal held sway with the Ciroma mafia hovering in the background?

The painful belly-landing suffered by Ciroma's mafia group that trailed the defeat of Atiku in the PDP's primaries will now be followed by another demystifying humiliation of everything Ciroma and his archaic group stands for. I honestly, cannot see Goodluck Jonathan losing the presidential election, rigging or not!

Anything outside a Jonathan's victory on April 09, 2011 will be a huge upset and absolutely unexpected.

***

Reality played out and Jonathan won the Presidency and finally pulled the curtain on the Yar'Adua's term.

IV
The Jonathan Days

The Jonathan days were ushered in in May 2011, with a lot of hopes and satisfaction. The constitution has prevailed, and the dominance of the almighty northern mafia broken. At 54, he was a relatively young President. He was an academic because he paraded the Ph.D title, which we were subsequently told by his mentor, former President Olusegun Obasanjo, he actually, did not possess. But that is a subject for a subsequent discussion.

No sooner had he taken the reins of power than his travails with inefficiency saw the light of day. I took my time to watch events unfold before I penned my first article in December 2011. My base was still the NigerianNews and lesser the Nigerian Village Square. Enjoy reading.

The Self-Created Problems of President Jonathan

By Frisky Larr

Since his ascension to the number one slot in Nigeria's political leadership, President Goodluck Jonathan seems to have perfected some expertise in moving from one political restiveness to another. Rather than clarity of purpose, most major actions of the President often leave more questions than answers.

It took some time to forget the FIFA fallout in the aftermath of Nigeria's dismal performance at the South African Soccer World Cup 2010. Without adequate consultation and planning by exhaustively weighing the pros and cons of his actions, the President hastily declared the disbandment of the Soccer Federation and the National Team. This was promptly followed by a foray of criticisms by opposition forces at home and abroad even though the President's action was widely applauded by a teeming majority of soccer-loving Nigerians. The President however backed down in a mild show of shame before the World Soccer Federation. Critics roared at the time that the career of several young lads was on the line. The rot in the soccer system that has so far persisted unabated has however shown that no career has ever been enhanced since the ill-fated retreat by the President. Soccer is still very much in a comatose state with players performing fine in their club sides and displaying automatic woefulness at the national side.

The President did not know then that the suspension of Nigeria's membership of FIFA on grounds of striving to put our soccer house in order, should have predated the disbandment of the domestic Federation. He simply needed to have consulted with professionals and legal experts who were versed in the standing orders and guiding rules of FIFA on the terms of quitting the world body on temporary basis. This would have been followed by further domestic measures and reform steps that the President should have kept close to his chest until perfecting the suspension of membership from FIFA. Unfortunately, the President placed the cart before the horse and the project failed.

Observers shook their heads in dismay wondering who the President's advisers were. It was termed a bumpy start and people were ready to give the President many more chances to prove his worth.

Knowing what the nation suffered in the hands of the Yar'Adua Mafia in a desperate bid to enhance casual tribal dominance, voters were in no mood to accept Buhari's tribalism-soiled political credentials over Jonathan's glaring leadership inexperience. Jonathan was voted in amid typical cries of foul from the losing party. But all signs at the present moment, point to the fact that several inexperience-induced political blunders committed by President Jonathan so far, would have been avoided under a President Muhammadu Buhari. This is the unfortunate price that we seem to be paying for striving to enhance geographical equilibrium in political leadership.

The President however started fine with the appointment of Ngozi Okonjo-Iweala to head the nation's Economic Team with a fistful of robust professional competence. He brought back Nuhu Ribadu and Nasir El-Rufai from unceremonious self-exile. From the moment that he refused to integrate these competent fellows into his government, however, his lack-luster disposition and romance of choice, with the enemies of yesterday became more than obvious for the eyes to see.

The President then gave a first elaborate presidential interview and lamented public clamoring for a more decisive and action-packed Presidency. He complained that he was not a Military General and could not go on the rampage in the name of governance. He chose the inauspicious example of Directors in government departments, who do not come to work at the official opening hours. Since he was not a General, he should not be expected to go after such erring Directors with the baton of discipline, he was quoted as saying. It was latest at this point it became obvious that the President did not have a talent for public communication. A well-prepared interview should not have given such erring Directors a blank check in flouting standing orders on official opening hours. In a nutshell, it became clear that this President cannot be let loose by his minders to give public speeches unguided.

On the policy front, the story didn't look different. To the astonishment of several African countries, Jonathan shot out a pronouncement to recognize the new and incoming Libyan government of Benghazi rebels who had just defeated the long-serving forces of Colonel Muammar El-Ghadaffi in a NATO-engineered civil war. The African Union had been boiling with fury over NATO's unilateral breach of the United Nation's resolution on a No-Fly-Zone over Libya and open support for the Libyan rebels. The mandate of the United Nation was clearly exceeded. While every political observer and activist agreed that no tears should be shed for Ghadaffi, the world was in no mood for this NATO's game of inordinate belligerence for the advancement of the private agenda of its individual nations. Without consultation with other Heads of State, Jonathan unleashed an unsolicited support for the rebels that eventually left him struggling for remedial explanations on the diplomatic front. No one was against the inevitable backing of the rebels' ascension to power and the President knew this. A balance only needed to be struck between support for the new government and admonition of NATO's errant ways, all possibly within the scope of a united front of the African Union. Aside reminding the world of late President Yar'Adua's awesome consternation at his presence in the White House and sudden jettisoning of the African High Command deal, President Jonathan by his pronouncement once again, left observers wondering who his advisers were. It seemed the President could stop at nothing to play the puddle of the West for some undisclosed reasons.

Then all of a sudden and in the style of a military General that he never was, President Jonathan went tough. He relieved Farida Waziri of her position overnight and unceremoniously. It was in the middle of her battle with corrupt Nigerian Legislators who sought her head for reasons that are yet diffuse. The world knows, however, that her prosecution of the former Speaker of the House of Representatives Dimeji Bankole, on charges of wanton corruption in which fingers are also pointing at the present Speaker of the House Mr. Tambuwal did not go down well with several Legislators who stand the risk of prosecution themselves. Till the present moment, the President is yet to come out with any single explanation let alone a credible one, for relieving Farida Waziri of her position with such an incredible timing. The result is that civil society is now agitated more than ever before, in its drive for lesser Executive freedom in the removal of the leadership of the anti-graft commission if the fight against corruption is to make any headway. The clamoring for a better legislation to amend the EFCC law is just beginning and people are wondering who the President's advisers are.

As if that was not enough, the President has been having to contend with another fully unnecessary but self-created battlefront of the removal of government subsidy on petroleum products. While several voters now cry 'betrayal' at the President's obvious obstinacy on an issue that hardly ever featured during electoral campaigns, the President seems to be biting far more than he may be able to chew in a very unnecessary and unwarranted battle.

At the moment, President Jonathan's success in making improvements on power supply and his bold moves to advance the NIPP for a lasting solution to the power sector problem is going down unnoticed. Like many other achievements of the government, reported progress in fixing the comatose Lagos-Benin expressway as well as several little strides made by the Ngozi Okonjo-Iweala's Economic Team in injecting fiscal discipline into the system, are all going down unnoticed. In the end, President Jonathan seemed more than determined to reduce his government to the damning judgmental fate of fuel subsidy alone.

Opposing parties on both sides of the aisle agree without reservation that fuel subsidy has to be removed. The most vehement and vocal party is simply asking the President to keep refineries functional and possibly build a few more and then allow subsidy to die its natural death. Only on May 13th, 2011 President Jonathan seems to have understood the rationale behind this argument. He had permitted the NNPC to sign a $23.8 billion deal with China State Construction Engineering Corp. to build three new refineries in Nigeria. For reasons yet unexplained however, no forward movement was ever recorded on this deal. Then barely six months later, President Jonathan will have none of it anymore and simply wants to take out the subsidy no matter whose ox is gored. It is deja vu all over again. The idea of putting the cart before the horse surely seems familiar to us.

But whose ox is truly gored but that of the common masses? Speculations hold sway that beneficiaries of the subsidies who are political financiers of the president have been working assiduously against domestic refinery. Yet the President does not throw down the gauntlet against these millionaires. Then this unfortunate and highly obnoxious interview once again! In another absolutely unguarded statement in this apparently yet unprepared interview a few days ago, the President was quoted as saying that he was ready for a revolution if that was the price he would pay for removing the fuel subsidy. A declaration of war on his own people, so to speak!

I read on an Internet forum today, someone reminding him of Ghadaffi's reaction when he was told of the starting of a revolution in Benghazi while on a foreign trip. He said: "Libya is not Tunisia". On returning home to confront the rebels, he was sure he would flush out those "rats" in no time at all. In the end, Ghadaffi was flushed out of a hole like a "rat" that he shouldn't have been. A word is enough for the wise!

***

In his early days as Acting President, one of Goodluck Jonathan's first acts was to ban the Nigerian national soccer team from international outing for two years. He disbanded the soccer federation the "Nigerian Football Association" (NFA) in the aftermath of the country's dismal outing at the just-concluded World Cup in South Africa. The flagship national team had underperformed beyond all expectations and the reasons were home-made. Corruption and mismanagement were rampant at and oozed despicably out of the NFA as in many other state institutions and it needed urgent reorganization and restructuring.

The President's decision was, therefore, greeted with a sigh of relief by the wider public, as something long overdue. Trouble, though, was that the President had not consulted widely with stakeholders and legal experts in the run up to the announcement of the decision. The President had no clue that there was a standing order of the world's soccer governing body, FIFA, which forbade political interference in the affairs of the national associations. While domestic pressure group began laying siege on the President for the damaging impact that the decision would have on the career of some soccer hopefuls, the world soccer body, FIFA, was reading the riot act to the Nigerian President and in the immediate aftermath, the President chickened-in. That was the general perception in public view. It was the very first misstep of an ill-prepared President.

As the substantive President in the wake of the general elections, he started off with brilliant appointments, not the least, of the technocrat and highly respected wall-street expert of the Ivy Lee elitist acclaim, Dr. Ngozi Okonjo-Iweala. He recalled erudite political characters from self-imposed exile in search of safety for their lives following vindictive harassments under his late predecessor, arguably, for the diligent duties these people performed under former President Obasanjo and stepped on powerful toes. Nuhu Ribadu and El-Rufai were welcomed back home under the new President Goodluck Jonathan but were not truly given any meaningful government appointment.

There was a lot of motion that signaled steps in the right direction and these positive steps were often appraised as achievements.

In a landmark move not too far from the early days of the Presidency, however, Goodluck Jonathan launched a move that he thought, would be the boldest and most daring that any President before him had ever undertaken. He launched a public debate on the removal of government subsidy on fuel consumption.

The following was my contribution to the debate at the time. I still wrote basically, under the auspices of the online site NigerianNews, where I had a column. At the time too, the reputable mainstream organ, This Day, often also released my works.

Extreme Caution Recommended As Fuel Subsidy Debate Heats Up!

By Frisky Larr

The heated debate on the recently announced plan to remove government subsidy on the downstream sector of fuel supply for domestic consumption is pulling out all the stops. Opinions have been running passionately high since the announcement of the move with each view on the political divide being strongly defended by proponents of and subscribers to such views.

Whichever way the issue is finally resolved however, it is becoming certain by the day, that none of the opposing views on the two sides of the fence rejects the removal of fuel subsidy. If anything, it has become increasingly clear that convergence of opinion prevails on the hazards constituted by the lingering subsidy on the overall Nigerian economy. The draining impact that it has on resources as well as the potential gains the removal of subsidy portends on infrastructural growth does not seem to be a point of disagreement.

The basic disagreement focuses on how the subsidy should be removed. Supporters of the government's position advance the notion that the beneficiaries of the current arrangement are a whimsical minority perpetrating fraud on the vast majority of Nigerians. Efforts are, therefore, required to redistribute these beneficial resources in a much more proper manner. This camp also advances the notion that the government should have no business whatsoever, building refineries, power stations or water supply plants since this can easily be left to private investors to handle. It is a typical market economy opinion advancing crude and cold capitalism subject to the dictates of market conditions. This camp subscribes to the example of several developed economies, which do not meddle in the running of infrastructural installations.

Living in Germany – a country that does not subscribe wholly to the dictates of perfect market conditions, the cold capitalist style – I am perhaps swayed by the notion of a softened welfare-oriented capitalist policy of "Social Market Economy". Indeed, many developing economies coincidentally embrace this trend of action in advancing a general state of social welfare. Nigeria has done this too since its inception as an independent nation and I do not think it is a wrong policy direction.

Like countless developing nations and economies, Nigeria started off years ago, with a policy of self-sufficiency in fuel consumption in the domestic market. It was in the aftermath of oil discovery. To this end, raw oil was refined at home and we had a handful of oil refineries.

When the transition to the second republic was effected in 1979, Nigeria was not importing refined fuel. Nigeria was self-sufficient. Nigeria had three oil refineries and the fourth was near completion and was subsequently completed by the government of Alhaji Shehu Shagari. I do not know precisely when it all started, but the transition to a regime of fuel importation was a fallout from declining oil prices and the general state of Nigeria's economy. The economy had taken a serious bashing from corrupt politicians who diverted resources to their own pockets that could have been saved for a rainy day.

Refineries were not maintained, and steady dilapidation set in. No new refineries were built, and production steadily ran short of domestic demand for refined fuel. Being short of money to fix the problem at the time, I suppose it was the government of Ibrahim Badamosi Babangida, which then resolved to import refined fuel from countries to which we had hitherto exported raw petroleum. After all the debate and rabble-rousing, the understanding at the time, was that the measure was tentative. The basic aim was to buy time to sort out the problem of fixing refineries for a reversal to self-sufficiency. After all, it is not an uncommon practice in oil-producing countries to allow the citizenry to reap the benefit of such a God-given manna from heaven. In fact, many see the idea of the citizenry reaping this benefit as a divine right. To underscore the tentativeness of the arrangement, however, government resolved to subsidize the importation of refined fuel so that the ordinary man in the street would not feel the harsh impact of importation until complete reversal to self-sufficiency is ultimately attained. That has been the psychology of the game plan surrounding the story of fuel subsidy.

In fact, General Babaginda implemented a very woeful policy of promoting private investment in the refineries and stripped the NNPC of the duty of maintaining refineries and keeping them functional. He encouraged private investors to engage in crude oil importation so that they will end up building more refineries. The reality however turned out differently. importers made their money and disappeared into thin air. This is an issue that I treated elaborately in my book "Nigeria's Journalistic Militantism".

In fact, one President of the Students' Union Government of the University of Jos at the time, personally led a protest movement to the military government of General Babaginda to impress upon it that the removal of fuel subsidy was "a crime against the Nigerian masses and a war against the poor". The President of the Students' Union government then, Mr. Labaran Maku is now the Minister of Information today, 're-branding' the government of President Jonathan. Today, he says that the removal of fuel subsidy is long overdue.

Somewhere down the line however, Generals and their cronies who ran the regime of fuel importation discovered the lucrative nature of the business to their private pockets. It fetched them millions in shortcut income. Fixing the refineries that are performing ways below capacity, thus became a problem that would pull the carpet from beneath their feet. In fact, the rising cost of raw petroleum and the loss of value of the Nigerian Naira, renders the cost of importation higher. These importers do not only bring in refined fuel, some of them also own filling stations. Today, many of them are politicians and lobbyists. Those who are not politicians simply sponsor the political aspirations of professional politicians thus making it difficult for politicians to engage them in a fight to force the notion of fixing refineries upon them.

The policy of fixing refineries with all vehemence has therefore become an almost impossible task because it will end up offending these rich oil Oligarchs. In fact, former President Olusegun Obasanjo is highly suspected to have also fallen victim to this reality. Renowned Economist Professor Aluko reportedly sounded it to him at the time of his inception as civilian President that Nigeria urgently needed the construction of new refineries to ease out the continued implementation of fuel subsidy.

In the face of all these constraints, the easiest backdoor solution left to politicians remains the removal of subsidy without solving the problem of refineries in the land. It simply drops the burden on the shoulders of the common consumer hoping that market conditions will drive investors to lay their money in the construction of refineries. But the policy had already failed under the government of Ibrahim Badamosi Babangida!

Short term reality will be the hiking of pump prices to cover up for everything that the subsidy had taken care of. In doing so, the government will maintain its peace and the Oligarchs will keep their millions in expectation of many more to come. Inflation will rise because salaries will not be raised proportionately. If the same money is diverted into the payment of the contentious minimum wage, the notion will be automatically defeated that savings from subsidy withdrawal will go into infrastructure building.

The poor consumer will then have to reach deeper down his pocket to meet the costs of boarding a bike, a taxi, a bus and a Molue or Danfo. He will reach deeper into his pocket to buy agricultural products that are transported from rural areas to the metropolises. He will reach deeper down his pocket to afford virtually every basic necessity of life since almost everything is linked with transportation and fuel for power.

Supporters of this government's move are holding on adamantly to the notion that the government should have had no business building refineries in the very first place. An inferred logic suggesting too that the government should have no business building power stations or water dams! They draw parallels to countries that are ways and many light years ahead of Nigeria in every ramification of social and infrastructural development. But they conveniently avoid comparison with countless other countries implementing beneficial welfare programs for their citizens.

The betrayal of public trust that was built up in the run-up to the tentativeness of the introduction of fuel subsidy seems to play no role at all. The reality of the very high chances of regained subsidy money going into private pockets without the refinery problem being fixed does not seem to play any role at all. The argument is advanced that public debate should focus on what to do with saved subsidy money rather than asking for the fixing of the refinery problem. They seem to present the notion that subsidy will be removed, and cash distributed to the hands of every household in return.

Indeed, President Jonathan, who has pledged to run for a single term, should ordinarily, not be caring about support from the millionaire Oligarchs. That is the beauty of the single tenure arrangement that should normally, have enabled the governing instance to concentrate on governance without thinking much of financial and political support for the next tenure. Unfortunately, however, President Jonathan seems to be in some fix unable to ply the road with the aim of fixing the subsidy problem in the interest of the masses.

Today, one Nelson Ekujumi has just told the President to cut the crap on complaining that N310 billion will be spent in the next fiscal year on subsidizing kerosene. He has reminded the President that it costs only N20 billion to build a new refinery while the time required is just two years. Unfortunately, none of these is being done in Nigeria for obvious reasons stated above. Everyone knows that the fixing of existing refineries and the construction of new ones will automatically translate into subsidy removal in the interest of the masses.

I am only hoping that the President will still use the time available to him to make the right choices before he sets the country on fire.

***

Alas, the President did not heed the words of wisdom in the interest of the masses. Unable to rein in his numerous friends and cronies, who exploded numerically as newcomers in the newfound business of fuel importation, fraud and corruption took control and subsidy payment got out of control. The President sought to introduce a solution in a slap-bang.

While pressure was mounted on the President to free up the market and surrender consumers to the mercy of the wolves, who have just discovered a new source of disproportionate profiteering in a country that could boast of no single welfare project for its poorest citizens, it did not take long to see that the President had launched the public debate only to prepare the public for the impending hardship coming its way. It was just the wrong time, and many warned against it.

It was the period of the Arab spring that had inundated the news media. The ordinary man on the street, professional protesters and mischief-makers were not short on inspiration. I wrote several articles, and this was one of them:

The Endless Saga on Fuel Subsidy: What the President Must Know

By Frisky Larr

I feel sad having to criticize the President of my country each time I have something to write about him. I feel sad not because my criticisms are not real or because they are not authentic. I feel sad because I detest being a critic all the way. I hold some die-hard optimism that no government is a complete failure. I therefore hold on to the dictates of old-school journalism of seeking the best possible proximity to fairness. The fairness of naming successes alongside failures! With President Jonathan these days, no matter how I try, it is very difficult to identify the positives and I hate being the propagator of pure negatives.

From baring a glaring loophole in the sophistication of counseling provided by aides and advisers to his poor quality of articulation in Public speeches, President Jonathan has played, every passing day, into the hands of critics who claim that he is not a good presidential material.

For once I was pleased the other day, when I saw the slightest sign of some professional Public Relations management in salvaging what was left of a poorly planned program of independence celebration. An October 1st celebration had been drowned in the shadow of terrorist threats and the President had to beat an unprecedented retreat to a low-key celebration. Exposed to an opposition ACN that was bent on capitalizing on the seeming weakness of the State that capitalized before terrorist threats, President Jonathan made one professional pronouncement for once at least. He stated that the low-key celebration was a child of economic expediency. A policy adopted by the government, so to speak, to last for three years and had nothing at all, to do with the terrorist threat. With this singular pronouncement, he pulled the carpet from beneath the opposition campaign and made a cowardly decision appear like some routine and laudable government policy. It showed some strength in what indeed, was a hastily taken decision to protect innocent lives from the stupidity of some brainwashed fanatics of a dark religious age. I had a feeling that he has been well managed in producing medicine after death, at least for once.

But who – for God's sake – is managing the President on the issue of fuel subsidy? Every Nigerian knows how contentious the subject of fuel and pump prices is to the average Nigerian. In fact, I remember the year 2007 during the transition to the government of late President Umaru Musa Yar'Adua. The incoming President implored his outgoing counterpart at the time to hike the pump price of fuel since he as the new kid on the block could not afford to

148

take the attendant controversy and public uproar of a price hike upon himself. Given his huge unpopularity anyway, outgoing President Obasanjo had nothing to lose having the buck passed on to him as the dreary boogeyman. He hiked the price to take the pressure off his successor but could not go the length of removing subsidy from the downstream sector. That alone added to anger against him and many would have been pleased to see President Obasanjo publicly executed at that time, for that singular act.

But there can be no doubt whatsoever, that the removal of fuel subsidy is highly economically prudent. Every observer, who doesn't even have to be an expert, knows fully well that the removal of fuel subsidy will free up a huge sum of money that will be used on other vital economic projects. The projects requiring huge expenditure cannot be over-emphasized. They range from road construction to the build-up of several other social infrastructures. For this reason, I will not blame the Finance Minister if she advices the President to remove fuel subsidy as quickly as possible to make her allocate the accruing money to other developmental projects.

Unfortunately, however, the welfare of the population is not managed on economic calculations alone. There are times that the most prudent economic consideration is deliberately allowed to crumble under the weight of overwhelming social realities.

As a nation blessed with these vital natural resources that is fetching the lion share of national income, less than one percent of the population reaps the benefit while the remaining ninety-nine percent continues to pay the bills *ad infinitum*. Soon Nigerians will copy the Americans to remind the elites who the 99% are.

99% living in a nation almost fully devoid of a welfare program! Social institutions are comatose and basic infrastructures a never-ending mirage. Yet stories emerge day after day how the elites are not affected in any way, by these grim, realities of a dark and dreary daily life. Our leaders fly abroad for medical attention and never get to know what power outage is all about.

Previous attempts to remove fuel subsidy have always been abandoned over fears of unnecessary public unrest amid an already volatile public security situation to say the least of painful cost of daily life to the ordinary man. This has been expressed on countless occasions by people in the know and government authorities have always been placed on the alert regarding the dangerous consequences of subjecting the ordinary man to yet aggravated hardships.

Unfortunately, the problem of freeing subsidy money for other development projects can be solved by other means apart from the removal of the subsidy itself. The reality however is the helplessness of the very government that should ordinarily be wielding the ultimate power.

The solution is the upgrading of existing and building of new petroleum refineries. That will in fact, bring an end to the regime of importing refined fuel from countries that we have exported raw petroleum to. That will automatically translate into the removal of the infamous subsidy.

The problem however is that there are many powerful millionaires in Nigeria today, who own refinery blocks and export petroleum products for profit. They import refined fuel for profit and also own endless chains of petrol stations, to which they supply the fuel that they have imported to reap maximum profit. The power that these people wield is the financial support that they give to politicians. Many of them are even richer than the state itself. The government – i.e. the President – fears them a great deal.

Improving existing refineries and building new ones will rob these powerful people of one more means of their crucial income. President Jonathan is not taking up the fight to confront these Oligarchs as one of his major personal sacrifice for the ordinary Nigerian. President Jonathan virtually leads a government, which actions seem to be defined basically, by fear. Fear of the Buharis and Babangidas, fear of Boko Haram, fear of the Niger Delta Militants and now fear of Petro-Oligarchs! This is a President, who has indeed declared several times, that he does not seek re-election and therefore, has no stake for which he seeks the inevitable support of influential interest groups. Why doesn't he then pick up the gauntlet and embark on a people-oriented infrastructural project?

It does not matter to these Oligarchs if Nigeria – the seventh largest exporter of petroleum product – sells refined fuel to its own citizens at prices far beyond what the average American pays, while America stands as the world's largest importer of petroleum products. What matters to the Oligarchs is the profit that they make and the power that they wield. Why is Jonathan just not assertive, bold and making the right choices? He fails to see countries like Saudi Arabia and Venezuela and reflect deeply on the people-oriented policy implemented in these countries of bringing fuel to the people at affordable rates no matter what it costs the government.

This alone is one compelling reason that people like me get worried and seek to understand just why President Jonathan is hell bent on removing this fuel subsidy. He is not new to expert projection of what the impact of such action will be in terms of short to medium-term hardships.

We are all aware that the tentacles of these Petro-Oligarchs spread virtually into every facet of existing political institutions. Falling out of favor with them often means the revelation of several scandalous skeletons in the closet and almost every politician has more than enough of them (except perhaps, my darling Okonjo-Iweala, who knows?). When these authentic revelations often come out in public domain, almost no one in public realizes then that someone is being sacrificed for fighting for the people.

But this argument does not hold at all times given the extent to which the Bola Tinubu mafia went even to impeach Babatunde Fashola in Lagos State. Unseating (through impeachment or whatever means) a leader who has succeeded in targeted propaganda, to make the public see and understand his fight for their own benefit, is not an easy task for the mafia itself.

Now does President Jonathan have so many skeletons in his closet that he fears will be uncovered if he takes up an aggressive fight with these oligarchs and build several new petroleum refineries? What stops President Jonathan from launching an aggressive and visible people's politics the Fashola style and bring the people behind him?

What we see in Nigeria today are Governors arrested on suspicions of embezzling horrendous sums of money. We hear of money squandered in the legislative houses for the purchase of new vehicles, TV sets and several irrelevant objects at amazing prices. We hear of a former Speaker of the Federal legislative house buying his former official residence at a laughable sum and renting it to his predecessor at an annual sum equaling the purchasing price. Public officers are milking the country dry at the expense of the tax-payer and voters whose ballots are golden in times of elections. President Jonathan surely knows alternative sources of freeing money for other developmental projects. He should encourage the Super Minister Okonjo-Iweala to enforce further fiscal discipline with the force of the law and assistance of the EFCC.

Unfortunately, President Jonathan chooses these very bad and trying times to intimate the general public of yet another hardship coming its way. What a pity!

***

No one knew at the time that the President, who had given his word to stakeholders, that he was committed to serving only one term as President, had other ideas. Time subsequently revealed that he was bent on having a second presidential term, while pundits were expecting him to unleash radical actions in his avowed single-term to cleanse the country of its social and political ills.

Then, the inevitable happened. After repeated assurances by the President that no decision had yet been taken on the removal or otherwise of fuel subsidy and citizens left their workplaces and traveled home from the metropolises to the hinterland for the end-of-year festive season, they were caught in a presidential ambush.

The President announced the removal of fuel subsidy with effect from January 01st, 2012. The prices of virtually, all consumer commodities, notably public transport fares, shot up. Many could hardly afford the costs of returning to their workplaces in the big cities. The largest trade union of the country, the "Nigerian Labor Congress" (NLC) and many smaller pressure groups launched public protests and public service and the entire country was grounded to a standstill and the military had to be deployed to stop a mob descent on the National Assembly that would have marked Nigeria's first taste of a popular revolution. Some lives were lost in the use of live munitions to quell the protest. It almost ran out of control and the government had to reverse a major part of its decision and met the demands of the public halfway in a *no-victor-no-vanquished* solution.

Read this:

Subsidy Removal: Whose Interest was the President Protecting?

By Frisky Larr

The rude awakening on New Year's Day is yet to be forgotten. The wounds have hardly healed, and the scars are all too visible. Yet more insults are added to injuries thanks to questions that never get answered. Every passing day in the Presidency of Goodluck Jonathan is increasingly characterized by questions piling upon one another. They never get answered.

As the only public institution that has now moved halfway on the side of the common man, the House of Representatives added even more questions to the yet unanswered ones through its report on the Fuel Subsidy Probe.

For the avoidance of doubt, it may be pertinent to repeat a few old and almost forgotten questions on whose heap the report has now piled additional queries. The President has till today, failed to reveal to the world who the Boko Haram agents in his own cabinet are. The President is yet to tell the nation his reasons for removing Mrs. Farida Waziri from the EFCC just when she was beginning to gather steam and drive her job in the right direction. The President is yet to tell Nigerians just one reason for telling lies to his fellow citizens through proxies, in the run-up to the catastrophic removal of fuel subsidy on January 01, 2012. The nation is waiting for an answer to the President's sudden and unexplainable breach of his own promise to PDP Governors in advance of last year's presidential election that he would serve only one term as President. The questions could go on and on.

Credulous analysts believed in good faith that the removal of fuel subsidy was in the overall interest of the nation's economy. Many carried out hypothetical and sometimes outlandish mathematical calculations. They trusted the President and believed he was doing his bit to move the country forward. The thought of some vested interests being in the focus of executive protection sounded just too remote. President Jonathan reaped the most praises from representatives of the World Bank and International Monetary Fund! Such protagonists believed that the President was opening the economy to the natural influence of market forces. They could be forgiven because they were non-Nigerians and could not know the depth of routine political romance with corrupt forces.

Sanusi Lamido Sanusi advanced several theories on "White Elephant projects" and sounded reasonable and intelligent. Diezani Alison-Madueke joined the chorus and hid behind the credibility clout of Ngozi Okonjo-Iweala. Together, they sounded academically formidable and indomitable.

Now that the House of Representative's committee probing the intriguing schemes of the petroleum sector has released its report, we are seeing the worms concealed in the can. Did Sanusi Lamido not have a clue that such underhand dealings were going on in the sector? Ngozi Okonjo-Iweala may know less about the extent of the rot in the sector due to her neophyte status in the Nigerian political arena. But what about the President at whose desk the buck stops? As a full-bred Nigerian politician from the Niger Delta, will President Jonathan claim innocence of all the crimes in the oil sector?

For a recap of the committee's findings, please join me on a brief trip into the wild world of the oil sector. The very first fact that the committee unearthed was the vast array of misleading information to justify the quick removal of oil subsidy. People knew the truth and deliberately circumvented it preferring to buy praise-singers to drum up support in public protests and treacherous newspaper articles, all in the bid to remove subsidy quickly and smoothly. Beneficiaries were those who would have escaped prosecution since the prevailing atmosphere was growing increasingly volatile. The subsidy for the continued importation would have been further paid by the poor consumers of refined fuel. Refineries could not be fixed. The cabal was declared more powerful than the government. But when Farida Waziri got audacious and began to turn her attention to the oil sector for possible arrests however, she was called off by presidential absolution and removed unceremoniously. Unknown friends in the oil sector were amongst the beneficiaries.

People were aware of companies that claimed subsidy payments and yet imported not a single drop of fuel. The House committee counted 20 companies that received importation allocation even before they got registered with the PPPRA. A Texas company called Eco-Regen with office in Abuja reportedly claimed N1.9 billion for importing absolutely nothing. In the year 2009, President Umaru Musa Yar'Adua removed subsidy on kerosene. The then Vice President Goodluck Jonathan was fully aware of the presidential directive. Retail prices for kerosene were hiked in the aftermath of the subsidy removal. Yet the NNPC had a total of N310.4 billion credited to its account as subsidy payment on kerosene for the period 2009 to 2011. NNPC characteristically made such illegal deductions from sales proceeds before paying the balance into the Federation Account. Was President Jonathan unaware of the directive issued by his erstwhile boss? Worse still, was Diezani Alison-Madueke, the Oil Minister, unaware of this illegality?

In an obvious cover-up of impeding consequences following the uncontrolled intrigue of a mob-gone-wild, the President's government resorted to using the wrong figure on the total amount of subsidy spent in 2011. Having massively and illegally exceeded the budgetary limit on fuel subsidy after satisfying cronies, allies and collaborators on payback time, the President's government began to panic. They had to pull the trigger in the face of virtual insanity. A high figure had to be announced to the public that should be high enough to scare the wit out of ordinary Nigerians and convince them to embrace subsidy removal. It was, however, not to be so high as to attract any inquisitive probe from the legislative arm of government. The government simply needed a figure that was moderately high enough to appeal to reason without creating complications for itself.

It thus declared having spent N1.3 billion on fuel subsidy in 2011. In the course of the probe however, the Accountant-General claimed to have disbursed a total of N1.6 billion for fuel subsidy. We all wondered what happened to N0.3 billion. The CBN added another twist to the drama by admitting that it paid out N1.7 billion to the Accountant-General for the same purpose. We wondered what the Accountant-General did to N0.1 billion. At the end of the day however, it was a bombshell. The committee ascertained that well over N2.6 billion was spent on fuel subsidy in the year 2011. This prompted speculations that a part of the money may have been used illegally to finance undeclared political activities. A clearly impeachable offence on the part of the President if proven to be true!

While Nigeria had only 19 registered fuel importers in 2008, PPPRA's register showed a record number of 140 importers in 2011. An ominous increase of almost 740% in just three years! Questions abound on how many refineries the amount of N2.6 billion (paid to marketers) and N310 billion (paid to the NNPC on kerosene) would have built for Nigeria since 2008. A total of N230.184 billion was paid to marketers that did not import or supply any fuel at all. President Jonathan ignored all these facts and sought to bleed the peasants deep from their heart. The question then arises why the President has never been keen on probing corruption within the Nigerian system. Who are these importers and marketers? What relationship do they have with politicians? Why did the government prefer to punish the masses rather than justifiably prosecute these blood-sucking vampires?

The report of the committee probe further reveals that the Accountant-General who was in charge of payments for the period covered by the probe paid N999 million for 128 times in a single day. The committee was unable to ascertain the names of the recipients of this horrendous payment. This Accountant-General is today the elected Governor of Gombe State.

So badly have pecuniary interests become interwoven with politics in this diabolic project of sucking Nigeria dry that presidential foot-dragging on the implementation of the committee's recommendations is all too comprehensible. After all, humans are naturally reluctant to bite the fingers that fed or still feed them.

As usual, President Goodluck Jonathan is unable to read the writings on the wall. Nigeria is undoubtedly drifting helplessly into the administrative era of a leader who has little or no talent in leadership. A President basking in the delusive safety of security provided by government functionaries and militants from the Niger Delta! It may do well to insert the footnote that Alison-Madueke was reportedly appointed as Minister of Petroleum Resources only after the intensive intervention of a militant. The political island of the Niger Delta with which the President has surrounded himself will quickly fade into a powder keg if he unwittingly triggers a revolution to engulf the land. He may end up unable to contain the stream of human blood that will color his hands when the toll is taken of the victims of his acts. In a nation where honor counts, the President by now, would no doubt have addressed the nation apologizing to the masses in humility and revert the pump price of fuel to its original state of N65.00 per liter while he sets out to cleanse the sector once and for all.

The time is now ripe for labor unions, students' unions and other civil society movements to swing into action yet again. Mass action looming for the second time in just six months in the middle of a spate of mindless terrorism! This time though, blood will be spilled from the very start since government will seek to protect strategic areas of demonstrations by the force of arms. As usual, President Jonathan is apparently oblivious of the strength of the inferno that he is choosing to handle with kid's gloves. Fire that may consume the entire edifice of his political existence! Kill the probe report and wait for the consequences. That's the only warning that anyone may wish to sound to the President's ears since a word, as they say, should be enough for the wise!

***

Events took their course and the mass uprising was quelled by the force of arms and massive intimidation in the course of conclusive negotiations with the labor unions. It marked the first and major litmus test for the young government in its inaugural learning process.

Yet, it did not mark the end of nearly all problems. One problem that was inherited from the preceding government had a particularly lasting and destructive impact on the body politics of the nation – the Boko Haram conundrum. A group of young religious radicals in the Muslim north of the country had gained public attention sometime around the year 2009 with the notoriety of launching attacks on government institutions decrying the influence of western education on day-to-day life. The law and order response to the brutal act of banditry led to the arrest of the ringleaders and the subsequent killing of same in police custody. Years later, the radicals regrouped and turned themselves into a rampaging formation of heavily armed brutes with a blurred evil mission of Islamizing the entire country.

Even though many sources point to the fact that the very strong resurgence of this – under normal conditions – ragtag army of rebellious civilians, was partly facilitated by political instability in the Middle East, the government of President Goodluck Jonathan did very little to stop Boko Haram. Unknown Neo-imperial Arab states were suspected of secretly financing and backing the Nigerian Muslim radicals in a bid to have the country Islamized. On top of it was the overthrow and killing of Colonel Muammar Ghadaffy of Libya – a development that has left Libya in political chaos ever after and set the flow of lethal weapons and trained fighters from that country on an uncontrolled path.

Since the brutal insurgency started from and was concentrated on the Muslim northern part of the country, the incumbent President of the time – Goodluck Jonathan – seemed to have focused more on preventing a spillover to the South and have the battle of Islamization confined to the North. In fact, his predecessor, President Olusegun Obasanjo went on record to quote the incumbent as saying he wouldn't care much as long as the Northerners were only killing themselves thus underscoring the dangerous subliminal religious divide distinguishing the north from the south of Nigeria.

It called for the penning of the following article that was widely circulated online and on paper:

Is Boko Haram just a Label? What Game is Playing Out Here?

By Frisky Larr

Nigerian readers will need no recap to understand what Boko Haram stands for. It is a phenomenon that trails the daily lives of individuals like a psychological shadow stretching over the entire country from Maiduguri. Yet for the sake of non-Nigerians it will suffice to explain that Boko Haram is a northern Nigerian group of jihadist militants whose violent campaign with heavy assault weapons came to public attention on July 26, 2009 with a raging attack on a police station in Bauchi, northern Nigeria. The violence which spread one day later, to other northern cities namely Maiduguri, Potiskum and Wudil with attacks on police stations and destruction of public properties culminated in the arrest of the group's leader. He was eventually killed in police custody under extremely questionable extra-judicial circumstances resulting in the interim reinstatement of law and order. It all happened in 2009.

Further trouble brewed, however, in the wake of the power tussle that followed the incapacitation and eventual demise of Nigeria's President Umaru Musa Yar'Adua in 2010. The ethnic and regional balance of power that political forces sought to foster on the nation by advocating the formula of the cyclical rotation of the Presidency suffered a huge blow with the death of the president. The contentious issue of the northern domination of political leadership since the attainment of independence in 1960 had long been a thorn in the flesh of southern politicians who felt marginalized by the northern domination of the military and political institutions that held the scepter of power.

The solution seemed found on June 12, 1993 when a western Nigerian Moshood Abiola of controversial political antecedents was presumed duly elected as President in a presumed free and fair election. The controversial background of this ticking political time bomb made the victor an unacceptable thorn in the flesh of powerful northern elites who ensured the annulment of that election without much ado. A complicated political chess game that ensued in the aftermath of the annulled election culminated in the questionable death of prominent political figures including a dictator and Moshood Abiola himself. Attempts to calm frail nerves saw the engineered re-emergence of the former military Head of State General Olusegun Obasanjo as President of Nigeria from 1999 to 2007 because Gnereal Obasanjo belonged to the same ethnic group as Moshood Abiola's. Obasanjo's largely successful efforts to re-organize and overhaul the entire system with a view to breaking the logjam of dominance of the military and political leadership by the northern elites stands in fact, at the heart of all disputes between the North and the rest of Nigeria today.

Sharp-tongued critics suspect that General Obasanjo who rebelled against his northern sponsors and sidelined them in active manipulations, had deliberately hand-picked a terminally ill successor to feign the transfer of power back to the north even though he knew that the Southern Vice President would automatically take the reins of power if the terminally ill northern President died mid-term. And so it happened.

The bitterness that trailed this feeling of perceived treachery and dirty tricks was poised against a feeling of "serves them right" by southern agitators who saw nothing wrong in short-changing the northern interest even if it meant a breach of moral commitments made within the ruling party. A choice had to be made between moral commitment and constitutional guaranties. While the rest of Nigeria stuck with the provisions of the constitution that guarantied succession by a Vice President (no matter his region of origin) when a President dies, leading Northerners sought to short-change the constitution in favor of intra-party arrangements to advance the morally agreed principle of rotation.

An acrimonious war of attrition ensued with opponents entrenched in overtly irreconcilable camps. Vitriolic charges began to thunder loud. Accusations and counter-accusations made the round. Several voices from the north threatened Sodom and Gomorra if the North failed to get its way. The language of violence was a matter of course. The paraphrase *"He who makes peaceful change impossible renders violent change inevitable"* symbolically summarized the prevailing northern anger and sentiments.

When the southern agitators finally prevailed in the aftermath of all the wrangling and manipulations, the sudden resurgence of Boko Haram that was presumed curtailed in 2009 with the killing of its leader fitted perfectly well into the picture of threats made in the run-up to the *Battle Royale*.

There was no question in the south as to who was behind the bloodshed that befell arbitrary targets and almost sought to spark a civil war. Defenseless citizens were killed and maimed in arbitrary attacks on bars, pubs, schools, churches and seldom mosques within the confines of northern Nigeria. This gave rise to the suspicion of aspirations to establish an Islamic state. Most often however, police stations and military installations were attacked, the highlight being the successful daring attack on the police headquarters in which the national police boss escaped death by the whiskers. It took an international dimension when the office of the United Nations also got bombed. It bore the hallmark of organized terrorism with mounting sophistication as time passed by. It became clear latest at this point that the work of the group was driven by a well-organized network of insiders and widespread support of highly placed and ordinary people.

The helplessness of the institutions of state to contain the situation was highlighted when the President finally cried out asking citizens to pray for the nation. He observed that the network of the terror group spreads through all segments of society – the paramilitary forces, the army, the legislature, the judiciary and even his own cabinet. Of course, when the President talked, it was assumed that he had credible intelligence report at his disposal. He seemed to have feared that he too would soon become the target of the assailants. Not long after however, the same President declared confidently that the institutions of the state had worked out a master plan to contain the menace and even specified a deadline for the eradication of the lethal movement.

Soon after, a legislator was identified as a collaborator and subjected to prosecution. Till the present moment however, the President's new-found courage in declaring the impending end of Boko Haram did not materialize in the identification of the cabinet members that the President knew to be members of the deadly jihadist sect.

In other words, the picture that meets the eye as time passes by, seems less clear-cut. The battle line now seems getting blurred and invisible. The more you look is the less you see.

My interaction with ordinary northerners who themselves resent Boko Haram and have very little in common with fanatical Islamism has now forced me to ask for answers to countless mind-boggling questions.

Is Boko Haram today still the Boko Haram of 2011 that sought to make Nigeria ungovernable for a Southern President? Have the institutions of state being badly compromised to shift goalposts in desperate midnight diplomacies? Many weird developments through the months now seem to signal a clandestine metamorphosis into a paradigm shift. The political atmosphere today is one, in which a Northern Bamakur Tukur has become the advocate-in-chief of a second presidential term for a Southern President Jonathan who only in 2011 was a factor that unified all northern foes to fight a common battle against the south.

The Joint Task Force (JTF) comprising combat-ready soldiers and law enforcement agents that was formed to address the combat end of the confrontation now seems to have transformed into the Boko Haram movement itself. I was forced to swallow my words in a recent intellectual exchange with a group of Northerners from Maiduguri who I accused of being too sentimental for blaming the JTF for high-handedness. After all, the ordinary folks will not provide information on suspicious activities of terrorists in their neighborhood. The answer I got shocked me. These friends painted a picture of ordinary folks coerced into sympathizing with Boko Haram. They reported widespread rejection of the terror group after so much bloodshed. They intimated me with stories of families that have been eliminated shortly after they passed on information to the JTF, of Boko Haram activities in their neighborhood. Someone was reportedly shot after he had informed the JTF of a terror kingpin in his vicinity. This did not surprise me as a Southerner since we in the south also witness similar situations, in which the police is offered information on the whereabouts of robbers and kidnappers. At the end of the day, more ordinary folks are driven into the waiting hands of Boko Haram for safety and security since the JTF cannot be trusted.

What I found disturbing however is that no single information of this sort has ever found its way into popular Nigerian news outlets. Many consumers of information are largely unaware of this development. Indeed, the wanton elimination and destruction of entire neighborhoods after a Boko Haram attack has been launched from a single spot often lead people to question the motives of the JTF. While this can yet be attributed to the presence of bad eggs within the JTF, the next example proves to be even more mind-boggling.

The name Kabiru Sokoto is today, no longer a mystery to Nigerians. It is the name of an alleged Boko Haram unit leader who was arrested and reportedly escaped police custody in dubious circumstances. Investigations further revealed that a Police Commissioner named Zakari Biu played a major role in facilitating his escape on January 18, 2012. He was eventually recaptured on February 10, 2012 and remanded in custody. Today more than one year after his re-arrest, no single information is available on the progress of prosecution or his whereabouts. Grapevine gossips that we are unable to verify now contend however that Kabiru Sokoto has long been secretly airlifted out of Nigeria and now enjoys a peaceful life either in Dubai or Malaysia. While the rumoring of a serious information of this sort cannot be guaranteed to be true or false, it is the direct impact of the actions of a government that refuses to provide information to its people and clad itself in dubious secrecy.

Commissioner of Police Zakari Biu was arrested in the course of investigations and released 9 months later in November 2012, according to sources *"on the orders of President Jonathan"*. In an intricate web of political intrigues, the media implicated the then Police Boss Hafiz Ringim in the exposure of Zakari Biu for career convenience. Till the present moment, no further information was released on Zakari Biu and the extent of his involvement in Boko Haram. The investigation report on which basis President Jonathan ordered his release was never made public. It therefore beats the imagination, what the President knows, how much he has tolerated or is tolerating or indeed if the President is under some quiet coercion or promoting a different agenda altogether. Why was the release of a terror suspect ordered by a President and not by a judge?

In fact, one of my northern friends in this informal exchange took it one step further and opines that the political Boko Haram that sought to make Nigeria ungovernable for President Jonathan shortly after the presidential election of 2011 may have long fizzled out. In his belief, what we have today is most likely to be a stage-managed Boko Haram exploited by the government for undisclosed political reasons.

To support his point, he drew my attention to the case of the Boko Haram's self-styled spiritual leader Abubakar Shekau who was reportedly shot in crossfire during a routine checkpoint interception. While some members of his entourage were killed, he was said to have escaped with two other persons after sustaining gunshot wounds. My friend raises questions on the feasibility of a successful escape to Mali from such a hotspot given the countless number of JTF checkpoints on this route. In fact, he does not rule out the fact that Shekau may have been deliberately airlifted to safety. I had no answer to his question on how the Nigerian government suddenly discovered the whereabouts of Shekau in Mali and did not know where the man had been in Nigeria all the preceding months.

In the absence of a clear positioning of government with defined and easily comprehensible policies on matters of national importance, rumors and insinuations of this sort will continue to shape the beliefs and convictions of local folks. It is yet a mystery today, what strategy the government of President Jonathan is pursuing in combating Boko Haram with such mysterious shielding of several identified and hinted perpetrators. Above all else, the nation is never offered progress reports to address the fears and apprehensions of the citizens. In its stead, the President's spokesmen concentrate resources almost exclusively on the abuse, denigration, disparaging and discrediting of anyone who dares to criticize the administration.

Where will this lead the government in the public desire to know the real game being played behind the Boko Haram label?

Follow me on Twitter @FriskyLarrimore! Read my new book "Africa's Diabolical Entrapment"

***

The Boko Haram menace then got a stranglehold on the nation. It took an international dimension and several countries began to worry what the whole mess was all about. Nigeria lost respect and value internationally being a country that the West looked on to for muscling international order through the geographical sub-region. Military intervention in Sierra Leone and Liberia was a part of its regional antecedents. It was not uncommon to hear journalists from neighboring countries asking themselves in consternation, what the hell was going on. Many murmured *"We're talking about the Nigerian army for God's sake"* – an open reference to the seeming inability of Nigeria to crush the insurgent ragtag army.

Aside the government looking the other way as long as the insurgency didn't spill southwards, i.e. as long as the northern Muslims kept on killing themselves (as the incumbent President was widely thought to have believed), it began to surface that collaboration or at best, indifference, was playing out also at the administrative level. Former President Obasanjo reported authoritatively that the incumbent President believed that Boko Haram was "a device by the North, to prevent him from continuing as President"[3] Therefore, he did not accord Boko Haram the necessary seriousness. It was no longer a secret that weapons flowed very easily from the rudderless Libya across borders, but Nigeria shares no border with Libya for the ease of weapon-smuggling. Yet, heavy weaponry like tanks, assault rifles and in some instances anti-aircraft missiles were seen with the insurgents.

Boko Haram assaulted Nigerian army barracks with ease and took them out and trained regular soldiers often fled for their lives abandoning heavy weaponry. A part of the arsenal of the insurgents came from looting barracks and the other part from cross-border smuggling that were obviously facilitated by administrative staffs manning land, air and sea borders.

They were widely suspected to have been financed by Middle Eastern countries that were sympathetic to their religious cause. Fingers often pointed to Saudi Arabia and Iran without proof. Yet, Boko Haram attacked banks and devised other sources of financial enrichment. It was a huge problem that ruined the government's image abroad and foreign intelligence agencies were also aware of the lack of seriousness on the part of the government, to confront and eliminate the menace. The ensuing refusal of the government of the United States to sell heavy assault weapons to the government of President Goodluck Jonathan at the time, thus marked the climax of mistrust.

The President was mistrusted for pursuing a different agenda than the upkeep of Nigeria's unity. Yet, his desire to purchase attack helicopters from the USA, the refusal to sell same by the the government of President Barack Obama and the subsequent smuggling of cash into South Africa through the hired airplane of an Evangelical, for the purpose of buying weapons from the black market marked a new low in the reputation of the Nigerian government because the money was discovered and impounded.

The entire development prompted me nonetheless, to pen the following article:

Who is Misleading America on Boko Haram?

By Frisky Larr

Recent unconfirmed media reports claim that the United States of America is leaning towards an official policy position on the wave of terror attacks perpetrated on Northern Nigeria by the Boko Haram group. There seems to be a movement against the listing of Boko Haram as a terrorist organization. A group that has unleashed a reign of street terror on Nigeria never before experienced in the history of the country.

These unprecedented vicious acts, which introduced the hitherto unknown element of suicide bombing into the general psyche of the Nigerian Muslim community, has become an omnipresent plague exacerbating a prevailing sense of general insecurity in the country. It is an act that has catapulted the Nigerian Muslim community overnight, to a level of parity with the dominant Jihadist version of political Islamist movements in the Middle East!

Militant Islamists from Indonesia to the Abu Sayyaf movement of the Philippines undoubtedly derive their inspirations from the Middle East – the spiritual seat and birthplace of the Prophet Mohammed. In their activities spreading death and bloodshed, they have never been left in doubt by western governments on how they are viewed and rated. No world leader minces words explaining that assaults on people who go about their daily lives in accustomed routine expecting nothing unusual, cannot qualify for anything else but terrorism.

Christians wake up on a Sunday morning in northern Nigeria. They dress themselves up and proceed with a sense of piety. They move to the only place they expect to find some abstract respite and escape from the pressures of the entire working week. They proceed to the **Church** hoping to drown their worries generated by daily occurrences in prayers and nurture spiritual hopes for the unforeseeable future through songs of praise. They arrive at the altar feeling at their best in physical composure and emotional unison with the calling of their God most high. The same God that Muslims believe in! Then something happens. A loud deafening sound is heard in the midst of all the prayers, singing and dancing. Consciousness darkens out all of a sudden! Some come around minutes after grieving in severe pains after losing several body parts. They are told the number of deaths before they realize that the numbers are not mere numbers. They include their own children, father, mother, relatives, neighbors and friends. They try to figure out what has happened. They try to understand who would wish them dead. Then they are told they had been attacked by Boko Haram for no offence they can imagine.

The search for an answer to the questions raised by these deadly attacks has always produced conflicting answers. The prelude was clear. Northern Nigerians lost out in a power game that it had long controlled unperturbed. It did not disguise its anger over the monumental loss. Prominent sons of the land threatened that a political leader who takes over the helms of affairs and deny the region what it perceived as its legitimate right to the Presidency following the unexpected death of a Northern President, would inherit a land that will stay ungovernable. When the results were declared, bloodshed began in the form of social unrest killing several young university graduates stationed in the region for obligatory national service. Prominent sons of the North sounded a loud tone with their conspicuous silence. Silence that sounded like: *"there you go! We warned you!"*

Then slowly Boko Haram began its own reign of bloodshed. First, it was declared as vengeance on the killing of their leader in Police Custody in 2009. That was the year in which the group rose to nationwide prominence. They attacked government buildings and police stations without warning. No one knew what informed these attacks, but the media reported the meaning of the name of the organization: "Boko Haram."

Boko (perhaps an Hausa word) was said to stand for Western Education. Haram – a known Arabic word – means "Abomination". Western Education was therefore a forbidden act that broke all the taboos of the values they understood, and their value was religion.

We then understood that they were fighting a battle against the westernization of their religious values. Law enforcement waded in and tracked down their leader. In a bid to underscore the fundamental political ideology of secularism driving the multi-ethnic and multi-religious Nigeria, the young man was to be prosecuted. In a manner that **superficially compares** to the outright execution of an unarmed Osama Bin Laden, however, the Nigerian Police took the laws into its hands. The young man was summarily executed in custody. Calm followed for a year or two.

The tempestuous presidential elections of 2011 came and went. The threats made are now history. The immediate aftermath of those elections in which scores of innocent lives were killed is no longer news. But what informed the resurgence of attacks by Boko Haram against government buildings, Churches, Bars, Police stations, etc. after the 2011 presidential elections and all the threats by northern politicians still makes headline news.

Today, Nigeria has woken to the reality that it is fighting a limited war with a group of radicalized young minds. Self-imposed radical Islamic scholars! Nigeria has cried out to the world for assistance – logistical and psychological. Within Nigeria, there is a consensus on the nature of the battle being fought with the combined efforts of law enforcement and limited military logistics. Unfortunately, however, the world is still groping in the dark trying to find a definitive status to qualify the violence.

With logistical and psychological assistance from foreign countries, Nigerian intelligence was fed data confirming Boko Haram's link with Al-Qaeda in the Maghreb. After all, the sophistication in their modus operandi could not be lost on any observer. Hardware weaponry and improvised explosive devises were amazingly similar to the ones used in Iraq by the defunct group of Abu Moussaf Al-Zakarwi.

Of course,there were criminal gangs who also raided banks time and again and stacked away millions in hard currency. This explained a part of their source of funding. No honest observer could however deny having suspected that politicians – Northern politicians – played a prominent role in preparing this violent onslaught while admonitions were vehemently being dispersed during the elections of 2009.

As time went on though, these suspicions gained concrete credibility. Having gained foreign logistical support, the Nigerian security forces were now able to record isolated successes in making high-profile arrests. The first prominent politician in the person of Senator Muhammed Ali Ndume was pinned down in the aftermath of the confessions of a murderous top-notcher. One after the other, more high-profile leaders of the group were caught in the net of law enforcement in quick succession.

Only then did prominent politicians – Northern politicians – suddenly begin to speak out. Before then though, their conspicuous silence had spoken volumes. One could not help suspecting that the dragnet was closing in slowly on suspected politicians up north who have at best, hitherto enjoyed and rejoiced over the new security challenges that rendered Northern Nigeria almost ungovernable. None other than the President had cried out openly in frustration that agents of this group were spread through strategic organs of governance in the country including his own cabinet.

A visibly lame duck President offered an involuntary proof of his incapacitation by failing to name and shame to say the least of prosecuting (at least) those agents of Boko Haram in his cabinet. The nation had long expected him to wield the axe on those voluble men and the men behind them, who issued tangible threats in the run-up to the Presidential elections. The President failed across the board.

Prominent Northern politicians began to speak out, some of them – not unsurprisingly – calling for immediate negotiations. Meanwhile, calls for splitting the nation along the religious line once suggested by Muammar Ghadaffi were getting louder. One could not help sensing the fear amongst the Northern elites that they were about to lose everything that they thought they stood to gain while launching the bloody battle. Very few courageous ones voiced outright condemnation of the killing of innocent souls.

Then the Guru of northern intellectualism – the Governor of Nigeria's Central Bank Sanusi Lamido Sanusi – joined the fold. He added his voice to the controversy and declared economic deprivation, unemployment and marginalization as the underlying cause of the carnages on Christmas day, Easter Sunday, United Nations building etc. perpetrated by Boko Haram. Others blamed police brutality in the killing of Boko Haram's leader in 2009 as the cause of the reign of terror which included the bombing of Nigeria's Police Headquarters in Abuja in 2011 and several Churches. The intellectual Guru went a step further donating government money to Muslim victims in one Kano blast and subsequently sought to remedy the situation by also donating a meager sum to Christian victims only after a public outcry.

For well-meaning Nigerians though, there has been no mistaking the handwriting of terrorism on the wall. The Americans saw it too. Washington moved to designate Boko Haram as a terrorist group.

All of a sudden, some Nigerian political groups launched an intensive lobby in Washington to sell the idea that Boko Haram was not a terrorist group. In a shocking and most amazing development, Sanusi Lamido Sanusi's arguments found their way into Washington. *The poor young killer boys are marginalized and economically deprived! They are pitiably frustrated in the face of police brutality! Their innocent young leader who could not harm a fly was murdered in cold blood in police custody.*

Nigeria as a country ruled by northern Muslim leaders for a large part of its years since independence, has failed to toe the path of development across the board. No single region was spared. The north was not singled out for economic deprivation.

This makes it all the more shocking that Washington is reportedly convinced by these simplistic arguments. Ambassador Johnnie Carson, Deputy Secretary of State for Africa, is reported to be leading this drive for a policy position. He is reportedly most convinced by the submission that the killing of hundreds if not thousands of innocent Nigerians by Boko Haram is the result of economic deprivation suffered by frustrated youngsters. It does not matter that no single church frustrated them. It does not matter that economic frustration will always be found in the biography of almost every terror foot-soldier from Afghanistan through Iraq up until Syria.

Ambassador Carson seems to have bought into the idea that police brutality is one point to consider in the reaction of Boko Haram. I do not know if anyone would blame the American special squad for excess brutality in the killing of Osama Bin Laden who was not armed.

The crucial question then remains "who on earth is misleading the Americans?" Nigerians have their suspicion and they center on northern politicians. There are names suspected too! But more importantly, will the Americans be so naïve, stupid or collusive to buy into such shabby and unmistakably self-serving arguments in the interest of obvious forces? There is also no shortage of suspicions of American motives in managing political matters in Africa.

To further darken the murky waters of political confusion however Boko Haram has declared in a recent statement that its mission is the total Islamization of entire Nigeria. Just so much for Police brutality and economic deprivation!

***

All along, the government has complained that the strength of the insurgents derived from the support that they received from the Northern elites that were bent on undermining his government because he was a Southerner. That, though, could at best, be just half the complete truth. Arming the military with superior weaponry did not seem to have been a priority for the most part of Goodluck Jonathan's Presidency. Indeed, fighting and defeating Boko Haram didn't seem to have been a priority beyond lip service too. The swift territorial gains made against Boko Haram by Goodluck Jonathan's successor bear witness to the fact of what could have been achieved if there was a serious desire to defeat Boko Haram by Goodluck Jonathan. On the contrary, Boko Haram under President Jonathan gained territories with ease, occupied military barracks with ease, seized territories with ease and governed territories within the Republic unchallenged and even had its own operational headquarters.

Shelving all other potent reasons aside, the run-up to Presidential elections in 2015 was marred by presidential blames on Boko Haram and its "Northern facilitators" of old, as a major reason for the poor performance associated with his rule.

Now, read this article that was written sometime in 2014:

Is Boko Haram the True Cause of Jonathan's Dismal Performance as President?

By Frisky Larr

These days, there is one argument that is persistently heard when a section of Nigerians attempt to explain why the President of Nigeria Dr. Goodluck Ebele Jonathan is largely perceived as having under-performed during his four-year tenure that is running out in a few months. This negative perception is so aggravated in some quarters that some disgruntled sharp-tongued commentators simply rephrased his name in some social media outlets to read "Goodluck *Ebola JoNothing*" while a now deceased Facebook commentator of blessed memory once described him as "Emir El-*Retard*-een Jonathan". These abuses underscoring the frustration of several hobby commentators often end up amusing the President's opponents while it is generally taken with utmost contempt by his admirers, who cannot understand why people are taking the freedom of expression to the extent of ridiculing the country's own President.

These days, we hear the argument that hardly anyone could have done better than this President under the atmosphere of genocidal and coercive insurgency that the northern political elite has subjected the country to. It is indeed, no secret that some northern leaders, in the run-up to the last Presidential election in 2010, vowed to make Nigeria ungovernable if Dr. Goodluck Jonathan insisted on becoming President, while the northern tenure under the zoning arrangement was cut short by the untimely death of the former President.

In fact, the rapid pace at which events have happened within the tenure of this presidency renders the chronicling of events almost impossible. Yet a fairly alert mind should be able to reflect on some events that unfurled within the past three and a half years of Dr. Jonathan's Presidency.

It started on a very bad note when the President – in reaction to the deeply-rooted chaos in the Nigerian Football Federation (Nigeria's governing soccer body) that saw the national team end up with a shameful performance in South Africa 2010 – disbanded the national team, dissolved the Federation and suspended international outings for two years. FIFA raised its voice a few days later and the President chickened in immediately. He had not done his homework properly and did not consult with the proper experts for advice before hastily announcing actions beyond the reach of his powers against FIFA. Boko Haram had not yet thrown a single stone, not even from a catapult.

Shortly afterwards, signs began to emerge that Boko Haram was stepping up its campaign of violence by striking at soft targets and taking scores of innocent lives. If anything, these initial actions signaled the need to address the issue head-on and as a matter of utmost priority. The President reacted and took the matter very seriously. He plunged himself into the politics of reaching out to those, who he thought mattered most and distancing himself from those, who he thought mattered less. The choice was his and his alone. He appeased them with some power-sharing arrangements, when he thought the people mattered most and offered them and their cronies, lofty government appointments. In return, he was repeatedly assured that the menace will be over not later than six months into the future. He took it all with deep satisfaction and took to assuring Nigerians with dates, by which the menace of Boko Haram would be confined to the trash can of history.

In his confidence and complacency, he turned his attention to another front. Without the requisite deep-thought, analysis of pros and cons and the need to take the bull by the horn, he lied and had his ministers lie repeatedly to Nigerians that he had no plans to remove fuel subsidy. Then on January 01, 2012 he gave Nigerians the demonic New Year's gift of subsidy removal against all wise warnings of risking a revolution if he did. The President unwittingly responded that he was ready for a revolution. He was not taken hostage by Boko Haram at the time. Inspired by the widely reported Arab Spring, traditionally fearful Nigerians took to the streets and the President escaped a full-scale revolution by the whiskers at the cost of a few innocent lives.

In the meantime, Boko Haram's insurgency was turning nasty and showing early signs of insurgent sophistication. His predecessor and mentor Olusegun Obasanjo offered himself for mediation – a task none of those people he appeased took upon themselves. He ended up ridiculing the former President and having his paid agents rain abuses on the old man with jeers and scorns. The choice was his.

Flashback to the subsidy protest: The nationwide uproar beamed the flashlight on the filth in the oil sector and all its attendant evils. The intelligent option of creating self-sufficiency in refining crude oil and discontinuing the regime of importing refined fuel was the final settlement that killed the nationwide semi-revolution. Investments were to be made in fixing old refineries and building new ones. A memorandum of understanding was even reached with Chinese engineering companies at the initial stage. We had no report that resources had to be withdrawn from the project to facilitate the fight against Boko Haram. No. Yet, the whole project died a quiet death while the regime of fuel importation continues unabated to the benefit of corrupt importers, who no one dares to question. Not because Boko Haram stops anyone at gunpoint! The President is simply held hostage by the corrupt power of the capital.

The speed at which the sins of people are exposed, who try to expose the scale of thievery in the oil sector underscores the excellence of President Jonathan's government when he chooses to expose thieves. Half of the energy invested in nabbing the lawmaker Farouk Lawan's acceptance of bribe to kill a part of his investigations on subsidy thieves was never invested in catching any of the oil thieves indicted. Yet Boko Haram did not incite this ineptitude. The mole planted in Ribadu's committee was never planted in any NNPC body to track corrupt officers.

Bursting the Nigerian Governors' Forum with undemocratic means had nothing to do with Boko Haram. Having the President's wife meddle in the politics of Rivers State and attempting to have 5 lawmakers rule over 27 others in the Rivers State House of Assembly had nothing to do with Boko Haram.

The President's only flagship project of success – the reactivation of the railway line from Lagos to Kano – was not disrupted by Boko Haram even though Kano is at the heart of Boko Haram's operation. Yet Boko Haram is blamed for making governance difficult for the President? Boko Haram did not force the President to grant a national pardon to former Governor Alamieyesigha, who has been officially adjudged corrupt and declared an international fugitive. Today this former Governor wields far more political influence in Jonathan's Nigeria than the cleanest of all public figures. Boko Haram did not incite the President to make lords of militant touts in the Niger Delta nor has Boko Haram stopped the arrest and public prosecution of powerful brains behind illegal oil refineries all over the Niger Delta region. Even Co-President Asari Dokubo declares openly that President Jonathan will "not dare" (repeat: "not dare") to refuse running for re-election. *"Else he can't come back home na! E no fit!"* No single comment was issued by the President to rebuke the young, exuberant slime ball. Did Boko Haram ask the President to grant that much power to a thug?

The Niger Delta insurgency did not stop Olusegun Obasanjo from negotiating away Nigeria's foreign debt. It did not stop him from pushing through with GSM, with NAFDAC and the installation of the EFCC even if its operations were more one-sided than otherwise. It did not stop him from building 6 power stations that would have been operational today if he had more time at his disposal. And I am not alone in the belief that an Obasanjo third term would have done Nigeria far more good than this disastrous Jonathan term has done. Obasanjo did not submit to militants who undermine him publicly like Asari Dokubo does Jonathan today. Obasanjo confronted as many powerful forces as he could, and they joined hands to give him a fight. Without prejudice to those areas in which President Obasanjo also had his failures, these powers it were, that successfully carved out the perpetual evil image for the old man with which many people associate him today in a convenient bandwagon effect.

On the contrary, President Jonathan shied away from confronting any force that is opposed to the interest of the state except those that challenge his personal ambitions. Today, his apologists are unfortunately in a desperate search of a scapegoat for the resultant dismal failure. First it was Boko Haram. But we know today that the President did not take on the background forces to nip the tragedy in the bud and tolerated if not partially participated in propping up a version of Boko Haram. Now, they blame the Americans for failing to sell weapons to defeat Boko Haram. We now know however that the Americans only refused to sell attack helicopters that can easily be bought from Russia and scores of other sources.

Now, they are engaged in shadow-boxing over political defections. But high-level defection from one party to the other is nothing new in the Nigerian democratic tradition. The overriding precedent case played out in 2007 when the Supreme Court of Nigeria validated the defection of a sitting Vice President from the ruling party to an opposing party. I am one of many Nigerians who thought – in the face of logical considerations at the time – that the Supreme Court Judges may have either been standing too tall on the high grade of intoxication or were simply drowned in their conspiracy to teach the overbearing Olusegun Obasanjo a very serious lesson. Whichever way it was, they did a serious disservice to the nascent democracy that is now hanging on the system as an albatross. The logic was simple. If for any reason then, Olusegun Obasanjo died as President, his Vice President, who was elected with and handpicked by him as a candidate of the PDP, would automatically have become the new President from another party, whose program the electorates knew nothing about and did not vote for. It was the second highest office in the land.

The lesson there was clear. Whether or not, the judgment was passed under the influence of intoxicants or emotions, and no matter how wrong the judgment was, it had definitely been passed and cannot be overturned. It is the law of the land until the constitution is explicitly amended to reflect another unmistakable reality. It, therefore, goes that the fact of being elected on the platform of one party should and does not automatically translate into the loss of an office upon defection to another party. It was the case with Governor Isa Yuguda, who defected from the ANPP to the PDP, Olusegun Mimiko, who defected from the Labor Party to the PDP, Governor Rochas Okorocha, who defected from APGA to the APC as well as Governor Rotimi Amaechi, who left the PDP for the APC.

I therefore wonder aloud, why President Jonathan simply refuses to accept his fate in the spirit of political sportsmanship each time a leading politician defects from his party even in these dying minutes of his presidency. The futile persecution of Governor Rotimi Amaechi does not seem to have shown the President the limits of his impunity. The same scenario is now being replayed against Aminu Tambuwal, Speaker of the House of Representatives. The botched amateurism of the Rivers State House of Assembly ended in dangerous bloodshed. It did not teach Jonathan any lesson. He sought to trick the House of Representative to re-convene under the guise of extending some worthless state of emergency only to attempt to stage-manage the impeachment of the Speaker. Now that this too has failed, efforts are said to be underway to arrest the speaker. I will dare to ask how Boko Haram has influenced this show of impunity which shows the President as constantly being petty, unintelligent and often failing to do the right thing at the right time.

But Nigeria will never be the colossal failure that it is today, if people do not routinely set the wrong agenda and priority every step of the way. Today, rather than focusing on the illegal and impuned invasion of the premises of the House of Representatives by armed policemen who would jump into the bush for safety at the shout of armed robbers, and soldiers who run away from Boko Haram, Nigerians are hurling stones at lawmakers who scaled the fence to frustrate the planned second illegality of impeachment. This should ordinarily have been a point, at which the fact of the Nigerian legislature being populated by celebrated and high-profile thugs ought to have occupied the back seat in the face of the more urgent issue of presidential impunity.

The threat by the opposition APC to form a parallel government if the presidential election is rigged is now the cry of brutal defiance by an opposition that smells a rat in the President's extreme desperation to retain the presidency. The recipe is clear. Insurgency is already on course in the north. A brutally aggrieved opposition will render escalation an easy task. The Niger Deltans – I assume – are ready as well. Obasanjo once cried out and warned of an army being built by the President with an arsenal of lethal weapons. Is 2015 the watershed to ending the amalgamation?

Of course, Nigeria is made what it is today with the immense help of hungry and willfully collaborative praise-singers, who give incompetent politicians like President Jonathan the leverage that they need to survive and drain the stability of national interests. After all, these are the same people who conjure the fairy tale of grand performance by the President that no one else sees but they alone! It simply remains to be seen where Jonathan thinks he will be taking Nigeria and how he will end as a person and page in the history of a now dejected Nigeria.

⁂

Yet, one major problem that Nigeria has always faced through several years of its political history since independence from colonialism, has been the concept of tribalism. As a resident evil of fusing several local tribes into one nation depending on the economic interest of the colonial master at time, Nigeria was made to house an estimated 250 ethnic groups of completely different cultural, traditional and structural orientation. Being tribes that historically fought one another for territorial expansion and leadership before the coming of colonial intruders, the emergence of political tension among the regions became a natural hallmark of existence in Nigeria as it was in every other identical post-colonial African country.

In post-independence Nigeria, political leadership was dominated by the North by virtue of its dominance of the Army, which often led coups to overthrow civilian and military governments. Leadership of the country by a Southerner was – till the present moment – always by accident than by design. The Southerner, Olusegun Obasanjo, ruled Nigeria as a military General simply because his boss was killed in a coup d'etat and he was next in line by rank. He was fielded as a Presidential candidate in 1999 after the return to civilian rule because the presumed winner of an annulled election that led to civil strife a few years earlier, was a Southerner and a person like Obasanjo, who had been tried and tested in the art of remote-controlled leadership was acceptable to the Northern elite. Since his re-emergence as a Southerner would pacify frail nerves being from the same ethnic group as the deceased fellow, who was denied the Presidency, the establishment believed it had killed two birds with just one stone. As for the Southern President Jonathan, he too was elevated to the podium because his boss died while President and he was next in line as Vice President.

The problem of tribalism or regionalism persisted and was even more intense under President Jonathan. It nearly cost him his constitutional entitlement to the office because the North believed it was been tricked out of it's rotational tenure. Tribalism or Regionalism was also believed to have played a role in the propping up of Boko Haram as a pressuring weapon of choice in the hands of the northern elite until it got out of their control.

It prompted me to write the following:

Can a Northerner ever be Detribalized in Nigeria?

By Frisky Larr

Let's face it. In the present dispensation, northern Nigeria has produced three brilliant Nigerians of the younger generation, on which Nigerians may build their hope for a better tomorrow. You may have guessed right if your mindset works like mine. To be precise though, my mind is set on Nuhu Ribadu, Nasir El-Rufai and Sanusi Lamido Sanusi. Many may disagree instinctively, but my point will be better understood when this submission is read to the end. As opposed to these three individuals, southern Nigeria currently has just Ngozi Okonjo-Iweala to boast of. In terms of focus and outstanding performance however, we will mention Babatunde Fashola. Unfortunately, though, Fashola is not the radical crusader that is created to fight evil. On the contrary, he is more the invisible crusader serving his people quietly and working for the good of his constituency.

For this reason, Babatunde Fashola – not being a rough fighter and an eccentrically voluble self-promoter like Adam Oshiomole – may have a hell of a time managing a Federal government in Aso Rock. I may be right, and I may be wrong in my speculations. But something tells me that Babatunde Fashola is the type that will serve Nigeria best in a position similar to Okonjo-Iweala's. An informal and imperial Prime Minister exercising her powers quietly but decisively. This is absolutely without prejudice to other superior qualities and qualifications that Okonjo-Iweala no doubt has. She has shown during the fuel subsidy crisis that she can also fight back if she is wrongly put in a pillory. She is not afraid of confrontation. On the contrary, Babatunde Fashola comes across as a man who is most comfortable operating smoothly away from the gaze of shine and glamour.

Comparing this attribute to the imposing characters of the three northern musketeers of our present dispensation, it will be easier to understand the point I wish to make. As the Jonathan example is presently showing, quietness and shyness from the limelight seem poisonous for the office of the President of Nigeria. Even worse is the lack of guts to take on rich and powerful exploiters to protect the interest of the nation even if it means ruining one's own political career. This fear of confrontation and preference for backstage dealings to foster business as usual is one character that Fashola seems to share with President Jonathan. The much-publicized dispute between Fashola and Bola Tinubu in the run-up to the last general elections and the manner in which the issue was resolved quietly in the aftermath of obvious horse-trading seems to show Fashola's glaring lack of appetite for confrontation. Confrontation however is an indispensable variable in the office of President.

On the contrary, we can all imagine how many rich and powerful exploiters will wet their pants in fear and panic if Nuhu Ribadu was suddenly picked to become President of Nigeria today. The Aondoaakas who subverted justice and probably enriched themselves illegally may run to exile overnight in the speed of Hussain Bolt. I do not know where High Court Justices like Marcel Awokunleyin who gave James Ibori a clean bill of health would choose to hide. Panic will definitely greet the rank and file of the powerful and stealing community. James Ibori tried to dare the fangs of President Jonathan but had to bolt helter-skelter when even Jonathan showed his teeth to fight his personal enemy the way he fought Timipre Sylva. Unfortunately, the same Jonathan will never fight the enemies of the State. That is the impression Nigerians have of the President at the present moment.

Imagine Nasir El-Rufai being called upon today, to take the reins of leadership in Aso Rock and figure out how many enemies of the Nigerian State will go on self-imposed exile. Imagine Sanusi Lamido Sanusi mounting the imperial throne that he no doubt, would personally crave and figure out how many people will bolt.

Now, my motive in this essay is not to assess the overall suitability of these three northern musketeers for the office of President but to highlight the boldness and courage that these men undoubtedly have in the things they do much unlike Goodluck Jonathan the President of the nation. They have shown it abundantly in the discharge of their duties. Coincidentally, boldness and courage are two key attributes that any President of Nigeria needs. Olusegun Obasanjo showed Nigerians how necessary these attributes are and Goodluck Jonathan is confirming it daily by forcing Nigerians to miss precisely these essential attributes of the Obasanjo days.

Northern Nigeria blessed us with these three young patriotic men and I have no doubt that every Nigerian will agree with me that these three musketeers are patriotic to the bone. They are all well read, intelligent and intellectual in their different capacities. The most outstanding quality that they all have in common however, is their love for their country! You heard me right "Their country"!

Even though they all share Nigeria with us all, questions abound as a matter of compulsion if these three outstanding northerners of our present-day love Nigeria as we all know it - Nigeria from North to South! I am deliberately refusing to include leading northerners of the older generation such as Ibrahim Babangida, Shehu Shagari, Umaru Dikko, Adamu Ciroma, Muhammadu Buhari or Abdulsalami Abubakar in this analysis. They are the known leaders of yesterday who laid the groundwork for the troubles of today - selfishly and inadvertently. We have therefore cried out loud for generational change and Obasanjo ushered it in – wittingly or unwittingly.

While many southerners of the younger generation excelled in thievery (see Lucky Igbinedion and James Ibori) Nasir El-Rufai and Nuhu Ribadu worked themselves into the hearts and minds of discerning observers. I personally became a die-hard fan of Nuhu Ribadu. Indeed, words could not describe how I felt when I heard that the ACN had nominated him for the presidential race in 2011. I mobilized very close and intelligent friends in my German abode and we all agreed to watch the situation very closely. We were ready to launch a vocal movement for Ribadu if we were sure that the game was genuine. We were very soon disillusioned when Nuhu Ribadu ran a very poorly managed campaign with what we considered to be a very inferior mode of strategizing. Nuhu Ribadu began to flirt with the self-declared committee of northern elders led by the infamous Adamu Ciroma. He was virtually begging to be named the northern consensus candidate after the demise of Abubakar Atiku. His focus was the north.

Sanusi Lamido Sanusi who has spoken himself into the hearts and minds of Nigerians, who love any semblance of intelligence, emerged from nowhere thanks to the late Umaru Musa Yar'Adua. Many of us opposed his appointment as Governor of the Central Bank when it was obvious that the late President was running a strategic course of northernizing leadership in Nigeria. We all began to have a rethink however as soon as we heard the man speak English. It sounds too simplistic and stupid, but it is the plain truth. He didn't only speak sound and clear English, he was also talking a whole lot of sense. We all became proud of him particularly when he courageously voiced out long overdue concerns about the legislative looting of Nigeria's treasury. He didn't care that he could lose his job. That was courageous.

Nasir El-Rufai stepped on toes as the Special Minister of the Capital territory. Till today he is paying the price for those patriotic deeds in an ungrateful society. He was courageous.

Unfortunately, however, the mere mention of the word "North" is enough to mark the end of courage, patriotism and neutrality for our three northern musketeers. In a manner symbolic and perhaps characteristic of a seemingly pervasive northern psyche, none of the three has the will or courage to mention some objective and courageous home truths when it comes to the north. Till the present day, I am yet to hear a single northern Nigerian with political leadership function coming out openly to show a little understanding for the complaints and suspicions of the south.

While the Northerners are absolutely correct in condemning the behavior of the ruling PDP in flouting its own zoning regulation to smuggle Goodluck Jonathan into the presidency, no single northerner has ever flipped the coin to see or even try to understand the other side of the debate. While the propaganda machine of the north makes haste to tell the Americans that the Boko Haram killers are no terrorists but merely economically deprived bunch of innocent young lads, no single northerner summons the courage to shout out loud and clear that northern leaders who ruled this country for almost three-quarter of the years since independence are responsible for the marginalization that a southern President should tolerate bombings for.

Neither Nuhu Ribadu nor El-Rufai stood up for one single day to say *"Come to think of it northern siblings, to some extent, I can understand the south."* The axiomatic and inevitable reality that the south will get up one day and say *"Come on buddy, we also have a right to rule this country"* was not factored into any intellectual reasoning whatsoever. The simple need to appreciate this basic fact before proceeding to pillory the PDP for flouting its own zoning policy was simply lost on the north in a collective and seemingly conspiratorial manner. This single courageous move alone would have made Nuhu Ribadu an immortal creature whose de-tribalized spirit would have hovered visibly above any serving presidential material until he is moved onto the throne of supremacy alive or as an unsung hero in the future history of the country.

While El-Rufai is busy blowing the trumpet of negotiations with Boko Haram, Sanusi Lamido is leaving no one in doubt that his constituency is first and foremost, northern Nigeria. I, therefore, ask myself a few crucial questions: "Will there ever be a de-tribalized northern Nigerian in this country to look across the borders of the northern states?" "Do northern leaders not have an obligation to pacify the rest of the country and chart a new peaceful path forward?" "Is Nigeria not for us all or is there a separate country for the Northerners?" "Are northern Nigerians truly immersed in the illusion that Nigeria is theirs to rule and theirs alone?"

If the realization dawns on our northern brothers and sisters that they have ruled this country for such a long period of time and are therefore largely responsible for most of the fundamental problems that we suffer, will they not understand that they owe a duty to restore peace and pacify the rest of the country rather than rejoicing quietly over Boko Haram's atrocities? There is indeed nothing wrong in adopting the enticing carrot approach to convince justifiably aggrieved southerners to sheath their sword and let Nigeria begin afresh. Instead, the northerners are aggressively beating the drums of war in a battle that no one stands to win but will ultimately end in the destruction of a promising Nigeria. It is so unfortunate that the foremost elites prefer to play the religious card to win the hearts and minds of ordinary northerners knowing fully well that the spread of Islam by the force of arms is absolutely impossible in today's world order of aggressive globalization.

***

In spite of all that, the tenure of President Goodluck Jonathan fell victim, largely to his personal incompetence and insufficiency as a leader. It was a regime that was largely devoted to compensating major political friends for their sacrifices in facilitating the Presidency than daring to take on the powerhouses that crippled the progress of the country. The regime devised a means of flooding the social media with foot soldiers, who engaged every critical entreaty with aggressive defenses. The praise-singing rhetoric that characterized the activities of these foot soldiers marked the regime's flagship drive to foster a positive public relations coup through every channel possible. Yet, the regime lacked seriously in achievements in the overall interest of the nation. On the contrary, signals came through on occasions that the government secretly nursed the hope of disintegrating the country into several independent entities in spite of vocal pronouncements to the contrary. The President was unmistakably torn between several advisory factions, which ordinarily, is a normal trait of a Presidency. Yet, this routine element of governance turned out to have overwhelmed President Jonathan. He often sounded confused in the grip of the faction that prevailed at any point in time.

The next article addressed the general ills:

Is Nigeria Drifting Uncontrolled Under President Jonathan?

Given the facts and figures available to the beholder, this question should ordinarily pose no match to the intelligent mind probing for an answer. Yet, the natural instinct of the average Nigerian that is configured to serve the cause of private and strategic interests often makes it difficult these days, to find even the simplest and most obvious answer to a very simple question. In the midst of incomprehensible polarization and subjective sympathies devoid of rational appraisal, it will be difficult in today's Nigeria to find common grounds even on the question if "Satan was truly evil or was maliciously painted black by God".

Judging by comments and analyses made by reputable international economic pundits and institutions, Nigeria's economy is growing impressively and performing adequately well to fuel optimism for a brighter future. In fact, nothing short of this judgment would have been expected of an economy managed by a powerful name like Ngozi Okonjo-Iweala. Unfortunately, however, the layman, the domestic consumer and millions of unemployed graduates in Nigeria express legitimate bewilderment at such claims in the face of indices and realities that glaringly contradict any semblance of economic progress.

News report at the end of the year 2013, unveiled a steady decline of the Nigerian Foreign Exchange Reserves to $39 billion from its peak of $48.85 billion in May 2013. In fact, records show that the sum of $1.33 billion was lost from this reserve in just one month (between August and September 2013). The Excess Crude Account in which the difference between the benchmark oil price and real market price is saved after sales stood at a peak of $10 billion at the start of the year 2013. Latest records however show that this account has been badly plundered down to $2.5 billion as at December 2013. Meanwhile, the foreign debt status that was zeroed down under Olusegun Obasanjo's government rose by 19.36% from $6.92 billion to $8.26 as at September 2013. It will surprise no one if the $10 billion limit is hit again as we discuss our problems in March 2014. Youth unemployment rate stood at 54% according to the latest figures for 2012 with prospects of a drastic rise in the run up to 2014.

Amid all these bleak and gruesome messages stands an upcoming highly contentious presidential election period in 2015. These badly depleted resources, which translate into the tragic reality of less money to share between the states, less money to spend on public infrastructural projects and difficulties in the payment of salaries and wages to public officers are rendering the government cash-strapped while the barrel prices of crude oil have enjoyed an all-time high in recent years and months. Yet, it is the proceeds from this single product that the central government relies on to finance the reelection ambitions of a President, who does not "give a damn" about the word he had given as long as there are Nigerians who will encourage such uncouth political behavior on the pretext of constitutional legitimacy.

In fact, talking about the gains realized from high oil prices, none less than Ngozi Okonjo-Iweala cried out recently: *"2014 will be challenging because of the elections. If we don't make it tight, **the elections will unravel all the macroeconomic stability we have achieved so far.**"* After all: *"The oil benchmark proposal is $74 per barrel. We want the National Assembly to push it to $76.5. We did $79 last year."*

In other words, the Nigerian economy cannot afford to finance the electoral machine of the ruling party. It is of extreme importance that the Coordinating Minister of the Economy and Finance cried out in this tone because she has lately been in the eye of the storm for her perceived transformation from Technocrat to benefit-seeking Politician. The fears that she expressed in these words are not a far-cry from the alarm raised by the suspended Governor of Nigeria's Central Bank Sanusi Lamido Sanusi.

Without prejudice to the accusations of financial recklessness and maladministration levied against the suspended Governor, which he – by the way – has debunked to the satisfaction of a huge number of non-Aso Rock affiliates, the notion that his revelation (claiming that oil proceeds are being habitually stolen) would have the ultimate consequence of robbing the ruling party of a vital source of financing electoral campaigns, is widely believed by many Nigerians. In the end, he was hastily suspended from office in defiance of strongly suspected misuse of constitutional powers by the President.

The absence of the same haste in clamping down on oil sector thievery since 2012 when the last wake-up call was sounded on the government by massive civil resistance, now raises questions on which direction Nigeria is heading. If anything, corruption in the oil sector has grown with impunity rather than diminishing. Cash-in-hand in the aftermath of the partial withdrawal of oil subsidy has dropped rather than increasing and the fall back on reserves and Excess Crude Account to augment public spending testifies to this. There is hardly any report of refurbished local refineries or newly built ones since 2012 as promised, nor is there any report of the prudent implementation of the subsidy reinvestment program (SURE-P). Now the audacious move to finally eliminate residues of subsidy is making the round again and Nigerians now seem fed up and may finally accept the total removal with the impending risk of loading the final straw that may break the camel's back.

While the anti-corruption agency EFCC is being openly scuttled and underfunded, actions like the Presidential pardon for an internationally acclaimed economic and financial felon in the person of Diepriye Alamieyeseigha are comfortably perpetrated without any care in the world. Facing no pressure of any sort in a move that many consider a ploy to intimidate political opponents of his reelection ambition, the President suddenly convened a National Conference allegedly to discuss the future of the country without compromising the unity of just that same Nigeria.

Worse still, the so-called delegates to the National Conference (numbering a total of 492) that are each rewarded with the whopping sum of Naira 12 million (approximately EUR 60,000.00) for the three months of deliberation are largely drawn from among friends of the establishment and their family members. It has so far been one of the government's closely guarded secrets, where the allocation for this payment will be drawn from.

Today, many forces have quietly designed strategies to hijack the National Conference from the President and alienate its outcome from the very objectives that the President has publicly propagated. In the end, the stage is set for yet another roof bearing a huge potential of collapsing on the President's head.

One can hardly help these days but compare the current leadership in Nigeria to a pitiable and helpless individual that is cursed with the gift of courting troubles when it least requires one.

The Nigerian military now witnessing strategic weakening through a combination of factors that includes corruption, is fighting a huge battle to contain misguided religious insurgency in Northern Nigeria – a battle that is yet anything else but won! On the flipside of constant strategic reformations of the military in processes that have seen the weeding out of experienced Generals and high-ranking officers to avoid *coups d'etat*, reports are reflecting a decimation of discipline and combat motivation. No doubt, the same military in its present state is making tremendous progress in fending off the consolidation of insurgency into a nationwide network. Reports however show that it works successfully in planning strategies and taking the enemy by surprise and recording enormous successes. Yet the same military will reportedly abandon defense posts and checkpoints when alerted of impending attacks by insurgents, it will refuse to appear for direct combat when insurgents attack helpless soft spots for hours unending and will require hours to repel attacks when they are taken to its barracks often with treacherous inside information.

This is a pattern that Nigerians have actually grown accustomed to by the Police Force. Reports often show under-equipped and poorly trained policemen removing uniforms to blend in with civilians, when insurgents attack their stations. That the Nigerian Police often shies away from appearing at scenes of robbery operations to take on robbery gangs in direct combat is no secret much like they are known to arrive at such scenes wielding heavy armory to intimidate civilians only after it is safely known that the robbers had long finished their operation of several hours and left the scene. If this mentality now moves to the military as reports seem to be suggesting, it will be a huge cause for alarm over the bigger picture of national security.

The dangerous drift in the country is further compounded by other social vices. Today, employment seems purchased rather than simply applied for. It has been pathetic enough that corruption and nepotism have always played a major role in securing gainful employment. It is now even more disastrous that hapless and poor job-seekers have to pay for forms, medicals and the like before being considered for employment interview in the first place. The employment process has now turned into a major source of internally-generated revenue (IGR) for government agencies. The natural result manifested recently in the death of innocent Nigerians when the Nigerian Immigration Service sought to conduct the shortlisting of employment candidates in stadia nationwide out of over 2 million applicants for just 5,000 jobs. Yet this does not preclude the phase of bribery after shortlisting. Mind you, we are talking of unemployed individuals with no source of income.

Then there is this issue of a Pastor-turn-Presidential Adviser on New Media. A Pastor that is expected to cover high moral grounds in matters of national unity! Yet Reno Omokri was reportedly caught recently in a willful campaign of calumny to smear a public figure-turn-enemy of the President in a dirty trick of sort. Till the present moment, Pastor Omokri's boss is maintaining sealed lips over this highly disturbing conduct much like he did in his frantic efforts to retain erring Minister Stella Oduah in the wake of her armored car scandal.

Steady progress on infrastructure and the wellbeing of Nigerians is echoed these days by government and given a beautiful face on paper and political rhetoric. The reality however, unmistakably shows a nation that is drifting uncontrolled in search of a quick redeeming action.

***

In all of these, the media led the polarization of the general populace. The once vibrant fourth estate that kept the government on its toes during the days of former President Olusegun Obasanjo simply turned out to be an empty bubble that was blown away in no time. The political interest of entrepreneurial proprietors dictated the direction and leanings of the various media outlets.

Occasional press briefings were held by the President in which he often ended up triggering consternation and head-shaking among viewers and listeners either for his poor use of language or the quality of messages he sent. On one occasion, the President was asked his reasons for seeking to run for a second term and he shocked viewers and listeners with his serious use of a very colloquial phrase in the Nigerian Pidgin English that is never expected in serious conversations let alone from a President. He said *"Nigerians will feel one kain"* if he failed to run. There was also an instance, in which he chastised Nigerians in a nationwide televised meet-the-press outing, for equating "common stealing" with corruption.

In the run-up to the presidential election that ousted him in 2015, he also met the press sometime in May 2014. After this session, one of his interviewers, a known Journalist called Jide Ajani, made his impressions public in writing in an article titled *"Goodluck Jonathan: A President in Need of Help!"*. In it, he addressed the weaknesses of the President and what he thought were the underlying facts.

That prompted my reaction in the following article:

A President and Journalists in Need of Urgent Help!

By Frisky Larr

Jide Ajani's article *"Goodluck Jonathan: A President in need of help!"* [4] was first published in Sunday Vanguard of May 11, 2014. It is a must-read. It is a daring exposé in clear deviation from the contemporary norms defining the state or plight of journalism in today's Nigeria. I find it an interesting masterpiece that is worth the follow-up it received in a Nigerian radio talkshow one week after. I will return to this issue later.

The reason I find this article exceedingly interesting is not because it said anything that no one else had said before in several strings of citizen journalism on blogsites and social media platforms. No. I find it interesting because it seems to signal a cautious break from the deafening collaborative silence of mainstream Nigerian media with the steady demise of all the opening gains made at the nascent stage of the current democratic experiment. There is simply no regular columnist in Nigeria's mainstream newspapers or presenters of programs on popular radio and television stations, who stand out today for being blunt on the steady collapse that Nigeria has witnessed at home and abroad under the incompetent leadership of President Goodluck Jonathan.

Whoever observed the bubbles and liveliness radiated by the Nigerian media during the second term of former President Olusegun Obasanjo will be forgiven for mistaking the Nigerian media of today since 2007 when Olusegun Obasanjo handed over power to Umaru Musa Yar'Adua, for a media training ground where aspirants are having some trial internship for the real thing that observers expected. After all, the dominant trait of a vibrant system is the insignificance of individual characters and the importance of the whole. Prolific denominators emerge with the speed of light and the disappearance of any individual character is hardly ever noticed in the scheme of things.

Where then today, are those media operatives, who wrote the entertaining serial stuff of a "Gbolekaja" president dancing naked in Public Square with all the despicable abuses and vilification that cared little about the sanctity of the office they disparaged? Where are those writers who wrote eloquent narratives of dreams and fantasies demonizing a President for daring to dream of a third term in office when the reality of today has now taught us better than we knew then? Jide Ajani had a view on this and I will address it further down this essay.

It will not help us any further now to look back at the days of Tai Solarin, who was not cowed by the forces of the barrel in a military dispensation. It will not help us now to shed tears over the demise of Dele Giwa or Gani Fawehimi, each of whom we would have all successfully abused and denigrated with varying adjectives if they were still alive today, to tell the tale as it is in all bluntness.

In a nutshell, the hope that the departure of Olusegun Obasanjo in 2007 aroused in the dawn of a new era of political accountability to be spearheaded by the Nigerian media quickly faded away when the media instinctively stayed dumb and watched Umaru Musa Yar'Adua dismantle one Obasanjo policy after the other without any viable replacement. The drawing back of the hand of the clock was also applauded even when it meant the celebration of a criminal James Ibori as the de-facto Vice President and the fight against corruption grinding to a halt. The vindictive tenor amongst media operatives was "serves Obasanjo right". This rapid drift by the media from the role of the aggressive gatekeeper to that of a collaborator-in-chief and unprofessional role model for future media aspirants drove me to write my first book "Nigeria's Journalistic Militantism". Unfortunately, this tradition has continued and has even been consolidated in the present dispensation.

What we now have is the celebration of Jide Ajani almost as a hero for expressing cautious discontent in words that were very carefully chosen. A far cry from the abuses that Olusegun Obasanjo suffered in the hands of Reuben Abati, Okey Ndibe, Simon Kolawole and also Jide Ajani himself. It didn't matter to any of them at the time that the office of President was sacred, and that Olusegun Obasanjo would come and go. Except for Reuben Abati, it is compelling to ask today where all these prolific writers have forgotten their poisonous stinger voices in full glare of Jonathan's destruction of anything left of political and diplomatic sanity.

Under the skilful pressure exerted by the radio host Jimi Disu (one week after the publication of Jide Ajani's article) to come clean on his obvious but poorly disguised critical view on the present administration, Jide Ajani shifted once again to the comfort zone of laying the blame of today's political problems on the one punching bag that is safe to hit – Olusegun Obasanjo! On the face of it, his reasons sounded plausible. But in truth to fairness, here are the naked facts:

It is no secret that Olusegun Obasanjo had to step on toes very brutally and recklessly to wrest power from the northern oligarchs that installed him in the Presidency. Else, there would have been no such opportunity like the badly misused Jonathan Presidency today. It is no secret that President Obasanjo fought people he did not like and those that offended him using their corrupt practices against them. It is also true that such people were very bitter seeing people who were friends with the former President getting away with the same corruption that he crucified his enemies for. In other words, corruption under Olusegun Obasanjo was not a free-for-all act for friends and foes unlike today where even enemies of today's President were virtually pacified in the hope that they would help bring Boko Haram to a quiet end and enhance a second term.

In the end, the corporate interests that President Obasanjo decimated and rendered irrelevant were indeed powerful forces in the political, judicial, economic, military and media sector. Bola Tinubu, James Ibori, Orji Uzor Kalu etc. were names in the media sector with corporate policies. Funny and illegal court judgments for vindictiveness were no rarity. Military pensioners training Niger Delta militants that were financed by economic powers featured on contemporary agenda. When finally, Vice President Atiku Abubakar seized the moment to rebel against the President and advance his political ambition, a non-palatable salad of political opposition was conjured to rally behind the Vice President. No one really liked him. No one really wanted him to succeed President Obasanjo but the "enemy of my enemy" was an automatic friend until the enemy is defeated.

Indeed, while many fought the battle supposedly rallying behind Abubakar Atiku, a strong majority did not wish to have this Atiku-type of insubordination setting an example for the future democratic tradition. Even a frontline hater and critic of Obasanjo - Simon Kolawole - acknowledged at the time, that a Southern Vice President would not have dared so much insubordination against a Northern President as Atiku did against Obasanjo. The field of presidential candidates in 2007 had characters that all sought to devour the incumbent President. Muhammadu Buhari had vowed openly that he would jail Obasanjo if he won the Presidency. Atiku didn't even need to say it. Atiku only declared his intention to jail Maurice Iwu.

It was therefore a "do-or-die" battle for Olusegun Obasanjo and he outsmarted his opponents by choosing a son of the respected Yar'Adua dynasty after eliminating many capable alternatives including Nasir El-Rufai that was long seen as the anointed successor. This is the excuse used today by Jide Ajani to justify shifting the blame of today's incompetences on Olusegun Obasanjo while comfortably negating the media's own share of the blame in unprofessionally attacking Obasanjo in all vehemence and in the service of interest groups, which ended up trapping the incumbent President in a corner from which he had to break free.

Everyone knew then that the choice of Goodluck Jonathan as Vice President resulted from the search for a calm and cool-headed deputy with no exaggerated ambition of his own like Abubakar Atiku to avoid repeating the scenario of a Vice President stabbing the President in the back and heating up the polity. Many observers saw the wisdom in this at the time. It was even the clearest proof that Olusegun Obasanjo did not pick on Yar'Adua in the hope that Yar'Adua would die soon and make way for an incompetent Jonathan. Goodluck Jonathan was simply the opposite of everything that Abubakar Atiku stood for and that was paramount to his thinking as the former President subsequently confirmed to me in one of my interviews with him.

On the other hand, if as critics like Jide Ajani would choose to say, former President Obasanjo truly 'deliberately' imposed Goodluck Jonathan on Nigeria without all the hostilities and challenges that he was personally subjected to, are we not talking here about a highly learned Doctor of Philosophy for God's sake?

Events that unfolded after the departure of Olusegun Obasanjo from the Presidency are characterised by the concomitant disappearance into perpetual oblivion, of the vibrant mass media that made the presidential throne a hot seat for Olusegun Obasanjo. Today, the only heat that President Jonathan feels is from citizen's journalism that is beyond his control. How did the mainstream media get so caged so easily? Jide Ajani made no secret of consequences that are feared if a journalist in a presidential media chat in today's format, tried to play the 'hero' by asking hot questions that could make the President look stupid. Yet, in the poorly disguised sentiments that Jide Ajani expressed in carefully chosen words, the President had already succeeded in presenting a not-very intelligible image of himself even without hot questions.

In the end, we are seeing a strongly impaired Nigerian President surrounded by exploitative interest groups of his own choosing. In front of him stands a professional mirror to show him what he looks like. Unfortunately, this mirror, which is the Nigerian media has been craftily manipulated to distort the image reflected under the pretext of not desecrating the Presidency. Since the professionals that the President should ordinarily take seriously are operating within this mirror, he is also badly misled by this same mirror that will not show the facts in all bluntness. The citizens package that is full of non-professionals but comes up with the necessary bluntness is not taken seriously and is fought hands-down with loads of paid 'counter-insurgents' as the presidency would choose to see it. It is the first Presidency to appoint a Special Assistant on New Media, while Obasanjo simply stopped reading newspapers. Now Nigerians should be able to understand why Obasanjo would not listen to advise from sycophants and acted as he pleased within the confines of his presidential powers.

It then beats my imagination, why media operatives who were privy to their own failings in contributing immensely to the emergence of the predicament that Nigeria now faces can simply not sit back and do the vital soul-searching. The need to survive in a collapsed Nigeria where jobs are hard to come by has now made Reuben Abati a dog that simply turns back to lick and enjoy what he had previously vomited. The courage to speak out bluntly will not secure the jobs of employed journalists as it did during Obasanjo's days. The few that are paid to do the yeoman's job often struggle to sound convincing in the face of so much presidential dumbness and incompetence.

Therefore, much like President Goodluck Jonathan, Nigerian journalists in the mainstream media need all the help they can get to salvage what is left of virtue in this unique profession.

*Further details on the failings of the Nigerian media can found
in my book "Nigeria's Journalistic Militantism"*

***

One major issue that was also addressed by the writer of the article that I responded to is another incident, without which any evaluation of the Jonathan Days will be simply incomplete. It was the abduction of about 270 schoolgirls from a northern town called Chibok by the Boko Haram militants. It was an issue that triggered worldwide protests and calls for the hashtag action #BringBackOurGirls by prominent personalities beginning with the then First Lady of the United States Michelle Obama.

It was difficult to comprehend that about 270 girls could be "loaded" into trucks like cattle, by militants that did not have comprehensive military training and the regular army of the land refused to appear on the scene to engage the militants for the countless hours that the incident lasted. Days and weeks after the incident, the President was lost in denial backed by his temperamental spouse, who went public shedding tears and speaking English language from the grammatic invention of yet unknown authors and calling "Diaris God oo!" in an apparent reference to what she considered immoral lies and tricks to show the President as incompetent. In other words, the President and his inner circle advanced the theory for several weeks, that the abduction was staged in order to highlight the weakness and incompetence of the President. Days and weeks that could have been spent strategizing on rescuing the girls were wasted by the Presidency, on conspiracy theories that the President thought were designed to malign him. He finally came around to admit the inevitable truth several weeks later after a commission of inquiry set up by him ascertained the veracity of the abduction.

Many adversaries of the President, some of who were former friends, who ended up disappointed at the turn of events in his outlandish and incompetent style of leadership that he unleashed on the nation, simply hoped that it will all be over when his term comes to an end. After all, he had assured all stakeholders in the heat of the cabal pressure to stop him from ascending the Presidency, that he would be satisfied with a single term as President. This became the focal point of an ideological war of attrition that was fought in the media and on abstract political battlefronts since the incumbent President was bent on retaining the Presidency by reneging on his words and having his party nominate him for a second presidential term.

The year 2014 was thus characterized by pre-election politicking preparatory to the election in 2015.

I felt, I had to write this as early as 2013, when the President's desperation for re-election slowly began to ring through:

The Dangers of President Jonathan's Desperation

By Frisky Larr

The body language of President Jonathan these days betrays everything but ease. It betrays defiance. Not often do we see the lips of this rather innocent and calm looking middle-aged man drawn tightly together and pointed, the wrinkles around the eyes drawn loosely upwards with the forehead pointedly squeezed to produce the unbefitting stern looks of a defiant rebel. These are the pictures that meet the eyes these days. The early days of striding effortlessly through the media aisles enjoying the expectant gaze of the audience from all directions now seem gone. Perhaps, forever too! Events unfolding in recent times also seem to give the President enough reasons to be ill at ease. The focus is on 2015.

In fact, the most closely guarded political secret that is indeed, no secret today, is the President's will to be fielded by his party and re-elected President, come 2015. To achieve this goal, the President's determination seems to know no bounds. He would even walk over corpses as a German adage would say. Yet he denies any intention to seek re-election publicly claiming to be consulting across the board to sample opinions. A pattern that is strongly reminiscent of the third term agenda of former President Obasanjo that the President denied until the bill got crushed at the National Assembly.

One way or the other, President Obasanjo survived this denting blunder and still remains a respectable domestic and international political personality till the present moment. Unfortunately, Dr. Jonathan does not have Obasanjo's clout. There are justified doubts that he will ever end up as lucky.

While neutral observers largely agree that a goal is hardly ever achieved in politics without a fight, many are however stunned by the extent to which Dr. Goodluck Jonathan is presently taking his fight to achieve re-election in 2015. In fact, there is near unanimity of opinion amongst neutral assessors that this 2015 dream is a near-insurmountable challenge for the President given his present record and public perception.

Therefore, every single time the President turns on the heat on opponents of this dream, he reveals to viewers from the outside that the opponents are growing stronger and have to be crushed. Each time the temperature is raised further to consume these same opponents, the world knows that the previous heat could not consume them. Further intensifications thereafter, simply serve to produce the image of a hopelessly frustrated and desperate President. Is Dr. Goodluck Jonathan unable to see these writings on the wall?

It seems to represent an element of the ensuing dynamics that the President is slowly drawn into a consuming labyrinth of manipulations when a single step simply refuses to snap. After all, all previous steps have functioned easily and effortlessly.

The removal of surrogates of the opponents from key party positions had gone very smoothly. The Chairman of the party's Board of Trustees was elected under the tele-guidance of the Presidency against fierce resistance from the opponent's camp and party business now rests on the platform provided by the presidency. The ease with which the President took over the party machinery from his powerful opponents in these intra-party squabbles seems to have given him a taste of the power of incumbency. But it was only the easiest part of the game. Problems begin however, when one single nut in the continuum refuses to snap into place. Prudent postulants would normally return to the drawing board thereafter and begin to wonder if they are slowly beginning to bite more than they can chew.

Today however, incumbent President Jonathan has opened up a new front to fight Governors perceived to be disloyal to the private cause. Rightly or wrongly every issue affecting the most prominent Governor at the center of the running battle is promptly perceived as a dirty trick whether or not it is related to the political dispute with the President. The grounding of Governor Amaechi's jet at a Nigerian airport for valid technical reasons of night flight precautions will be spontaneously seen by many as another presidential dirty trick to intimidate an opponent. The public perceives this, and it is the public that votes in the President.

A new political coalition emerges and chooses the name All Progressives Congress (APC) waiting to be formally registered. All of a sudden, a group crops up to overtake it and declares its intention to register a party with the same abbreviation APC. A move that was aimed at frustrating the successful registration of the coalition since another party would have then been registered with the abbreviation before the coalition! The public takes note of this and registers a dirty trick looking over the shoulder straight at the Presidency, rightly or wrongly.

But how frustrated would a President be to then come out from nowhere and tell a discerning audience that he alone has the wherewithal to keep Niger Delta militancy in check and empower the reign of peace in the oil producing region? Media reports have very lately reported the Presidency as highlighting the dangers of the resurgence of Niger Delta militancy if this administration is ditched in 2015. Another mild expression of the possible replacement of Boko Haram with a resurgent MEND or the double jeopardy of both after 2015 if President Jonathan is not re-elected! The discerning public takes note, and many shake their heads in endless disbelief.

Then all of a sudden, the public begins to hear hitherto unknown quantities reporting of an ex-President who ran a Killer squad and a Robbery squad and also had a hand in the assassination of Bola Ige – Nigeria's former Minister of Justice. This, in fact, is an issue that I examined with sufficient attention in my book "Nigeria's Journalistic Militantism". Indeed, any qualified journalist or mass communicator who watched this web TV and saw the highly unqualified toilet journalism that packaged the interview or read the subsequent article that summarizes the interview with two attention-seeking young men with a very poor sense of expressional articulation will know immediately that there is absolutely nothing in the brouhaha to be taken seriously. As viewers and readers' comments in that childish website subsequently betray, the timing of these so-called revelations, the facts and the tele-guided journalistic questioning are all pointing to yet another dirty trick. The public takes note and keeps watching in dismay.

Not forgotten is yet the trouble of the oil sector. Troubles that were investigated assiduously albeit not without a dose of self-interest, by legislators led by Farouk Lawan! Findings were made and valid revelations too. But a very dubious and amateurish sting operation nabbed and exposed the Nigerian sense of greed in Farouk Lawan and all the findings and revelations were conveniently dumped in the waste bin of a President seeking re-election. The former no-nonsense Czar of the anti-corruption Commission EFCC was also drawn into the game to give it all he has and only ended up being conveniently rubbished by another highly coincidental procedural flaw uncovered by a subordinate member of his committee. The songs of dirty tricks have all been sung for times unending. Yet the public watches and it is the public that decides elections.

No one is in doubt that President Jonathan is aware of his very negative public image at home and abroad that will be a liability to any political party in any credible election. With a hand-picked party Chairman who has his own ambitions however, the President is not-surprisingly, being urged on by sycophants and dreamers with private agenda and political dreams.

Amid legitimate questions over tangible achievements by his government, the President does not sit up tight to achieve as much as he can in the remaining period of his tenure. No. He accuses the media of under-reporting his achievements.

So much has happened in governance to earn the President the title of "Mr. Clueless" that observers now seem to agree that President Jonathan's governmental cluelessness has now been replaced by expertise in fighting opponents. But he was elected to govern and not to fight opponents.

Addressing the issue of consulting on 2015, the President has often cited the necessity of not being diverted from the business of governance through the politics of 2015 as a reason for not yet making up his mind in public. Yet the President stands out for having long thrown the business of governance overboard to concentrate on 2015 even though he had reportedly agreed to run just one term in the run-up to 2011.

Even one of the most credible, internationally-acclaimed brains in the administration who, hitherto has been considered by many as a hot presidential material has now been actively drawn into the business of telling petty lies to enhance the President's standing. Dr. Ngozi Okonjo-Iweala had shamelessly posed before a world audience on CNN lately in a futile attempt to launder the overall image of the presidency and government's achievements with one blatant lie. She downplayed the enormous consequences of corruption in Nigeria claiming that 99.9% of Nigerians are honest people with just 0.1% who are mischievously corrupt and hit the headlines all over the world.

Today, President Jonathan has commenced the process of irreparably destroying his party to sound the lesson of the consequence of his eventual demise in 2015. In other words, the party will be scattered if it fails to nominate him for re-election and he will not drown alone in the fecal pool of ominous stench. How far he also intends to take the corporate existence of Nigeria along with his doomed ambition is presently anyone's guess.

If anything, the prediction of MEND's resurgence will not portend good tidings. It is yet unclear that the insecurity of Boko Haram will be solved under his presidency. There is virtually no doubt that a faction of disgruntled elements would love to pick up arms again and fight the central government if the millions they presently earn in legally sanctioned brigandage are no more paid upon the demise of Jonathan. Combined with the raging violence of Boko Haram if not resolved soon, MEND resurgence will usher in the threat of a watershed civil war that may decide the fate of Nigeria.

With its high arsenal of nuisance weapon, the political architecture that has so far been constructed by the Okupe's and the hungry Abatis under Dr. Goodluck Jonathan is recklessly strolling down the hellfire path without a care for the foreseeable consequences. All because a single man has grown an insatiable appetite for political power!

After all, political Nigeria had long witnessed strong popular hatred of former President Olusegun Obasanjo and thought no one could be hated more. If Nigerians now begin to consider it an insult on Olusegun Obasanjo to compare Goodluck Jonathan with the former President, then the alarm bells should be sounding very loud in Goodluck Jonathan's inner circle. I received this post on Twitter just a few days ago:

"Can u compare obj to Gej? even dough obj is evil,this one is a demon.Frm looting to lawlessness to wickedness."

Voices of reason will no doubt urge Jonathan to back down from 2015 NOW! After all, he has always left a back door open for an exit strategy by claiming that governance is more important to him than 2015. At the moment, however, vested interests telling him that the opponents also have the choice of backing down are having the President's ears. Dr. Jonathan will prefer to toe the most convenient line and probably lose sight of a dangerously bleak political future awaiting him if he fails to back down NOW!

***

After several months of denial, the President finally came clean and declared his intention to run for re-election. One could hardly miss out on the impression that seemed subtly transmitted by accident or by design, that the unity of the country was at stake if the strongly opposing political establishment refused to back down and let the President re-contest. The problem though, was that the level of the President's incompetence and the scale of corruption that took over the country was known not only to critical observers at home. Resident diplomatic missions that have observed the situation with keen interest, have also filed several reports to their home countries confirming what critical domestic observers have been echoing loudly.

At the fore of the critical establishment that was fighting vehemently to stop the President's ambition, was former two-time leader of the country, President Olusegun Obasanjo, who had carefully formed a formidable international opposition against the continued reign of President Goodluck Jonathan in a second presidential term.

The incumbent President's strategy was obvious and dangerous. He had deliberately empowered militants in the creeks of the oil-rich Niger-Delta region, arming some with about 6 refurbished warships from Norway, while the country's own armed forces were under-equipped. Money earmarked for weapon's purchase – as subsequent probes uncovered – were carefully disbursed amongst the President's friend to facilitate his re-election. Those who had the President's ears had never relented in assuring him that the power of incumbency would see him through and that they would do all in their powers to have him re-elected. In the meantime, all opposition forces had united behind a replacement that the forces sold to the international community as highly credible.

A coalition of forces at home and the international community led by the American President Barrack Obama resolved, without compromise, not to allow a second ruinous term for President Goodluck Jonathan. The incumbent President was hell-bent on defiance with the backing of well-armed militants that threatened to declare multiple independence in several regions of the country in case the incumbent President was denied a second term in the upcoming 2015 elections.

In the meantime, the soldiers of neighboring Chad, Niger and Cameroon had marched into Nigeria unsolicited, to help fight Boko Haram, fully encouraged by the USA and without prior consultation with or permission from the Nigerian government. All intruding armies had argued that they needed to secure the pathways for commercial exchange between Nigeria and their countries, that were marred by the growing strength of Boko Haram that was even launching cross-border operations.

Many experts saw in this move, an American-aided preparation for an anticipated civil war in the aftermath of President Jonathan's failure to secure a second term. The intruding armies were to assist the under-armed and badly weakened Nigerian Army that would be split in the aftermath of the anticipated independence declarations by sections of the country. The international community was in no mood for a destabilized region in West Africa.

The tense political situation led me to write the following that found wide coverage on the Internet:

Desperate President Jonathan Weighing Suicidal Options?

By Frisky Larr

When news first broke out that the secondary school leaving certificate of the presidential candidate of the opposition All Progressives Congress (APC) was to become a campaign issue in the Nigerian presidential elections, every right-thinking Nigerian dismissed the idea out of hand and considered it a huge joke. After all, the retired Major-General was not running for the Presidency for the first time. The supposed joke soon developed into headline news, became talk-of-the-town and subject of a satirical musical denigration before finally ending up in court in surrogate litigation. It was the continuum of a desperate bid to secure the return of the incumbent President for a second term in office.

In the course of the malicious propaganda drive applied exclusively by the ruling party of President Jonathan that attempted to utilize all forms of dirty tricks in the hope that one would stick, an obviously outraged aide to the President's Senior Special Assistant on Public Affairs came up with very angry verses transmitted through the Blackberry Messenger. Mr. Deji Adeyanju left no doubt about what he considers the sheer unthinkable option of a Buhari Presidency in a democratic Nigeria. *"Buhari can never be President of Nigeria. Quote me any day, any time. A military coup will even be allowed than for Buhari to become the President of a democratic Nigeria"* Conclusively, he repeated *"Quote me any day, any time!"*

More than a fortnight has passed since campaigns for the coveted office of President was launched in Nigeria. Again, another joke is brewing in the political horizon.

Media information is simply not going away insinuating that the President of Nigeria is mulling several incredible options to short-change the democratic process if he is unable to stop the present momentum from translating into palpable electoral gains for the ex-General of the opposition party come February 14, 2015. In testing the waters to feel the depth of public reaction, the President had obviously delegated a junior Officer in the person of his National Security Adviser, Sambo Dasuki to call for the postponement of the elections that is due in barely 10 days. The ensuing aftershock reverberated far beyond the shores of the Federal Republic of Nigeria.

Unfortunately, one cannot help but live with the impression that Nigerian politicians have failed to draw any useful conclusion from the Wikileaks scandal of 2010. At least we do know today, thanks to Julian Assange, that the foreign diplomatic missions of major powers all over the world are hardly anything else but intelligence-gathering stations. It did not seem to have dawned on Nigerian politicians that the election campaign was and is still being monitored closely by foreign agents with reports wired back home by the invisible observers of the United States and the European Union covered by diplomatic immunity.

In the end, the Secretary of State of the United States had to squeeze an unscheduled visit to Nigeria into his itineraries. In the ensuing consultations that saw him meeting with the President and the opposition candidate on Nigerian soil, he successfully extracted assurances from both sides that the presidential election will be peaceful and above all, will not be postponed. The President gave him his word and no government functionary came out ever since, to call for the postponement of the election. With knowledge of how such meetings are held however, every objective observer will report of stern warnings and coercions that the strong often uses against the weak.

As the days pass by, it has become obvious that the President is losing more following in a groundswell of public disenchantment with his image and general performance since the past six years.

In place of government functionaries, investigative reports now do the talking and the gist just won't go away, that the postponement option is still very much on the table if other options fail.

Other options are the judicial disqualification of the opposition candidate in cases filed by surrogates of the President himself while the threat that was messaged by Mr. Deji Adeyanju has suddenly taken center stage all over again. The military may be allowed to take over government rather than permit the handover of political power to the ex-Major General of the opposition in an impending and largely forecast landslide victory. In an Obama-type juggernaut cruise, the momentum and pendulum that have unmistakably swung the way of the opposition is bringing out a degree of massive desperation in the President's camp that transcends all the imaginations of any mortal observer.

The truth however is that all the options on the table mean trouble for the incumbent President no matter the choices made. In the characteristic fashion that has defined the Presidency of Mr. Jonathan for the past six years, a realistic appraisal of the prevailing situation with a view to working out the best solution in the interest of the country doesn't seem to be a choice to make. The belief and trust in the power of incumbency seems to be so massively exaggerated in the President's camp that a defeat seems to sound like a sacrilege in their ears particularly if that defeat is suffered against the man called Muhammadu Buhari. For this reason, national interest is sacrificed at the altar of personal ambitions to keep the clique feeding fat.

Given the bitterness and desperation with which the campaign has been prosecuted so far by the President's men (with chains of trivial muds thrown at the opposition candidate unnecessarily), it will be difficult to appeal to a sense of goodwill and benevolence on the part of General Buhari if eventually, a smooth transition is enforced by any chance. On the other hand, should Major-General Muhammadu Buhari get disqualified by any corrupt and compromised judge (that is not hard to come by in today's Nigeria) in spite of all the clarifications offered so far, not only by the secondary school attended by the candidate in his childhood days but also by Cambridge University, which was a major player in the high school leaving examinations of those early years after independence, Nigeria will surely descend into uncontrollable anarchy. The fuel subsidy protest of 2011 will be a child's play in comparison. In the end, the merit of the case will be of no interest to any single person anymore in and outside the country since the plot is known to be a deliberate design of the incumbent power to perpetuate itself in office.

Furthermore, if the President's tribal companion and hatchet man General Kenneth Minimah who was elevated over forcibly retired senior officers into the position of Chief of Army Staff to guard the President's back, takes a shot at a military coup d'état, he will have to march over hundreds of corpses to consolidate whatever power he may have left. He will quickly realize then that Nigeria in front of the United States of America does not command such strategic importance as Egypt does to get away with the massacre of innocent civilians in the name of securing and consolidating political power.

It is true that there is hardly any world power, for which Nigeria commands so much importance as Cote d'Ivoire does for France. It can therefore be safely expected that no country will march into Nigeria to arrest Goodluck Jonathan (like France did in Cote d'Ivoire to arrest Laurent Gbagbo) if Jonathan plunges Nigeria into chaos for his own selfish ends. Yet there are several countries that will not fold their arms and watch Nigeria disintegrate. Intelligence gathering has already armed several key countries with all possible and plausible scenarios that may unfold under the heightened tension unwittingly sowed on Nigeria by Goodluck Jonathan.

The fear of the scale of his involvement in large-scale corruption that has now enveloped Nigeria and his involvement in the atrocities of Boko Haram that Jonathan probably fears will be unveiled by Muhammadu Buhari will be hastened with even more intensive consequences if collaboration with foreign forces finally enforce the defeat that Jonathan will ultimately suffer.

In each of the scenarios that may play out in the aftermath of Jonathan's unavoidable defeat, armed resistance by his militants that he has so well equipped with weapons that he has denied the Nigerian Army, will be crushed with the help of foreign alliances despite misleading and superficial successes they may achieve at the onset. How quickly warships can be destroyed with missiles that are remotely fired from a comfortable distance will be realized by these illiterate perpetrators and probably awaken the much-needed sobriety in the consciousness of these intoxicated sons of Jah-most-high in the Marijuana creeks.

Today, the magic that the presidential election has worked is made manifest in the sudden permission of 7,500 armed fighters of the African Union into Nigeria in its battle against Boko Haram where American military trainers were unceremoniously kicked out in controversial circumstances. The fact that the Americans and the Israelis have refused to sell sophisticated military hardware to Nigeria should be warning enough for President Jonathan that the international community has no appetite whatsoever to help the President arm his private army in the creeks of the Niger Delta to the detriment of the Nigerian army. And we know only of these two countries.

In the end, Mr. Jonathan hardly has any alternative to the staging of a free and fair presidential election devoid of any misuse of the judiciary, the military and the electoral commission. He has no choice but to concede defeat on the 15th of February 2015 when he will be declared beaten hands down. Nigeria will not survive international economic sanctions on top of the present hardship endured by the common man to satisfy the political whims and caprices of a single person. Jonathan will end up an international fugitive and a candidate for the International Criminal Court if he allows the worst-case-scenario take hold on Nigeria. Then he may quickly realize how the 7,500 soldiers of the African Union may be quickly bolstered by aids and agitation from all over the world to not only crush the resistance of his private army but also to facilitate his own arrest. Once again, a word should be enough for the wise!

***

In fact, the naked reality of the presidency under Goodluck Jonathan also includes one major fact. His political intrusion and total destabilization of the workings of the Nigeria's Governors' Forum (NGF) – a group that has always worked to promote the cooperation of Governors in speaking out for or against the central government with one voice on crucial political matters. Since this body became too powerful for the President's liking, he simply lobbied a few Governors to have them dislodge the serving Chairman of the forum and replace him with a Governor that was more favorably disposed to the President. In the internal election that went awfully wrong for the President, the incumbent Chairman of the body, who was badly hated by the President for his assertive nature, won the votes by 19 against 16 for the President's favored candidate. The President, nonetheless, chose to recognize the candidate with 16 votes as the legitimately elected Chairman of the Governors' Forum thus encouraging the splitting and dysfunction of the body for as long as his presidency lasted.

This article reflects the general weaknesses of the President's regime:

The Presidential Joke Called Jonathan!

By Frisky Larr

Were it not a matter as serious as ruling over a strategically important country called Nigeria, the man Goodluck Ebele Jonathan would have been a highly interesting and enjoyable subject of ridicule in late night comedy shows. A subject of entertainment in banters over mugs of Palm wine at the palm frond bar in a typical African setting! Banters that should trigger a spate of uncontrolled laughter in the casual beer parlor in every busy urban district of an African metropolis! Unfortunately, however, this is not a joking matter. It is a matter that borders around the serious crime of toying with the collective destiny of millions of people and the existence of an entire nation. It is a matter of playing the game of personal enrichment and enjoyment of pleasures and goodies without a clue whatsoever, on the serious responsibility of holding a nation in cohesion and fostering a common identity.

It has always been a poorly guarded secret in the rumor mill that the President of Nigeria Goodluck Ebele Jonathan (a man of questionable academic integrity) is one who loves indulging in sessions of nocturnal boozing in one of the private wings of the Presidential palace. The veracity or otherwise, of this claim is better left to his conscience and the conscience of those who are close to him and work hard to exploit his position for corrupt gains of a personal nature. We will address this issue later in this discourse.

I recall a comment made by President Jonathan in one of his media outings very early in his Presidency. The comment was roughly in the tone that he was not a military General and could not be expected to move around with a whip in the hand to flog Directors of government agencies in line, who are notoriously acclaimed for making a mockery of the opening hours of government offices and come habitually late to work. I was one of very few commentators at the time, who spotted the President's serious problem with public communication and the articulation of progressive ideas. Many admirers applauded the President agreeing with him that the dictatorial days of military repression were a thing of the past. The underlying stupidity however, of indirectly encouraging late-coming to work by Directors of government agencies by issuing them a blank check in this respect, was obviously lost on the "follow-follow" admirers. Even the President, who did not intend to transmit this impression, hardly knew any other way of expressing himself without sending the wrong message.

It, finally, came to a head when the Present a few months later, did a roadshow interview for CNN in the snow-cladded streets of the Swiss town of Davos on the sidelines of the World Economic Forum attended by world leaders. The stage-fright, the stutters, the incoherent articulation of loose facts and the outright delusional self-aggrandizement as the ultimate achiever of the comatose power sector was lost on no conscious observer. It was even made worse by the President's outing in a series of Meet-The-Press sessions before a domestic audience of nationwide television viewers that often go viral on social media. If he was not declaring that he does not give a damn what the constitution demanded of him, he was busy lecturing the nation that stealing cannot be equated with corruption. Never mind, though, that the entire world considers corruption as a form of stealing. These became moments, in which many viewers simply felt ashamed to describe Goodluck Jonathan as the President of the country they belong to. He was suddenly no longer the charming poster boy that many people admired and proudly fought for in the battle against the Yar'Adua cabal.

It was a similar scenario – again – very early into his Presidency when he disbanded the national soccer team to reorganize the soccer federation that had long been riddled with corruption and cronyism. The nation soon learnt that the President had not done his homework properly before declaring the disbandment of the soccer federation. He had not factored in, the reaction of FIFA and the pressure that would be brought to bear on him by interest groups profiting from the filth of the system before making the public pronouncement. He backtracked and chickened in when FIFA bared its claws. He moved on to fuel subsidy and tried to do what no leader before him had ever dared to do talking big about being ready for a revolution when the political soil was more than fertile for a consuming social upheaval.

It became clear latest at this point that the President did not have a Masterplan of any sort when it comes to ruling and building a nation. One got the impression that the President was taking a lot of things for granted believing that political leadership was a self-operating system that simply requires the fixing of one notch here and there without much ado. The finesse, the intricate process of managing and confronting several interests and motions at the same time with the requisite astuteness of an intelligent mind seemed like factors that were and still are extremely foreign to the President.

How easy and simple the President thought the system would work was even more obvious in his celebration of the privatization of the power sector as a major achievement. Many intelligent minds who have all it takes to know and comprehend the situation better, simply rallied behind the pathetic President in celebrating this bankruptcy. It was the same calculation that informed the attempted removal of fuel subsidy. To get out of the way of powerful mafia gangs holding both sectors hostage, the President chose privatization as an alibi stone that would be catapulted to strike three birds at the same time. First: His cronies and financial facilitators would be left off the hook without public clamoring for arrests and prosecution. Second: The constraints of the sector would ease tremendously, and a lot would improve under the mechanism of the competitive market economy. Third: His financial facilitators, who made up the same criminal mafia would buy off the sector from the government and thus stay richer and happier and still remain the President's friends.

The first and third calculations have worked very easily in the privatization of the power sector. Unfortunately, however, the power situation has not improved for consumers and the public. In all my years of sojourning in foreign countries (and I still stand to learn a lot), I have never seen any sector privatized by any government that has not first been developed and made functional by the same government over a longer period. The operation of such sectors by government often serves to set the standard and threshold for subsequent private operators that should not be fallen short of. After all, every lame duck knows that the primary concern of every private investor is nothing but profit. A system of public control and standards set in advance of privation often force the hands of private investors to keep the standard floating.

President Jonathan hardly seems to have a clue on all of these. In the same vein, he had ignored the Boko Haram menace in the belief that those behind it were not making governance difficult for him but merely killing themselves in the name of religious sanctity. Somewhere down the line however, he seemed to have discovered the amount of profit that could be drawn from the bloody insecurity. Budgetary allocations on security became a looting ground for government elements in collaboration with Generals. After all, no one renders accounts on security votes. It is the most prominent no-man's land for government looters. The result today is the emergence of a ragtag army that is poorly equipped in spite of huge budgetary allocations that are routinely stolen with impunity. The exacerbation of violence in crucial northern states has suddenly become recognized as a political capital if elections are not held in populous states over which the opposition holds sway.

Caught in the act with the game-plan oozing transparently, all the government does today, is to deny without yet furnishing a credible and convincing plan on how elections are to be held in states, where the insurgents have made serious gains and are ruling unchallenged. Over 2,000 victims were reported massacred in the past few days with an entire village wiped out in an insurgent onslaught. Yet, the incident hardly found a mention in the domestic media. The President did not lose a single breath of verbal articulation on the tragedy. All the military does is to declare an exaggeration of figures.

Now, the nation is debating how best to fight corruption with the President unwittingly triggering consternation in the wake of his utterance that corruption cannot be fought by jailing people. Never mind that corruption is a capital offence in China that is punishable by death and long-term imprisonment in very many other countries of the world including the USA with the array of high-tech at its disposal. Yet, Nigeria's President contends that his focus is not set on punishing corrupt people with imprisonment but on creating a high-tech system that will disengage when people seek to divert funds for purposes other the ones they are meant for.

What a joke! The President doesn't seem to ask himself what high-tech system would stop a government officer from collecting kickbacks. He doesn't seem to ask what system would prevent the inflation of contract costs. He doesn't seem to ask what system would stop officers from seeking gratifications before the award of contracts etc. etc. This is the extent of the boundless intelligence of a man ruling over Africa's most populous nation.

Speaking in clearly unacceptable English grammar for a holder of a doctorate degree, the President even goes further to chastise his opponent for having jailed a former Governor, while he was a military head of state, for *stealing* an amount of money that was not even enough to buy a "Peugeot" (with all due respect to the French brand). He has been widely quoted as saying *"How much did Jim Nwobodo* **stole***? Money not up to the price of a Peugeot and Buhari regime sent him to jail. Is that good enough?"* Suddenly the President seems to smell a clue that *stealing* may possibly be equated with corruption after all. The President now sticks persistently to the fully nonsensical claim that he does not believe in fighting corruption with imprisonment. Yet, Governor Sule Lamido knows too well what his son suffered on charges of corruption in EFCC dungeons in the President's bid to persuade the Governor to stay with the ruling party and not defect to the opposition. Femi Fani Kayode knows too well what he feared so badly that made him defect back from the opposition to the ruling party and lick back the entire stench that he had vomited about the President and the ruling party.

Now, the President is telling the world that the amount of money stolen by Jim Nwobodo should not have warranted imprisonment. This is no doubt, a comment that was made on the spur of the moment in the hyped spirit of crowd agitation and super-stardom. It brings us once again to the notion of disastrous public communication.

For a President who has been making the headline for confining all meaningful committee recommendations on fighting corruption to the dustbin, this joke couldn't have soiled his image any better. It raises the question if truly, alcohol or other intoxicants do play any role in the President's mien and routine countenance, given the dogged information on the rumor mill pointing precisely to this direction.

On the other hand, it has become not only a national embarrassment to citizens of the country that a supposedly highly educated President of such an influential nation often struggles to articulate himself in public speeches making frequent grammatical blunders on top of poor expressions, but eminent personalities of the academic world have also begun to question the viability of his academic degrees. More importantly, the overall perception of President Goodluck Jonathan as a holder of a doctorate degree awarded by a Nigerian university now seems to be throwing in tatters, anything that is left of reputation for higher institutions of learning in Nigeria.

Today, whoever criticizes the President is his enemy. No trace of reflections to admit errors to say the least of learning from mistakes. Decorum and high moral grounds are phrases that sound just foreign to the presidential psyche of our times. Gutter languages from the highest seat now mark the peak of the preludes advanced by foot soldiers parading the most despicable of political theatrics. A few days ago, some foot soldiers boasted of plans to arrest a former President of critical acclaim stating clearly that the man will die in the prison where he belongs. Today, the President is crawling on all four begging for an audience with the same elderly President that he described only a few days ago, as a motorpark tout.

What a joke!

***

In the end, the election came after a desperate postponement by the incumbent President to gain him time for quiet machinations and re-strategizing. In the end, the President lost. A novum in the history of Nigeria's political history, in which incumbents never lose elections! The new President-elect **WAS** the nightmare of many, who advanced and brought the practice of corruption and looting of the public coffers to new and outlandish heights.

V
Enter President Muhammadu Buhari

Former Major-General Muhammadu Buhari became a rallying point in the run-up to the Presidential elections in 2015, in the search for a credible replacement for the incumbent President Goodluck Jonathan. So bad was the filth and rot in the system that a leader with an iron clad and hand was badly needed to reset the button back to where Nigeria was in the 1980s and take it from there again.

Muhammadu Buhari was seen as a last resort in the quest to instill discipline into the psyche of a completely wrecked and lawless society, where firmaments have virtually, gone out of control. It was a land standing on its existential precipice.

Muhammadu Buhari ruled Nigeria as a military Head of State from December 1983 to August 1985 when he was deposed in a counter-military coup. He was subsequently retired from the military with the rank of a Major-General.

For Muhammadu Buhari, this two-year reign constituted the political liability that marred his dreams of becoming a civilian President early into the experiment of the fourth Republic. With a draconian iron fist, he and his then Deputy and Second-in-command in the hierarchy of governance, Brigadier (as he then was) Tunde Idiagbon sought to force the entire nation to its knees to instill discipline and fundamental human values. The price was high in terms of rights violation and disregard for individual freedom. Press freedom was also tampered with in a period that Nigeria boasted of the freest press in the region.

Characterizing Muhammadu Buhari in his opposition to the candidature of the former Major-General for President of Nigeria in 2007, Wole Soyinka (Nigeria's only Nobel Prize Winner for Literature) deemed the possible ascension of the former military leader to the office of civilian presidency as *"a far graver looming danger"* than the prospect of another government-sponsored candidate. Soyinka saw it as a mistake that must never be allowed to happen. Speaking at the press conference, the Nobel laureate reminded his audience that the *"complaints that were tabled against (Buhari) involved a career of gross abuses and blatant assault on the fundamental human rights of the Nigerian citizenry."* He recanted an example of wasteful executions on a retroactive decree for an offense that did not carry the death penalty at the time it was committed, ethnic favoritism in the implementation of a foreign exchange law, etc.

In 2015, however, even this renegade Professor of public political conscience became a strong advocate of bringing Muhammadu Buhari to power. It was more a case of ensuring the departure of President Goodluck Jonathan's corrupt government at all costs. In the field of contestants, the need for a stern disciplinarian that would pull the nation by its horns began to stare Nigerians in the face.

All of a sudden, General Muhammadu's Buhari's atrocious past, began to turn into his political blessings. His political capital.

Unfortunately, however, the man who led the War Against Indiscipline (WAI) in that short-lived military regime, General Tunde Idiagbon, had died a few years back under mysterious circumstances. Without doubt, a crucial reset was needed in the overall scale of national discipline. The truth though, was that Muhammadu Buhari, who was more or less, the figure head of that military government, excelled in contradictions whenever he took center stage in the actions of that government between 1983 and 1985. One glaring example was the case of some thirty-something suitcases that were smuggled into the country while the draconian law against such acts was still fresh and sound. Wole Soyinka reckoned they could even have been fifty. To keep the drain on resources in check, the government had halted the outflow and inflow of specific goods through Nigerian borders (land, sea and air). In the direct aftermath, the legendary Afrobeat singer Fela Anikulapo Kuti was jailed for taking foreign currency with him for an oversea trip, that he needed for his concerts.

At the same time, some northern traditional ruler was allowed to travel into the country with so many suitcases unchecked in direct breach of the same law. Wole Soyinka:

"Yet a prominent camel was allowed through that needle's eye. Not only did Buhari dispatch his aide-de-camp, Jokolo - later to become an emir - to facilitate the entry of those cases, he ordered the redeployment - as I later discovered - of the Customs Officer who stood firmly against the entry of the contravening baggage. That officer, the incumbent Vice-president is now a rival candidate to Buhari, but has somehow, in the meantime, earned a reputation that totally contradicts his conduct at the time. Wherever the truth lies, it does not redound to the credibility of the dictator of that time, Buhari whose word was law, but whose allegiances were clearly negotiable." (Annex 11, page 321, "Nigeria's Journalistic Militantism" Frisky Larr, Authorhouse U.K.)

In 2015, all that changed. Even General Olusegun Obasanjo became a strong protagonist of the installation of a Muhammadu Buhari's presidency. The far graver looming danger of yesterday became the very serious hope for redemption, wholly unforeseen.

On one hand, the transgressions of Goodluck Jonathan created a vital necessity. On the other hand, Muhammadu Buhari became the redeemer that everyone looked up to because minds were simply reconfigured to accommodate the uncomfortable truth that he was not the real disciplinarian that edified the short-lived government. I wrote this article at the time:

Nigerians Largely Want Jonathan Out, but Do They Want Buhari In?

By Frisky Larr

A few months ago, I wrote an article in which I implied that Nigerians should blame the arrogance of the Northern elite if our lame-duck President Jonathan is returned to Aso Rock in 2015. Five months to the scheduled elections in February, all signs are pointing to the fragility of the opposition in a self-staged display of self-laceration. While Nigeria may be a land of chronic and negative wonders, where unimaginable treats are achieved in all aspects of life, the current political scenario playing out in public gaze is simply unusual if not unprecedented in democratic settings.

For some time now, I have invested some efforts in the project of straining my brain for a recollection of any democracy in living memory that has witnessed the persistent and serial feature of one and the same circle of actors for competitive political offices. It is not so much the trouble of featuring the same circle of persons in a land that is rich in competence and fallacies that bugs my mind so badly, but the reality that such persons have failed serially in the tasks they set themselves.

The names Abubakar Atiku and Muhammadu Buhari are the names of frontline political personalities in Nigeria, whose mention should ordinarily command respect in the face of their antecedent and dispositions in years gone-by. While the first may have been an actor of yesterday, the latter is a doyen and political principal of yesteryear. From Germany through Great Britain to the United States of America, it is a rarity to find the same political personality running for the same office three to four times consecutively after failure on each occasion. After all, the saying goes that time is no respecter of persons and waits for no traveler.

Customarily, politicians move on and define new objectives to live up to when the adventurous quest for political power fails to yield the desired result. Never in Nigeria!

Today's Nigeria is such that is rife with intense political bickering and social calamities in a scale that has never before been witnessed in over 40 years of the country's inaugural history. From corruption through homicide to the serious yearning for secession, instability has never been as bad. It is a country, in which a gang leader declares in a television interview that naturally goes viral on the social media, that the President of the country *will not dare* to decide against running for re-election. The celebrity gangster makes this declaration with all imaginable doses of self-confidence not even mulling the fear of a presidential reprimand or contradiction by the President's men to say the least of the President himself. He is after all, the President's man in flesh and blood.

Never in the history of Nigeria has it become so clear that the President shares political power with clandestine forces that are unknown to the electorates. The level of the entrenchment of corruption with untouchable powers of the oil sector and the level of government collaboration with warring and divisive sectional separatists for the purpose of salvaging what is left of the limited scope of power that the President has carved out for himself has left Nigeria ostracized internationally. The country now struggles with the pariah status next to Sani Abacha's Nigeria.

In other words, the setting couldn't have been more conducive for the definite and sure removal of the incumbent President in the elections five months away and his prosecution thereafter. That would be the case in a normal democracy. Never in Nigeria! Today, there is a murmured consensus that the President may be returned "unopposed".

"The reason?" you may want to ask. Arrogance, misplaced priorities and the egoistic sense of overestimated relevance! In the absence of a credible replacement that the electorates can trust across-the-board, the result is the persistence of the status quo with the less foul of all bad eggs. Short: the Nigerian opposition is in shambles.

With the name of a former Vice President featuring prominently in the opposition's list of potential replacement for a fragile President that has virtually been counted out, the opposition cuts a pathetic figure today, from the cake of electability. This is a politician, who stood out predominantly for insubordination to his former boss and was used by friends and foes whose priority was to get rid of the common enemy at the time. He is a former Vice President who was marked so conspicuously as an unmarketable presidential material by the false friends who allied with him in his unholy battle and stands accused today, of corruption by major foreign forces. If this is the hope that the opposition presents to a downtrodden and weary nation, then it stands to be pitied and consoled for its impending defeat that will have been forced down the throat of a reluctant crowd.

The most prominent and even more controversial is the retired General Muhammadu Buhari who has a track record of modesty in his personal disposition. Some attribute a no-nonsense attitude to him because it was the flagship tenor of the "War Against Indiscipline" that symbolized his era as a military head of state. His track record of modesty is informed by the fact that no single finger is pointed at him on suspicion of being the 6th richest African leader through wealth that is suspected stolen in his days as the military head of state.

While it may be most probably true that General Muhammadu Buhari is a modest personality in terms of living an ordinary life and does not amass wealth or condone larceny of any sort on public properties, there are yet some indisputable and credible facts informing the fears and suspicions that people have against his die-hard dream of ruling Nigeria again at all costs, after his military adventure. This stubborn insistence alone raises questions about his personal motives. Some sharp-tongued assertions even suspect his regrets at choosing to live a modest life that leaves him as the laughing stock of peers being the last among equals. This suspicion is however, not founded on any objective or credible premise.

If the truth must be told, the charismatic personality and poster-child celebrity of the Buhari military days that wore the cap of discipline and no-nonsense attitude was his own deputy General Tunde Idiagbon of blessed memory, who seemed to have served in a functional power-sharing arrangement. With Idiagbon today as a Presidential candidate, there would have been less controversy in the rank and file. Our literary Professor Dr. Wole Soyinka rightly pointed out in 2007, the most potent scare radiated by General Muhammadu Buhari. Citing several examples of double standards in General Buhari's conduct, he stated thus: *"The conduct of the Buhari regime after his coup was not merely one of double, triple, multiple standards but a cynical travesty of justice"*.

One prominent example was Buhari's decision to keep former President Shehu Shagari, a Northerner from the same geographical region, who was toppled from the seat of power by the Buhari coup, under house arrest while his powerless Vice President Dr. Alex Ekweme, from the "rival" region of East Nigeria, was locked up in the then maximum-security prison in Kirikiri. A former Permanent Secretary in the Ministry of Finance Abubakar Alhaji Alhaji, who was caught in flagrante in some hormone-driven escapade in far-away Austria was entrenched in a foreign exchange scandal. *"Alhaji Alhaji kept, not one, but several undeclared foreign accounts, and he had no business being in possession of the large amount of foreign currency of which he was robbed by his overnight companion."* Buhari's government looked the other way only to slam a draconian prison sentence on Fela Anikulapo Kuti for possessing foreign currencies required for the upkeep of his band on overseas trip

If anything, General Muhammadu Buhari does not make any secret of his personal sense of intransigence, religious embrace and sectional alignment.

At this dire and critical juncture of Nigeria's existence standing on the brink of disintegration, the prominent thug of the Niger Delta refers to himself as one who clamors for the dissolution of Nigeria. This indeed, is the period, in my humble opinion, in which Nigeria requires a unifying but resolute and strong leader.

Muhammadu Buhari is resolute and strong and is indeed, the type of leader that Nigeria would need at the present moment were it not for his divisive nature. General Muhammadu Buhari unapologetically transmits the impression that he is a Northern Nigerian before being a Nigerian. Any pretense that these antecedents will not be made manifest in an eventual Buhari

Presidency will be sheer wishful thinking on the part of anyone who wishes to keep Nigeria above regional and sectional divisions.

General Muhammadu Buhari's insistence on being the king at all cost rather than the kingmaker will always remain a source of stunning consternation. After all, his moral authority would have given him all the leverages he needed to groom a worthy replacement for the ill-fated Goodluck Jonathan, who he may now force down the throat of Nigerians again with his obstinate disposition.

I have no doubt that an eventual Buhari's Nigeria will stand a good chance of crushing the diabolic mafia of the oil sector and the mafia of the power sector that the lame-duck Goodluck Jonathan has simply capitulated to. The crucial question however, will be the extent to which he may wish to assert his passion for the northern domination of the entire country – an imbalance that Olusegun Obasanjo had largely corrected in favor of meritocracy. After all, the General has never made any secret of his clamor for the return of power to the north, which on the face of it is so irrelevant to every well-meaning Nigerian after the Jonathan disaster, as long as any such northerner places Nigeria first. This is the core factor that informs the general fear and suspicion of Buhari's sincerity.

In the face of all these, it becomes compelling to ask why the opposition APC – the only party, on whose shoulders popular hope for the removal of Jonathan rests at the moment – forced itself into this tight corner of uncertainty. Why wasn't the usefulness of General Buhari tapped in other more efficient capacities? Does anyone expect heaven to fall if General Buhari loses the election? Should his popularity in the north make people lose sight of the deep suspicion of his motives in the south? After all, until their performance in their various offices, no one knew Nuhu Ribadu and Nasir El-Rufai. Was there no one to be groomed for proper leadership? This is one of the predominant weaknesses of African leaders, who characteristically place themselves above all collective considerations.

While advanced age is and cannot be a factor for judging competence and eligibility, serial failure in one venture should serve as a moral burden on any reasonable contender, who chooses to stake a reputation for national salvation.

At the present moment though, it is yet too early to foretell Buhari's failure against Jonathan. If it happens all the same, no one should be surprised and pretend not to have seen it coming. Then posterity and history will be left to judge the saboteurs of national interest when Nigeria needed them most. Should Buhari however succeed in achieving the impossible against all odds, by removing the Jonathan burden from Nigeria's back, we will wish him all the best and caution him very strongly, to make amends to any desire for regional dominance and focus on keeping Nigeria one and making Nigerians proud to belong to the union.

***

In the end, Buhari won the elections against all odds and a new chapter was opened. To the grievous disappointment of all, the expected iron man did not hit the ground running. He opened up with a lousy inaugural speech claiming to belong to everyone and then belong to no one. He wasted months assembling a cabinet and betrayed his utter unpreparedness for the intricate job of a civilian President. Prior to the selection of a cabinet, the President had a few months to rule as a sole administrator. Events then happened in quick succession. The election of leaders of the two chambers of the legislative arm, the National Assembly (NASS), was hijacked by the former Governor of Kwara State, Mr. Bukola Saraki. The accustomed tradition was the involvement of all stakeholders, particularly the party, to ensure the election of leaders that will steer the ship of legislation in sync with the Executive arm of government to minimize the risk of conflicts.

The President and his lieutenants had their own ideas, what to make of the process and when to begin it. In what was a foreboding of things to come, the President and his camp was thrown off guard and Saraki spat on the principle of party loyalty and went ahead with his personal ambition.

That prompted me to write this article in the early days of the Buhari administration:

Disarray in Buhari's Camp Amid Saraki's Insubordination and Signs of Things to Come!

By Frisky Larr

If there is anything that many observers agree upon, it is the fact that Muhammadu Buhari could have had a better start into his civilian presidency. Most disheartening and uninspiring was his inaugural speech, which left many people wondering what message he intended to send and why he made the choice to send such a message. The calculation seems obvious. The President simply sacrificed the all-important notion of toughness and popular reassurance at the altar of pacifying the team of the outgoing President, who has been locked in the fear of high-handed persecution.

Before the gaze of foreign dignitaries and backdoor facilitators of the smooth transition from the feeble and militant-backed former government, President Buhari seemed to have staked his cards also in reassuring the different interest groups observing the transition that he was out to calm the political temperature and not heighten tension any further. This was however, not the expectation of the teeming masses of Nigerian voters who yearned for change and had enough of the passive patronage of overbearing insiders by a weak government that was erroneously labeled as "Pacifist". President Buhari's inaugural speech simply failed in balancing the need to reassure those who fear persecution and the need to reassure his constituency that he was out to address their needs.

In the end, the meaningless message of belonging to all and belonging to none was the only substance that was left to be extracted from a long-drawn speech that many expected to be fiery and momentum-laden. Yet, it was easily skipped and quickly forgotten with the brave face of disappointment underscoring the need to keep heads high and simply move on. Many have been quietly nursing the uneasy trepidation deep within them ever since, hoping that Buhari may not end up a complete flop and a major disappointment.

After all, the President had all the opportunities in the world to reiterate his commitment to fighting corruption by revamping the anti-corruption agencies. He had all the chances in the world to reassure Nigerians on how he intends to work to strengthen regional military cooperation with neighboring countries to eradicate insurgency until the Nigerian Army is put back on its feet again to stand alone. He had all the chances in the world to reassure Nigerians, how he intends to clean the oil sector, enforce fiscal discipline in government institutions and carry party soldiers along in enforcing a new era of discipline in the national psyche, etc.. The President simply allowed this noble and golden opportunity of popular appeal to escape and slip through his fingers. It is an opportunity that was lost for good. It was his first own goal and an unforced error that barely stopped short of being an outright gaffe. It is a major blunder that he shares collectively with his handlers and perhaps, speechwriter(s).

Yet, as is typical of the honeymoon period, the need to stay calm and allow the President some time to understand the situation has so far dominated the reasoning of many critical observers, who are still waiting and watching out for just one decisive step from the President to reassure them that he is very much on course with his own agenda. So far, it has been to no avail! It does not matter though that the President was supposed to have understood the situation perfectly well even as a candidate with a blueprint to hit the ground running. On the contrary, signals keep trickling out, painting the picture of a President's camp in utter disarray. From all indications, the President now seems trapped in the fangs of party interests, regional interests and the interests of scattered loyalists, who fought tooth and nail and against all odds, to ensure his electoral victory even if also in protection of inordinate selfish interests.

Now, there are reports of regional powers wanting key ministries to be headed only by persons from a particular geographical region. There are loyalists, who now seem to have been suddenly understood as too ambitious and power-hungry to be given government appointments in spite of their excessive commitment and personal contributions to electoral success. There are now stories of the Vice President being locked out of Security meetings with service chiefs. There are stories of the President's wife wearing a $50,000 wristwatch to the Presidential inauguration. There is the outright gaffe of the President referring to his wife as 'Her Excellency' after promising to abolish the office of 'First Lady'.

In the midst of all these, the President is nowhere to be seen before his own folks. Barely two weeks into his administration, the signs perceived by the public are that he has no clue just yet, who should make up his cabinet. It is yet the picture of a very weak and unprepared Muhammadu Buhari that is presently meeting the eyes.

Reaction to this image has not waited for too long. Even though Senator Bukola Saraki belongs to the class of featherweight activists, who fought to install Buhari as President and does not need to be sidelined in disgrace, he is now one character, who has clearly shown to Muhammadu Buhari, how people will ride on him if he does not make amends very quickly and take charge of the country in a very decisive manner without fear of stepping on toes. Rather than ostentatiously declaring non-interference in the selection of National Assembly leaders, it would have taken the President one decisive word or two into Bukola Saraki's private ears before heading for the G7 summit in Germany to help Saraki beat a very quick retreat from his overblown ambitious rebellion. But when a President tries to be everybody's darling seeking to appease minds and win friends, he soon learns, how others will strive to stretch the limit before his very eyes.

If reports are anything to go by, Bukola Saraki has simply called the bluff and disgraced the President with impunity before ranking APC members of the legislative houses, who gathered with the President for a crucial meeting while Saraki was busy ordaining himself as a renegade priest in the midst of gleeful death-wishers. While opponents are now relishing the spoils in schadenfreude, a word should now be enough for the President if he wishes to toe the path of wisdom. Bukola Saraki and his friends know too well that the last word has not been spoken on the hijacked Senate Presidency. If anything, Olusegun Obasanjo can help Buhari out very quickly in teaching him methods of stamping his authority in constitutional arrangements of this nature. This is where Buhari still seems to be struggling to come to terms.

By declaring Saraki's hijacked election as "constitutional" while sticking to his new-won image of a loyal team player subjected to the dictates of his political party, President Buhari now seems to have managed to throw his doubters in a slight state of disarray. He has managed to stand out still as a mysterious winner. The aura of fear that Buhari emitted by declaring the hijacked senate election as "constitutional", is cladded in indiscernibility much like his declaration of being for all and being for none. For now, no one seems to have a clue, what to make of the President's comments.

Buhari's pattern of whipping people in line, if he chooses to travel down that path, will no doubt be strongly rested on the principle of constitutionality as time progresses. After all, what Saraki can do, one would guess, Buhari should be able to do better. It is however, yet a mystery, which path Buhari wishes to toe in this nascent Presidency. The cards have been thrown on the table and Nigerians are waiting to see his sense of cohesion and execution.

He had appealed to Nigerians, particularly on the social media, to exercise a sense of responsibility in practicing citizens' journalism. Precisely for this reason, many responsible and professional operatives in the conventional world of mass media and social media have been waiting patiently to catch a glimpse of the President's choices and policy direction particularly in the corruption-ridden petroleum sector. With the understanding that the role of importers will be abolished in favor of hiring the services of foreign companies to refine our crude oil until our refineries are fixed, there is hardly any Nigerian that is not impatient to see the removal of fuel subsidy. This alone, will be a giant stride in freeing up resources for other developmental projects in the near and medium-term.

First however, President Buhari will have to sit up tight and very quickly too if he is to upset the yet suppressed general suspicion that his elevated image of a no-nonsense General may be a serious misunderstanding after all since the late Tunde Idiagbon was the major architect with the disciplinarian credentials.

***

While struggling to cope with the unintended election of Bukola Saraki as Senate President, another renegade Lawmaker in the lower house – the House of Representatives – garnered his own crowd of assemblymen to elect him as the Speaker of the House of Representatives ahead of party horse-trading. In what looked like a coordinated rebellion, Yakubu Dogara emerged as the Speaker of the House of Representatives. The outsmarted ruling party, the All Progressives Congress (APC), was left dumbfounded in this first-of-a-kind maneuvering in the political history of the country. It was an unprecedented case of disloyalty to party in a newfoundland that placed the focus on the political ambitions of individual politicians.

In the last-ditch effort to save the party's face, overtures were made to have the Principal Officers of both chambers chosen in line with party wishes. Again, Bukola Saraki defied his party and followed the pre-planned script of his renegade mutineers. Yakubu Dogara obliged the party.

It was the sign of things to come. The battle line seemed drawn for the presidential ambitions of Bukola Saraki, who, by his actions, was cautiously spewing disdain for an incumbent President that was erroneously thought to be a no-nonsense character.

I wrote this article in the wake of the early signs of things to come:

Is Buhari Confused while Saraki Rampages and Jonathan Boys Go Insane?

By Frisky Larr!

What is truly going through the mind of President Buhari at the present moment has become a task for fortune tellers and tea leaves readers. In these early days of his Presidency, he reminds me very much of former President Olusegun Obasanjo in the second term of his Presidency. The former President, who had a very clear idea what to do with Nigeria, made a clear point of refusing to interact with Nigerians through the mass media and allowed the opposition to use the media as a playground to throw mud at him uncontrolled. Much of that mud does stick to the former President today in his public perception.

On the contrary, former President Goodluck Jonathan had no idea whatsoever, what to do with the Presidency and the country at large. To him, being a President was divine blessing enough, than the overwhelming task of moving Nigeria forward. The latter was a burden that he simply did not bargain for. Yet, he used the media. He communicated regularly with the people no matter how much trash and childish messages he communicated. His aides hired foot soldiers to write irksome comments on articles and even sponsored media outlets with public funds while the President stayed far away from stepping on toes. Today, remnants of these foot soldiers have gone haywire and purely insane propagating anti-Buhari messages simply for the sake of malignity.

But Buhari is not helping matters either. Having missed the golden opportunity of his inaugural speech to brace Nigerians for things to come in the clearest language possible, President Muhammadu Buhari is yet missing out on another opportunity to woo the hearts and mind of ordinary Nigerians. He seems stubbornly and deliberately refusing to address the nation almost one full month into his Presidency while his inactions are leaving far more questions than answers.

Like Obasanjo, there is no doubt that Buhari has a very clear idea what to do with Nigeria. His numerous international consultation travels primarily to woo allies for the overall security of the country, show his serious commitment to solving the overriding security problem of the country as quickly as possible. And that is precisely where it ends. Every other issue has become a guessing game.

While this approach of talking less and letting results speak for themselves is a very legitimate approach often adopted by action men and honorable people of authority, it is yet a dangerous public relations strategy that may make any achievement whatsoever amount to naught in the face of unnecessary public anger. Former President Obasanjo can tell a thing or two about this. This leads to the next pertinent question, if Buhari is resistant to advice from his aides or if his aides are sheer incompetent.

A professional drafting of an inaugural speech will only end up in futility if the speech fails to come down to earth and address every citizen in the language they will understand. Coded and well-packaged messages that are meant to be decoded by a select target audience on a day of inauguration is the first own goal and a hallmark of professional inefficiency. Then the gaffe of *"Western Germany", "President Mitchell"* and all that stuff!

So far, these have all been mitigated by very positive rumors that are in sync with public expectations. Nigerian refineries are reportedly working towards the commencement of full-scale refining operations in the early days of July 2015. A move that will surely relieve the pressure on public funds wasted on subsidizing the importation of refined fuel by larcenous importers with the credentials of former presidential alliance.

While insane old-time foot soldiers of former President Jonathan relish the wishful thinking of crediting this feat to their defeated presidential principal, I have always craved the provision of proof that the former President commenced the turn-around maintenance of the refineries. Indeed, I have no memory of any such public information that the former administration was ever interested in the domestic refining of fuel to say the least of awarding any contract to this end. The priority of that administration was either the unconditional lifting of subsidy (as was already proposed in the next fiscal planning) or the continued importation of refined fuel by surrogate thieves. Not even in the heat of the presidential campaign did the losing party make any mention of (the non-existent) efforts to revitalize refineries. The conclusion can therefore, be just one: The fear of *something* has simply become the beginning of wisdom in such a way that turn-around maintenance was done in such a very short time contrary to fears that the work and costs were ways too enormous. Whatever the truth may be though, we keep our fingers crossed. If refineries commence work in July and subsidy disappears, the credit will go to Muhammadu Buhari since goals are always credited to scorers and no to midfield assists.

There are rumors that the EFCC will be merged with the ICPC – a laudable move in the fight against corruption that has suddenly seen the EFCC now brazenly arresting big names after sleeping through Jonathan's 5-year reign. Then we hear that power supply has now improved dramatically. There is a vow to recover stolen funds and in fact rumors are making the rounds that quiet deals are being struck to bring back stolen money by different individuals. The days of a rampaging "First Lady" is now over with Aisha Buhari openly telling the nation that she is just not "First this or First That" simply because her husband is President.

On the other hand, the wave of uncontrolled corruption and the massive flow of donations in foreign currency as were seen during electioneering a few months ago are enough to leave anyone with the premonition of a *"virtually empty"* treasury. The President said this without mincing words. Of course, Jonathan boys will not be true to their name if they did not try to capitalize on this to launder the inherently soiled image of their clueless principal. They have either not understood the meaning of the "virtual" or missed out on the word altogether, in the President's comments. Today, remnant Jonathan foot soldiers have launched a sort of brainless Tea Party campaign hurling stones at Buhari simply for the sake of it.

They are just not being silenced in shame yet partly because the President does not seem to have fully understood his responsibility and is stubbornly – and with all due respect – "foolishly" refusing to address the nation to outline the state of affairs.

As if this was yet insufficient, renegade Senate President Bukola Saraki continues relishing the image of a determined spoiler relentlessly fanning the embers of disunity and party insubordination. Precisely this issue is the crucial stroke that has sealed the confines of President Buhari's cage and trap. It has defined the scope of his virtual incarceration and personal confusion.

While Buhari was quick to switch gears from electoral campaign to the practicality of the Presidency, he has taken to heart, the looming danger of an overbearing Bola Ahmed Tinubu in the running of the Presidency. Having tried and failed in efforts to impose himself as Vice Presidential candidate against the wise counsel of many well-wishing stakeholders, the former Governor of Lagos State does not seem to have any intention whatsoever, to take a prominent backseat at the present moment. On the contrary, he seems to clad himself in overbearing cloaks relishing insatiable hunger for power and wealth. With the huge ballast of negative image that he brings along with him into government by his party, any prudent and strategy-inclined activist would have toed a line that is less burdensome to government and his party. After all, the fight against corruption and nepotism, which Tinubu prominently stands accused of, is one major pillar of his party's credentials.

Does he then wonder that alliances are subsequently forged against him with the President gleefully taking a backseat in the "indirectly complicit" hope that the result may bring Bola Tinubu to his badly needed senses? Moreover, President Buhari seems to be resisting vested interests – be they Governors or divisive regional leaders – in the selection of his lieutenants. Unlike former President Obasanjo, he is just not YET being openly defiant in the "To-hell-with-you-all" pose. The need to pacify and keep the friendship of electoral facilitators – no matter the degree – seems to be yet taking the better of the President.

In the process, the President seems to be taking his time to understand the true position of things even though this sounds outright irritating given that he was once a leader of the country and has a long history of failed application for the coveted office.

Bukola Saraki and people around him now seem to be taking undue advantage of this temporary impasse in stamping presidential authority to advance their own agenda beyond reasonable limits. After all, for a cross-carpet frontliner, it should not take a sage to impress it upon Bukola Saraki that he is being overtly too bellicose and crossing the crucial red line. Having landed that huge coup of emerging President of the Senate with the help of members of his former party, Bukola Saraki should understand the limits of stretching the demarcating line. With perhaps, the "unspoken" support of the President in trimming Tinubu's wings, there is no gainsaying that no elected officer would get anywhere without the party and its programs. As with many things Nigerian, Saraki is losing it and doesn't seem to have a clue, when and where to slam the brakes before they consume him. Openly acting to and encouraging others to defy and ignore his party will not only expose him to the suspicion of crossing carpet to advance a clandestine agenda for his former party but also to the anger of the electorates, who elected a specific party of their choice. Proceeding to fill principal positions with members of his former party in total disregard for party directives can only be counter-productive to his political ambitions and interest.

In fact, Buhari may now be getting far more than he bargained for in Saraki's rebellion to establish a balanced equation with Bola Ahmed Tinubu. After all, the same party sponsored primaries to produce the presidential candidate Muhammadu Buhari. No losing candidate rebelled to fight the other openly. Then candidate Buhari relentlessly emphasized the relevance of the party in defining his campaign and programmatic agenda. Coming out openly to defy the majority choice of his party caucus in preliminary mock election of the Senate President was negative news enough for the overall image of the ruling party and team. Going further however, to encourage party indiscipline and open defiance in the selection of a majority leader, chief whip etc., is a declaration of an all-out-war on his own party.

Muhammadu Buhari now seems to be faced with the constraint of seeking a total realignment of forces to push his personal agenda forward as President. He will no doubt, seek to pacify Bola Ahmed Tinubu while at the same time keeping his reach to presidential policies as moderate as possible. Will he be however forced, to take up a fight in trimming the wings of an overtly over-ambitious Bukola Saraki? So far, the President seems to be shying away from being drawn into any distraction.

On the whole however, while I regard Buhari's slowness in announcing his team of aides to the country as unhelpful to his general perception, I do not see extreme damage being done to his presidency on the short to medium term since he still has ample time to correct all flaws and unfold mitigating achievements that may send town-criers singing another tune. With all the information at my disposal however, I have no doubt, he will strike the right nerve.

***

Soon, a loophole was found and the serving President of the Senate, who has no immunity from prosecution, was allegedly found to have made a wrong declaration of assets in breach of statutory mandate. The asset declaration form that was completed by Dr. Bukola Saraki and deposited with the Code of Conduct Bureau (CCB) was allegedly found to have contained anticipatory declarations. In other words, assets were declared that were not owned at the time, thus prompting speculations that such assets were to be retrospectively acquired, apparently through looted public funds. Charges were subsequently filed against him at the Code of Conduct Tribunal.

This was subsequently followed by criminal charges in a regular court after Bukola Saraki and his Deputy, Ike Ekweremadu, were found to have allegedly tampered with the Senate Rules for selecting leadership officers of the chamber.

None of both litigations bore fruits in terms of conviction in the face of a strongly compromised judicial system that is open to corruption and influence-peddling as well as a President that is highly incompetent in playing the political strongman card to carve out a unique identity for the country's democracy. Letting the trial drag on for so long with extensive periods of adjournment, the President exposed himself to lobbying by the interest groups and the deep state until the entire process ended up in ridicule.

This article sums up the early problems the President confronted and his difficulties in tackling them:

Buhari's Slow Pace Stifling Momentum and Breeding Rebellion!

By Frisky Larr

These days, almost every Nigerian with a computer keyboard and the ability to formulate any sentence in English (no matter the quality) is a political analyst. Such self-styled talents and geniuses parade themselves on private blogs and postings on the social media drawing often, primitive and substandard conclusions on matters of serious political relevance. In the face of it, this shouldn't be a problem to any actor and participant in the democratic process. After all, freedom of expression is a fundamental column of the democratic edifice. It does not forbid grammatical blunders. It does not forbid the poor command of any language of choice. Yet there are limits that every informed mind is also fully aware of. Slander and treason are very popular limitations to freedom of expression. But we'll come to that later.

As already stated above, no one would ordinarily care about the rascality and disingenuousness of the several millions of "certificated illiterates" (to quote Pat Utomi) littering the Nigerian social media scene, were it not for the inordinate exploitation of this mean manifestation of emptiness by interest-prone politicians. Since the last presidential elections that produced retired General Muhammadu Buhari as President of Nigeria, the social media have witnessed a stark proliferation of self-ordained political gurus and Master of Political Intelligence. They seem to have no other function but rabble-rousing to the detriment of intellectual growth and personal maturity. They never engage in debates for the academic exercise of learning and teaching i.e. giving and taking as it were, but furiously seek to impose their own will on dissenting voices while drawing support from like-minds in a comfort zone that reassures them that they are right on track.

Then you realize the game of sponsorship that was launched by former President Goodluck Jonathan that culminated in the appointment of a Special Assistant on New Media. The Special Assistant recruited foot soldiers that were planted in every critical online forum to glorify mediocrity with a level of commitment that bordered on submission to the guru of a doomsday sect. They paid websites to scuttle critical thinking and sing the praise of government. To them, life began and ended with Goodluck Jonathan and the mindset with the consistent construct of a skewed and very badly calibrated perception of reality persists till the present day.

Unfortunately, however, there is a new kid on the block. Since Olusegun Obasanjo (no matter what view anyone may hold about him), Nigeria once again, has in Buhari's leadership, a government that is set on a clearly defined course. Like Olusegun Obasanjo, I have my doubts that Muhammadu Buhari ever reads Nigerian newspapers. I have my doubts that Buhari has the time to care about petty naughtiness and trivialities on Facebook and Twitter to warrant the waste of public fund on the appointment of Simlins and Renos.

Today, government is being showcased with more sophistication and less volubility. There are no more gutter languages from purported medical doctors functioning as presidential mouthpieces or certificated Abatis, with little clue on media ethics and professionalism. Today, public pronouncements by government spokesmen are terse, professional and to the point. No ranting on perceived enemies. No more incitement of President to fight the wrong enemies for personal aggrandizement.

Precisely this quality now seems to be going down as a sign of weakness in the minds of the gullible rabble-rousers and losers in the battle of "yesterday's men".

Yet, the new President is not wholly without guilt. While the uncouth agitation of political enemies that are bent on testing the limits are often allowed unfettered grounds in the name of upholding the principles of constitutional democracy, President Muhammadu Buhari, is today, also partly being haunted by his own political past that bears a baggage of bitterness and recklessness.

There are very many who believed for good reasons too, that the misuse of Boko Haram at the turn of the millennium was predicated upon the notion of making Nigeria ungovernable to a Southern President. Top on the list of frustrated politicians at the time, was retired General Muhammadu Buhari who was kept away from the seat of power in elections that were contrived by both sides with the stronger getting his own will. Comments are not hard to come by, which showed Muhammadu Buhari at the time, as spreading the protective cover of fellowship over Boko Haram. The comments *"An attack on Boko Haram is an attack on the whole of the North"* was attributed to the former General at the time. This adds up to previous pro-political sharia comments of all shades and color that sought to destabilize the government of former President Obasanjo. Nothing is known (at least in public) if former General Muhammadu Buhari walked the talk at any point in time and did anything to actively build-up such anti-stability forces of evil.

Since the destructive activities of Boko Haram were largely confined to the North of the country, former President Jonathan is known to have adopted the now infamous lackadaisical approach and seemed to have allowed Boko Haram to fester uncontrolled and was even quoted by former President Olusegun Obasanjo as saying: *"It is the North killing themselves"*. Indeed, there were some suggestions that former President Jonathan probably also tried to use Boko Haram to his own advantage at some given point in time and this notion was backed by several questions that begged for answers.

In the end, Boko Haram grew out of the control of those who founded and funded it, those who pampered it as well as those, who ignored it. In one case, even Muhammadu Buhari had to thank his stars that he did not end up a flattened victim under the rain of Boko Haram bullets.

Today, obvious plans by those, who probably seek to make Nigeria equally ungovernable to a Northern President is clearly manifesting. The attempt to give Muhammadu Buhari his own taste of Boko Haram seems to be playing out in a carefully orchestrated but self-defeatist game of wits in Eastern Nigeria featuring miscreants and hoodlums, who hardly have a clue what the war of secession entails.

In all of these, the President's slow pace of action often plays into the hands of the professional architects of mischief. Every blacksmith who knows his onions will always recite the old saying to anyone who cares to listen, *"strike the hammer while the iron is hot"*. For some reasons, however, President Muhammadu Buhari often prefers to strike the hammer when the iron has tremendously cooled down and stiffened beyond bending.

Bukola Saraki ushered in the new era of change with a taste of rebellion against his own party. The President had all it took in the world to send a strong message to such extreme and unprecedented acts of rebellion against the party and his personal authority that embodies the presidency. While the subsequent but legitimate prosecution of the same individual may be seen as a slow and steady approach at achieving sound results, it also has the collateral impact of forces teaming up against him to test his resolve and the length he would go. If the information available is accurate and anything to go by, one Justice John Fabiyi with the collaborative influences of the "Belgores" and other Justices are already firing the warning shots.

The uncouth, uncultured and wayward character personified in the name of Fayose is well known to every observer of political events as a resounding misfit in the comity of decent politicians. If anything, his thug-like composure and conduct, which fit better into the activities of the Association of Road Transport Workers are least desired in a serious world, where the business of governance is conducted. In the characteristic thug-like disposition, the fellow single-handedly dislodged the function of a state legislature with the force of gangsterism. Yet, Muhammadu Buhari let the time slip by, to send the rascal the strongest message possible and place him where he truly belonged. Now, he takes very little steps further every single passing day. The military investigation of electoral malpractices that may end up indicting the process that brought Fayose to power may come too little too late with an unholy example disbursed to evil fighters probing for avenues to resist the well-intentioned onslaught of a democratic convert.

All-in-all, President Muhammadu Buhari talks less and follows his path regardless of slanders and abuses in a manner that would remind everyone of Olusegun Obasanjo's approach but with a more pronounced touch of democratic leanings. This is now pushing skeptics to ask the crucial question if a nation as disorganized and lawless as Nigeria will understand this language of controlled decency. In spite of early promises of a wave of prosecution of corrupt individuals, six months on, there seems to be no distance covered amid the gyre and motions. On the contrary, critics now fear that the President may have buckled under the noises of the "Kukahs" and other fools.

The aggressive drive that many thieves and saboteurs feared in their initial reaction to the now infamous 'body language' is fast dissipating and individuals seem to be finding their ways around it in a language summarized by an Agbero Governor that *"Buhari is, after all, also a human being"*.

Quiescence and a well-meaning constructive design to install political decency now seems to be making way for heightened rascality and the resurrection of decaying agents of trouble and professional waywardness. Whatever happened to regular intelligence gathering to say the least of military intelligence that no one saw funded and orchestrated upheavals brewing underground? Demonic characters such as Asari Dokubo, who should have long been confined to spaces of their peers in a determined and pro-active disposition, may now be unwittingly allowed to get up to no good again as Jonathan did Boko Haram.

Muhammadu Buhari obviously lacks the talent of nipping issues in their bud and clamping down hard also within the confines of constitutional democracy. If anything, Nigerians fear decisiveness and resolve the most. If the President fails to change course anytime soon and run out his claws and teeth for the sole purpose of deterrence, he will end up being overwhelmed by issues creeping up one after the other and in different regions such that he will hardly know where to begin. The need to make an example of representative figures and instances cannot be over-emphasized if President Buhari is serious about making any meaningful impact within his four-year tenure. How quickly time passes will dawn on him much sooner than later.

***

Then sometime close to the end of the year of his inauguration, the President unleashed his fangs and dragged a high-profile corrupt officer into his anti-corruption net. Retired Colonel Sambo Dasuki was the National Security Adviser to the government of the defeated President Goodluck Jonathan. He was accused of large-scale corruption. This came as a surprise as all indications pointed to a retention of the retired Colonel in his position since the new President had allowed him stay on till the point of his arrest several months after the inauguration of the President.

Colonel Sambo Dasuki was accused of having misappropriated about $2.1 billion defense allocation, on the campaign expenses of the defeated President. In a period, in which the country was struggling to free itself from the stranglehold of a ragtag army that was blowing off military positions in the Northeast of the country, the amount of $2.1 billion was reportedly earmarked for the purchase of military hardware from external sources. Rather than purchasing weapons, sources say, the money was diverted to the campaign processes of the incumbent President for the 2015 presidential elections.

Weird stories began to make the rounds. The former National Security Adviser won the nickname "ATM" of the defunct government because he was reportedly vested with the duty of disbursing the said amount to various interest groups that were expected to facilitate the victory of the incumbent President. Sources report that about €290,000.00 and € 150,000.00 were paid into two private accounts of unknown individuals as gratification for prayers for the former President in the run-up to the elections.[5]

Parallel to this, credible rumors had it that the smooth transition from the defeated ruling party to the victorious opposition party (first of its kind in the political history of Nigeria) in 2015, was incumbent upon a deal brokered by foreign powers, between the outgoing President and the newly elected opposition candidate. It was claimed that the outgoing President was to face no prosecution on any charge and was to be left alone as a price for facilitating the smooth transition.

As time went by, however, media headlines began to dominate the airwaves claiming several corrupt activities on the part of the ousted President. Individuals fingered in the Dasuki affair often sang the refrain of acting on the orders of the former President. One prominent and known example was one of the former President's media spokespersons, Olisah Metuh. Calls began to mount, for the minimum act of inviting the former President for questioning. It looked increasingly likely that the former President would be invited for questioning and thus set the stage for a possible prosecution in breach of the rumored gentleman's agreement of smooth transitioning.

Then, the bubble burst on the prevailing uncertainty. Suddenly, a new militant group sprang up in the Niger Delta region calling itself the "Niger Delta Avengers" (NDA). A wave of economic sabotage attacks was launched blowing up pipelines, ostentatiously aimed at stopping the President from pushing ahead with any prosecution of the former President if he had contemplated it.

The following article was written, precisely at the peak of the bombing campaigns that successfully crippled oil production and revenue inflow on top of the unexpected crash in the global market price of oil:

Attacks on Buhari: How pathetic they've become!

By Frisky Larr

It's been quite amusing since the inception of the Buhari administration barely one year ago, observing self-styled critics of the new government, who are driven by diverse motivations. I have identified them in three different categories. The first group comprises those, who have set out to criticize the government from the very beginning, no matter what the regime does. This group has now become popularly christened as *"The Wailing Wailers"* very much in disrespect to *"Bob Marley and The Wailers"* of classical Reggae fame! The second group includes those who believe that they are being objective by being seen as criticizing the government after throwing their full weight behind Buhari's watershed election in a juicy grand style. The third and final group comprises those, who are genuinely angry that things are not proceeding the way they had hoped would uplift the common man in a very short time.

I have issues with all three groups with varying degrees of understanding. I tend to show the least understanding of the position and attitude of the first group, which set out from the very beginning, to attack and disparage the government at all costs no matter what it does. It is the group that exemplifies the "ideal" form of despicable attacks and criticisms like it should never be practiced in a healthy democratic culture. Confronted with the levity of their actions and illogicality of their utterances, their most commonly advanced argument is *"What does it now feel like getting back a taste of what you dished out to Jonathan?"*

This extremely infantile and pubescent approach to important matters of state and the destiny of a nation can hardly be qualified by any discerning mind, with any flattering or polite adjective for the sake of decency. The actors are aware of the sense of immaturity that their actions reflect but they are very well driven by the impact of Group dynamics. What an individual would never do, left to himself, he will now do very easily with a sense of justification and righteousness, feeling not alone in the company of like-minds. Educated minds that would ordinarily weigh the pros and cons in words and deeds simply metamorphose into cyber touts and rabble-rousers, spewing hate and mischief for the simple sake of angering the state because they feel secure in the comfort of a mob group. Their most popular stock in trade so far, has been the habit of jumping on every issue perceived as negative in relation to the government of Muhammadu Buhari and ripping all facts apart and out of context if need be, as long as it serves the purpose of boosting a negative perception of the government in public view.

They celebrate in ecstatic fascination, the shortage of cash in the state's treasury as incompetence in the management of financial and economic affairs knowing too well what the impact of dwindling prices can be when it affects the mainstay of the economy. They celebrate the padding of a budget as incompetence and hypocrisy, conveniently ignoring the criminal dimension to the despicable act perpetrated by remnants of decadence and the preparatory environment under which the habit thrived. They celebrate the emergence of buyers' queues at filling stations as an opportunity that can never be missed to cut a pound of flesh, willfully negating the reality that the folks also suffered same in the reign of their hero. They suddenly find the megaphones to announce the random criminal killings perpetrated by northern cattle rearers as a new crime-in-town introduced by the hated northern President. The truth that they know so well, however, is that the problems have existed in varying degrees over several governments. They know so well too, that it is one thing to point out the urgent need for a solution and another thing entirely, to label a problem as the poster-problem of a hated regime.

Then they are led by people who should have known better with an intimidating background of academic experience and financial resources, lending credence to pettiness and idiosyncrasies. They tweet half-truths and sponsor ads for political ambitions and clearly negate the consequences of the political tradition they are breeding for future generations within and outside the senate.

The tweeting senator with a not-so-covert presidential ambition simply ends up spearheading a movement of half-truths and willful manipulation in reckless abandon and reminds me of the foul seed of journalistic analyses that was sown by the likes of Reuben Abati, Okey Ndibe and Simon Kolawole at the peak of their activism against Olusegun Obasanjo. Today, the behavior of the so-called Wailers is a partial manifestation of this academically misplaced tradition that I strongly condemned in vain at that crucial point in time.

The tweeting senator who saw all the ills of the preceding government and made no commonsense to challenge the fundamental spread of decay has now suddenly rediscovered and redefined the word "commonsense". In all his tweets and rants, he cleverly forgets to make commonsense on Dasukigate or Badehgate. He makes no commonsense on the financial recklessness of the red chamber. Femi Fani Kayode has long gone silent under the yoke of a corruption cover-up that went awfully wrong and no tweeting senator saw a commonsense factor to tweet about.

Then it dawned on me that the folks are trapped in a state of mind from which they have failed to free themselves. They are yet to grow past the problem of the North-South dichotomy that has plagued Nigeria for several decades past. To them, Buhari is always a Northerner before being Nigerian and they themselves remain Southerners before being Nigerians. It "Us" versus "Them"! It does not matter to them that even President Muhammadu Buhari, who in the past, was a personification of sectionalism with reckless pro-Northern utterances, has now grown past that stage and continued on the footpath of former President Olusegun

Obasanjo, embracing the Federal Character mandated by the constitution for the good of the country. No.

In their perception, a Southerner who embraces the anti-corruption project of the President (which, in their view, is nothing but hypocrisy because Buhari is also a thief) is nothing else but a traitor and a sellout. The fight against corruption has suddenly become a misplaced priority of governance as long as the thieves may end up being predominantly Southerners. Never mind though that the hated government has so far, focused far more disproportionately, on his northern kindred.

This is the point in time, in which we recognize the pitiable state of mind that the critics have long degenerated into.

The second group of critics for which I show a limited dose of understanding seeks to wear the cloak of objectivity by being seen to be criticizing the administration having staked a lot of energy backing the same regime. I am sometimes irked by this group for the simplicity, to which it reduces itself to be loved and adored as everybody's darling. For want of subjects to criticize, they hop aboard the bandwagon of trivialities and irrelevance. With a vast and radiant array of positive mental and rational energy, they unwittingly obscure their hard-earned reputation needlessly flip-flopping on the murky stream of dirty water lilies. They suddenly find favor in unleashing attacks on a President's honesty that promises foreign partners the resolve to rein in the rampant culture of crime and dishonesty, for which a section of Nigerians is known all over the world. They dance upon the carnival wagon showcasing budgetary irregularities to be seen as fair and square. Then they fail to make amends when news unfolds, of the criminal syndicate underlying the embarrassing plot. They suddenly begin to hinge on the President's distinctive slow pace in prosecuting his signature policy of War Against Corruption. They occasionally stray into the Wailers' terrain, illogically asking if this was the Change they sought with their votes only to provide the relevant answer when they start defending the President again.

This is a group that basically, means no harm to the national interest, but seems to crave the notion of advancing their personal image with a simplistic approach to popular appeal.

The last group, with which I sympathize and empathize, is the group that is simply reacting authentically, to the persistence of pains against all expectations. My grudge with this group, however, is bedded in its involuntary supply of needless ammunition to the camp of the grumbling wailers. This is the group that heaved the most sigh of relief when power supply suddenly surged upon the assumption of the Presidency by Muhammadu Buhari. It enjoyed every bit of the moment, in which our comatose refineries swung into action and did outlandish magic. We called it all the body-language impact. Deep within though, we all knew, it was a transient knee-jerk reaction. After all, the fear of the unknown was leaving a livid track on the comportment of those who had axes to grind. With revenues dwindling, however, and culprits compelled to spit out the "yam" that they have eaten, the fear of who may be the next person in line, now seems to drive the panic reaction of overnight saboteurs.

Yet, I must not fail to pay tribute to all these men and women in this last category of involuntary critics, who live in Nigeria and bear the brunt of hardship that daily life demands and still remain level-headed enough to separate the wheat from the wasteful chaff. I doff my hat for all courageous men and women who go through hours and days of power failure, weeks and months of fuel shortage, unpredictable days of armed robbery, and the uncertain days of kidnapping. I adore their resilience and doggedness for making ends meet in extremely challenging conditions. Yet, they keep their cool and know where to lay the blame and help to craft a blueprint.

The missing link of added patience that is required in the face of mounting pressure signals the weight of the burden that they bear. Yet, it will all get worse before it becomes better.

Little wonder then that the group of the Wailers, in its isolation and desperation, seeks to capitalize on the pains of the vulnerable third group in the hope that it will bring it relief. But the nagging and wailing of the third group is as transient as the pains that it endures. It simply requires a heightened dose of reality check.

By the way, if I were a tweeting senator, I'd imagine myself saying right away, *"My name is Frisky Larr, I'm doing some reality check"*.

***Coming up soon: Watch out for my exclusive Video Interview
with former President Olusegun Obasanjo!*** [6]

***

Then came the issue of fuel subsidy that almost led to Nigeria's first ever revolution in history under President Goodluck Jonathan. It is an area that Presidents seem to make an endless array of unforced errors. Buhari tackled the issue early enough while he still enjoyed the goodwill of a huge section of the electorates. But not without his mistakes.

Read this:

Buhari's Inconsistent Management of Fuel Subsidy leaves Loyalists Confused in a needless Own-Goal!

By Frisky Larr

An unnecessary own-goal indeed. Who doesn't remember Muhammadu Buhari's infamous interview (Here: https://www.youtube.com/watch?v=YmG_dYY7YRA) before he became President? He talked elaborately about fuel subsidy stressing very clearly that the measure was a fraud and that he hardly understood what it was all about. So far, so good. He went further to express his dismay, how we got where we are, asking repeatedly who was subsidizing who. He emphasized clearly, how shortfalls in domestic supply were managed during his days as Minister of Petroleum Resources when the refineries were dysfunctional in the wake of Turn Around Maintenance. Muhammadu Buhari, the private person then, explained how he, as Minister of Petroleum Resources, employed the services of multinational oil companies to take out crude oil, refine and bring them back again without Nigerians noticing the shortfall. Such foreign companies marketed a part of the end-product directly through their outlets within Nigeria and were paid commission. That was Muhammadu Buhari the retired General and a private citizen.

When he subsequently became President, however, Muhammadu Buhari inspired a lot of hope – lots and lots of it too. After all, who will not embrace a man as President, who openly did the mathematics of what a liter of fuel should cost the average Nigerian given the readily comprehensible to the negligible cost of production and transportation of the refined product?

It, therefore, goes without saying then, that intelligent Nigerians who viewed that footage logically expected fuel subsidy to be removed swiftly, under a Muhammadu Buhari's Presidency. That much is proper and logical. Beyond that, however, such Nigerians also expected this President to ensure a low-priced disbursement of fuel at the proper outlets having heard the underlying mathematics. They also expected a Buhari government to move swiftly to replace fuel importers with those same multinational oil companies, with whom he struck those deals in his years as Minister. After all, the same companies are still around. In fact, one would have expected the then President-elect Muhammadu Buhari, to have moved straight into negotiations with such companies that were still known to him from his days as Minister, to explore the scope of assistance that they could render, when he becomes President.

The reality that he met on the ground will, no doubt, go a long way to define the pace and nature of action to be taken by the President. One of such realities is the huge debt owed to importers who were friends, cronies and surrogates of yesterday's people and some hidden people of today. The refineries were inoperable and simply comatose. Depot facilities were largely in the hands of importers and other criminals that were propped up by agents of previous governments. These are seriously negative conditions to meet for any meaningful effort in this project no matter how well-intentioned it may be.

In an overbearing atmosphere of pervasive corruption and fraudulent minds, no doubt, a government will face a sense of confusion, knowing where to begin and telling what to prioritize.

In my honest opinion, the government did set the right priority by beginning with corruption and taking up all other issues on a parallel train. Indeed, the falling price of crude oil in international markets, couldn't have come as a better opportunity. So, it came as no surprise, when news broke out, a few months into the new Presidency, that fuel subsidy has been removed. That was just a few months ago. The issue was passionately debated and many unrepentant supporters of the ousted regime of Goodluck Jonathan had poured venom and vitriols on people who supported the removal of subsidy but almost brought down Jonathan's government for the same reason. Again, that was only a few months ago.

Obviously, there have been some quiet back-and-forth within the government that may have entailed policy somersaults. We were told at a point that the NNPC was now the sole importer of refined fuel and that other importers had been weeded out. A few days later, the story changed. The NNPC was reported to be the **largest** importer and was assisted by **a few select private importers** for whom subsidy continued to be paid even though we had long been informed that subsidy was no more, and we were done with the weeping and wailing.

Following the sudden outbreak of fuel scarcity, apparently, in the aftermath of sabotage actions by disgruntled losers of the subsidy equation, frantic efforts were made to normalize the situation and the Junior Minister of Petroleum Resources and General Managing Director of the NNPC Mr. Ibe Kachikwu, addressed the nation directly in a video footage. Precisely this, is the lesson that President Buhari has, so far, refused to learn. The art of talking to the nation.

Former President Goodluck Jonathan ran into trouble trying to remove subsidy because he did not only ambush Nigerians amid denials and childish tricks in bad faith, the project was soaked in oozing corruption that he was just not willing to face up to. With the high price of crude oil at the time, the removal of fuel subsidy would have simply handed over Nigerians to the mercy of profiteering vampires. Today, the price of crude oil is down. Corruption is facing a head-on challenge and opportunity is rife. But that is just is just one segment in a chain of prerequisites.

We asked Jonathan to work on old refineries and build new ones given the resources available at the time and first kill the regime of fuel importation. Subsidy would have died a natural death and the process of privatization would have been smoother. Today, some of the refineries are functional again that were not in Jonathan's days. Government-owned outlets sell refined fuel today, at a far cheaper rate. Not the private ones.

Given the fact that the requisite conditions for the removal of fuel subsidy have not been fully met to make the transition to private enterprise less painful to the underprivileged, it is pertinent to ask why this government is caving in so quickly to the demands of neo-liberal economists who cannot wait for the cushioning groundwork prior to privatization. This is all the more painful because this is a government that is believed to be not anti-people. The pains of substandard living remain high with ordinary Nigerians.

On the other hand, however, there is hardly any Nigerian today who still thought in all seriousness that fuel subsidy was still being paid. So high is the confidence in President Buhari that many believed in the automation of the process to fix the sustenance of refined fuel either through importation by the NNPC as sole importer or through the refinement of crude by international oil companies or whatever.

Today, the picture that meets the eyes is one of a government that didn't seem to know how to get out of the subsidy quagmire in the aftermath of quiet policy reversal probably necessitated by prevailing circumstances and a government that doesn't seem to know the mood and trend of thoughts among ordinary Nigerians. After all, Nigerians have already known that the new budget for 2016 made no provision for subsidy payments. Legislators knew it. The Labor Unions knew it too. This has been tacitly accepted across-the-board.

Where then did the idea suddenly spring up from again to re-announce the official removal of fuel subsidy? Are there no public relations experts within this government, who should measure and gauge the public mood and know the manner of measured communication to dish out to the public? Government communication is never done on whims and caprices.

Publicly revisiting the issue in this fully amateurish manner has offered the opposition a fresh lifeline to get noticed. Now, a high-level Ambassador (plenipotentiary) and self-proclaimed anti-Nigerian citizen of the Republic of Corruption is screaming out loud from the balcony of the Senate to lead a march on Aso Rock. Civil Society Pretenders have now found a voice so suddenly. Labor Unions who offered cosmetic cries and shed crocodile tears when Senators were padding and *unpadding* the budget and holding our collective progress to ransom have now suddenly found their voices to Occupy Aso Rock. Unfortunately for them, however, the widespread backing of 2012 will prove elusive this time, simply because of their ingenuous hypocrisy.

In spite of all that, this reactionary pressure on the government will not be wholly counterproductive. It will, indeed, be a partially welcome idea to keep the government on its toes while standing and on the edge of its seat while sitting. In spite of all public admiration and approval over the ferocious war against corruption, Muhammadu Buhari should not take us for a ride. He should learn to communicate with Nigerians more frequently.

Irrespective of the amateurish nature of a government that is acting confused on the subsidy issue and the constant manifestation of unprofessional public relations exposures and incompetent media management, the premature removal of fuel subsidy is just wrong. If it was wrong yesterday, it is wrong today still. More so, it is an unforced own-goal.

***

Slowly, opposition to the President began to mount, also from fully unexpected quarters. With mind-boggling revelations of the massive scale of looting that took place under President Jonathan hitting the headlines almost on daily basis, even hitherto respected clergies came out in condemnation of the President's drive. One known Catholic Bishop even came out to tell the President, he should face the real issue of governance rather than wasting precious time fighting corruption. No outrage. No consternation at the scale of looting uncovered.

The following two articles address precisely, this anomaly:

Matthew Kukah's Christian Values and Misplaced Priorities

By Frisky Larr

When I wrote the book "Africa's Diabolical Entrapment", in which I examined Black Africa's plight in its self-imposed religious trap, I stopped short of crossing several thresholds. Contrary to speculations advanced by people who read articles, reviews and intros about this work, the content did not concern itself with the existence or otherwise of any supreme deity. I did not concern myself with the relevance or otherwise of atheism. Indeed, on the contrary, I highlighted the importance of religion in society as the recognized custodian of moral and ethical values.

This is not because atheism does not have good enough reasons to question the existence of God. No. It is not because there are no reasons to call the existence of religion into question. No. The bottom line was to pointedly highlight the troubles we see in the practice of religion and its negative impact on people and development without passing judgment.

Alas, the more Preacher-men in the Nigeria of today thrust themselves into the limelight of public exposure and perception, the more reason they provide doubters to question the existence of God and the holiness of religion.

In a society that is faced with the enormous moral challenges of recognizing the value of life, particularly human life, one would ordinarily assume that religious establishments already have their duties carved out for them. Taking it from the most basic of all social ills that has metamorphosed to a higher level, one asks when things got so badly out of control in Nigeria that the sight of corpses on the street does not cause revulsion. In the early post-independence days, the only place to see a dead body in public space were the scenes of public execution by firing squad. A priest administered his last prayer on the victims, they said their last words and were shot dead and quickly packaged into the coffin for burial in respect for the sanctity of human life.

Today, seeing the dismembered body of a human being on the street for days if not weeks unending, is as common a sight as seeing a dead rat in the corner of a blind alley. These days, scores between young men in cultist associations are settled using the barrels and the cannon. Simple disputes over girlfriends, cash or rank in cultist associations are met with death to the ringing sound of a short gun. Whence then, will the value of life emerge when young ones at their tender age have no sense of awe and reverence for the human lives they take without care or at the sight of lifeless bodies that they spit upon?

The duty of religious leaders has been naturally carved out or so you may think. The sanctity of life alone, makes a resounding subject for lessons from the mosque podium or the church pulpit on Fridays and Sundays for weeks unending. The society offers it as one of numerous subjects.

Yet, no. Let us not get into the daily fear of armed robbery and kidnapping in a society that seems to have lost it all completely. The daily struggle of the ordinary man with the harsh realities of normal life – from power failure to the non-availability of pipe-borne water – is often crowned by the fear of being confronted to handover meager savings at gun point. Assailants often do not hold back from gunning down their victims. Ordinarily, this is a serious subject for Preacher-men to pick upon and play their role in fixing the human mind that is growing in the vicious circle to breed more generations that may know no sanity.

Yet no. Just what then, is this obsession that Nigerian self-styled "Men of God" have with dabbling into politics leaving serious issues that are naturally designed for religion through the ages? What constituency does religion seek to address in politics to the detriment of more urgent moral and ethical issues in society?

Most notorious these days, is one Bishop Matthew Kukah of the Roman Catholic Diocese of Sokoto. Prominence and guidance are attributes that make the rank of a Bishop in the catholic faith a big deal indeed. It is a level, at which the stakes of moral guidance are high that are expected of the embodiment of such designation. For several reasons, Bishop Matthew Kukah has played several roles on the moral wing of the Nigerian political scene since the start of the new dispensation. From human rights investigations to the Ogoni reconciliation efforts, Mr. Kukah has had reasons to contribute his quota to the building of a political moral standard in the country.

Yet political assignment for clergies is often a calling that is answered and done with. It is not a primary assignment that defines the role of religion. The saying *"Give what is God's to God and what is Caesar's to Caesar"* was a clear demarcating line that the Bible drew for the propagation of the scriptures and impact on society.

Today however, Nigeria has a Christian Association of Nigeria (CAN), which seems to see itself, first and foremost as a political body. From a blin-blin pastor that excelled in all worldly riches defined by nearness to political power to all other peripheral associates of CAN, the primary goal of religious leaders today seems embedded in material wealth.

In my book "Africa's Diabolical Entrapment", I highlighted the catholic church as one different entity of the Christian faith today, that has not been consumed by prosperity evangelism. In a setting of several fraudulent new generation churches performing fake miracles and exploiting parishioners, the catholic church stands out as one that does not conduct cheap rallies and spit deceptive rhetoric. The catholic church in Africa does not parade private jets for its Bishops and Archbishops. It does not task its members to build universities for the children of the political elites to enrich the preacher-men. Their trademark dress is the catholic robe of different colors. Not the blin-blin chains and suits of some shameless Oritseja-Fool!

Yet, the catholic church embodied by Matthew Hassan Kukah is fast turning out to be a far cry from the role that society expects of the Church. To underscore his relevance these days, Bishop Kukah seems to find compulsion in making political statements on how best to govern. While appreciation will always be shown to the moral instance represented by the Church in the affairs of state, people and governance, there is hardly any evidence that reposes expertise in governance on a Bishop with theological education at various levels.

Not for once has any headline captured a call from Bishop Kukah laying out an action plan to realign the mindset of our youths from 419, cultism, robbery and kidnapping. Not for once have I heard Bishop Kukah speak out against the generous donation of blood money to churches after plundering the public chest and robbing at gun point. Not for once has Bishop Kukah taught the nation about the wrath of God at taking another man's life.

When Bishop Kukah speaks out, he speaks to condemn the government's approach to fighting corruption. At the start of the government of President Muhammadu Buhari, Bishop Kukah spoke out against the fight against corruption and urged the government to focus more on the central issue of governance than fighting the *"symptoms of corruption"* as he puts it.

Not for once has any headline captured the Bishop condemning the brazen mentality of greed in the looting of public property. With names exposed and figures poured out in public domain, not once has any word of encouragement been heard from the mouth of the Bishop urging the government to carry on in its quest to sanitize the system. Not a word of support. All that comes from the Bishop's mouth, is to express doubt as to the government's ability to solve Nigeria's problems. In one very brazen utterance, one media outlet quoted the Bishop as saying: *"I will advise that rather than chasing the 'thieves', the president-elect should address the issues of the misery and squalor that have become Nigeria's lot, as development will raise the best army to fight corruption."* In other words, the Bishop had counseled the then President-elect to leave those who have already stolen, to God and simply go on governing as if nothing had happened.

It was at this point, in my humble opinion, that Buhari missed the golden opportunity to read the riot act to this errant Bishop and place him where he truly belongs. A respectful church leader speaks out once and retreats and does not make activism out of his views like a politician. Check Father Mbaka.

Not for once has Kukah called on God to forgive those who stored billions in a private house. Not for once, has Kukah appealed to the conscience of the people who disbursed military budget amongst themselves while Boko Haram was killing innocent souls. Now, voices are claiming that Kukah himself is often agitated each time the fight against corruption makes headlines, and finds faults in the process because he too, may have been a beneficiary of corruption under the immediate past dispensation. This insinuation alone would have been sufficient for an intelligent and honest adviser to retrace and recalibrate his steps. Not Kukah. Instead, he doubles down and complains about the commando and propagandist-style attack on corruption as if he was more pained by the sufferings of the apprehended than the sufferings of the masses at the receiving end.

Aside having no expertise and scientific authority to tutor anyone on good governance, Mr. Kukah does not even find the need to attempt a delicate balancing act when audaciously dabbling into a field that is naturally not his home domain. The need to condemn the crime, praise efforts to heal the malaise before suggesting steps to perfect the process of combating the affliction, does not appeal to Kukah as a well-meaning diplomatic approach. That he thus ends up as being the nominal mouthpiece of people who society seeks to hold accountable for crimes against the populace seems lost on him in its entirety. Worse still, is the fact that he commits all these moral atrocities wearing and abusing the robe and moral authority of the catholic church. Will he be surprised if skeptics begin to wonder what God he serves and what church he represents, where this God exists and what this church stands for?

Frisky Larr is the author of Nigeria's Journalistic Militantism,
Africa's Diabolical Entrapment and Lost In Democracy

***

Of Pharisees and Cardinals in the Buhari Equation!

By Frisky Larr

To the objective mind, the Christian religion in Nigeria today seems to embody a story that is yet to be told to a generation that is struggling to identify the goals, functions and aspirations of this religion. In a corporate society like Nigeria's that has been smashed and battered to its barest fabrics, this is a daunting task. When I set out to write the book "Africa's Diabolical Entrapment", I was determined not to give the Christian religion any semblance of wholesale condemnation in the face of the socially and politically useful moral values that the religion incorporates to the benefit of any society that cares.

Today, like a few years ago, when I commenced the project of doing that literary discourse, the motivating factors that drove me to its completion are still persistent. In fact, they have significantly worsened.

The trouble no longer ends with robbers and kidnappers going to Church every Sunday to pray for God's guidance and assistance in the execution of criminal and murderous projects. It does not end anymore, with criminals paying stupendous amounts as tithes to their gleefully excited and highly gratified pastors and preachers. No. The game has gone far beyond.

If I reported authentic instances of unbelievable and mundane pastors in that work, if I discussed fraudulent pastors and corporate tricksters in the glittering robe of peace and the bling-bling flash of splendor, today I can only talk about preachers and pastors, who have taken the game to the very foundation of the edifice that they seek to destroy.

To my readers, who expressed appreciation for my efforts in that work and told me how informative they found the work and enjoyed reading it, I owe you all a big apology.

I apologize for highlighting the unique position of the Catholic Church in Africa, which seemed clearly shielded from the racketeering mischief of new generation Churches that seem to have metamorphosed from the traditional blend of the Cherubim and Seraphim of old. Today, actors within the Catholic enclave seem to have long quietly devised a means of concealing their own version of racketeering behind the mask of ordinariness and avoidance of fraudulent sensations in the performance of miracles.

Indeed, I will make bold to say that Africans precisely Nigerians, do have reasons enough to express gratitude to the self-imposed men of God, whose stock-in-trade is flamboyance and the public display of silver and gold and jets and coats. They show us who they are and save for a few gullible and helpless minds, they are known to everyone else for their insatiable greed for material wealth and larceny based on sycophancy. They were not the least, very visible at the seat of power advancing prophetic and treacherously divine justification for all ills and evils in the last political dispensation under the Presidency of Mr. Goodluck Jonathan.

Not just a few observers suspected that many of these *counterfeit* men-of-God enjoyed gratifications from political sources and saw nothing wrong in being pampered for the nurturing of political support base at the expense of the tax payer's resources and labor. But no one knew for sure, the prevalent *modus operandi*. In all of these, the Catholic Church soared high and enjoyed a level of respectability that shielded it from public scrutiny.

It all began to change however, when one Reverend Mbaka cried out that attempts were made to have him launch a money-induced political campaign laced with spiritual cronyism to garner support for the now defunct government of Goodluck Jonathan. He mentioned names. He mentioned locations and even mentioned amounts. None was denied.

We knew then that a lot happened behind the scene that did not meet the eye and Reverend Mbaka's pronouncements lent more credence to the belief in the uniqueness of the Catholic Church.

Unfortunately, however, this illusion began to break apart as early as May 2015 shortly after euphoric hopes began to mount on the potential cleansing impact of a Buhari administration. None other than one elderly and hitherto highly respected Cardinal Anthony Okogie fired an initial shot warning Nigerians not to expect much from the then President-elect Muhammadu Buhari. He hinted at the possibility of a selective probe. It sounded mundane and absolutely normal at the time coming from a Catholic Clergy.

Barely a few months into the Presidency of General Buhari in September 2015, however, this same Cardinal Okogie came out again with a call to stop the public castigation of looters of public funds. In his view, the solution lies simply in calling such thieves to a national dialog probably for the purpose of reaching an honorable understanding for a meritorious award.

Then came another Cardinal Kukah shortly after, decrying what he regarded as an undue focus on anti-corruption measures to the detriment of what he considered other '*important tasks of governance*'. Till the present moment, he has failed however, in credibly explaining to Nigerians, what more important *task of governance* former General Buhari has sacrificed to the war against corruption amid dwindling national revenues.

As if that was not sufficient, a third Catholic Cardinal – a position that qualifies the Clergy to contest for Papacy – came out to inform Nigerians that the war against corruption will get nowhere if the government failed to flirt with religious leaders and secure their favor (probably like Goodluck Jonathan did).

What is most noticeable in all of these though, is the absence of outrage at the huge amount of looted public funds that are highlighted in the daily headlines. The commensurate collapse of public infrastructure and the glaring destitution of a complete nation with huge initial potentials do not seem to drive these men mad in the height of their elevated podium. Yet these voices are the voices of the moral instance of society – or so we thought – coming from within a religion that is known for the Mother Theresas of this world and a serving Pope, who stands out for abjection and humility.

They do not cry out and appeal to the conscience of the looters and launch an unsolicited campaign for voluntary submission to amnesty. No. Not a bit of that. They do not apologize on behalf of the looters, for the lives lost in conquerable insurgency. No. Not one bit. They lose no thought on instituting an unsolicited moral campaign to educate the minds towards virtues and fallacies. All that matters to them is the integrity of the thieves of our commonwealth.

Then it dawns on me to ask if Africa is doomed and condemned to the shelters of Charlatans even in religion. Do they worship a different God in Africa than does the Pope in the Vatican? What favor have these voices hitherto enjoyed that is presently taking its toll on their standard of living and self-exaltation? For short: Are we dealing with Pharisees in Cardinal skins?

It then beats my imagination so badly to figure out that a section of our intelligentsia does not only condone and identify with these fundamental evils, they also come out in staunch defense of such elementary folly. This hardly catches me off-guard though, since the group dynamics that has been driving the concept of Anti-Buharism in cyber space, seems to be robbing individuals of the urge to summon the need for a deeper rethink of shallow positions.

Yes. Any scholar of Social Pedagogics will smirk a bit hearing the phenomenon of 'group dynamics'. It is this social phenomenon, which gives an individual a sense of security and reassurance, when acting in the company of like-minded individuals. He will do things that he wouldn't have done left to himself. The need and urge to rethink one's position is often obliterated in the face of empowering solidarity. I know many individuals, who invest a lot of personal capital in elevating their intellectual profile. What the simplistic, skewed and in part, tribal identification with Goodluck Jonathan has ended up doing to these individuals, however, now looks like a perpetual damage to their faculty of simple intellectual perception.

They are driven by the sheer number of people on the social media, who share this lower stratum of intellectual challenges and do not care anymore, to give a proper scrutiny to the positions they represent for a basic commonsense compatibility. The number of people, they are able to team up with, gives them the needed psychological reassurance that they are simply holding a *"different"* and not a *"fundamentally flawed"* position that basic logical reasoning would hitherto, have forced them to think about. This indeed, has also galvanized a desolate President Jonathan (who ordinarily, should have retreated into solitude never to be seen or heard for the time being), into truly believing that he has a genuine place not only in the good books of Nigerian History but also in international reality. The weighty burden of the mess he plunged the nation into does not seem to have dawned on him quite yet.

And then there is this position trending these days that the President has morally desecrated the image of Nigeria by admitting in overseas trips that his priority presently lies in cleansing the deeply-rooted rot in his own country. Many who hitherto, have spent their time and energy pondering over serious issues now seem to have found time to promote the efficacy and sanctity of a worthless state of denial.

Hearing this simplistic and superficial postulation, I asked myself if people truly expected a meaningful and purposeful cleaning of our own home with the assistance of outside forces that have served as safe sanctuaries for looting and exploitation if we simply took to denying the obvious and papering over the filth and stench. Who doesn't know how rotten Nigeria is? To whom will that be news for the love of Mike? Is there anyone in his true senses, who actually believes that Nigeria can recover from its present disaster without assistance from outside forces? Not the least, the recovery of loot is proving this otherwise. Is it now that we fear the collateral impact of the vociferous vampires in economic and political superpowers? The same superpowers that housed loot from the Atikus and Iboris of this world! All these happened before the war on corruption was declared. The looting and exploitation had desecrated the image of the country badly enough and everyone knows from Abuja to Zurich. Who should then to be the foolish and hilarious Statesman to go around the world denying the obvious?

It is precisely at the back of such elementary and pedestrian logic and reasoning (that no one indeed, should ordinarily, be wasting his/her energy upon, who is serious about moving forward) that the Pharisees in Cardinal skins conceal themselves from the glare of reason. They appeal to the gullible, who are ever ready to swallow hook, line and sinker and without in-depth consideration, anything that makes shallow sense to them.

Going at this rate, however, I'm afraid Nigeria will be doomed. Yet, I have my hopes that the new direction will fathom a rescue path that will make generations smile even after we quit the stage.

***

All signs were pointing at an impending questioning of the former President since more and more voices were singing from the same hymnbook after arrest for graft and misuse of public funds. Several lieutenants of the former administration often refereed to instructions from the President for whatever vices they were subsequently associated with. Even the once adored and even revered former operative of the World Bank, who served the Jonathan administration as a Super Minister of Finance and Coordinator of the Economic Team, Ngozi Okonjo-Iweala, took pains to point out that she carefully channeled all her activities through the President for every major action she took. The buck stops at the President's desk. Cardinals and Pharisees that were then lecturing the President on how best to govern all seemed to be working towards one goal: Forestall the impending arrest of the former President.

I wrote the following article amid this atmosphere of uncertainty. The fire-brand nature of the article meant, I did not even bother to send it to any major news outlet for publication and wider coverage but simply confined it to my personal website (www.Friskylarr.com) and the social media alone:

Arrest Jonathan Now, Declare State of Emergency and Blow 'em all up!

By Frisky Larr

It would have been so easy if anger could solve problems. We would have chosen the path of the prophecy of the legendary Bob Marley of blessed memory. *"A total destruction, the only solution. They aren't no use, no one can stop them now!"*

Quite obviously, the civil war that seemed to have been avoided in March 2015 on the heels of former President Jonathan's concession of defeat to retired General Muhammadu Buhari, is now looming large more than ever before. Who didn't feel a chill up the spine when the carefully choreographed theater of the absurd played out at the collation center of election results on that fateful sunny day when ex-Minister Orubebe starred as the notorious bad boy and angel of doom? Who didn't feel the eerie air of silence that seemed to have paralyzed the nation in expectation of the second Act?

Again, who did not heave a sigh of relief when Goodluck Jonathan finally did the needful and called Muhammadu Buhari on telephone to concede the obvious defeat that was only waiting to be announced? Who?

Of what relevance is that today, though, in the face of dreadful realities portending danger and misery for the Niger Delta and the rest of the country?

Indeed, every fair-minded analyst knew what it meant for Nigeria, when news broke out that former President Jonathan performed the historical act that was done before him only by Dimeji Bankole at a lower level, to concede electoral defeat and congratulate the rightful winner. We knew the pit of hell that Nigeria was rescued from and agreed that Jonathan deserved accolades.

Tragically too, we knew very many things that we did not want Jonathan to get away with. One generally known fact is that no nation on earth makes budgetary provisions for the re-election campaign of any political leader. Nigeria was no exception. Yet information dominated the airwaves, of the free flow of hard currency for gratifications to mobilize support from all nooks and corners, for Goodluck Jonathan's re-election. Ridiculous pictures hit the airwaves, of an incumbent President kneeling and crawling for prayers before witches, pastors and imams. Millions of dollars were paid for spiritual salvation and physical manipulations.

Today, thanks to the dogged but expected efforts of President Muhammadu Buhari, these issues are no longer speculations but common knowledge that will soon be widely validated by judicial pronouncements. Government and party officials, who knew so well that there was no budgetary allocation for the re-election campaign of the President, are now trying in vain, to feign ignorance of the source of the money that was disbursed to them to prosecute the President's re-election campaign. The giver and the taker of stolen money are often considered trapped in the same cage in the spirit of the law. Ignorance is no excuse.

The same applies to a cousin or next-of-kin of the President, who is officially awarded a $40 million contract and is paid upfront in full for doing nothing.

A lot happened prior to the elections too. Sanusigate ended up in some Pricewater charade with whistleblowers rather than the perpetrators of crime being hunted beyond all bounds. The perpetrators reveled in triumph and emptiness believing in the power of the highest political instance. The brigandage of an elitist clique called the shots in the land much to the amazement and fury of the discerning minds. A nation was simply bastardized by drinkers of liquor and many who should have known better.

No doubt that the anger was immense that Jonathan sought to paper-over with the virtue of conceding an electoral defeat that was not orchestrated to look as such. The sweetness of the moment was compounded by memories of the vicious rape committed on a single nation in the belief of raping the nation on a turn-by-turn basis and from region to region. Worse still, it was led by a man who, Nigerians erroneously believed, was blessed with the highest possible academic decoration as a symbol of intellectual superiority.

Now, we know that former President Jonathan is immensely constrained intellectually by virtue of his actions and omissions. Discerning Nigerians – not the half-educated and emotionally overwhelmed soldier-bees – had long come to terms with this reality and accepted that an internationally brokered soft-landing (even though only speculated) for the ex-President may be grudgingly accepted in the interest of peace. That much was the status quo until Sahara Reporters threw the bombshell. We will come to that later.

No one anticipated the enormity of the theft that the former President supervised until fingers started pointing at him repeatedly, as the legitimator of the loots that turned the Central Bank to a self-service snack bar. The deliberate weakening of the Nigerian Armed Forces through the free ride granted the Generals to loot the coffers blind was complemented by the suspected arming of rebel forces in the creeks with warships from Norway as far as we know in public space. Former President Obasanjo worried aloud about fighters sponsored by President Jonathan, who were receiving military training overseas. His open letter claiming the stock-piling of weapons by Jonathan's men, is no secret to the nation. Today, some militants are boasting of missiles to strike the presidential palace.

It all started with the curious and sudden resurgence of secession agitation led by one pathetic but fully misguided agent of the invisible forces that was quickly tamed and quarantined by the forces of re-organized authority. Having been frustrated in that angle, the forces obviously regrouped and activated the alternative option of restarting the Niger Delta militancy, again, under the pretext of marginalization.

They proceeded to launch treasonable sabotage attacks on the economic lifeline of the country and did not care that they were subjecting their region to the more serious collateral impact of environmental hardship. While speculations have been rife on the evil project being the brainchild of political sponsorship, no one saw the bombshell coming that indeed elected and trusted officers of state in charge of public funds would come anywhere near sympathizing with the diabolical notion of the criminals in the creek.

Indeed, like me, many Nigerians are waiting and hoping they will wake up soon from a deep sleep and understand that the bombshell exploded by Sahara Reporters was just a dream after all.

The yet-unrefuted Sahara Reporters report contends that Governors of the Niger Delta region with the exception of Cross-River and Edo State are presently in an open and brazen gang-up to kill the war against corruption as it affects their region by calling for the abandonment of corruption charges against politicians from their region. This is supposed to be in return for the cessation of pipeline-bombing hostilities. In this extremely outrageous ploy, it is yet unclear if they enlisted the support of the only government Minister so far perceived to be hardworking and productive, or if this Minister – himself from the region of the tamed trailblazing secessionist agitators – has been a part of the criminal design all along.

No surprise that the teeming majority of Nigerians who voted for a clean-up of the system to reset the button of decency, is now up in arms and extremely infuriated. The blackmail that was planned by these Governors, who now stand under the serious suspicion of at best sympathizing with the criminal activities of the Niger Delta militants or at worst, having sponsored them all along, seems predicated on the obnoxious thought to fall back upon, that the resources being from the Niger Delta justifies corruption by politicians from that same region. They, therefore, hold the belief that the state can be legitimately blackmailed in this respect.

Many have been wondering why former President Goodluck Jonathan in his abundance of wisdom has so far, failed to speak up on the atrocious act of his kinsmen. Now, there is a sense of knowing why it has been so. Yet, a more intelligent approach of openly disowning the rampaging criminals, whether he sponsors them quietly or not, would have been the least strategic move to expect. It is reminiscent of the game that he played in the run-up to the Presidential election of 2015. Even though all indications pointed to his re-election ambition and efforts, he kept mute on the issue for a very long time and even denied it outright when confronted directly. On one occasion, he was quoted as telling his predecessor, Olusegun Obasanjo that "I have never told anyone I wanted to run for re-election".

With the bunch of pedestrian advisers surrounding him, he will, sooner or later, end up ostracizing himself in the international community, where the same people who have been awarding him questionable democracy prizes, will begin to question his integrity and the role he is playing in destabilizing his country. Most pathetic of all, is the lack of constructive remorse in the attitude of the former President under the evidential yoke of consuming vices. With evidence mounting by the day, of the unprecedented monumental scale of corruption directly coordinated by this former President, he still nurses the hope of bullying his way out of the stinking quagmire.

In his failure to learn from history, he is unable to see what his presidential bullying has turned his party (the PDP) into. He bullied his way into presidential candidacy in the spirit of 'having it my way or the highway'. Denying his party, the option of a strategically more qualified candidate, he ran for re-election and lost woefully and today, his party is in tatters. Again, he is trying the same diabolical tactic using the Niger Delta as a springboard. His pawns are the ganja-smoking sons of Jah and militant-minded Governors of Nyesom Wike quality that was foisted on us by corrupt Supreme Court judges. In the end, all signs are pointing to the fact that the Niger Delta may as well be left in tatters like PDP as a historical presidential souvenir. If the meaning of "Goodluck" is to leave a trail of disaster wherever the former President goes, I will gleefully wish the Niger Delta good luck.

For now, though, the fury and outrage that the so-called Governors of the South-South plus Ibe Kachikwu have triggered in the public should be encouraging enough for President Muhammadu Buhari to bring out the General in him pretty quickly in spite of age-induced frailty. Indeed, in the depth of my anger at this willful sabotage to spite the aspirations of a nation for good governance and a return to casual sanity, I would have advised the President to summon an emergency meeting of the Council of State to declare the urgent need to arrest former President Goodluck Jonathan there and there, declare a State of Emergency in the rebel states of the Niger Delta, arrest the Governors and have them tried for treason, and declare an all-out war on the Niger Delta until the militants are wiped off the face of the earth.

Unfortunately, though, anger does not solve problems and innocent souls will bear the brunt. No matter what happens, this is a battle that Muhammadu Buhari must win by hook or by crook. By defiance and doggedness! Without surrendering, without retreating! No region in any nation is ever granted a free ride to corruption – golden egg or not. Nigeria will not be an exception.

Every well-meaning Nigerian will now be best advised to brace up for the impending revolution to topple the forces that will not let Nigeria be. At individual level and at the level of voluntary, non-governmental organizations, the time is fast approaching to seize the scepter and grab the bull by the horn. Preparations should start here and now, to pick up the gauntlet and deny evil forces the taste of victory. Nigeria must survive and together, we will blow 'em all up!

***

While the enemies of the President, who are largely, drawn from sympathizers of the old guard, grew louder on the social media, one couldn't help suspecting that the old guard itself, was busy fomenting trouble for the new government. First, information trickled out that the Niger Delta Avengers was, indeed, founded by the defeated President Goodluck Jonathan preparatory to the 2015 presidential election in an intimidatory and vengeful bid to secure his hold on power or react to an eventual defeat.

"In fact, the name 'Avengers' came from the lips of Goodluck Jonathan. … As Election Day approached, certain stakeholders were mobilized to form a force to standby and ensure total anarchy in the South-South and the South-East within 24 hours if the election results were not favorable to Jonathan. It took everyone by surprise to learn that Mr. Jonathan had conceded defeat even before the final results were released. The standby force that was supposed to attack specific targets was told to stand down. They were all compensated in US dollars cash." [7]

The sabotage actions of the Niger Delta Avengers that involved the blowing up of oil pipelines ended up decimating Nigeria's revenue derived from international oil sales. Production dropped from 2.2 million barrels per day (Bpd) to 1.6 million bpd.[8]

Subsequently, unverified and unconfirmed rumors swirled around claiming that the explosives detonated by the Niger Delta Avengers had been planted during the tenure of the former President in anticipation of attempts to deny the then incumbent President, a second term in office and only required the green light to have them detonated. At the time it looked increasingly likely that the former President would be called in for questioning, the orders were said to have been given, to blow them all up.

Secondly, a hitherto, little known organization that called itself the "Indigenous People of Biafra" (IPOB), with a ragtag radio station broadcasting from London and led by an extremely vulgar young man named Nnamdi Kanu, sprang from nowhere and resurrected the secessionist Biafran provocation that was long defeated in the early 1970's. This young man adopted unprintable and extremely inappropriate gutter languages in describing Nigeria, the incumbent President Muhammadu Buhari and any dissenting voice of Igbo origin that was supposed to make up the Biafran Republic of his dreams and those that sympathized with him. In an attempt to bring the struggle deep into Nigeria by installing technical possibilities of receiving the radio transmission in Nigeria, his travel to Nigeria became a nightmare and he was arrested and locked up for a very long time.

There were also widespread assumptions that the young man and his movement, which gained a huge following amongst his secessionist-minded natives, was also sponsored and financed by members of the old guard in a bid to avenge what they consider, an unjust defeat.

Then, information began trickling out once again, on piecemeal basis, that the President's health was taking a big hit. He embarked on occasional travels to the United Kingdom in the fashion of many other politicians, past and present. Many things happened in quick succession. The President's own wife cried out that the presidential clinic within the President's fortified palace, "Aso Rock", was embarrassingly and shamefully ill-equipped. The President that was called in to fix the ills of the system but failed to start with the basic necessity of putting the presidential clinic in shape, ended up seeking treatment in a foreign country. On top of this, he told the world press, in response to the scathing criticism made by her, that she belonged to his kitchen and his bedroom.

Accusations surfaced, of one close aide of the President, spending millions of taxpayers' money on weeding the soil where a camp for Internally Displaced Persons was to be erected for victims of the Boko haram insurgence. The President, who everyone had in mind as a no-nonsense character, was surprisingly, slow to action.

I wrote this article in the wake of these contradictions in the President's actions and projected image:

How President Buhari Played into the Hands of his Adversaries

By Frisky Larr

The political career of President Muhammadu Buhari is fast playing out as a tragic political thriller of sort. It is a career that is filled with suspense, perseverance, celebration and also marred by complacency. I will shed more light on this as the discourse proceeds. But first, let us take a look at President Buhari's antecedents.

Before becoming President, he was a seriously polarizing figure. He was either hated bitterly or loved unconditionally. One section of his haters was disturbed and petrified by his perceived sense of strictness, sternness and savvy stubbornness. Another section based its rejection strictly on the tangible facts extracted from the draconian (but in hindsight, highly missed) days of combined rulership with the late General Tunde Idiagbon.

In his submission that was widely publicized in Nigerian newspapers on January 16, 2007, Professor Wole Soyinka outlined Buhari's crimes in the following order:

Disregard for constituted authority by treating the Oputa panel with "unconcealed disdain", execution of a 29-year old chap (Bernard Ogedengbe) on drug-smuggling charges by retroactive legislation even though the crime did not carry a death penalty at the time it was committed, the stifling of civil rights and the indiscriminate imprisonment of activists such as Tai Solarin, extreme tribal leanings in locking up Vice President Alex Ekwueme in the maximum security prison of Kirikiri, while his boss, the head of the regime that was overthrown on charges of corruption – Shehu Shagari – was kept in the comfort of a house arrest in Ikoyi, the long detention of the septuagenarian, Governor Adekunle Ajasin, even though he was acquitted in repeated trials and finally, "the story of the thirty-something suitcases" that Buhari allowed a northern traditional ruler to bring into the country in spite of strict laws prohibiting the inflow and outflow of goods through the country's borders, while Fela Kuti had to languish in jail for having currencies that he legitimately needed for an overseas performance.

In other words, Professor Wole Soyinka was strongly representative of the voices that saw in Muhammadu Buhari, a bigoted tribalist and religious fanatic, who felt comfortable, creating privileges for people of his tribal and religious extraction, to put it mildly. Even though this formulation may not be perfectly accurate as it relates to Wole Soyinka, the accusation nevertheless, sums up the sentiments of the anti-Buhari camp over several years. It, however, took a few years of one Goodluck Jonathan from a minority tribe to run down the entire fabric of political correctness and threaten the unity of the nation to make Nigerians, including myself, forget the serious dangers that were hitherto associated with the name Muhammadu Buhari. He was given a second chance with his "War Against Indiscipline" (WAI) conveniently called to mind in a nation that had simply taken to the celebration of crafty larceny and idolization of talents in transgression. The prominent role that the late Tunde Idiagbon played in the instilment of discipline under WAI, was conveniently relegated to the background while the background role of Muhammadu Buhari under that dispensation was raised to the forefront by a country that was in desperate need of redemption and the resetting of the values button.

Archenemies like Wole Soyinka and Olusegun Obasanjo suddenly became converts and Buhari-sympathizers against Goodluck Jonathan, to save Nigeria from imminent collapse.

All through the years, though, the man Buhari, had witnessed transformations in the aftermath of serial failures in political adventures. There was suspense in his molding of political alliances and perseverance in his resilience. Yet, when celebration finally came with the involuntary help of Jonathan's obnoxious designs and incompetence, age had already taken its toll on Muhammadu Buhari. His health had taken a hit, but above all else, he had learned some crucial lessons.

Those, who felt passionate about dissolving the union that they called a contraption, which a continued Jonathan's Presidency, would probably, have done little to stop, remain bitterly angry till the present moment, over the disruptive victory of the secretly ailing Muhammadu Buhari in 2015. On the contrary, those who remembered the War Against Indiscipline and the good-looking Major General of the youthful days, yearned for the General to pick up the pieces, tidy up the stall and reset the values button.

Since his victory was facilitated by forces from within and without the shores of the country, Muhammadu Buhari learned the art and craft of political compromises through the days of electioneering in an almost effortless manner. His minders and tutors in the deal of civilian leadership were sure that they had formed in him, the perfect mix of dictatorship and compassion to retake Nigeria from the wolves. The voters were convinced that Nigeria will witness the dawn of a new era in General Muhammadu Buhari. The phrase General versus President was coined with the latter representing the weaker option caged by a mindset of political compromises in the spirit of constitutionality. The new President, who assured the important forces behind his success that he will strive to be more democratic and be guided by the constitution, was, however, also aware of the expectations of the masses and the schadenfreude of his adversaries.

President Muhammadu Buhari started failing surprisingly, when he negated the need to carry the folks along and deliver a fiery and reassuring inaugural speech to keep the momentum alive, while pilferers and kleptomaniacs still had the fear of the General in mind. Instead, he came up with a very uninspiring and 'unspinnable' slogan of belonging to everyone and belonging to no one. The new President did not stop at that. He kept everyone guessing if he was overreaching the need for commitment as a newborn democrat.

In a third world country that is demonstrably more in need of discipline than democracy, the new President played seemingly feeble and indifferent to shocking manipulations in the installment of a Senate President. He turned a blind eye and a deaf ear to the thuggish disengagement of a state assembly by a Governor in Oyo State. All these developments fresh into his Presidency were yet forgivable and were forgiven too, because he was assumed to have opted for a concentration of efforts on battling the menace of the Islamic ragtag army in the north that his predecessor allowed to blossom and grow in an apparent attempt to weaken the union. Yet, many could not understand, why the President's pushback against a rogue party member, who stole the Senate Presidency and consistently undermined his authority against in-house consensus, was not done in a decisive and terse counterattack.

History is awash with narratives and examples of the incompatibility of democracy with poverty and weak social fabrics. Successful democracies in today's world are generally rich in material and educational opportunities and often have a healthy groundwork of social stability. Successful poor countries often thrive when leaders stretch the limit of their powers imposing their will, sometimes, in outright dictatorship too, to create affluence and boost the standard of living of their citizens. Citizens often care less about a dictator, when the proper standard of living is put in place. Constitutions do not make countries rich without the requisite educational mindset and compatible social setting that African countries do not have. Details in this regard, are contained in my book "Lost in Democracy".

When the teeming majority of Nigerians popularly ushered in Muhammadu Buhari, many expected the General. Not the President.

The 'General' moved swiftly to confront Boko Haram and launched a clampdown on corrupt judges. The 'President', however, retreated from cleansing the Judiciary either in the aftermath of a clandestine blackmail or out of a sheer lack of fortitude to follow through. With the faint-heartedness of a caged President, he has continued to ignore credible and outrageous reports of corruption, arrogance, high-handedness and overreaching authority by members of his inner circle.

As if he had completely forgotten the persistent suspicion of tribalism that trailed him since his days as military Head of State and his travails as a failed candidate, the 'President' seemingly chose to display a part of the General's arrogance and complacency by confining himself to the provisions of the constitution in meeting the demands for the Federal Character and making all other appointments thereafter, a northern Nigerian affair. While I, personally, do not care at all, who the President chooses to work with, since Jonathan also chose his kinsmen and heaven did not fall, commonsense has, nonetheless shown that Goodluck Jonathan could not have been a viable barometer for measuring credibility in this regard. Having lived through the color-blindness of Olusegun Obasanjo in terms of tribes and appointments, it is strongly pathetic that President Buhari still seemed to have nursed this archaic sentiment of promoting northern dominance in his appointments.

The 'General' moved swiftly to confront misguided agitators and political pawns, who nursed unrealistic hopes for a disintegrated Nigeria. Now, who was it that simply turned a blind eye and a deaf ear to the Fulani Herdsmen? The 'General' or the 'President'?

In the end, in spite of all his major achievements in struggling to diversify the nation's economic base, to streamline the flow of federal revenue through a Treasury Single Account, to bailout states with funds to pay salaries, wages and pension, to pay government debts owed by his predecessor, to take Nigeria out of recession largely caused by a plunge in revenue intake, to edge towards self-sufficiency in rice production and other agricultural sectors, and in spite of countless ongoing infrastructural projects, the revamping of the foreign reserves that were plundered in times of plenty etc., he played into the hands of his adversaries by simply allowing the Benue massacre and the Boko Haram abduction to happen under his watch. Now, revisionism and denials are compounding his achievements and echoes of his major blunders are overshadowing any narrative that may attempt to be fair on him. Thanks to Buhari, Nigeria now knows that our budgets have been criminally padded through several regimes. Yet, he failed to clamp down on the legislators decisively with the necessary prosecution of perpetrators. On the contrary, he sided openly with the principal officers of the legislature and threw whistleblowers to the wolves.

To make matters worse, the President's own reaction to charges that he refuses to dialog with Nigerians on matters of political importance, when he is most needed, simply seems to signal to the world that he prefers to take his time in reaching decisions. Taking the time needed to reach decisions can never be equated with ignoring serious charges and refusal to act on offenders that have been made public. After all, it is the same Buhari that did not bulge long to execute criminals on retroactive laws.

This is the tale of willful self-desecration and self-demystification. How history will judge Buhari's legacy will, in part, strongly depend on how much he continues to leave the narratives to his adversaries to tell and how quickly he makes amends to fix his weaknesses and rebrand his image for the rest of his tenure. I strongly doubt though that he will have a second term in the face of health challenges and a hostile establishment.

One more issue:

Omoyele Sowore

I strongly commend the courage of Omoyele Sowore in his bold move to run for the presidency of Nigeria. All talks about a new breed will have to have a starting point. This hardly compares to those unseasoned social media dreamers, who seem to be toying with party politics these days, amid ideological contradictions and a lasting chain of inconsistencies. On the face of it, it sounds very ridiculous because Omoyele Sowore has zero political experience in any political office. But underrate this young man at your own perils. Sahara Reporters started from nowhere and seems to have taught many syndicate journalists in Nigeria, a serious lesson on what investigative journalism and the sophistication of sources should be about. Hardly anyone knows today, who Sowore's backers are, if there are any. He has, nonetheless, been elevated to an outstanding pedestal in the journalism of exposure reaching from England through the United States and deep into the heart of Nigeria. Who doesn't remember his adventurous secret travel to Nigeria as an enemy of the Jonathan's regime during the 2015 elections and his successful utilization of credible sources to unearth accurate election results ahead of any other outlet? I, personally, do not expect him to defeat President Buhari, if the President chooses to recontest. Yet, I expect him to give any mainstream candidate a good run for his/her money. A lot will depend on the kind of friends he chooses down the line. Close association with inconsistent Facebook dreamers can only impact negatively on this laudable project. Underrate Sowore only at your own perils.

Frisky Larr is the author "Nigeria's Journalistic Militantism", assessing the role of the media in the image of Olusegun Obasanjo, "Africa's Diabolical Entrapment", assessing Africa's obsession with Religion and "Lost in Democracy" outlining the futility of democracy in a society with other priorities

***

Before then though I had written an article appealing to the conscience of Nigerians, who were keen on having the nation rescued from the annihilating fangs of the previous administration:

Brush the Mistakes Aside and Help Buhari Save the Revolution!

By Frisky Larr

The name Eddy Grant is still a household name to a particular age group all over the world. The Guyana-born Reggae star once sang the lyrics that I remember so well. One of several memorable verses. *"Another revolutionary; He is fighting for us righteously; But he can't paddle waves with his hands..."* Whoever watches the Nigerian political scene of today and does not see Muhammadu Buhari reflected in these verses is either indifferent to the Nigerian scene or is an avowed adversary of the current President of Nigeria.

Within the past few weeks and months, there have been reasons to be angry at the President. Very many reasons too. Indeed, even if not clearly articulated or expressed in public space, Nigerians, who voted Muhammadu Buhari to power in March 2015, actually voted for a revolution, no matter the type. His admirers knew this and his enemies too. The desperate drive to stop his candidacy at all cost (with certificate, health records, etc.) was borne out of a premonition of the troubles ahead. The revolution. Steering the nation from one extreme to the other was and still remains a daunting task. From insane corruption that broke all bounds under Goodluck Jonathan back to normalcy and sanity! From disintegration to a unity of purpose. It was a movement from one extreme to the very other.

The realization that the filthy system will always fight back has been with us since the days of Nuhu Ribadu. We have, therefore, genuinely asked ourselves umpteenth times, how come President Buhari allowed himself to be duped and cornered by the cabal both within and without.

In all honesty, though, a lot is easier said than it is done. It is also easier to watch and criticize from the comfort zone of an armchair quarterbacker than it is to be the real actor on the throne of power. Precisely this power is President Buhari's strongest enemy today. We will come to this later.

To become a President, Muhammadu Buhari mounted the candidate's saddle in three futile attempts. Each of these three attempts fielded the real revolutionary Buhari, who sought to enforce (*"by fire, by force"*) most of the radical changes that Nigeria constantly yearned for. At least, for the most part. Upon the third consecutive failure, however, the Ex-General saw the steam in him dissipating. The age factor could not be wished away. He vowed to call it quits. There was no way the powerful establishment of Nigeria at the time, could have allowed him to mount the throne of President. No way. His views were yet, too radical. They were too divisive. They were yet, too tribalist.

A Softened Buhari

When Jonathan took the rot to further extreme, however, and many observers got disappointed, thinking they had seen the worst of filths long before Jonathan, a part of the establishment had to swing to action. The need to shake and overhaul the system was recognized and Buhari became the only bride available. This time though, the rules of the game were not to be dictated by him alone. The radical line, the divisive line and the tribalist line had to be reworked. He had to shed some baggage. Getting Muhammadu Buhari to play by the rules of the powerful domestic and international establishment meant the birth of a softened Buhari. This, indeed, was the veiled message that Muhammadu Buhari constantly sent to Nigerians, amongst others, when he told Chatham House in a speech that was primarily directed at the international establishment, that he was a born-again democrat, who regretted his dictatorial past.

Unfortunately, however, revolution is nothing but the radical displacement or reversal of the status quo and existing conditions against the desires and wishes of the establishment. The establishment never leads a revolution to rob itself of power. In other words, the day Muhammadu Buhari became marketable as a presidential candidate democratic election, was the day Nigeria lost the original and authentic revolutionary Buhari.

Since old soldiers never die, revolutionary instincts are also, never lost completely. Within the scope that still makes his silent gentleman's agreement with the establishment tenable and workable, Muhammadu Buhari set out to face the onerous task of walking the electoral talk, once becoming President. All within his possible authentic limits! He was serious. He was hell-bent on succeeding. Each time, he lets out these revolutionary instincts in a bubbling crescendo, however, the domestic establishment descends on him to take him back to the limits of marketability and electoral assurances.

The best proof of what every observer has long thought and speculated, was provided lately, by the Publicity Secretary of the All Progressives Congress in Lagos State, Mr. Joe Igbokwe while commenting on the excesses of former President Goodluck Jonathan. *"He is supposed to be the one that should be held responsible but because other heads of state (keep) pleading for him, that is why he is busy junketing all over the place."* He was quoted as saying.

Indeed, those persons, who step in to caution and whip President Buhari back into line for whatever agenda they pursue, often adopt all measures possible. Some choose the instrument of invisibility through conspiratorial intimidation. This partly entails the **avenging** of peace and tranquility in delta environment as well as **agitation** for the loss of innocent lives in the eastern region to warn the President of an impending chaos.

Veiled Household Betrayal

In other words, while President Buhari took off the gloves and began to step on powerful toes, he was ready to stretch the limit to the constitutionally permitted leeway. Sabotage set in, though, through viciously hostile and bellicose acts that was then smoothened out by the *innocent* intervention of *well-meaning* establishment characters. They urge soft-pedalling. They urge the recognition of untouchable geographical regions in the war against corruption. They sugar-coat their psychological persuasion. They urge a cooling of the political temperature.

Since this powerful and massive pressure is often difficult to overcome by one man alone, the President's doggedness caved-in and opened up another vacuum for die-hard opportunists. Slowly but steadily and before the President knew it, his own inner circle seems to have formed another dirty cabal just before his nose.

In this collaborative network of criminal actors, which requires several hands washing each other for dubious cleanliness, the President now seems alienated in his own world. Who would not be in the trap of unsuspected predators, when fighting back against righteousness is a matter of life and death? It is in this light, that I have begun to view the President's heap of contradictions in the fight against corruption.

This is no longer the time to fume over the President's unforced errors. Countless unforced errors! This is no longer the time to turn our back on the President in anger as the childish agents of hate and vindictiveness do, saying "I told you so". After all, the revolutionary instinct still lives in President Buhari.

The Revolution lives!

His historical, unprecedented and dare-devil strike on the judiciary that gladdened the heart of all well-meaning Nigerians, is one little drop of water on a glowing rock. It shows to us that even though further planned arrests of more corrupt judges have been stalled, yet again, by intervening establishment maneuvers, Nigerians should rally round the President to bring out the best in him. It also shows to us that this President strikes in the dark of night to take his adversary unaware in spite the constant stumbling block of the establishment.

He may have missed the golden opportunity to fall back on his rock-solid base of people's power. He may have missed the chance to damn the establishment and relate directly with the masses. But the opportunity of the masses to get him back to their side is inexhaustible.

A true revolutionary seeks the instrument of power by all means and implements his agenda without a care for the consequences and whose ox is gored. He leaves the end to justify the means. President Buhari may have underrated the readiness of committed Nigerians to take to the streets and whip the enemies of the country into line on his behalf, but Nigerians will never underrate their inexhaustible opportunity to get the President back to their side. The Occupy NASS movement and the spontaneous march on the Supreme Court by a few aggrieved Nigerians are just a taste of the gathering storm that the Germans would refer to as the cleansing thunderstorm.

While the world always expects a revolutionary to confront the system and the establishment, it is also aware that revolution is akin to a gathering hurricane that will raze many edifices to their foundation for a better and guided reconstruction bearing all imaginable precautions. Nigeria is overdue for the reset button and for now, we have no Tunde Idiagbon on the horizon. We have no Murtala Muhammed left. No Gani Fawehimi. No Tai Solarin. All we have left, is Muhammadu Buhari. Even though trapped in the tempest and the violent waves of a brutal sea, he cannot paddle the waves with his bare hands. Brush his costly mistakes aside and help him save the revolution. Let us reassure him now, of the needed support to break free from the fangs of the evil cabal.

Watch out for my upcoming Book "Lost in Democracy" - An Inquest into Africa's Problems with Democracy and Exploration of Possible Alternatives! Don't Miss It!

***

Somewhere down the line though, the President's health began taking a turn for the worse rekindling memories of a presidential clinic in the President's palace that is being left to dilapidate. Whatever happened in the President's palace, no one outside the inner circle can say with any degree of certainty today. Rumor has it that the President suffered food-poisoning and was rescued by the prompt reaction of some of his closest confidants. What is certain, however, is that the President went on a medical vacation to England and underwent treatment for good three months after duly handing over power to his Vice President to run the country in his absence. That too, was a novum and a clear sign of forthrightness on the part of the President.

I wrote this article at the height of the controversy that trailed the President's absence:

Buhari's Leadership Disappointment and Confused Nigerians!

By Frisky Larr

Who doesn't remember the dirty tricks in the presidential elections of 2015? A medical report was released, ostensibly engineered by the incumbent President of the time, from the Teaching Hospital of a reputable Nigerian university. The content was explosive and a potential game-changer. It purportedly revealed the negative medical record of the then opposition candidate, Muhammadu Buhari. A long-standing impact of advancing prostate cancer was poised to take a toll on his fitness for the office he aspired to hold, so the report claimed. Remember the misstep at a rally stage and the hyped reports of a slump on the campaign trail?

The medical report was subsequently retracted, and no one claimed responsibility for authoring it at the Teaching Hospital of the reputable Nigerian university. Today, memories are revisited for highly informed reasons. The opposition candidate, who went on to become the President of today's Nigeria is indeed, now known to be truly suffering from an undisclosed illness. Backdoor rumors point to prostate cancer.

In spite of all that though, and not the least, based on what we know today, every citizen, who wishes his country well, will still rejoice that the truth was suppressed, and the ill-health info did not mar the chances of ousting the corrupt and disastrous regime of Goodluck Ebele Jonathan. In the same vein, however, it offers reasons for regrets and lamentations, basically, because it uncovers a deeply rooted culture of political manipulations to entrench the will of the political establishment. What you see is not what you get. The decision to remove Goodluck Ebele Jonathan from the driver's seat was paramount to everything else. Thank goodness for it though!

The manipulated electorate, however, nurtured high expectations and saw a small-ax messiah that was configured to take a no-nonsense stance and cut down the mighty tree of corruption. The corrupt ones feared for their lives too. The scramble for cover-ups and obliteration of traces and desperate moves to intercept the President-elect on planes to strike a deal for mercy, were the least that the evil caucus could allow itself. Many took ill overnight, and overseas medical check became a pastime exercise. In panic and desperation, journalistic white-wash propaganda was employed as well as the sudden exposure of cardinals and pontifices to rationalize the negative impact of fighting corruption.

The scammed electorates trusted in the man and the man struck the right nerve to usher in the birth of a new era. For starting the fight from the top and docking the powerful and the mighty, the President was forgiven for his unpreparedness for the routine demand of the office he fought repeatedly, to occupy. After months of preparation as a President-elect, the President had no clue, how to constitute his cabinet for good six months. He was forgiven. For observers of the scene, it was re-assuring, however, to understand that the President was prepared to shake the establishment from top to bottom and *"give corruption a bloody nose"*.

Unfortunately, however, the President derailed and allowed the powerful to fight back while he, obviously, in consideration of the transience of life, saw no need to make too many enemies. He saw no need to overheat the polity. President Buhari betrayed the trust of the excited and frenzied masses and sold away the soul of hope in the birth of a silent revolution. He spat on the euphoria of a people that were prepared to run down the powerful in the fight for the heart of a sane Nigeria.

Today, we know that the President is sick. On a medical vacation and represented by a buoyant Vice President, Nigerians were served a little taste of the dish that everyone expected of a radical and revolutionary President Muhammadu Buhari. In the aftermath of an unannounced visit to Murtala Muhammed Airport, the Acting President made heads roll, when he discovered the depth of management filth that kept the system from functioning. That is precisely the type of action that brought fame and regards for Samuel Osaigbovo Ogbemudia of the defunct Bendel State. It is the kind of actions that Nigerians expected of Muhammadu Buhari.

Today, a lunatic Governor Ayodele Fayose makes a mess of a once-dreaded General Muhammadu Buhari. A red-eye Wike runs a state like an uncontrolled drug addict while the President watches helplessly dumb. The President is surrounded by interest groups, a part, of which seems to be working to wholly Jonathanize the system that he sought to sanitize. The Economic and Financial Crimes Commission (EFCC) is now reported to be operating in the opaquest of systems imaginable. EFCC operatives are reported to be running around town in opulent wealth and corrupt enrichment from incompletely submitted wealth recovery. All under the watch of the once-dreaded General Muhammadu Buhari.

A welcome clampdown on the judiciary rekindled hope in a thorough cleansing of the system only for the President to stop it half-way and "Sarakize" the process once again.

Unfortunately, however, Nigerians do not help matters. In spite of boasting of a huge number of university graduates in a comparative continent-wide statistical distribution, Nigeria suffers a huge shortage of intellectuals with the capability of reasoning scientifically – a virtue that is taken for granted in saner climes. Engaging purportedly educated Nigerians in armchair beer-parlor debates sometimes, you'd be forgiven if you thought you were debating with pre-colonial village elders, who believed they too could have made good intellectuals if they were educated. The glaring shortage of sophistry, empiricism and rationality that is often reduced to popularly applaudable traditional intelligence, notwithstanding, many such pseudo-intellectuals believe so passionately and strongly in the superiority of their reasoning and calling that you'd simply end up pitying the country and the wasted generation that drives its destiny.

Believe it or not, there are educated individuals in today's Nigeria, for whom Ayodele Fayose serves as a formidable role model. There are educated Nigerians in today's world, who do not see any wisdom in fighting corruption since no Nigerian alive is qualified to lead the fight. There are Nigerians, who for one selfish and emotional reason or the other, will not see anything wrong in a legislative chamber populated by gangsters and run in the spirit of Gangsterism. And they are all educated.

Prosecution for the forgery of standing orders by a self-imposed gang of principal officers in the legislature will be rationalized by educated Nigerians as victimization.

This glaring intellectual deficit with which no nation can ever witness meaningful advancement, was first laid bare in all facets during the regime of Olusegun Obasanjo, who did his best to re-arrange the Nigerian political space for the equitable accommodation of all the regional entities in the nation away from Northern domination. But guess what! His strongest adversaries were the Southerners, who benefitted most from his mission of political inclusiveness. Purportedly educated minds did not only take to the vicious condemnation of those things that he got wrong, everything he did right was subjected to the relativism of malicious condemnation. A few years after, having had a savory taste of the late Yar'Adua and the "Ph.D Jonathan", many of these voices sing a different tune today. They were all educated.

In the same spirit of talking before thinking, many unleash venom on Muhammadu Buhari for picking lieutenants that he can best work with, claiming the progression of a clandestine Northern agenda and ignoring all other facts of the inherited federal spread that are constitutionally unavoidable. Yet Obasanjo's blindness to ethnic coloration was ignored at the time and glaringly portrayed as the devil's deal by precisely those same minds that choose to characterize Muhammadu Buhari today, as the brainless cattle-rearer.

Impunity in anticipatory and manipulatory asset declaration, forgery of senate rules, forgery of import documents and many more vices and acts of banditry are willfully ignored by Nigerian pseudo-intellectuals to elevate destructive role models to survive peak positions in notable political spaces. Today, the Dino Melayes, the Ayodele Fayoses and the red-eyed Wikes excel in thuggery and the desecration of institutions that are ordinarily meant to be noble and charitable. They are cheered on by educated persons.

While legislatures in exemplary democracies represent nobility and display exceptional political intellectualism in committees and plenary sessions, the Nigerian upper house is bent on ignoring all important matters of state to force someone to appear before it in uniform. Trivialities and perfidy now stand out as virtues for representatives that are regularly engaged in emptiness and low academic tagging. Yet, educated friends mistake ours for a grown democracy and worry more about the impact of disobeying the legislature by not wearing uniforms and comfortably ignoring the need to grow a tradition by drawing the limits for all parties in the game including legislators. The overblown sense of self-exaltation ignoring the chance factor in being in one position at a given time seems lost on many of our schooled but non-educated legislators in their perception of self. If a democratic tradition is to be grown, no doubt, they will need to learn the limits no matter how many pseudo-intellectuals cheer them on.

A combination of these qualities of Nigerians and the apparently health-impeded agility of the President of a nation that has betrayed hope and enormous expectations, has presently seen Nigeria treading a hopeless path of no redemption. It is yet not too late for President Muhammadu Buhari to damn the impact of his own health and fix the health of Nigeria for a lasting legacy. It does not matter when he goes to his grave as we will all do; enemies and friends will be there for eternity. Cozying up to the wrong friends in Dogara and Saraki and allowing the wrong establishment characters like Ibrahim Babangida or the power-hungry Atiku Abubakar preach the toxic message of not overheating the polity, will only betray the deal of moving Nigeria forward.

*Follow me on Twitter @friskyLarrimore, Frisky Larr is the author of the books "**Nigeria's Journalistic Militantism**", "**Africa's Diabolical Entrapment**" and "**Lost in Democracy**".*

***

In the absence of the President, however, one issue got on the front-burner. The Igbo Agitation. The leader of the movement who got bailed under strict conditions, from a lengthy pre-trial incarceration, was finally released on the intervention of highly placed ethnic representatives, who negotiated with the government. He was expected to be of a better behavior. In the period of the President's coincidental ailment and absence from the country, the secessionist agitation intensified gaining headlines at home and abroad but without support from any meaningful international source whatsoever. It added, immensely, to the deep polarization of the country with virtually, every other part of the country pitched against the Igbos.

The poisonous atmosphere of deep polarization that had previously been fueled by the anti-Buhari and pro-Buhari divide, took a drastic turn for the worse, with the self-appointed leader of the agitation pulling crowd after crowd, of his disgruntled, disenchanted and complaining secessionist folks. The Vice President, who was the Acting President of the time, seemed to have deliberately avoided any concrete action to address the situation.

Political leaders of the agitating ethnic group suddenly seem to be lining up behind the extremely flippant and uncultured leader of the agitation. Shamelessly. None could or was willing to prevail on him. Common voters on either side of the divide hurled abuses at each other on social media rationalizing inanities and all forms of senselessness as long as they suit their purpose.

I held the view that the greatest supporters of oppression in Nigeria are the oppressed Nigerians themselves.

The Enemies of Nigeria are the Oppressed Nigerians!

By Frisky Larr

The thesis suggested by the title of this essay will not come as a surprise to any political observer within the Nigerian experimental space by any standard. Since our subject will be governance and society, however, our standard for evaluation will also be governance and society. In every society, governance is always about the people. While some systems of governance pretend that power emanates from and rests with the people, other systems make no secret of their disdain for the notion of "People's Power".

Yet the struggle for the liberation of the Blackman through history has always been based on the slogan "Power to the People" symbolized by the black power salute shown in the thrust of the clenched fist. Today, even in the black continent as represented by its most populous nation Nigeria, "people" are the most powerless. After all, the saying "United, we stand and divided, we fall" is a very popular one amongst Nigerians.

For some reasons, however, Nigeria in its miniature ethnographic reflection of virtually, every other society in Africa, is home to an edifice that is strongly divided against itself defying all senses of elementary logic. It is a patchwork nation (and which African nation is not?) that breeds millions of self-acclaimed philosophers, self-proclaimed geniuses, self-ordained prophets, self-made scientific inventors waiting to be discovered, self-declared apostles of perfection and even self-imposed billionaires. While all the others may be fake by virtue of emptiness and wishful thinking, the self-imposed billionaires are unfortunately, the only segment in the fold that is real. It is the segment that thrives on larceny and willful usurpation of people's rights and imposes itself on society.

Yet it is precisely the same people, whose rights are usurped and trampled upon that have discovered a new and fashionable hobby in obvious oversize activities surpassing their individual capacities on daily display on social media. The average Nigerian of the present generation of youths often lives in the delusion of academic omnipotence with no readiness to concede ignorance even when it stinks to high heavens in the face of a deeply submerged quality of education. He is the bedrock of all facets of political and social activity no matter how good, bad or ugly. Vain and ignorant positions are often defended with the vile and vicious proliferation of emptiness as if basic existence depended on them.

Such has been made manifest in the most recent encounter of the polarized population, with the emerging authority of political leadership.

The dividing lines are often obscure but defined by whims and caprices and the power of cash. There are divisions along party lines. There are divisions along tribal lines. There are also forced loyalties defined by circumstances. The most typical example of forced loyalty is that of political defectors, who saw the pecuniary or strategic convenience of defecting to a different political umbrella only to be stuck to the losing end and forced to feign loyalty amid internal confusion. Femi Fani Kayode is topmost on my mind!

The popular elevation of partisanship is not uncommon in periods of elections wherever democracy or some semblance of it is practiced in any form. In fact, it is the fan that blows the flame of electoral democracy. It is also not unusual to see the business of governance dominated by partisan and biased manipulations. After all, a party wins the stakes and sets the agenda, which is promptly followed by strategizing on the political field with all players taking their defined positions. While the opposition also influences governance with informal contacts and clever or dumb politicking, the masses, who cast the ballot often end up the biggest loser with a very marginal impact on practical and day-to-day policy implementation. After all, the masses only have a say at the ballot box once in every legislative period.

Misplaced attacks on authority

When partisanship, however, becomes much more strongly pronounced with the voting class than it is with political actors along the corridors of party houses, then there is a fundamental flaw somewhere in the system. This is crucial because every element of the voting class all over the world, often meets on common grounds. They are the 99% of the "Occupy" fame, whose commonwealth is criminally misused by a coalition of political and economic interest groups. They are the victims of oppression. They are the impoverished victims of corruption. They are numerically stronger in Black Africa than anywhere else in the world.

Today, however, precisely this class of Nigerians is up in arms in a staunch but unconscious defense of corruption under astonishing guises. In the plethora of crimes that have been perpetrated on the common man in Nigeria in such a way that the nation has systematically been robbed and virtually thrown back to the 'stone age' of our times by progressive and cyber standards, I still wonder what business the ordinary man has, crying 'selective persecution' when thieves are caught. Nigeria of our present day is at a crossroad seeking to redefine guilt in corruption on the basis of political or tribal camps and the numerical strength of beneficiaries. The real guilt of the crime committed now seems a non-issue in the face of overtly loud and vehement agitation. The notion seems to stand that prosecution will be fair and acceptable only if all and nothing, but ALL perpetrators are picked and charged in one fell swoop. Everything else is selective. The need to encourage the reigning authority to broaden the search for thieves also within its own ranks is now taken as a compelling criterion for measuring the guilt of certified thieves and the daylight robbers of our own commonwealth. I, therefore, say this for crying out loud: *"What business has the oppressed and suffering son of the land, crying 'selective prosecution' when the thief is real?"*

All of sudden, a vocal section of precisely, these downtrodden Nigerians has now found its voice behind Kukahs and charlatans raising the alarm that the core issue of governance is being sacrificed for the fight against corruption. After all, the fight against corruption is not a part of governance as long as the person caught is not from the camp of the governing party. The Oshiomoles have suddenly become the bad boys of the creek seeking nothing but the destruction of the land simply for vehemently unveiling the mask of corruption that should ordinarily have attracted heightened interest and detailed inquisitiveness. For every indictment of governmental armchair quarter backers, the ordinary Nigerian is waiting to rally around his hero. No excuse is shameful enough. No excuse is embarrassing enough. No reckless excuse is a shame on the face of worthless mitigation.

The Stockholm syndrome

Precisely the downtrodden Nigerian now summons elements of pity and sympathy to proclaim the innocence of robbers who have dragged them down decades into the depth of a swampy sludge. Suffering from cancer now renders a looter innocent. The sudden heart attack suffered by an adjudicated looter leading to an unfortunate fatality suddenly leads to canonization. It is the picture of a folk that has learned to feel comfortable in poverty and oppression not having really known the opposite standard in real terms.

It is the picture of a folk that has learned to live with a wrongly calibrated mental structure thriving on trivialities and superficialities, sticking vehemently to irrelevant facts that sound consistent to the wrongly configured mind yet making him proud of a self-perceived level of heavenly intelligence.

At a point, I am forced to think about the Stockholm syndrome that I elaborated in detail in my book *"Africa's Diabolical Entrapment"*. A section of Nigerians now seems to sympathize with their captors and oppressors having been too long encapsulated with them in a common dungeon of unfettered brainwashing. The detailed mental challenge of setting priorities for national development has now been voluntarily ceded to the heritage of pettiness and nothingness.

The few amongst the misguided, who manage to see a few steps beyond the tip of the nose, complain about the absence of a blueprint for economic recovery. They celebrate every misfortune like suicide attacks on soft targets to declare leaders brainless and say it's payback time. Anyone will be speechless and short of words at the vanity of this stance on the part of helpless masochists, who mortgage the collective welfare of a nation for the passion to weep over spilled milk.

But excuse me. Who on earth has ever performed the trick of working out a successful economic blueprint with a treasury that has been badly looted amid dwindling revenues? With the volatility of the price of crude oil today, which is the mainstay of Nigeria's economy, can a budget be planned with any certainty in the first place to say the least of an economic blueprint? Can revenue projections be made even for 6 months? In a nation where treasuries were brazenly looted through multiple peripheral accounts, pension funds personalized by a few individuals and salaries are owed over several months, what meaningful economic blueprint can be worked out on the short-term without first fixing the leakages? A single treasury account has now been ordered in a frantic effort to take the country back to the early eighties where sanity gave us hope of a brighter future until politicians did us part. Yet, Stockholmers find fault in what they term brainlessness.

No one plans an economy without first knowing, what resources and capital are available. The drive to recover as much of the nation's looted fund as possible as a basic groundwork for better planning is now suddenly derided as negligence of the real business of governance. The same voices derided a predecessor, who failed to fight corruption as being ignorant of governance. Could this be the stuff that the African is made of?

Is it a coincidence that revolutions never happen in Black Africa? Will anything good come out of a house that is divided against itself? Who expects a revolution from Nigerians with the aim of a thorough cleansing of society when Nigerians defend and protect their own oppressors? Who will hold the looters to account in all seriousness? Secessions may come and go. Smaller nations may emerge in a unifying global village. But the mental, developmental and collective inferiority of the black African will persist as long as this low level of intellectual disposition persists. With the generation yet unborn that will take the lead in the quest to rebuild nations, Nigeria simply has a very long way to go!

***

The President finally recovered after three months of treatment in a London hospital that was cladded in secrecy and a sickness that has, so far, not been revealed to Nigerians. Upon returning home, he devoted time to solving the agitation problem and launched the military exercise codenamed "Python Dance" in the region of the secession agitation, where law and order had, virtually, collapsed and was ceded to the agitation group, whose wings grew broader by the day.

Calm returned to the nation, with several regional political leaders, who had kowtowed to the whims and caprices of the leader of the agitation by gleefully posing for photos with him, sounding secretly satisfied that the overbearing young man, who they didn't challenge openly, was finally removed from a position of dominance that overshadowed their own existence.

Questions over the whereabouts of the young man in the aftermath of the military operation that is reported to have taken several lives, was obscured and seems unsolved till the present moment, at least, before the public eyes.

Yet, the country could not experience political calm thereafter. Even if not on the same widespread and sensational scale of the Biafra agitation, another issue of a more brutal and bloody dimension took over the airwaves. The herdsmen killings.

Through the years and cutting across several governments, Nigeria has been faced with the problem of accommodating itinerant cattle-rearing herdsmen, who continue to live their age-long tradition of walking long distance with their cattle in search of healthy grazing fields to feed their cattle.

In changing times, however, free grazing fields have become a rarity. Plots are now owned by individuals, who often use them for farming, largely, in rural areas. The generally uneducated herdsmen, whose labor provides meat for the nation and have practiced their trade over several generations, have not been able to cope with this situation, to the overall benefit of all the parties concerned. They would move through farmlands with impunity and have their cattle feed on cash crops that meant a livelihood for the peasant folks. In the aftermath tension rose to a boiling point. Folks rustle the cattle while the herdsmen were and still are, unrelenting in ravaging farmlands. The resultant clashes meant death on a massive scale. The herdsmen are often seen, very well armed, sometimes with automatic rifles. With time, the conflict took on a political dimension, with powerful personalities suspected of owning the cattle that are reared by the herdsmen and rustled by organized gangs.

In effect, this translated into suspicions that unknown powerful personalities were arming and sponsoring herdsmen in their occasional raids on folks with countless number of casualties. Media focus was and still is, however, much more on the repeated 'slaughtering' of humans in, often, organized nocturnal armed raids on unsuspecting compatriots in the refuge of their homes. Counterclaims contend that the flipside of the coin involves rustlers stealing cattle and dislodging the means of livelihood of the herdsmen while also conducting counterattacks on herdsmen. The bulk of these incidents happened mostly in Benue State – a region that is popularly referred to as the Middle belt.

In all of these pervasive and headline-catching incidents, the President of the country simply kept quiet and seemingly indifferent. This fueled unproven suspicions that the President privately sympathized with the herdsmen because they come, largely, from his own ethnic group – FULANI.

Then, from nowhere and fully unexpected, former President Olusegun Obasanjo threw a bombshell. He wrote an open letter to the President chastising him clearly, for yet, another incident of herdsmen attack on innocent civilians with a huge number of casualties. Former

President Obasanjo accused the incumbent President of failing to revive the economy and spending much time apportioning blames. He advised the President to dispense of any idea of being re-elected for a second term also in view of the uncertain development of his health problems.

It was the dawn of massive politicking again. And it prompted me to write the following lengthy article that provided a detailed recap of how we got to where we, presently, are. It gained wide coverage in the mainstream media both online and print.

Buhari's Inconsistencies Denting the Integrity Image Amid the Rescue Mission.

By Frisky Larr

There is hardly any well-meaning and patriotic Nigerian today, that will dispute the fact that retired Major-General Muhammadu Buhari was elected President of Nigeria in 2015, to rescue the country from the self-immolating path that was designed by his predecessor. Three years on, there is also, hardly any well-meaning and patriotic Nigerian that will deny that this goal has been largely achieved. Yet, the President is faced with a huge load of popular disenchantment that comes close to re-echoing the unsavory tunes of the year 2007.

It was the year, in which Nigeria made history with an elected civilian President handing over power to another elected peer without a military disruption. Yet, that year stands out not for this historical feat alone, but also for the level of anxiety that gripped the entire civil society. The nation stood on the brink of a boiling point, sharply divided between lovers and haters of the outgoing President of the time.

Today, history seems to be repeating itself. The term Buharists and anti-Buharists have not only become household words, they are also, distinctively marking the dividing line of a deeply polarized society that never ever seems to have enough of tragic divisions.

On one hand, is a once buoyant and hopeful section of Nigerians, who invested a lot of expectations in President Muhammadu Buhari to transform Nigeria in a radical manner without **fear** or **favor**. This group nursed a near-puritanical stern belief in the infallibility of the former military head of state, whose government once fought an abstract War Against Indiscipline. Today, this group of Nigerians is reaping the fruits of utter disappointment, at least, in their own perception. This group is also joined by non-Buharists, who are still struggling to recover from the electoral loss suffered by their principal in 2015. This latter section of non-Buharists have been traditionally hostile to the Buhari agenda and deliberately refuse, in the most irrational, abusive and destructive manner, to appreciate any achievement, whatsoever, by the President.

On the other side of the divide are Buhari loyalists, who have supported the President from the very beginning and remain irrationally loyal to him as well, no matter the odds. This group it is that will inadvertently and unwittingly manipulate facts in every form possible, to rationalize irrationality in favor of their Principal.

As in 2007, the middle ground is, again, occupied by very few analysts that are often open to attacks from both sides of the divide.

Now, as a pundit without expertise in the economy, I will dare to reiterate at this point that President Muhammadu Buhari has done quite a lot to put Nigeria back on track from the realms of destructive insanity, no matter how many faults economists may attempt to appraise. Many of his political adversaries today, will, no doubt, agree with this assessment.

President Buhari turned the tide in the officially approved looting of government coffers by departments and agencies, which ran individual bank accounts without accountability. Buhari tried to tidy up the finances of individual states to reset the fluency of financial management with particular reference to regular salary payments and met resistance. This, in spite of starkly decimated revenue inflow. Buhari seized the right opportunity to revoke the payment of fuel subsidy and curtail brazen fraud in the oil sector, where fraudsters made bogus imports and milked the country voraciously in the recent past. Buhari invoked strenuous efforts to settle inherited debts with contractors that were accumulated in the midst of plenty. Salaries are now, not only paid regularly, to Federal Government employees, pensioners now receive their gratuities as fathomed in the founding principles of the nation. Arrears have been paid where pension funds were traditionally looted in the past, without a pinch of conscience. The President has struggled to boost the foreign reserves that were willfully looted by his predecessor while income was high. Feeding of children at school in a country with little or no social welfare program is now a daily reality, at least in some schools. Efforts to diversify the economy seems to have yielded results with agriculture reportedly being at the center of self-sufficiency in rice production while work is in progress to galvanize the utilization of opportunities in the area of solid minerals. A massive buildup of physical infrastructure is, reportedly, on course.

Even without a mention of the government's success on the security front, displacing and dislodging Boko Haram, the achievements are so numerous in three years to set the nation back on the path of sane statehood again, that anyone would be guilty of bare-faced calumny, to refer to the government of Muhammadu Buhari as a complete failure. Yet, there are serious failings.

A large part of President Buhari's failures centers around his personality and his approach to public issues. This is also compounded by poorly articulated campaign promises that have so far, ended up unfulfilled.

In fact, contrary to the belief of many of his supporters, the democratic toppling of President Goodluck Jonathan's government in 2015 was not hinged on a popular love for the person or personality of Muhammadu Buhari. Many of his enemies at the time, swallowed their vows to rid the country of a more urgent and serious plague that was configured to damage the corporate existence of the entity. Buhari's antecedent as a no-nonsense former General with no publicly known or conspicuous trace of illicit wealth made him attractive and not necessarily lovable to voters across the ethnic divide as a potential revolutionary, since general discipline and patriotism were the most lacking political commodity.

Without dwelling on his lack-luster inaugural speech, which in hindsight today, clearly symbolizes the Buhari that no one expected or his failure to hit the ground running in forming a government after his inauguration, his approach to the first major test of his political skills took many admirers by surprise. Contrary to astute maneuvers that in-party politicking required for the production of leaders for the two legislative chambers, a known politician, wearing the secret cloak of clandestine political forces dared the President to do what he could. He defied party actions and schemed for his own majority in the chamber and got himself elected President of the Senate. He was soon followed by another renegade bloke, who grabbed the leadership of the second chamber by private scheming in defiance of party and President. The President, who was taken by surprise, was largely expected by his supporters to wield the big stick and assert his authority to pave the way for smooth governance since he needed all the support available on the rescue mission. Hiding publicly, behind the shield of constitutionality, the President exposed his ignorance of the legitimate constitutional means, with which he would have stamped his authority on the long-awaited cleansing process. It lingered on until he got outmaneuvered by the evil forces.

Campaign promises

While the President's supporters were still licking their wounds from the President's shocking inefficiency in political scheming, it became incumbent on all, to put up a brave face and move on hoping that the bigger picture will vindicate the President on the long run.

The President picked up the gauntlet and declared war on the thieves of the oil sector, having done the mathematics of the subsidy fraud many years before his election. He had reminded the electorates how foreign companies had quietly refined crude oil into consumer fuel in his days as a military actor, against the payment of commission in such a way that importers were not required. All that the country needed was the NNPC. The President successfully seized the moment of favorable public opinion and abolished fuel subsidy. Alas, there was no quiet refining by foreign companies in the wake of the abolition. Fuel continue to be refined overseas and reimported in the usual fashion. NNPC was crowned the principal but not "sole" importer of refined fuel. A select number of favored importers were and are still allowed today, to import refined fuel alongside the NNPC. In other words, despite abolition, the payment of subsidy continues till the present moment even if on a drastically reduced scale.

The following web links contain further details of the President's other campaign promises including the abolishment of medical tourism that have been left to the wolves to feast on: https://www.vanguardngr.com/2015/05/what-buhari-promised-nigerians/ and https://www.thecable.ng/documented-promises-buhari-apc-made-nigerians.

Integrity

Soon after inauguration, the President went ahead to keep some refineries running (Port Harcourt and Warri) at least, as announced by the NNPC after a quick turnaround maintenance. The President fed hopes that new refineries will be built to fuel self-sufficiency in refining crude oil. For some reasons, however, the issue disappeared completely, from the agenda. All hopes began to hinge fully on the Dangote's refinery that is presently under construction. Dangote is the same man that Olusegun Obasanjo sold refineries to for private upgrading and construction. Yar'Adua had reversed the move without a viable replacement and was loudly applauded by self-styled pundits with hardly any argumentative substance to match. President Buhari's agenda of indigenous operational refineries became a story for the marines and the entire nation's hope and destiny in the oil sector, now rests exclusively on the project led by one single private individual.

From nowhere, came a surprising bombshell. The year was 2016. Media outlets began reporting, barely 9 months into the presidency, of a secret staff recruitment exercise at the Central Bank without a public advertisement for applications in a country, where highly qualified workforces were and are still roaming unemployed. People that were employed in the process reportedly included a relative of the President himself, relatives of serving and former Ministers and of high-ranking politicians including a former Vice President. The Central Bank responded and claimed to have broken no law in its actions. The President remained mute till the present day. Not few observers looked back there and then, to the days in which a former President publicly revoked a property acquired by his own wife with a not-too-quiet rebuke.

Then came the issue of budget-padding, again, in the year 2016. An issue that the nation got to know about because Muhammadu Buhari exposed it for the very first time in the history of the Fourth Republic. Yet, the same President Buhari failed to follow it through with the doggedness and vehemence of a true revolutionary without **fear** or **favor**. One young assemblyman, Abdulmumin Jibrin, probably seeking to exploit the situation for personal political gains, came up suddenly, with public pronouncements incriminating the leadership of the House of Representatives. He claimed to be in possession of valid evidence to prove that the budget to which the President had twice refused to assent on grounds of padding and finally accepted after a third attempt, was still padded. It was an ultimate litmus test of the administration's commitment to the anti-corruption war. However, rather than treating this assemblyman with all the seriousness that the anti-corruption war demanded, the President held several audiences with the leader of the House of Representatives, who was at the center of the accusation and shunned the complainant, who requested an audience with him, repeatedly. The complainant eventually ended up being illegally suspended from his elected seat, humiliated and made miserable, precisely by the same people he accused without any support – public or private – from the President. Yet, the government's priority was fighting corruption.

Without a doubt, President Buhari has done much to disorganize the hitherto, uncontrolled appetite for looting in the legislature. Yet, information crept out reporting millions of public funds that each legislator immorally takes home every month in a country with scarce resources for human development. The President kept mute showing no leadership. No reassurance for the common man that he detested this blatant breach of trust or that he was in consultation with the legislature to discuss means of curbing such abuses in the future.

For the first time in the history of Nigeria, President Buhari ordered the arrest of corrupt judges in a bold effort to cleanse the judiciary, which the public knows to be riddled with corrupt judges, who pass judgment, often, for the highest bidder. Yet, he lacked the will and balls to follow it up to its logical conclusion by relying solely on people's power against any legal provision or stern opposition. If the law truly and foolishly permits corrupt judges to hide behind the shield of the Nigerian Judicial Council to circumvent the course of justice in the country for their personal enrichment and at the expense of the country's development, a worthy President would a) either have mobilized voters in a direct address to the nation as was typical of Ronald Reagan, for the purpose of having the law quickly amended, or b) defied the law for the good of the country and with the backing of the people for whom the laws are made and by so doing, expose the bad eggs in the judiciary. That is what makes a revolutionary that is devoted solely, to the good of his country. Unfortunately, the President chickened in upon the first cry of the separation of powers and the dubious functions of the Nigeria Judicial Council prompting speculations of a blackmail since the President may also have had skeletons in the closet in the face of his cost-intensive electoral campaign.

With the prompt suspension and subsequent dismissal of Babachir Lawal, former Secretary to the Government of the Federation, and Ambassador Ayo Oke, former Director-General of the National Intelligence Agency, over graft accusations, the nation caught a glimmer of hope that the fight against corruption was beginning to turn the corner in earnest. Yet, the Osinbanjo's report that indicted both men, has remained cladded in utmost secrecy.

There is also the issue of appointments. Having met the constitutional requirement of the Federal Character in key appointments, the President went ahead to make every other appointment that is not liable to Senatorial approval, almost exclusively from his regional base. While it makes a lot of sense and must even be encouraged that principals habitually appoint lieutenants that they can best work with and I am an advocate of this school of thought, the path to tread in a democracy, however, is often, a most delicate one. Since democracy rests on numbers, there is no strategy as good as carrying the majority along as often as possible.

After all, Nigerians had believed that the issue of excessive ethnic leanings in appointments had been left behind since the days of Olusegun Obasanjo. The loudest complaints chastised the appointment of all military service chiefs from a particular region. The President damned all public outcries and kept mute on the issue till the present moment.

Then, there is the crucial issue of herdsmen roaming the country, killing and maiming the natives in their peasant environment in search of grazing land. It is the issue that finally brought it all to a bitter head, pitching the incumbent President against one of his predecessors with the support of many other former leaders. For a long time, the President remained mute. He refused to address the public on what he intended to do to halt the senseless killings until he visited the President of the United States and saw the issue presented to him and simplistically reduced to that of Muslims killing Christians, which the United States was not going to allow. His proposal, of creating ranches for cattle rearers has since been on paper without any precise action to see practical implementation. Now, that the problem has long metamorphosed into a politically-sponsored onslaught far detached from the search for grazing land, the President still remains mute. This resultantly led to speculations of ethnic bias against the other tribes that are pitched against the Fulanis, the President himself being a Fulani.

No sooner had former President Obasanjo pitched his tent against the incumbent than the order was made for the arrest of Babachir Lawal, who was long dismissed as Secretary to the government but remained apparently shielded from prosecution for so long. The Presidency denied though that there was any link between both incidents. The President finally summoned a meeting with service chiefs to address the issue of herdsmen killings and reprisal killings. Inconsistencies that would have long been avoided if the President was a man of prompt action without **fear** or **favor**.

The issue of his ailing health is another crucial subject on the front burner. Amid rumors of food poisoning in Aso Rock as a counter-effect of his anti-corruption war, the President found himself absent from his seat of power for three valuable months undergoing treatment in the United Kingdom. He had dismissed the printed information on his battle with prostate cancer as unfounded rumors during the presidential campaign. Amid all these, there is no indication whatsoever that the President is doing anything to improve health services in Aso Rock, to say the least of the rest of the country. At a point, his own wife complained of a shortage of facilities at the presidential clinic as she also did about other political inconsistencies of the President. With a well-equipped presidential clinic, an expatriate surgeon or specialist may be employed, for all anyone cares. The President seems to be doing none of this.

The Second Term Debate

The seriousness of his health problems is even underscored by a rumor in the international media that he may have died in the United Kingdom while undergoing treatment. Yet, the nation does not know what the President presently suffers from and how well he is, to complete his first term or even go for a second term. At a point after his election, the President went on record as lamenting that he was not elected in his more youthful and vibrant years, seemingly making a clear reference to age-induced strategic deteriorations.

The President himself has, according to information, had reasons to sit back and think deeply, if he should truly run for a second term as President. It took him a long time to decide in favor of running for a second term, in the end, apparently as a posture of defiance in the face of establishment opposition. There is no indication whatsoever, that he has considered grooming a worthy successor with a clear understanding of his own vision to foster a plan of continuity. The worthy Governor of Kaduna State, who hit the ground running upon assuming office or the worthy incumbent Vice President, who, as Acting President during the absence of the President, occasionally displayed qualities that were initially expected of the President himself, readily come to mind. If there are no thoughts in this direction, this may be the time to kickstart the process since no one can comfortably say, how the health of the President will evolve in a possible second term.

Today, the polity of the country has been suddenly overheated because former President Olusegun Obasanjo, with the support of several other establishment forces, has declared his stern opposition to the re-election of the incumbent President. In an initial show of political maturity, President Buhari expressed thanks for the criticism, corrected a few notions here and there and warned his lieutenants strictly against any disparaging comments to denounce the former Head of State. As the opposition of the former President, to the re-election of the incumbent heated up through consultations and alliances, however, and the incumbent saw the looming threat, he suddenly remembered that there was an unsettled case of $16 bn allegedly wasted on the power sector between 1999 and 2007 by the opposing ex-President. It didn't matter anymore that the incumbent had said long before his election that he would limit his investigations on corruption to the immediate past administration of President Goodluck Jonathan.

Clarifying this in July 2015, Presidential Spokesman, Femi Adesina, reportedly said:

"It is a simple thing. Before he was inaugurated, the President said that it will be a distraction for him to start digging deep into past governments. He said so. I don't see anything new."

When it got to the battle of re-election, however, distraction was suddenly seen as a political capital putting at stake once again, the question of personal integrity.

To launch the massive infrastructure offensive that is presently on course and to keep the economy running as well as finance obligatory projects, the President has had to resort to heavy international borrowing. In 2006, the then President Olusegun Obasanjo paid the Paris Club a total of $12.4 bn to secure the forgiveness of $18 bn and obliterate a total debt of $30 bn. Today, the same former President is watching and seeing the debt profile steadily hiked once again, to a total of $18.9 bn as of December 31, 2017. Complaints are loud. Criticisms in this regard are difficult to silent. Yet the President does not speak.

In all, the President comes across as grossly underrating the power of public communication. Aside from the disaster of demystifying his image of a radical revolutionary by displaying the inconsistencies highlighted above, the President has unwittingly added the image of a snob to his portfolio as it pertains to his relationship with the public and by implication, the voters. No doubt, Nigeria has not been endowed with the gift of eloquent Presidents, the Obama style, in its recent political history. Yet, even Goodluck Jonathan in his mastery of the art of gaffing, obligated the public with regular communications and often explained, albeit inadequately, the direction of his actions.

Today, President Buhari has opened up avenues for staunch attacks on his personal attitude prompting speculations that his health or fear of rhetorical inadequacies are behind his failure to communicate with the masses as often as helpful. Never has a President squandered this much goodwill and popular followership with a formidable block of mass support. A minimum of two spontaneous movements has attempted to mobilize peoples' power in support of the President, to defeat the legislature's anti-people padding of budget and resultant delay in the passage of same. Rather than enjoying support from the Presidency, demonstrators were dispersed by the police at least, on one occasion. Does the President fear a blackmail in invoking peoples' power?

By suddenly bringing $16 bn power probe to the front burner of the political agenda without any pressing cause whatsoever, except electoral expediency, the President has demonstrated a needless degree of desperation and the will to tap into public sentiments at the expense of personal credibility for the sole purpose of hanging on to power. While no one can have any objection to the probing of perceived but unproven grand larceny in the power sector by former President Olusegun Obasanjo and the punishing of culprits if identified, the willful peddling of inaccurate figures and instrumentalization of public sentiments for electoral expediency can only be condemned since it undermines the seriousness that the battle against corruption requires. All of a sudden, the enormous sins of, and damage done to Nigeria's economy by the immediate past administration no longer command urgency. The activities of a regime that paid off the country's debts and grew foreign reserves in spite of very many weaknesses, now qualify for urgent probe while respected personalities like Femi Falana and Wole Soyinka cheer on in partisanship and schadenfreude, partly asking what problem the leader in question has ever solved.

A President like Muhammadu Buhari with such a comprehensive list of laudable achievements, in spite of his serious integrity lapses, should, ordinarily, have no need for a blackmailing probe to secure mass support. If he had a good mastery of public communication with the voters with the aid of proper communication coaching, the perception of him as a hero and aspiring revolutionary would have been a monumental reality. Timing and style are key in politics and no doubt, President Buhari will live long enough to yet, learn a whole lot of lessons.

Frisky Larr is the author of "Nigeria's Journalistic Militantism",
"Africa's Diabolical Entrapment" and "Lost in Democracy"

***

This head-on collision between the incumbent President and former President Olusegun Obasanjo, is presently trending on social media while this book is being prepared in mid-2018. It brings, once again, to the fore, the numerical strength of ordinary people, who nurse extreme anger at the former President on the basis of media-promoted issues that are not necessarily accurate but largely interest-driven in nature. These issues were analyzed and presented in one of my books "Nigeria's Journalistic Militantism".

The battle between the two former Generals reached a head with the former President crying out that the incumbent President was planning to frame him up for arrest and was promptly supported by his former Vice President, who then called on the incumbent to retrace his overzealous steps derived from a populist momentum on the social media. In other words, while the incumbent President Muhammadu Buhari feared the interruption of his Presidency through sustained campaign against him and the relentless formation of alliances by former President Olusegun Obasanjo (a friend-turn-adversary), the former President suddenly feared being arrested again and confined to a dungeon by a serving leader. I coined the episode, "The Jitters of the Generals". This article received wide coverage online and a massive reaction by readers:

The Jitters of the Generals: President Buhari's Needless Assault on the Populist Front!

By Frisky Larr

The import of the tirades against Olusegun Obasanjo on social media since President Muhammadu Buhari launched his vengeful assault on the former President has largely been the expression of accustomed hate, schadenfreude, and the childish serves-him-right fascination. Outside the social media, traditional die-hard Obasanjo-haters like Professor Wole Soyinka and Femi Falana have been having a field day of feasting on their favorite object of pastime denigration. In one of the most unobjective, hate-filled and clearly envy-driven tirades, Femi Falana even strayed shamefully, into the murky waters of suggesting a government seizure of Olusegun Obasanjo's landmark Presidential Library. An edifice that does not represent personal enrichment but does Nigeria proud, promotes education and serves as one indispensable official archive of Nigeria's history and everything Nigeria may stand for in generations to come! Indeed, such unequivocally nonsensical show of deep-seated abhorrence devoid of any appreciative sense of goodwill will rather be ignored for what it truly is.

Retaliating the former President's rejection of his Presidency and apparently, effective drive to unseat him and deny him a second term in office, President Muhammadu Buhari has taken to tapping into these hate-filled, populist sentiments to resist and perhaps, fight back in very surprising desperation. That is the very first jitter that has triggered this fully unwarranted feud in a roller-coaster relationship.

I remember vividly, one summer evening in the comfort of my summer residence in Turkey in 2015 in the wake of President Buhari's victory over President Goodluck Jonathan in the polls. I had this call from President Obasanjo's Personal Assistant, who gave me the rare privilege of talking to the former President on the telephone on that calm evening. I remember President Obasanjo's pleasure and excitement over Muhammadu Buhari's triumph and his reassuring words: *"My son, we can't afford to fail this time. We will get it right!"* These, in my opinion, are the words of a patriotic legend, whose personal interest far transcend the celebration of the victory or defeat of any individual and was focused more on fixing the country. In fact, in a statement released by the then, presidential candidate, Muhammadu Buhari, in March 2015 on occasion of the former President's birthday celebration, Muhammadu Buhari had these words for Olusegun Obasanjo:

"Former President Olusegun Obasanjo is a courageous patriot and statesman who tells the truth to power when he is convinced leaders are going wrong ... he is a nationalist, whose commitment to democracy and good governance are worthy of recognition and praise ... Obasanjo is a true statesman and nationalist who doesn't abandon his country when it needs his voice to jolt the conscience of leaders to listen to those they govern."

Again, these are authentic and deeply-felt words of honest appreciation against the backdrop of the tragic direction that the Nigerian state was heading under former President Goodluck Jonathan. The reality though, was that President Goodluck Jonathan at that time did not agree and would never have agreed with Muhammadu Buhari that Olusegun Obasanjo's public efforts to unseat him from the Presidency had anything statesman-like or patriotic in them. He was at the receiving end. So, just what does President Buhari think he is doing here and now?

Where did this relationship go sour? Judging by the open letter written by the former President, it is glaring that he has his grudges in clearly defined areas and he minced no word highlighting them. Agree or disagree with him, he blamed the incumbent President for his performance on the economy and his constant apportionment of the blame on others and not taking responsibility for failures where necessary. He buttressed his point with one clear example amongst others, of the President blaming the Governor of the Central Bank for the 70% devaluation of the Naira. He criticized the President's lack of flair and instinct for the handling of subtleties in the dynamics of politics. Indeed, many pundits have had cause to voice out criticisms in these same areas on several occasions too. A President, who refuses to dialog with his citizens, seemingly snubbing them and simply ignoring matters of crucial significance can only end up having the country deeply divided. Many will disagree with President Obasanjo on these two issues in view of the enormity of the economic problems that Buhari inherited and the progress he undeniably, made on several fronts of the economy. From my own layman perception though, I will not discount chances that President Buhari may have made significant errors of judgment and implementation at crucial moments, on the economy. Yet, I do need stronger arguments to convince me that President Buhari has failed woefully on the economy. Many will also disagree with President Obasanjo that the deep polarization in the country today, is attributable solely, to President Buhari's lack of the requisite political finesse. After all, the nation was deeply polarized in the days of President Obasanjo as well.

On another point, though, the former President wrote about an area in which:

"President Buhari has come out more glaringly than most of us thought we knew about him. One is nepotic deployment bordering on clannishness and inability to bring discipline to bear on errant members of his nepotic court. This has grave consequences on the performance of his government to the detriment of the nation."

It is on this point that President Obasanjo, in my opinion, has clearly hit the bull's eye. He cited the example of Maina and talked about *"collusion, condonation, ineptitude, incompetence, dereliction of responsibility or kinship and friendship on the part of those who should have taken visible and deterrent disciplinary action"*. He then asked how many more cases may have been concealed or remained unseen by the public eye.

Now, looking back at the year 2007 in the heat of presidential campaigns to succeed Olusegun Obasanjo as President, candidate Muhammadu Buhari did not hide his disdain for President Olusegun Obasanjo. In different ways, he insinuated that he would subject Olusegun Obasanjo to one persecution or the other. It was at a point, in which the polity had been badly overheated, and the nation was deeply polarized.

Part of the problem at the time that badly angered the northern establishment was Obasanjo's radical break from the normative political order that several northern-led military governments had established through several years of dominance. Key government offices were reserved solely for Northerners. The Governor of the Central Bank, the Inspector-General of Police, Chief of Army Staff, Secretary to the Government of the Federation, Minister of Finance, Minister of Defense, Minister of External Affairs to name but a few, were posts that were often reserved exclusively for Northerners.

As the first leader of its kind, Olusegun Obasanjo displayed color-blindness as far as ethnic coloration was concerned, when it came to making appointments to government posts. Olusegun Obasanjo reorganized the military in a manner that ensured the less frequency of coups and equal opportunities for all irrespective of tribe and geographical origin. Many Northerners, who commented on this issue at the time, considered this a frontal attack on the North. As I elaborated in my book "Nigeria's Journalistic Militantism", one serious consequence of this perception, was the unilateral declaration of Sharia Law in individual northern States to undermine the constitutional laws that defined the legal system of the country as well as to dare the incumbent President of the time to take any action to restore constitutional order. So, when candidate Muhammadu Buhari made it clear that he would hold Olusegun Obasanjo accountable for whatever vices he had in mind if he became President, it wasn't difficult to figure out, where the grudges were coming from. Yet, he won a lot of applause from his target audience across the board because Olusegun Obasanjo had a multitude of media-influenced enemies and the media were driven by the individual political interest groups that owned and controlled them. It made the 2007 presidential election a do-or-die affair for the incumbent President Olusegun Obasanjo, who had to fight for his own political and personal survival.

Fast-forward to 2015. All these animosities died in the wake of President Goodluck Jonathan's extremely clannish and corrupt approach to Governance. Very much as it is with President Buhari, there is no doubt that Olusegun Obasanjo had his moment or moments of disagreement with President Goodluck Jonathan as well, which made him part ways from his political foster son. At the time, this parting of ways meant courageous statesmanship and patriotism to candidate Muhammadu Buhari. After all, he was the beneficiary. Olusegun Obasanjo committed to him as a candidate and campaigned relentlessly to secure international endorsement for the removal of Goodluck Jonathan's threatening disintegration of the Union.

Now, upon proclamation by Olusegun Obasanjo, of his parting of ways with President Muhammadu Buhari, the initial reaction by President Buhari was measured and respectful, probably hoping to dissuade from a further deepening of the rift and to nip the crisis in the bud. He had clearly instructed his aides to desist from disparaging the former President because they would be too young to disparage an elder in the spirit of African courtesy. Aside the factual and impersonal response provided by the Minister of Information, Lai Mohammed, the President's bar on disparaging comments does not seem to have applied to Festus Keyamo, who he had recently appointed as his campaign and not necessarily, government or personal spokesman.

As soon as President Obasanjo started acting out his script of working against the reelection of the incumbent President, making consultations and forming alliances as he did in the days that nourished the candidacy of the incumbent President against Goodluck Jonathan, President Buhari suddenly remembered that $16 bn had been wasted on electricity that was not provided in the wake of the year 2007. Never mind that the figures were not quite accurate and never mind that the President was also personally aware of the controversy surrounding the accuracy of the figures. Never mind too that the Economic and Financial Crimes Commission had officially investigated the issue exhaustively over the years, with conclusive reports – fair or foul! It became the most urgent issue on the front burner.

There are yet no charges prepared or filed against Diezani Allison-Madueke to be taken up whenever she returns. No. No investigation is deemed urgent on the reason for the depletion of the country's foreign reserves while earnings were high. No. Instead, another lie is advanced that the price of crude oil between 1999 and 2007 averaged $100.00 per barrel. No probe is being ordered on why fuel subsidy blew out of proportion and why many surrogates and cronies were allowed to get away with false subsidy declarations without prosecution. The urgency of prosecuting such looters publicly has not been highlighted. The stupendous looting of the country's resources in the immediate past administration is not a subject of any urgent public scrutiny. No. It is the power sector spending under President Olusegun Obasanjo, who, coincidentally, is championing the cause of stopping the reelection of the incumbent President Muhammadu Buhari that is now on the front burner.

Then from nowhere, President Buhari discovered the sanctity of the June 12 movement and its democratic significance for Nigeria and the ecclesiastic infallibility of General Sani Abacha.

Now, while I have no judgmental input whatsoever, into the injustices of June 12 and the atrocities related to it, I have opined in one article several years ago that I, personally, shed no tears for Moshood Abiola, irrespective of the attacks and abuses this will generate. The man Moshood Abiola played a crucial role in the unfair demise and dismantling of Obafemi Awolowo in the early days of the Second Republic to advance his own political ambitions. In the battle of the Nigerian Concord against the Nigerian Tribune, the most brutal form of political propaganda journalism was put on display in the hope that Moshood Abiola would be nominated the presidential candidate of the ruling National Party of Nigeria at the time when the tenure of President Shehu Shagari was expected to end. A move that would have guaranteed him electoral success while the more brilliant and popularly adored brain would have wasted away and fallen prey to the power of some ITT-financed monetary prowess. Alas, when the time came, the party constitution was manipulated and amended and Moshood Abiola was shown his rightful place in an era that saw ethnic and regional politicking at its highest peak. It was the first warning shot that he failed to heed.

As a practicing Moslem, Moshood Abiola had always considered himself a brother to the North and was highly connected with the political powers of the time since the North dominated political leadership and Abiola cherished hanging out with such political leaders and sponsoring them for favors. Unfortunately, there was no indication that the Northern leaders were ready to reciprocate his heavily money-guided overtures in any way. In the end, he suffered the inevitable fate of dining with the devil too closely in the hope of a cheaper path to fame and power and Obafemi Awolowo would have turned in his grave and cracked his ribs laughing. That much for my unfavorable personal opinion.

Now, if the conduct of the historic June 12 elections was the freest and fairest Nigeria has ever had and the activists involved were unjustly persecuted and victimized, no doubt honor must be given where and when it is due. But why didn't it occur to President Muhammadu Buhari to shower these accolades on the recipients in 2015 (shortly after his inauguration), in 2016 or in 2017? Why did President Buhari have to wait till his feud with Olusegun Obasanjo to suddenly remember that there are people to honor, who posterity may have been unfair to? This is where a dose of childishness may serve to neutralize the goodwill of men. It is highly reminiscent of President Jonathan's act in promoting the election of Governor Ayodele Fayose to spite Olusegun Obasanjo in the heat of his hopeless bid for reelection. History repeating itself in different cycles in the gaze of those, who choose to react with hate emotions and spitefulness.

Even though President Olusegun Obasanjo now seems to have betrayed the second jitter of a General by ringing the alarm bell on attempts to incarcerate him, I will encourage President Muhammadu Buhari to truly go ahead with such plans if indeed, he has them in mind. The making of a legend will be realized not too long after the fading of the music. In spite of all hatred and abuses that President Buhari is willingly and knowingly tapping into, Olusegun Obasanjo's place in Nigeria's history has long been defined and cemented. The social media rascals – professionals and novices – who believe in the power of blind submission giving the incumbent President the feeling of heroism in setting the wrong agenda out of obvious desperation, may not be the determinant factor in reelection.

Then, the President comes out to declare that he had allowed the Governor of the Central Bank – a Jonathan appointee – to remain on his post because he, basically, wanted the Governor to correct the mess he had created in the economy. An unforced error of this sort often prompts one to wonder, if our Presidents are never guided by capable advisers. With a statement of this nature, the President is clearly dropping the hint that he had no blueprint of his own to salvage the ruinous economy left by President Jonathan in the wake of grand larceny. President Buhari's belief in reviving the economy through reverse engineering that he expected Emefiele to perform is the most potent declaration of his own bankruptcy of ideas. He could as well have allowed President Jonathan to stay on to correct the mess he created, and this is without prejudice to the continued stay of Emefiele as Governor of the Central Bank.

In the end, opportunism and desperation are the last attributes anyone would have expected of General Muhammadu Buhari, in whom we all saw the Messiah and Revolutionary. No doubt, General Olusegun Obasanjo deserves to be punished, jailed and disgraced if, indeed, corruption and massive wrongdoings are proven against him. But please do not sell opportunism and desperation to the world as a fight against corruption and the final touching of the Untouchables.

Knowing the criticisms directed at him by Olusegun Obasanjo, it would have been incumbent upon President Muhammadu Buhari to seek immediate dialog with the former President to defuse further tension particularly after the coincidental meeting in Addis Abeba shortly after the open letter was written. That would have been the only logical move to make while acting in good faith. The goal would have been, to carry the former President along by explaining details to him if there were issues, which in the view of the administration, he had not properly understood. Whether any such move was made or not, we do not know from the outside. The current turn of events, however, indicate that such moves were either never made or ended up in failure.

Whichever way it is, the growing bellicosity and grandstanding tapping into negative sentiments to intimidate or silent Olusegun Obasanjo will only end up overheating the polity in the most unnecessary manner since Olusegun Obasanjo will continue to defy all odds at an age, in which he has virtually, nothing more to lose. By taking this barrage of vengeful counter-measures, President Muhammadu Buhari is doing nothing else, but making his reelection battle his own personal "Do-or-die" moment.

Frisky Larr is the author of "Nigeria's Journalistic Militantism",
"Africa's Diabolical Entrapment" and "Lost in Democracy". Watch
out for the upcoming book "A Journey Through Times"

While the battle raged, and no party seemed ready to relent, the mounting pressure on the incumbent President grew in tactical and numerical strength. The ruling party began to suffer internal divisions comparable to the split in the party that it defeated in 2015. The methods adopted to secure a second term for the incumbent President began to look more and more like the tactics adopted by the President, who was defeated in 2015 save for the lavishing of bribe and appeasement money for votes, at least, as of mid-2018. Above all else, President Buhari had tangible achievements to show for his three years in office as opposed to the President he defeated in 2015, who didn't have much for his 5 years. Yet, in his desperation for a second term in office, incumbent President Muhammadu Buhari seemed to have borrowed a leaf from his immediate predecessor in his battle against Olusegun Obasanjo by empowering people in line with the principle *"The enemy of my enemy is my valued friend"*. A former Governor and sworn enemy of Olusegun Obasanjo was suddenly nominated and chosen as the Chairman of the ruling party but not before the Ex-Governor called for the arrest of former President Obasanjo claiming that heavens will not fall, while he too faced a court action on corruption charges, filed by a Cleric and private citizen, to force law enforcement to investigate the source of his disproportionate wealth, in which the incumbent President didn't quite seem interested.[9]

In fact, the characteristic feature of Muhammadu Buhari's government, no matter how it ends or fares, will definitely be defined by the widely-held perception that he is personally a modest and incorruptible personality, who nonetheless lacks the substance and iron will to fight corruption and illegality ruthlessly even if it involves his own mother and next-of kin. His poor performance as a strategist and tactical politician was underscored by his exposure to repeated outmaneuvering by political foes that he failed to recognize in good time. In the end, the President resorted to hiding behind the mask of being tolerant and keeping to the rules only to launch a desperate and even poorly-planned fight with enemies – perceived and real – in the wake of a struggle for re-election.

I penned the following article to conclude my perception of the President's government before going to press with this compilation:

When Foolish Failures Overshadow Important Achievements. Yet no Substitute for Buhari in Sight.

By Frisky Larr

Unlike haters of President Muhammadu Buhari, I will not relent in stressing the reality that his ascension to the Presidency truly saved the nation from imminent collapse in the hands of dormant secessionists lurking in the dark from the North, South and East. More importantly, he rescued the nation from prominent and unrepentant looters! I will not relent in pointing out very many important achievements that have been made since his ascension to the Presidency and many things that have moved Nigeria forward. Some of such achievements are recorded in areas that other leaders before him did not delve into with the necessary commitment and doggedness. We will return to the subject as this discourse progresses.

Unlike his hailers and die-hard supporters, however, I will also not relent in pointing out his unforced errors and blatant failures, some of which are very uninspiring and absolutely unnecessary. Some are so dire that they have currently placed the nation on the brink of catastrophe. Most annoying though, is that they are all, absolutely avoidable.

While it is true that the nation has, for long, been held hostage by its greedy and often, egocentric leaders, it is also true that the hostage takers of today are a combination of such leaders and the largely half-educated and pseudo-intellectual citizenry, who beat the drums of praises and irrational support, sometimes for no reason other than sheer admiration and clannishness. Some are inspired and driven by the type of blind followership they show to religious leaders, who are scammers in trade but have the tragic position of leadership over non-discerning flocks, who are prepared to follow blindly to the bitter end. In the clad of such blindness, many have buried the need for questioning leaders and understanding more and perfected the craft of inventing eulogies and outlandish characterizations. They conjure logics and subscribe to weird spinning arguments that sound rational to them alone in the tragic world of make-believe that they choose to thrive in.

Diehard supporters of President Muhammadu Buhari are brilliant examples in this category.

No doubt, President Buhari has merited huge accolades, not the least for good intentions and records of achievements that many of his critics acknowledge as well. From the suppression of Boko Haram through the TSA implementation, salary bailout to states, giant strides in promoting self-sufficiency in agriculture, moving forward on solid mineral exploration, loot recovery, the exemplary prosecution of tribal affiliates before other tribes on corruption charges, up until the launching of massive infrastructural build-up, clearance of inherited salary and pension backlog, clearance of inherited government debts to contractors, etc. Indeed, some previous administrations supervised the stealing of pension and salary funds as well as made away with payments for infrastructure. Military chiefs stole money with ease that was meant for purchasing military hardware. In fact, President Buhari's short-lived assault on the Judiciary to weed out corrupt judges was one daring area that none of his predecessors openly stepped into. Today, one big case trails the other in corruption prosecution. Thanks to Buhari, Nigerians know today, what budget-padding means and how legislators enrich themselves at the cost of impoverishing the entire nation. None of his predecessors found the need to expose this deadly cancer that was growing from one regime to the other.

These are immense achievements for a short period of three years that flies by in the speed of a whirlwind.

Unfortunately, however, President Buhari's failures often lie precisely within the ambits of his celebrated successes. A logical oxymoron that simply beats the imagination while trying to make sense of it all! Taking the budget-padding issue as a typical example, the President, while exposing a long-standing criminal activity spanning several regimes and periods in the legislative chambers, also failed to follow up on exposing and prosecuting the criminals. On the contrary, he seemingly proceeded to even accept a lesser level of padding in the first budget that he signed into law after refusing to sign it on two previous occasions. A whistleblower, who triggered the alarm on the padded budget was shockingly ignored by the President and handed over to the wolves to feast upon.

In the 2018 budget that the President signed into law in the wake of reelection politicking, Muhammadu Buhari took a highly laudable step that broke with the tradition of several predecessors. Following an obnoxious eight months of delay in considering the budget by the Senate, the tinkered and highly altered version was sent to the President for assent. For the first time in the history of Nigeria, the President cried out to the public reporting that the Senate has usurped his rights of budget-drafting and strongly and arbitrarily altered allocations for infrastructural projects in favor of hiking the Senate's own voracious appetite for larceny. This exposure did not solve the problem, though. Yet, it constitutes a major step in the right direction that any successor can take forward. Unfortunately, however, he proceeded to sign it into law without telling the public what he intends to do to curb the excesses. Even though information swirls on social media that legal action is pending in court that is challenging the Senate's right to tinker with the budget, the public has no limited, to say the least of full-scale information, on what precise legal action was filed and what holds back quick judgment on the issue or what arguments the parties are advancing to support their positions in court. In other words, there is no indication whatsoever, in public space that any such litigation is on course. This, thus, leaves room for the speculation that either a systematic and state-sponsored social media disinformation to support the President is on top gear or there is an overall media incompetence in performing the duty of informing the public. A situation that would be tantamount to the echo of the complaints that I aired in my book *"Nigeria's Journalistic Militantism"* blowing hot air to bring down personalities but oblivious of the performance of sacred functions!

Today, Muhammadu Buhari's government is flying on second-term re-election mode setting all active configurations to play to the gallery amid the drumbeat of blind and endless praises by the President's admirers. Yet, all is not well. The President has had a chain of serious failings that MAY cost him reelection in spite of all illusionary appraisals, the type that misled Goodluck Jonathan to his political no-man's-land. The only reason that Muhammadu Buhari still looks astoundingly good for reelection today, is simply the absence of a credible replacement for him, far and wide. But we will come to that later.

The hugely avoidable sins of President Buhari are much more important an issue for the present moment than the absence of a replacement for the next four-year term. Else, there would be little understanding for the need for plurality in the field, by the wider voting masses.

In spite of several years in the doldrums struggling to become President, it came as a huge surprise that Muhammadu Buhari was not fully prepared for the challenges of the Presidency that he so cherished. He seems to have run repeatedly for the Presidency with his mind set basically, on two formidable principles: *"Fight corruption"* and *"Return political powerbase to the North"*.

The train of *"Fighting corruption and decay with zero tolerance"* is one that every Nigerian will appreciate and jump upon every single day of their life, if the fighter was serious, ruthless, impartial and uncompromising. From the days of Olusegun Obasanjo as President, Nigerians have shown a degree of extreme sensitivity towards selective prosecution. While President Obasanjo did an unprecedented and laudable job in setting up the EFCC and prosecuting many corrupt politicians, the whole achievement was marred by the public perception that the enemies of the President alone were prosecuted giving his friends a free ride to unperturbed looting. Right or wrong, the perception stuck. Unfortunately, President Buhari doesn't seem to have learned much from this mishap.

With actions and inactions, the President showed huge reluctance in calling out people that were close to him even when the deeds had gone far beyond nasal perception. Even if Babachir Lawal, Ayo Oke and co. are facing prosecution today, the President, like a child, who despises class attendance for learning, is still displaying the greatest reluctance to face the tragic issue of Kemi Adeosun head-on. In fact, there are times in the history of humanity, when we all take a deep bite on a sour apple and make deeply regrettable amends on crucial spots. That is the character of consistence. The sitting Minister of Finance, Kemi Adeosun, is reported to have forged a certificate of National Youth Service – the rough equivalent of post-education military service in many other countries – to qualify for appointment as a Minister. So far, this report by a reputable news outlet has not been compromised. Yet, the government seems completely immune to consequences for the culprit, even in the face of seeming admission of guilt and a weighty public outcry. No political price to pay. No comment from the President.

The vengeful re-opening of the corruption file of ex-President Olusegun Obasanjo in the pettiest manner possible, only after the ex-President had openly rejected the incumbent's second term bid was another glaring display of "unseriousness" on the part of President Buhari. Telling wanton lies in anger and desperation, the President reported of an ex-President, who went about "bragging" that he wasted money on electricity, when the nation knew just nothing of any bragging ex-President anywhere in the public information square. Buhari even went on to quote figures that he knew and actually knows to be at best, controversial, if not outright inaccurate. In the most childish and pettiest of forms possible, he asked an applauding audience of packaged haters, *"Where is the power? Where is the power?"* Indeed, the need to re-open a file that had long been processed by two previous administrations while worse scenarios were playing out right before his very nose in the judiciary, legislature and even his immediate environment, underscored President Buhari's penchant for needless populism and pandering to hate sentiments for political sympathies. In fact, his immediate predecessor left him a can of worms to unearth and it is doubtful that he has gone through one-third of such serious cases. Unfortunately, however, very few Nigerians prefer feeding the *hate-pleasure* in them to seeing through the odious design in moments of overwhelming emotional and irrational obsession.

Just on March 03, 2017, a lengthy American report on democracy, human rights and labor in Nigeria (*https://www.state.gov/j/drl/rls/hrrpt/2016/af/265288.htm*) stated unequivocally that *"Impunity remained widespread at all levels of government. … pervasive corruption affect all levels of government."* It is worth remembering that Buhari rode to the Presidency on the cloak of a no-nonsense arbiter. Abdulmumin Jibril had a dossier on thieves in the legislative chambers, with whom he interacted, wined and dined. The President was not interested any bit in knowing who they were or what they did, not even at the cost of also prosecuting Jibrin along with the people he accused if dirt was also found on him. No. Invariably, he sent the ultimate message that the country could well do with some dose of corruption and malpractices since he couldn't take on everyone. The fact that budgets were padded, ordinarily, with the help of individuals in the bureaucratic establishment, is not a secret. Yet, no investigation has been carried out to weed out the bad herbs in the midst of a raging battle. All the subsidy thieves of the Jonathan days are still a mystery locked in some secret boxes. These are a part of President Buhari's *"One step forward, two steps backwards"* philosophy no matter how many imperfect steps he believes he may have taken to curb budget-padding. Reversibility and the human factor remain incurable diseases.

The reality that has not dawned on the President for now, however, is the fact that a lot of vices and evils may have been chopped off today, but perception will ultimately remain the final judge in history. Who will bother to know that the *Ghana-must-go* moneybags are no longer exchanging hands freely in the lobbies today? Who will care if railway lines run from Abakiliki to Zaria? If Senators and Representatives are still becoming overnight millionaires before the eyes of an anti-corruption crusader, who seems to tolerate them without a care, all those positive steps will simply pale into insignificance. The same applies to the decimation of Boko Haram that the President set his eyes upon only in the latter days of his quest for the Presidency. No one will remember this feat, which by the way, is now suffering serious setbacks, if the President allows it to be overshadowed by avoidable foolish mistakes. President Buhari does not seem to have learnt much lessons from the Obasanjo days, in which unnecessary enemies set off the Niger Delta militancy and the kidnapping of expatriates. After all, the President's refusal and failure to prosecute his anti-corruption war with zero tolerance as exemplified by his backtracking on cleansing the judiciary, betrayal of Abdulmumin Jibril, bickering on Adeosun and a host of countless other cases, he has little choice than to tread with caution when making political enemies. This would have been irrelevant if he had been ruthless in uprooting every corrupt tree on his path and won the formidable support of the masses to be his advocate.

Indeed, it is the highly simplistic execution of these two apparent political objectives of fighting corruption and returning the powerbase to the north, that speaks more in favor of their veracity than much other ancillary evidence. The fight against corruption has been compromised in the most simplistic manner possible almost re-sounding the echo *"Touch not my anointed but blow up my insulted."* On the other front, the calculation seems to have been the fulfillment of the constitutionally laid-out prerequisites for the Federal character, while the age-long anger at the divulgence of powerbase from the north and spreading it throughout the federation by Obasanjo, was to be given a free ride to re-actualize the post-independence northern grip on power.

While the rift with former President Olusegun Obasanjo topped the political agenda, voices emerged on social media citing the refusal of the President to accept some Obasanjo's nominees for political appointments as the root cause of their dispute. The loudness of the outcry from both sides of the political aisle, however, seems to suggest that President Buhari's agenda in the rejection of several nominations from different quarters was simply his deep commitment to the *re-northernization* of the political establishment. If true, this short-sighted calculation simply seems to have negated the reversibility of such futile exercises.

I have, indeed, represented the view that a President should always be free to choose people that he can best work with irrespective of their region of origin. Unfortunately, however, team-compatibility is something else altogether, than ethnic divisiveness.

As if there wasn't much pressing issue to tackle on the national stage than such pettiness, the President seems to have taken this issue so seriously as exemplified by the appointment of all military service chiefs from a specific region, that he even allows it to get between him and many of his political facilitators in his ascension to the Presidency.

Today, the engine of the President's infrastructural ambition is being oiled by a widening debt profile after the drastic reduction of same by a predecessor. The outcry across the aisle is that of incompetence on the economic front and is echoed by people, who know far better than I do, on this important discipline. Moreover, the simple battle for survival on the part of Fulani herdsmen that spans several administrations and years, was allowed to spiral out of control under the incumbent President through a long period of sheer indifference that some observers believe, speaks to petty tribal sympathies. Killings attributed to Fulani herdsmen today, evidentially have nothing more in common with the struggle for grazing land. It has long metamorphosed into contract killings as a political statement at the cost of innocent lives, boiling down still to political inexperience in the delicate craft of making political enemies and playing forces against one another.

Now, it is becoming a major benchmark for presidential efficiency or inefficiency like Boko Haram was in adjudging the President's predecessor. Reports now emerge, of armed attacks on defenseless villagers lasting 8 hours and spanning 11 villages in the Boko Haram fashion of old, without security forces coming anywhere near, while a total of 52 villages have been reportedly sacked since the start of the conflict. After it galvanized hidden critics from general silence into open agitation as the last straw that broke the camel's back, the President turned vindictive and became confrontational, once again, out of sheer political inexperience. Today, the subject remains high on the political agenda overshadowing almost everything else that the President has achieved.

As a potent political subject that will always capture top-spot on the agenda, the sponsored killings are likely to continue to keep the President on edge and torment him as his strongest political weakness. It may be utilized by forces that he failed to confront while the sun was shining. Yet, the President had a choice. Inter-personal disputes and conflicts that should have never been allowed to take a strong foothold on the periphery were stubbornly nurtured to fester into monstrosity. Where dialog was needed, precisely after an open letter, the President chose conflict unnecessarily to attract applause from petty minds on the advice, also of petty thinkers and half-baked strategists – the type that buried Jonathan.

Today, his adversaries mock him quietly because he had set himself the wrong priorities in an attempt to flaunt the credentials of a democrat-extraordinary and is now finally turning around to face a bitter reality.

The Fayoses and the Sarakis, you name them. The President had the opportunity to tame them all and keep governance on the course of calmer waters without diversions and side shows for the gallery. Yet, he chose to pretend that he was presiding over a matured democracy, where everyone knew the rules and the limits. He pandered to western sympathies and pampered characters that were bent on killing the fabrics of a nascent democracy. Yet, characters like Ayodele Fayose and Bukola Saraki would never even have been tolerated in grown democratic climes in the first place. Today, Saraki is reportedly sponsoring criminal gangs and defection gangs. The President defied experienced counseling at the appropriate time and is now, suddenly waking up to the dawn of reelection campaign to trim the wings of a flying poison.

The name of the deplorable petty game has now been defined as the sharing of returned Abacha loot as campaign bribes to an electorate that may sometimes choose porridge over treasure. Is Muhammadu Buhari not far above this petty level of politicking? What has happened to the presidential clinic in Aso Rock? Has it been equipped to a presidential standard? No update. No public information. What about hiring high quality doctors to man the presidential clinic and halt the incessant overseas flight for treatment? Wherein does the President see the urgency in money distribution aside electoral favor?

In spite of all these weaknesses though, Nigeria keeps waiting for the opposition to put forth a candidate that has the requisite appeal and acumen to dislodge Muhammadu Buhari. A candidate that will take the positives of the incumbent President one step or even two steps further! Move Nigeria two steps forward where Buhari took just one step. A candidate that will be prepared to jail his own wife or mother, if he finds her guilty of criminal malpractices! It must be a candidate that will not bicker or lose time like the incumbent President does each time decisiveness is expected of him. Vice President Osinbanjo showed Nigerians a taste of decisive and positive actionism with his infamous visit to the Nigerian international airport when his principal was sick before he was quickly tamed by the President's men. Yet, Buhari has not got the message. Nigeria today, cannot afford an Umaru Musa Yar'Adua type or the Goodluck Jonathan type of President, who refused to move the nation forward from where they found it.

Today, only the spirit of Tunde Idiagbon would have been in a position to topple Muhammadu Buhari. A Nuhu Ribadu properly nurtured through the years without amateurish political prostitution, would have come halfway to dislodging Muhammadu Buhari.

For now, President Buhari's weaknesses may be plain angering and have disappointed all the expectations of a revolutionary. Yet, finding a replacement from the current breed of politicians lining the public space that will satisfy and promise Nigerians a better stewardship than Buhar's seems plain utopian and an impossible task. That is public perception as it stands today.

*Frisky Larr is the author of **"Nigeria's Journalistic Militantism",** **"Africa's Diabolical Entrapment"** and **"Lost in Democracy".** Watch out for the upcoming work **"A Journey through Times"***

***

This article was immediately followed by the following article highlighting the intriguing times in the run-up to the 2019 presidential elections and the role of the incumbent of President. Once again, the helplessness of the country in search for a redeemer and crusader could not have been more exposed. The last hope that was reposed in the incumbent President has proven to be a bubble. Enjoy reading:

When Integrity Became Questionable! President Buhari Can Be Replaced!

By Frisky Larr

At about the same time in 2014, the news media – Social and Mainstream – were busy showcasing the deep polarization that ripped through the Nigerian political landscape in the common quest to salvage Nigeria. The country was in the suffocating grip of a very clueless leader, who sought to hang on to power by all means, even though the real power was wielded by everyone else around him but himself alone. Today, we are back to square one in the infamous pattern of "Same Procedure as every year".

In the euphoria that greeted the contrasting personal qualities of candidate Muhammadu Buhari in 2015, as opposed to President Goodluck Jonathan, expectations were hyped, not the least, by the very actions and pronouncements of the candidate Muhammadu Buhari. *"We will give corruption a bloody nose"* was one of his most popular propagandist slogans. The earth tremored in trepidation and angels bowed before him. Humans panicked in real-time fears. Some thieves had cause to flee overseas after failed personal overtures. The petulance of hustles and whitewashing political journalism that followed, bore immense testimony to the tremor of the earth upon Buhari's ascension to power.

Now the time has come to take the stock and strike a balance again.

The lack-luster inaugural speech aside, Buhari enjoyed a huge amount of goodwill and trust even in spite of his failure to hit-the-ground-running. He wasted six good months before installing a government. It was the first assumed pointer to his comfort zone of sole rulership without much input from lieutenants and subordinates. Yet, the inner circle that he subsequently constituted, still manages to pull a fast one, sometimes ignoring him and sometimes, keeping him in the dark and usurping his powers at will. We will come to this in much details as this discourse progresses.

Starting with his immediate clampdown on looters and reorganization of the military in its fight against insurgency, President Buhari made a very good start, chasing terrorists into hiding. He could not be accused of tribalism or nepotism. The fight against corruption began with his own kinsmen. He moved swiftly to restructure the regime of fuel subsidy having lambasted the running of the project under his predecessors, particularly under President Jonathan. President Buhari swung into action and had refineries functioning again albeit temporarily and promised to build new refineries and ensure that existing refineries will work at installed capacities. It was the breath of a new life.

He aroused expectations (https://www.youtube.com/watch?v=YmG_dYY7YRA) that he would negotiate with foreign companies to refine crude oil against a token commission and have them bring back the refined product for public consumption. This way, the public would not even realize that crude oil had been sent out and reimported as refined fuel. That was the expected interim solution before refineries would work in full swing. It was supposedly the way he did the trick in his military days when they suffered shortfalls. His infamous sloganeering question then, was *"Who is subsidizing who?"*

Today, there is hardly any refinery functioning anymore. The nation is now at the mercy of just one man – Aliko Dangote – waiting on him to complete the construction of his private mega-refinery. Never mind that Olusegun Obasanjo foresaw this early enough in 2007 and sought to have precisely, this same investor, sanitize and completely refurbish and overhaul existing refineries. He was sabotaged by the late Umaru Musa Yar'Adua and accused of selling government properties to cronies at a token price, also by a persistent psyche of hateful antagonism, that does not care for facts and truism. Subsidy payment, although sold publicly as nominally abolished, continues today, as ever before, even if with lesser fraud and the hitherto, insanely crowded field of importers. Yet, in spite of the integrity mantra, transparency continues to be a rare commodity in the oil sector. Precisely this is where President Muhammadu Buhari began to derail.

As in many other fields, the President never considers it necessary to communicate directly with the nation and inform its citizens, when things happened that may have changed the trajectory of his promised policy implementation. Today, Muhammadu Buhari counts as one President that has shunned his electorates with the most arrogance and ignorance. Even Goodluck Jonathan met the Press regularly and dialogued with his folks.

Integrity became a huge problem once again, when the President, who rode on the waves of honor and glory for his own election, now travels abroad repeatedly for medical treatment (surpassed only by a late President, who stayed and died abroad for months unending). A practice that he, reportedly, vowed not to encourage. He does this today, without still making any project-based effort to create a world class hospital in his own palace, not to mention the country, manned by highly qualified doctors even if they needed to be flown in time and again. He just doesn't care.

Confirming stereotypes

That President Muhammadu Buhari survived a grievous assassination plot in the Abuja presidential palace through a deliberate food-poisoning attempt in 2017, is known only in rumors. It was the run-up to his long stay in London on medical treatment. Many insiders have confirmed the accuracy of this rumor in hushed tones only. Yet, we are facing a political structure that should set historical records straight for the public and possible successors for a clearer understanding of the working of power in Aso Rock under the first self-proclaimed leader of integrity from whom openness should be the least expected. Never mind that the citizens have a right to know the state of health of their leader. Nigerians give it to themselves in their self-confessed acceptance of political immaturity by not pressing hard. The President has, thus, successfully hidden behind the veil of privacy to keep his sickness secret from the public that he governs. That much is called integrity.

And then, there was this lengthy submission written by Prof. Wole Soyinka in the run-up to the Presidential election of 2007. The Professor had warned Nigerians urgently, to desist from voting in Muhammadu Buhari as President (never mind that he now sings Buhari's praise more than he tries to keep him in checks) in the face of his ugly clannish acts of nepotism and merciless execution of young souls while he was a military Head-of-State. The suitcase saga of shielding a Northern Emir from accountability for a breach of an extant draconian law that was brutally enforced on a non-Northerner, was a particular point in question.

Today, many actions of the President seem not only to be confirming and entrenching Wole Soyinka's fear and warning of clannishness, the President does not even seem to care if he hurts public sensitivities or not. In the most spiteful of attitudes towards his own citizens, the President stays stoically silent and unnecessarily defiant, when public outcry grows deafening and unbearable on crucial issues. The cry of the massive northernization in the appointment of service chiefs (some complain of a trickle down even to the level of Divisional Police Officers) is a major point in question. As I have said in previous exposés, it has long become obvious that one of President Muhammadu Buhari's key agenda in his quest for political power was the return of power to the North. His second priority was to *"Give corruption a bloody nose"*. Today, the level of northernization in the choice of service chiefs, far transcends the choice of people he can best work with.

On this same issue of extreme north-leaning appointment of operatives into crucial political and security positions, Vice President, Yemi Osinbanjo, was once on record as declaring publicly that the issue will be looked into and corrected. Yet, the President by his actions, never seeks to explain his rationale – directly or indirectly – for public discernment and never tries to be seen as actualizing his deputy's drift, which should be assumed to have been a coordinated pronouncement.

The President allowed the so-called herdsmen's killings to go on for ages with hundreds of innocent souls wantonly slaughtered by blood-thirsty marauders, without uttering a single word to reassure the restive, insecurity-weary public in the geo-political divide. Some observers claimed openly that the President seemed to have had a positive leaning towards his Fulani kinsmen, who seemed to be asserting themselves above a rival ethnic group in the aftermath of the senseless killings. Thank goodness, no more report of these atrocities is heard today. It was Buhari's own Jonathan-type Boko Haram moment. He kept mute. Just mute.

Integrity took another hit, when former President Olusegun Obasanjo couldn't take it anymore and vented his anger through an open letter, with yet another mass killing by supposed Fulani herdsmen, serving as the last straw. The incumbent President in the most simplistic, petty and unpresidential outing possible, took to telling outright lies as a counter-attack, claiming that a former President went "bragging" about spending $16 billion on power. No former President bragged, and no former President spent that amount on power. President Buhari knew and knows it but allowed anger and frustration to get the better of his emotions while he was deceitfully applauded by a lot of people to his incoherent chant: *"Where is the power? Where is the power?"*. Integrity never encourages lies.

Shielding confidants

Early into his Presidency, information surfaced about millions of Naira spent on grass-cutting by very close aides of the President circumventing extant rules for personal enrichment. Evidence flooded the public domain. The President kept mute. The blatant abuse of power by close personal aides stopping Ministers from seeing the President when they desperately needed to, came up high on the political agenda. Everyone heard it. Only the President seemed left out. The President shielded his aides from prosecution for as long as he could until the pressure threatened to weigh in on his re-election ambition. In the end, the big stick was wielded on the Babachirs and the Okes but not before stretching the reach of integrity to its very limits.

Then came the revelation of the forged NYSC exemption certificate. At the center of it all, was a highly respected Minister of Finance (whose competence was roundly certified) and a reputable online news portal. Kemi Adeosun, was, by all accounts, a senior cabinet member. In the eye of the storm, she posed a serious threat to the integrity of the man she served. Yet, the President let it drag on for months unending until it was finally recognized as a threat to the re-election bid.

The Adeosun-gate then became one issue that finally got me questioning the President's pattern of reasoning and that of his advisers. Is the President resistant to counseling or he simply has substandard counselors like his media team? In saner political climes, one of several options that would have been mulled and adopted to finally retain Kemi Adeosun, as the President, obviously intended to do, would have been to launch a Public Relations offensive. After all, the continued services of Kemi Adeosun in the government seems to have been more of a prized asset to the President and his confidants than her exit. Yet, they were absolutely clueless on how to weather the storm. A wave of media interviews by Kemi Adeosun, explaining her own side of the story for public understanding (no matter what pundits may analyze thereafter) would have laid the groundwork for remorse and innocence and above all, clearer understanding. After all, the issue is clear. The certificate is fake, and it is a crime and it must be prosecuted. For an integrity President, who cherishes the services of a highly qualified vicarious agent, swift prosecution would and should have been facilitated with the resultant payment of a fine or other minor punishment. This could have been followed by the belated issuance of the proper certificate and the rejection of any resignation she may have tendered to the President. By this means, the President would have taken full responsibility for his decision and explained this to the public for better understanding. It was a failure of intellectual leadership and the Minister was probably not worth the stakes in presidential reckoning.

In the end, the President reinforced his long-standing image of being too hesitant to wield the big stick when his own close confidants err and break the laws. It was a major blow to integrity once again much like the Abba Kyari debacle that is currently playing out before his very eyes. The element of swiftness in action is just not a Buhari trademark.

The President's Chief of Staff, Abba Kyari, is reputed for arrogance and self-aggrandized lordship over all other subordinates of the President. The rumor mill also fingered him in the successful effort that relatively tamed the Vice President in the second and long absence of President Buhari on medical leave. Today, he is in the news for all the wrong reasons. A corruption scandal allegedly involving the scamming of an unsuspecting kinsman of Abba Kyari to the tune of 25 million Naira, by Abba Kyari himself in collaboration with other accomplices has been publicly unveiled in a videoed Radio talk show within the past few weeks and months. The live-streaming online show had in attendance, the accuser, his corroborator and also sympathizers of Abba Kyari. The accusations could not be clearer, more direct and more forthright. Abba Kyari was named as the principal culprit in misleading the accuser into a non-existent contract for the supply of vehicles to the government, for which no budgetary allocation existed. The victim was required to make advance payment that was never to see the light of day. Abba Kyari was insinuated to have abused his office by influencing the Department of State Security (DSS) to incarcerate people, including a senior police officer, indiscriminately without trial as well as humiliate them and plot further schemes on them in a matter that has nothing to do with State Security.

The lid was blown open on the incident because the helpless and frustrated victim went to the media to cry out for help. Naturally, the accused, Abba Kyari, by virtue of his position, will not appear on a radio talkshow to wash his dirty linens in the public. He will not speak out and will not comment on the accusations. Yet, his boss, whose integrity label is quickly called into question will not show – directly or indirectly – any discernible reaction to salvage his integrity. Not the least, the involvement of the President's Chief of Staff in such a petty case of 419'ing should be of concern to the President himself. Worse still, the abuse of the Department of State Security should call for heads to roll. The least that a serious government of integrity should have done, would have been to set up an inquiry without delay, to recommend measures on curbing such excesses in the future. The President is mute and will neither act nor comment in his wrong priority of stubbornly ignoring the very wrong issues.

Open to blackmail?

The President's actions in his attempted clampdown on the judiciary to clear the rot in that third estate, is one for which he still has my admiration and highest regards to the present day. It is, at the same time, the singular action that exposed him to me as not being the long-awaited Messiah. It was the action of a leader, who, even though, had the good of the nation at heart, lacked the strength of will and skills to fight it to the bitter end. Why did he not stubbornly follow through the way he stubbornly insists on maintaining service chiefs almost exclusively from the North? After all, democracy is nothing but people's power. The constitution derives from people's power. Revolution is nothing but people's power. What more support could the President have wanted but the people's support? Did the President finally end up being blackmailed? What skeleton could the President have had in the closet? That the electoral victory that made him President cost a lot of money that he did not have, is not a secret. In the non-transparent electoral system that Nigeria operates, Nigerians will never know, where the President got his funds from, who contributed what and what anyone may want to get or actually got in return.

Till the present moment, the nation is not aware of any single subsidy fraudster of the past dispensation that the President has successfully docked and held accountable. Like a novice in the game of politics, some powerful intra-party opponents have played on his intelligence like a brawling tiger tamed with a snap of the finger.

This is not to say that nothing good has come out of this President. So groundbreaking are some of his achievements that I admire in the field of agriculture, infrastructure projects, streamlined economic discipline in paying off inherited debts in salary and contracts, fuel supply etc. that some of my readers often erroneously accuse me of being a Buhari image launderer. On the whole however, the President has been a massive disappointment in his failure to live up to the expectations that he aroused and his failure to show intellectual leadership and uncompromising patriotism.

Take his choice of media and public relations management as an example. One is shocked sometimes, seeing his media operatives and image-makers behave no differently from cyber trolls in their choice of words negating the highness of the office they are working for. It is not unusual, for instance, to read a presidential spokesman irresponsibly using the word "Wailers" to describe opponents of the President, precisely the same way substandard online trolls would do, even though the President is there to serve both his own enemies and his own friends. Even worse to observe are those Internet foot-soldiers, who often claim to be irreconcilable Buhari loyalists, either because they are being paid or are truly voluntary fighters, who blindly defend and do more damage to the image of the President. The blind, laughable and outright double-standard defense of Kemi Adeosun's indefensible crime played out pathetically in this regard. Some of such Internet loyalists are so superficial, shallow and unconstructive in their overblown endorsement of their self-worth, one would be forgiven for thinking they are emeritus academics of the Cambridge and Oxford world. With often very shallow analysis and superficial facts, they win the applause of the beer-parlor-type online cheerleaders and consider themselves superstars with little to zero knowledge of the scientific and empirical rules of objective and rational analyses that learned minds routinely plough their trades in.

In the overall assessment, it is obvious, from all ramifications that President Buhari's decision to run for a second term was a highly controversial one even by his own personal standards. With his last so-called leave-of-absence in London that was in fact, a medical leave for routine treatment, President Buhari knows so well that his health is a very major issue in the scheme of things. It was, definitely, not an easy task deciding to run for reelection. As it stands today, my gut feeling tells me that there is, certainly, no single candidate in the ranks fielded by the opposition that can come close to beating Buhari in a presidential race. Not because of the President's perfection. No. Not because his so-called integrity mantra has not been put to test with dismal failure in several instances as shown above. No. Muhammadu Buhari is generally perceived as not being personally corrupt. This is yet to be proven wrong with objective facts and figures. The crucial question then is whether or not, President Buhari is placing his personal ambition ahead and above the interest of the country. Is it his desire to defy the establishment, which doesn't want him to return to power or his sheer lust for power? How far he is prepared to make compromises and not fight all the way to protect the interest of Nigeria against vested interests has been exhaustively analyzed above.

Today, foreign outlets report military gains by the Islamic State of West Africa (ISWA) and Boko Haram pushing back on the military gains made on the national security front as early as 2015. The ill-equipped Nigerian Army is reportedly, falling victim to superior assaults in ambushes. As many as hundreds of soldiers are reportedly being killed in one single attack with little domestic reporting. Morale has reportedly dwindled dramatically, and scared soldiers hardly dare to leave their barracks. (https://af.reuters.com/article/africaTech/idAFL3N1VZ544) Time and again, Vice President Yemi Osinbanjo has shown with swift and prudent actions, what Nigerians actually expected of President Muhammadu Buhari. Saboteurs within the President's own kitchen cabinet worked hard to frustrate a smooth working relationship between the President and his deputy. The President stood firm and secured the honor of his deputy.

Then, why does President Muhammadu Buhari not simply make way for a more vibrant Yemi Osinbajo that he has so groomed?

Frisky Larr is the author of several political discourses. Watch out for the upcoming collection of essays "A Journey Through Times"

***

Today, the Nigerian nation could not be more polarized in its entire history. While the opposition (backed by powerful establishment personalities comprising retired Generals and silent powerbrokers) is frantically working to displace the incumbent President in the 2019 presidential election, the odds seem to favor the re-election of a President, who has strongly disappointed his deliberately encouraged high expectations. In the end, Muhammadu Buhari proved to Nigerians that he may be everything but not at all a messiah that Nigerians should have rested their hopes upon. Too many unfulfilled promises, half-hearted policy executions and even some about-face in key policy areas (e.g. continued subsidy payment on the importation of refined petroleum products in spite of loud-mouthed philosophies in advance as well as failure to build refineries) have left negative indelible marks on the President's track-record no matter what his admirers may say.

Endnotes

1 https://nypost.com/2007/06/08/cnns-bad-new/

2 "96 months of Obasanjo: A gruel of mixed tastes" (VANGUARD newspaper) By Adekunle Adekoya, Deputy Editor Posted to the Web: Saturday, May 26, 2007

3 https://punchng.com/jonathan-believed-bharam-was-sponsored-to-remove-him-obasanjo/

4 Reproduced in Annex 2

5 http://saharareporters.com/2015/12/11/how-former-nsa-dasuki-shared-n30b-%E2%80%98loot%E2%80%99-anenih-ayu-pdp-reps-delegates-and-prayer

6 https://www.youtube.com/watch?v=a6_Tak9ijSM (Frisky Larr's Exclusive Interview with former President Olusegun Obasanjo)

7 http://punchng.com/jonathan-formed-avengers-2015-polls-rnda/

8 https://www.dailytrust.com.ng/news/general/renewed-attacks-in-niger-delta-we-ll-soon-expose-sponsors-of-niger-delta-avengers--dhq/146746.html

9 http://saharareporters.com/2018/06/15/oshiomholes-fraud-efcc-blindness-and-buharis-endowment-corruption-bishop-dr-osadolor

Annex 1

THE WAY OUT: A CLARION CALL FOR COALITION FOR NIGERIA MOVEMENT

Special Press Statement
By
President Olusegun Obasanjo

Since we are still in the month of January, it is appropriate to wish all Nigerians Happy 2018. I am constrained to issue this special statement at this time considering the situation of the country. Some of you may be asking, "What has brought about this special occasion of Obasanjo issuing a Special Statement?" You will be right to ask such a question. But there is a Yoruba saying that 'when lice abound in your clothes, your fingernails will never be dried of blood'. When I was in the village, to make sure that lice die, you put them between two fingernails and press hard to ensure they die and they always leave blood stains on the fingernails. To ensure you do not have blood on your fingernails, you have to ensure that lice are not harboured anywhere within your vicinity.

The lice of poor performance in government - poverty, insecurity, poor economic management, nepotism, gross dereliction of duty, condonation of misdeed - if not outright encouragement of it, lack of progress and hope for the future, lack of national cohesion and poor management of internal political dynamics and widening inequality - are very much with us today. With such lice of general and specific poor performance and crying poverty with us, our fingers will not be dry of 'blood'.

Four years ago when my PDP card was torn, I made it abundantly clear that I quit partisan politics for aye but my concern and interest in Nigeria, Africa and indeed in humanity would not wane. Ever since, I have adhered strictly to that position. Since that time, I have devoted quality time to the issue of zero hunger as contained in Goal No. 2 of the Sustainable Development Goals of the UN. We have set the target that Nigeria with the participating States in the Zero Hunger Forum should reach Zero Hunger goal by 2025 - five years earlier than the UN target date. I am involved in the issue of education in some States and generally in the issue of youth empowerment and employment. I am involved in all these domestically and altruistically to give hope and future to the seemingly hopeless and those in despair. I believe strongly that God has endowed Nigeria so adequately that no Nigerian should be either in want or in despair.

I believe in team work and collaborative efforts. At the international level, we have worked with other world leaders to domicile the apparatus for monitoring and encouraging socio-economic progress in Africa in our Presidential Library. The purpose of Africa Progress Group, which is the new name assumed by Africa Progress Panel (APP), is to point out where, when and what works need to be done for the progress of Africa separately and collectively by African leaders and their development partners. I have also gladly accepted the invitation of the UN Secretary-General to be a member of his eighteen-member High-Level Board of Advisers on Mediation. There are other assignments I take up in other fora for Africa and for the international community. For Africa to move forward, Nigeria must be one of the anchor countries, if not the leading anchor country. It means that Nigeria must be good at home to be good outside. No doubt, our situation in the last decade or so had shown that we are not good enough at home; hence we are invariably absent at the table that we should be abroad.

All these led me to take the unusual step of going against my own political Party, PDP, in the last general election to support the opposite side. I saw that action as the best option for Nigeria. As it has been revealed in the last three years or so, that decision and the subsequent collective decision of Nigerians to vote for a change was the right decision for the nation. For me, there was nothing personal, it was all in the best interest of Nigeria and, indeed, in the best interest of Africa and humanity at large. Even the horse rider then, with whom I maintain very cordial, happy and social relationship today has come to realise his mistakes and regretted it publicly and I admire his courage and forthrightness in this regard. He has a role to play on the side line for the good of Nigeria, Africa and humanity and I will see him as a partner in playing such a role nationally and internationally, but not as a horse rider in Nigeria again.

The situation that made Nigerians to vote massively to get my brother Jonathan off the horse is playing itself out again. First, I thought I knew the point where President Buhari is weak and I spoke and wrote about it even before Nigerians voted for him and I also did vote for him because at that time it was a matter of "any option but Jonathan" (aobj). But my letter to President Jonathan titled: "Before It Is Too Late" was meant for him to act before it was too late. He ignored it and it was too late for him and those who goaded him into ignoring the voice of caution. I know that praise-singers and hired attackers may be raised up against me for verbal or even physical attack but if I can withstand undeserved imprisonment and was ready to shed my blood by standing for Nigeria, I will consider no sacrifice too great to make for the good of Nigeria at any time. No human leader is expected to be personally strong or self-sufficient in all aspects of governance.

I knew President Buhari before he became President and said that he is weak in the knowledge and understanding of the economy but I thought that he could make use of good Nigerians in that area that could help. Although, I know that you cannot give what you don't have and that economy does not obey military order. You have to give it what it takes in the short-, medium- and long-term. Then, it would move. I know his weakness in understanding and playing in the foreign affairs sector and again, there are many Nigerians that could be used in that area as well. They have knowledge and experience that could be deployed for the good of Nigeria. There were serious allegations of round-tripping against some inner caucus of the Presidency which would seem to have been condoned. I wonder if such actions do not amount to corruption and financial crime, then what is it? Culture of condonation and turning blind eye will cover up rather than clean up. And going to justice must be with clean hands.

I thought President Buhari would fight corruption and insurgency and he must be given some credit for his achievement so far in these two areas although it is not yet uhuru!

The herdsmen/crop farmers issue is being wittingly or unwittingly allowed to turn sour and messy. It is no credit to the Federal Government that the herdsmen rampage continues with careless abandon and without finding an effective solution to it. And it is a sad symptom of insensitivity and callousness that some Governors, a day after 73 victims were being buried in a mass grave in Benue State without condolence, were jubilantly endorsing President Buhari for a second term! The timing was most unfortunate. The issue of herdsmen/crop farmers dichotomy should not be left on the political platform of blame game; the Federal Government must take the lead in bringing about solution that protects life and properties of herdsmen and crop farmers alike and for them to live amicably in the same community.

But there are three other areas where President Buhari has come out more glaringly than most of us thought we knew about him. One is nepotic deployment bordering on clannishness and inability to bring discipline to bear on errant members of his nepotic court. This has grave consequences on performance of his government to the detriment of the nation. It would appear that national interest was being sacrificed on the altar of nepotic interest. What does one make of a case like that of Maina: collusion, condonation, ineptitude, incompetence, dereliction of responsibility or kinship and friendship on the part of those who should have taken visible and deterrent disciplinary action? How many similar cases are buried, ignored or covered up and not yet in the glare of the media and the public? The second is his poor understanding of the dynamics of internal politics. This has led to wittingly or unwittingly making the nation more divided and inequality has widened and become more pronounced. It also has effect on general national security. The third is passing the buck. For instance, blaming the Governor of the Central Bank for devaluation of the naira by 70% or so and blaming past governments for it, is to say the least, not accepting one's own responsibility. Let nobody deceive us, economy feeds on politics and because our politics is depressing, our economy is even more depressing today. If things were good, President Buhari would not need to come in. He was voted to fix things that were bad and not engage in the blame game. Our Constitution is very clear, one of the cardinal responsibilities of the President is the management of the economy of which the value of the naira forms an integral part. Kinship and friendship that place responsibility for governance in the hands of the unelected can only be deleterious to good government and to the nation.

President Buhari's illness called for the sympathy, understanding, prayer and patience from every sane Nigerian. It is part of our culture. Most Nigerians prayed for him while he was away sick in London for over hundred days and he gave his Deputy sufficient leeway to carry on in his absence. We all thanked God for President Buhari for coming back reasonably hale and hearty and progressing well in his recovery. But whatever may be the state of President Buhari's health today, he should neither over-push his luck nor over-tax the patience and tolerance of Nigerians for him, no matter what his self-serving, so-called advisers, who would claim that they love him more than God loves him and that without him, there would be no Nigeria say. President Buhari needs a dignified and honourable dismount from the horse. He needs to have time to reflect, refurbish physically and recoup and after appropriate rest, once again, join the stock of Nigerian leaders whose experience, influence, wisdom and outreach can be deployed on the side line for the good of the country. His place in history is already assured. Without impaired health and strain of age, running the affairs of Nigeria is a 25/7 affair, not 24/7.

I only appeal to brother Buhari to consider a deserved rest at this point in time and at this age. I continue to wish him robust health to enjoy his retirement from active public service. President Buhari does not necessarily need to heed my advice. But whether or not he heeds it, Nigeria needs to move on and move forward.

I have had occasion in the past to say that the two main political parties – APC and PDP – were wobbling. I must reiterate that nothing has happened to convince me otherwise. If anything, I am reinforced in my conviction. The recent show of PDP must give grave and great concern to lovers of Nigeria. To claim, as has been credited to the chief kingmaker of PDP, that for procuring the Supreme Court judgement for his faction of the Party, he must dictate the tune all the way and this is indeed fraught with danger. If neither APC nor PDP is a worthy horse to ride to lead Nigeria at this crucial and critical time, what then do we do? Remember Farooq Kperogi, an Associate Professor at the Kennesaw State University, Georgia, United States, calls it "a cruel Hobson's choice; it's like a choice between six and half a dozen, between evil and evil. Any selection or deflection would be a distinction without a difference." We cannot just sit down lamenting and wringing our hands desperately and hopelessly.

I believe the situation we are in today is akin to what and where we were in at the beginning of this democratic dispensation in 1999. The nation was tottering. People became hopeless and saw no bright future in the horizon. It was all a dark cloud politically, economically and socially. The price of oil at that time was nine dollars per barrel and we had a debt overhang of about $35 billion. Most people were confused with lack of direction in the country. One of the factors that saved the situation was a near government of national unity that was put in place to navigate us through the dark cloud. We had almost all hands on deck. We used people at home and from the diaspora and we navigated through the dark cloud of those days. At that time, most people were hopelessly groping in the dark. They saw no choice, neither in the left nor in the right, and yet we were not bereft of people at home and from the diaspora that could come together to make Nigeria truly a land flowing with milk and honey. Where we are is a matter of choice but we can choose differently to make a necessary and desirable change, once again.

Wherever I go, I hear Nigerians complaining, murmuring in anguish and anger. But our anger should not be like the anger of the cripple. We can collectively save ourselves from the position we find ourselves. It will not come through self-pity, fruitless complaint or protest but through constructive and positive engagement and collective action for the good of our nation and ourselves and our children and their children. We need moral re-armament and engaging togetherness of people of like-mind and goodwill to come solidly together to lift Nigeria up. This is no time for trading blames or embarking on futile argument and neither should we accept untenable excuses for non-performance. Let us accept that the present administration has done what it can do to the limit of its ability, aptitude and understanding. Let the administration and its political party platform agree with the rest of us that what they have done and what they are capable of doing is not good enough for us. They have given as best as they have and as best as they can give. Nigeria deserves and urgently needs better than what they have given or what we know they are capable of giving. To ask them to give more will be unrealistic and will only sentence Nigeria to a prison term of four years if not destroy it beyond the possibility of an early recovery and substantial growth. Einstein made it clear to us that doing the same thing and expecting a different result is the height of folly. Already, Nigerians are committing suicide for the unbearable socio-economic situation they find themselves in. And yet Nigerians love life. We must not continue to reinforce failure and hope that all will be well. It is self-deceit and self-defeat and another aspect of folly.

What has emerged from the opposition has shown no better promise from their antecedents. As the leader of that Party for eight years as President of Nigeria, I can categorically say there is nothing to write home about in their new team. We have only one choice left to take us out of Egypt to the promised land. And that is the coalition of the concerned and the willing - ready for positive and drastic change, progress and involvement. Change that will give hope and future to all our youth and dignity and full participation to all our women. Our youth should be empowered to deploy their ability to learn, innovate and work energetically at ideas and concepts in which they can make their own original inputs. Youth must be part of the action today and not relegated to leadership of tomorrow which may never come. Change that will mean enhancement of living standard and progress for all. A situation where the elected will accountably govern and every Nigerian will have equal opportunity not based on kinship and friendship but based on free citizenship.

Democracy is sustained and measured not by leaders doing extra-ordinary things, (invariably, leaders fail to do ordinary things very well), but by citizens rising up to do ordinary things extra-ordinarily well. Our democracy, development and progress at this juncture require ordinary citizens of Nigeria to do the extra-ordinary things of changing the course and direction of our lackluster performance and development. If leadership fails, citizens must not fail and there lies the beauty and importance of democracy. We are challenged by the current situation; we must neither adopt spirit of cowardice nor timidity let alone impotence but must be sustained by courage, determination and commitment to say and do and to persist until we achieve upliftment for Nigeria. Nothing ventured, nothing gained and we believe that our venturing will not be in vain. God of Nigeria has endowed this country adequately and our non-performance cannot be blamed on God but on leadership. God, who has given us what we need and which is potentially there, will give us leadership enablement to actualize our potentiality.

The development and modernization of our country and society must be anchored and sustained on dynamic Nigerian culture, enduring values and an enchanting Nigerian dream. We must have abiding faith in our country and its role and place within the comity of nations. Today, Nigeria needs all hands on deck. All hands of men and women of goodwill must be on deck. We need all hands to move our country forward.

We need a Coalition for Nigeria, CN. Such a Movement at this juncture needs not be a political party but one to which all well-meaning Nigerians can belong. That Movement must be a coalition for democracy, good governance, social and economic well-being and progress. Coalition to salvage and redeem our country. You can count me with such a Movement. Last time, we asked, prayed and worked for change and God granted our request. This time, we must ask, pray and work for change with unity, security and progress. And God will again grant us. Of course, nothing should stop such a Movement from satisfying conditions for fielding candidates for elections. But if at any stage the Movement wishes to metamorphose into candidate-sponsoring Movement for elections, I will bow out of the Movement because I will continue to maintain my non-partisan position. Coalition for Nigeria must have its headquarters in Abuja.

This Coalition for Nigeria will be a Movement that will drive Nigeria up and forward. It must have a pride of place for all Nigerians, particularly for our youth and our women. It is a coalition of hope for all Nigerians for speedy, quality and equal development, security, unity, prosperity and progress. It is a coalition to banish poverty, insecurity and despair. Our country must not be oblivious to concomitant danger around, outside and ahead. Coalition for Nigeria must be a Movement to break new ground in building a united country, a socially-cohesive and moderately prosperous society with equity, equality of opportunity, justice and a dynamic and progressive economy that is self-reliant and takes active part in global division of labour and international decision-making.

The Movement must work out the path of development and the trajectory of development in speed, quality and equality in the short- medium- and long-term for Nigeria on the basis of sustainability, stability, predictability, credibility, security, cooperation and prosperity with diminishing inequality. What is called for is love, commitment and interest in our country, not in self, friends and kinship alone but particularly love, compassion and interest in the poor, underprivileged and downtrodden. It is our human duty and responsibility so to do. Failure to do this will amount to a sin against God and a crime against humanity.

Some may ask, what does Obasanjo want again? Obasanjo has wanted nothing other than the best for Nigeria and Nigerians and he will continue to want nothing less. And if we have the best, we will be contented whether where we live is described as palaces or huts by others and we will always give thanks to God.

I, therefore, will gladly join such a Movement when one is established as Coalition for Nigeria, CN, taking Nigeria to the height God has created it to be. From now on, the Nigeria eagle must continue to soar and fly high. CN, as a Movement, will be new, green, transparent and must remain clean and always active, selflessly so. Members must be ready to make sacrifice for the nation and pay the price of being pioneers and good Nigerians for our country to play the God-assigned role for itself, for its neighbours, for its sub-region of West Africa, for its continent and for humanity in general. For me, the strength and sustainable success of CN will derive largely from the strong commitment of a population that is constantly mobilized to the rallying platform of the fact that going forward together is our best option for building a nation that will occupy its deserved place in the global community. May God continue to lead, guide and protect us. Amen.

Annex 2

Goodluck Jonathan: A President in need of help!

An encounter inside Aso Rock
By Jide Ajani

This was to be the fourth meeting between the man, Goodluck Ebele Jonathan, and this writer. However, last Sunday's meeting with the man who is now President brought home some truth. From the preparation for the live broadcast of the PRESIDENTIAL MEDIA CHAT, to the post-event dinner at the President's residence, one point remained very critical: Nigeria's President needs help.

Before your imagination runs riot, this report presents the details of the encounter which lasted about three hours and thirty minutes; situating and contrasting it with a similar encounter with former President Olusegun Obasanjo. And after all said and done, you can then make up your mind on the type of help President Jonathan needs.

The President of Nigeria needs help from a wide range of people: His wife, his aides, friends and associates; foreign governments; Peoples Democratic Party, PDP, leaders; opposition politicians; and just about any individual who believes in Nigeria. But the context of the help is what needs to be properly situated. The boy who wore no shoes to school and who used to put his books on his head is now the President of Nigeria. Grace and good luck don't come any better! That is the lot of Goodluck Ebele Jonathan, who hails from the dingy, sleepy creek community of Otuoke, in Bayelsa State.

A simple, very simple man by nature, Jonathan's life has been one dominated by grace and good luck. The story of his ascendancy is too familiar to be retold here.

But last Sunday, May 4, 2014, the encounter with Jonathan was like none other. For some 10minutes, apprehension, occasioned by a massive dose of excitement and anxiety, reduced the esteem of this writer as he entered one of the chambers inside Aso Rock Presidential Villa in the company of Funke Fadugba of AIT/Faaji FM; Cyril Stober of NTA; and Bashir Saad of the BBC.

The first pleasant surprise was that there was no schooling – that is, no government official came to tutor the quartet on what to ask or what not to ask President Jonathan.

Pre-recording formalities done, in came Mr. President in the company of some aides and friends who had come for one appointment or the other. Jonathan looked cool.

After warm handshakes, he took his seat.

Sensing that this writer was already sweating, the President dropped the hint about government's plan to build a standard studio for recording; with all the necessary facilities and equipment. Some 20 seconds before 7pm, the cameraman signaled that we "would soon be live".

Stober, the anchor for this edition of the media chat, set the ball rolling with the issue of insecurity, specifically the abducted CHIBOK girls, as agreed by the quartet.

It was at this point that the enormity and reality of the challenges confronting President Jonathan reared their heads like a multi-headed monster. Though he was very emotive, feeling helpless and displaying what can be described as real signs of pain, the verbalization of the emotions left much to be desired.

The President said all he wanted to plead for is that the parents of the missing girls should help government; that they should cooperate with government; that they should come and volunteer information and tell government where the girls are. He confessed, rather helplessly, that government had no information regarding the location of the girls.

But that response on national television belied a deeper challenge, steeped in frustration that Jonathan was facing.

Sunday Vanguard gathered from Aso Rock insiders that a meeting the day before, between President Jonathan; Governor Shettima of Borno State; CP Lawal Tanko, Police Commissioner in the state; Mrs. Asabe Kwambula, the school principal; Comrade Inuwa Kubo, Education Commissioner; and the DPO for Chibok, Hezekiah, had caused more muddle. It was discovered by Sunday Vanguard that the four actors from Borno gave different versions of the incident of April 14.

Challenge of capacity

A source inside the Villa disclosed that this development threw every effort being mounted from the Presidency into a kilter. "Even Mr. President could not believe what he was hearing from the principal, the education commissioner, the police commissioner and the DPO. Those at that briefing listened with mouths opened wide". It was this sentiment that President Jonathan re-echoed on national television. From the gesticulation of hopelessness that he displayed regarding the insecurity in the country, what was clear was a challenge of capacity. Even an attempt to help Mr. President place some of the blame where it really belongs – at the door step of leaders in the North, who allowed the Boko Haram insurgency fester and blow out of proportion – he condescended and rationalised this leadership failing, explaining that leaders in the North were dealing with terrorism and not militancy.

Corruption and Stealing

On the question of corruption and the NNPC, President Jonathan missed some points. He did not need to attempt to define corruption and its relationship with stealing. He did not also need to drag the legislature into it – by saying he smelt legislative dictatorship in the conduct of the activities of the House of Representatives; he also did not need to attempt to draw a parallel between corruption, inflated pump-head price of petrol and the popular rally of January 2012.

Governance and Politics

On the issue of governance and politics, President Jonathan said he wasn't ready to declare whether he would seek re-election or not. He voiced out the same mantra of not wanting to be distracted. That response was expected any way.

On the need to curtail the excesses of petroleum products' marketers who are selling beyond the official rate, President Jonathan sounded very distant. There is the Department of Petroleum Resources, DPR, statutorily mandated to monitor activities in the sector. But Mr. President first embarked on a voyage of disbelief; that he finds it difficult to believe that the claim was true; and that Nigerians were responsible for the serial inhumanity against fellow Nigerians. Then suddenly, Mr. President remembered that there was DPR which, he admitted, should begin to do its job.

Jonathan also responded to questions regarding the need for a sound electoral system. He tackled, quite well, the need to ensure that the Independent National Electoral Commission, INEC, gets good funding to prosecute next year's general elections.

The National Conference going on in Abuja got a fair share of mention. Tackling the need to provide a legal framework that would ensure that resolutions from the confab found their way into the Constitution, Jonathan assured Nigerians of the genuineness of his intention. He provided a pan-Nigerian vision which he said should be the abiding mantra. He made it clear that it would be better for Nigerians to buy into the resolutions so long as they are meant for the enthronement of a nation built on fairness and equity.

Reality check

At the end of the two-hour session, the coterie of staff and a few friends were all smiles. 'Mr. President, well done'; 'Mr. President, that was a good one'; 'Mr. President, that was great'. Those were the comments from virtually everyone around. So, you needed to do a reality check: Were these guys referring to the same media chat that had just ended; a chat that saw Mr. President avoiding some questions and instead launching into a series of expeditions. But then, you were quickly reminded that by Mr. President's own standards, this was one of the best performances.

To be fair, not every man is blessed with the magisterial elocution or oratory of Obama; therefore, we cannot hold President Jonathan accountable on that score.

However, we can hold his handlers culpable for dereliction of duty. Was Mr. President not coached properly on how to handle questions? Was he not prepared on the art of effective response to issues raised? Whatever you say of President Jonathan, he is a thorough gentleman who appears to mean no harm. He may be limited as all mortals are. He may also have been catapulted, by grace, beyond his wildest imaginations as he is wont to admit. However, President Jonathan has spent enough years on the seat of power to realign the realities of his present situation by desisting from constantly disappointing some of his admirers. What one saw last Sunday was the same man whom one had met twice at Government House, Bayelsa, between 2000 and 2004; and the man one met, through the facilitation of now Senator Smart Adeyemi, at Eko Hotel in 2006 – his very early days as governor of Bayelsa State. Verdant, innocent, unacquainted and untried, four years on the seat of the President and Commander-in-Chief of Nigeria is more than enough time to recreate a man.

And whereas an old adage says you cannot teach a man to become left-handed at old age, and while not being totally dismissive of the token transformation of Jonathan the village man to Jonathan the President and Commander-in-Chief, there is still much work to be done. And this is where Mr. President's need for help starts.

At Dinner

He invited the quartet to his residence for dinner. First was the weight of the dining chairs! Only God knows what material was used. Just pulling out the chair, it felt like the weight of a 25kg bag of rice. One of the guests could not but voice "these chairs are heavy, very heavy".

And if one had thought the needless effusion of praise about his performance was absurd enough, more was to come at dinner table. We would need to be charitable here. Apart from Mr. Vice President, Namadi Sambo; Chief of Staff, Gen. Arogbofa (rtd); Dr. Reuben Abati; and Labaran Maku, Information Minister; the dinner table was filled with jesters. Some would not even allow Mr. President to finish a sentence before they would interject and complete the sentence for him.

Real help

When Jonathan tried to explain the complexities involved in the abduction saga and why he remained disappointed in the way the episode is turning out, some people around the table would not let him finish. 'Yes, the state government should be blamed Mr. President'; 'the school principal is not fit to head a school'; 'Mr. President, this looks like a set up'.

Emotive as the crisis at hand was, some individuals cracked jokes that were at once dry and unproductive. Yet, some of these persons are aides who are very close to the President. But the real help Jonathan needs must be offered by all well-meaning Nigerians. He remains the leader. Whatever shambling of issues you may accuse him of, he remains the number one citizen of the country. Those who are guilty in this regard are legion. His wife, for instance! Patience Jonathan may be a wonderful wife on the inside but each public intervention by her comes with a heavy baggage of collateral mishap, which, in turn, only breeds public opprobrium. Giving instances here would be impolite but the social media videos of her intervention did more damage than good – even infusing the abduction issue with some sordid comic relief.

But Jonathan's friends and close aides are the guiltiest of the lot. They appear to have ring-fenced the man from reality. Those who would have been able to offer good counsel and meaningfully contribute for the success of his administration are either kept at bay or do not enjoy quality time for strategic and serious thinking. What you then have is a miss-mash of ineffectual policy pronouncements. Those who seem to think the disgrace being suffered by the Jonathan Presidency – yes, disgrace – because of the abduction should not glory in it. It is a disgrace for the whole nation. The party leaders, the former heads of state, the elder statesmen who labored to ensure that Jonathan got his 'Doctrine of Necessity' should carry part of the blame of what this Presidency is turning into. Is it that they offered counsel and were rebuffed? True, he cannot be held responsible for this insurgency but he can be blamed for the way he handled the abduction of the girls.

Throes of evil

True there may have been political undertone in the beginning but when the Presidency is quick to splash the tar of politics on every act of insurgency, this belies the fundamental issues which are related purely to a lack of capacity. There was once the sharia movement in this same country. A President dealt with it and even proclaimed that it would fizzle out. President Jonathan was on CNN mid last year waxing pontifical that Boko Haram would be forgotten in three months, that he would reappear on CNN to tell the story. Sadly, the story on CNN today is about a nation in the throes of evil occasioned by the insurgency.

Still on this issue of abduction, how did the Defence Ministry come out within 24hours to say all the abducted girls had been rescued? Was it PR gimmickry? For all of three weeks, the Presidency was asleep. Until the weekend of the media chat, there was no momentum. In times of national crisis, every nation needs a leader. A leader who means well must be seen to be doing well. In the case of the Jonathan Presidency, from what the naked eyes could see, there appears to be a great disconnect between the desire to accomplish and the capacity to deliver.

Mr. President needs help from all Nigerians because at least, as of today, he is still the President. We have had leaders who were rambunctious, some deceptive, others meek, and yet some clueless and uncoordinated. How would you describe President Jonathan?

In terms of assistance, mercifully, at the time of going to press, many countries of the world have shown considerable concern about the state of affairs in Nigeria and are sending help. Nigerians, the elites should help their President in the area of capacity-building. Watching our Information Minister on CNN, shouting and attempting to use decibel to break down their microphone smacks of panic response. Yet, I can bet you, as indecorous as that action may be, there would be some people in the Villa who would say, 'Well done, Mr. Minister,' 'You did well Mr. Minister'.

That is the way we are. But the way we are would not help President Jonathan.

Printed in the United States
By Bookmasters